Springer Series in Supply Chain Management

Volume 21

D1823643

Series Editor

Christopher S. Tang, University of California, Los Angeles, CA, USA

Supply Chain Management (SCM), long an integral part of Operations Management, focuses on all elements of creating a product or service, and delivering that product or service, at the optimal cost and within an optimal timeframe. It spans the movement and storage of raw materials, work-in-process inventory, and finished goods from point of origin to point of consumption. To facilitate physical flows in a time-efficient and cost-effective manner, the scope of SCM includes technology-enabled information flows and financial flows.

The Springer Series in Supply Chain Management, under the guidance of founding Series Editor Christopher S. Tang, covers research of either theoretical or empirical nature, in both authored and edited volumes from leading scholars and practitioners in the field – with a specific focus on topics within the scope of SCM.

This series has been accepted by Scopus.

* * *

Springer and the Series Editor welcome book ideas from authors. Potential authors who wish to submit a book proposal should contact Ms. Jialin Yan, Associate Editor, Springer (Germany), e-mail: jialin.yan@springernature.com

Omera Khan • Michael Huth •
George A. Zsidisin • Michael Henke
Editors

Supply Chain Resilience

Reconceptualizing Risk Management
in a Post-Pandemic World

 Springer

Editors
Omera Khan
School of Business and Management
Royal Holloway University of London
Egham, UK

Michael Huth
Department of Business
Fulda University of Applied Sciences
Fulda, Hessen, Germany

George A. Zsidisin
Department of Supply Chain and Analytics
University of Missouri–St. Louis
St Louis, MO, USA

Michael Henke
Faculty of Mechanical Engineering
TU Dortmund University, Fraunhofer Institute
for Material Flow and Logistics IML
Dortmund, Nordrhein-Westfalen, Germany

ISSN 2365-6395   ISSN 2365-6409   (electronic)
Springer Series in Supply Chain Management
ISBN 978-3-031-16491-0   ISBN 978-3-031-16489-7   (eBook)
https://doi.org/10.1007/978-3-031-16489-7

Preface

Risk in supply chains has existed for as long as we have had commerce. For many years, the risk of supply chain disruptions and financial volatility were considered just "part of doing business," and were often mitigated by maintaining ample inventory levels, ensuring dual or multiple sourcing, acquiring insurance, hedging, or simply building it into the business model.

The 1980s and 1990s, highlighted by insights from the Toyota Production System (TPS) and popularized with the publication of *The Machine that Changed the World* (Womack et al., 1990), witnessed a significant shift for many business and supply chain processes. The new philosophy and business practice of lean provided justification for firms to reduce or eliminate the traditional risk mitigation strategies and adopt lean production and just in time delivery processes. The financial rationale for adopting these practices is to free organization cash flows by reducing the need for both current assets (such as inventories) and long-term assets (like warehousing and production equipment). Unquestionably these practices contributed toward significantly increasing the profitability and market share for many organizations.

The structure of firms and supply chains likewise started to shift in conjunction with the adoption of lean business practices. Additionally, considerable advancements in technology development in combination with shorter product life cycles made it difficult for companies to remain "experts" in a wide variety of industries. As highlighted by Prahalad and Hamel in their classic 1990 *Harvard Business Review* publication, firms in response started to "focus on their core competencies" and significantly increased their outsourcing practices. As a result, many of these enterprises experienced greater efficiencies and profitability but, at the same time, became more dependent on other firms in their day-to-day operations of producing products and services for customers.

Although supply chains have existed globally (among continents) for millennia, the sheer quantity and complexity of international trade skyrocketed from the 1980s onward. The further advancements of intermodal shipments through containerization, the development of computers, data analytics, and the Internet, in conjunction with political policy changes in China, provided a ripe environment for opening new global trading partners. Many companies in Western Europe and North America started to exploit opportunities for low-cost country sourcing, initially with a focus on Chinese suppliers and then stretching to other Asian markets. These shifts in production sources, including key industries such as pharmaceuticals and electronics, further provided financial benefits for many Western firms and lower costs for consumers, but also started the journey toward greater dependence on global supply chains.

The confluence of these factors created vulnerabilities in many supply chains. Unfortunately, managing risk and ensuring supply chain resilience often became secondary issues.

There are debatably several different events that can be identified for fostering industry and academic interest in supply chain risk and resilience. These include the well-cited supply chain disruption experienced by Ericsson in 2000, hoof-and-mouth livestock disease outbreak in the UK during early 2001, and the terrorist attacks on the World Trade Center on September 11, 2001.

These incidents provided the initial baseline for a large-scale inquiry into supply chain risk and resilience, with the intention of providing insight and solutions for firms and industries to ensure efficient supply chain continuity. It was during the turn of the millennium that we started seeing the publication of empirical studies investigating supply chain risk, resilience, and ultimately supply chain risk management (SCRM) from a behavioral perspective. In order to start advancing this nascent field of supply chain risk and resilience, scholars from the UK, the USA, and Sweden decided to meet and hold a 3-day seminar in 2001 to share our ideas and recent research findings. This became the genesis for the International Supply Chain Risk Management (ISCRiM) network.

The inaugural meeting of what became ISCRiM occurred on October 11–14, 2001, hosted by Professor Bob Ritchie in Crewe, UK. The initial members, including Bob Ritchie, George Zsidisin, Andreas Normann, Ulf Paulsson, Robert Lindroth, and Clare Brindley, spent 3 days sharing insights on the nascent discipline of supply chain risk. From this initial meeting we decided to (1) establish a network with the title ISCRiM as a collaborative, informal organization to share insights on supply chain risk and its management, (2) publish a book highlighting our recent research projects, and (3) meet on an annual basis, with the second meeting occurring in Lund, Sweden, in 2002. From these foundations and throughout the years, we have and continue to meet as a collective group to share our work and insights on supply chain risk. To date, we have published four books as a network, including *Supply Chain Risk* (2004; Ashgate), *Supply Chain Risk: A Handbook of Assessment, Management, and Performance* (2009; Springer), *Handbook for Supply Chain Risk Management: Case Studies, Effective Practices and Emerging Trends* (2012; J. Ross), and *Revisiting Supply Chain Risk*, Springer Series in Supply Chain Management (2019; Springer). Below are the dates and locations of our (almost) annual meetings throughout the past two decades.

- October, 2001—Crewe, UK
- September, 2002—Lund, Sweden
- October, 2003—Crewe, UK
- October, 2004—East Lansing, Michigan, USA
- September, 2005—Cranfield, UK
- October, 2006—Oestrich Winkel, Germany
- October, 2007—Verona, Italy
- September, 2008—Trondheim, Norway
- October, 2009—Cullowhee, North Carolina
- September, 2010—Loughborough, UK
- October, 2011—Denton, Texas, USA
- September, 2012—Porto, Portugal
- September, 2013—Verona, Italy
- September, 2014—Dortmund, Germany
- October, 2015—Richmond, Virginia, USA
- September, 2016—Steyr, Austria
- September, 2017—Lappeenranta, Finland
- September, 2019—Copenhagen, Denmark
- September, 2021—Online

Our most recent meeting in person occurred in Copenhagen, Denmark, during September 2019. This seminar was bittersweet. During our seminar we had the honor of providing Ms. Celia Ritchie, the wife of Bob Ritchie (one of the founders of ISCRiM who recently passed away), a signed copy of our most recent book which was dedicated in his name and to honor the work he had done in supply chain risk scholarship. However, we were not aware that this would be the last in-person meeting for the foreseeable immediate future.

Initially reports and stories of a virus started emerging from China in December 2019 with little fanfare. There had already been several other outbreaks in recent years, such as SARS and the avian bird flu, which had unfortunately resulted in the deaths of thousands of people. However, the effects of these outbreaks had relatively temporary detrimental effects on commerce and supply chains. However, by mid-March 2020, the world appeared to have stopped, and COVID-19 became a harsh reality throughout the entire globe. The pandemic also provided a platform for the term "supply chain" to become part of the everyday language and lexicon of the public—something not quite experienced before.

It became quickly evident to the ISCRiM community that COVID-19 will provide us a once-in-a-lifetime opportunity for studying supply chain risk management and how firms ensured (or failed) to create resilience in their operations and supply chains. What are the critical learning lessons we can take away for ensuring organization and supply chain resilience? We cannot think of any other incident occurring within our lifetime that has had such a long-term influential effect on local, regional, national, and global supply chains.

Shortly after experiencing the initial shocks of product shortages (we all remember the lack of hand sanitizer, toilet paper, and masks) and widespread lockdowns, we decided to virtually meet as a network to determine an appropriate course of action we can pursue as a scholarly association. It was quickly decided to start our fifth book as an organization. We had already published two prior books with Springer Publishers with great success, and decided, with the assistance of Professor Christopher Tang, to publish again with Springer. This edited book is the result of the hard work done by scholars investigating how COVID-19 has affected supply chains and the risk management and resilience strategies pursued by firms for ensuring supply continuity and profitability in meeting customer and societal needs.

There has been no shortage of recent research examining the effects that COVID-19 had on supply chains. These studies are still being published, frequently with special issue calls for papers by various scholarly journals. In addition, one of the first books examining the effect of COVID-19 on supply chains was published by Yossi Sheffi titled *The New (Ab) Normal: Reshaping Business and Supply Chain Strategy Beyond Covid-19* at the end of 2020. However, we are not aware of any other books bringing together a variety of industry observations, practices, and research studies in one volume.

The purpose of this book is to provide insight from research and practice in how organizations were able to sustain resilience in their global supply chains during the COVID-19 pandemic and to advance our understanding of supply chain risk management. The individual chapters of the book contribute to a considerable gain in knowledge in science and practice by:

- Explaining empirical and analytic findings from research
- Examining new models and methods
- Providing examples of best and effective risk management practices

The emergence of COVID-19 and how it has affected supply chains globally has made us "re-conceptualize" how we understand supply chain risk and resilience. In some ways, we are entering the phase of "Supply Chain Risk Management 2.0." The initial impetus for supply chain risk and resilience scholarship started near the turn of the new millennium. Slightly over one score later, and especially from our experiences with the pandemic, we clearly see that supply chain risk is not going away anytime soon. However, from the challenges almost every firm encountered during the various stages of COVID-19, and even continuing today as of the time this book is published, we believe many of the learning lessons promoted in this book provide insight for firms to more effectively and efficiently ensure supply chain resilience from a multitude of threats. Recent events such as the Suez Canal blockage, the war in Ukraine, and global inflation provide us with constant reminders of the pressures that supply chain professionals face in managing supply chain risk.

Ultimately, the intention of publishing this book is to provide the reader greater knowledge, strategic approaches, new methods, and practical tools for proactively ensuring global supply chain resilience. It is only by better understanding supply chain risk and resilience that we can create more robust supply chains that withstand the ever-present threats existing in today's supply chains. COVID-19 has provided us a "petri dish" for investigating how organizations addressed one of the most, if not most significant, large-scale supply chain disruption in our lifetime. We hope that this book takes us one step closer in re-conceptualizing supply chain risk in order to create resilience in a post-pandemic world.

Egham, UK   Omera Khan
Fulda, Germany   Michael Huth
St Louis, MO   George A. Zsidisin
Dortmund, Germany   Michael Henke

References

Brindley, C. (2004). *Supply chain risk*. Ashgate. isbn:0754639029.

Khan, O., & George, A. Z. (2012). *Handbook for supply chain risk management: Case studies, effective practices and emerging trends*. J. Ross. isbn:978-1604270389.

Prahalad, C. K., & Hamel, G. (1990). The core competence of the corporation. *Harvard Business Review, 68*(3), 79–91.

Sheffi, Y. (2020). *The new (Ab) normal: Reshaping business and supply chain strategy beyond Covid-19*. MIT CTL Media. isbn:978-1735766119.

Womack, J. P., Daniel, T. J., & Roos, D. (1990). *The machine that changed the world*. Rawson Associates.

Zsidisin, G. A., & Henke, M. (2019). *Revisiting supply chain risk* (Vol. 7). Springer Series in Supply Chain Management. Springer. isbn:978-3030038120.

Zsidisin, G. A., & Ritchie, R. (2009). *Supply chain risk: A handbook of assessment, management, & performance*. Springer International. isbn:978-0387799339.

Contents

Editors and Contributors

About the Editors

Omera Khan, Ph.D., has gained international recognition for her research and thought leadership in supply chain risk management and resilience. Following an academic career spanning over two decades, she has joined Maersk as their Head of Supply Chain Insights and Trends Lab within the Corporate Strategy department. Omera has led numerous research projects, commissioned by government agencies, research councils and companies, and is an advisor to both businesses and universities on the broader topics of strategic supply chain risk management, sustainability and resilience. Her research is published in several peer reviewed journals and book chapters. She is a highly acclaimed speaker and is regularly invited to deliver keynotes and speak at global conferences and corporate events. Omera was awarded her PhD from Alliance Manchester Business School, UK and she started her academic career at the Centre for Logistics and Supply Chain Management at Cranfield University. Omera held several senior academic apointments before moving to Denmark, as a Professor of Operations Management at Denmark Technical University (DTU) and she has held a number of adjunct Professor positions in the Nordics. Omera is a Chartered Fellow of the Chartered Institute of Logistics and Transport and Fellow of the Chartered Institute of Procurement and Supply.

Michael Huth has held the professorship for Business Administration, in particular Logistics, at the Department of Business at Fulda University of Applied Sciences since 2006 and is the scientific director of the "HOLM" research network. Prof. Huth's research focuses on supply chain risk management, process management, digitalization, and sustainability in supply chains. From 2009 to 2011, he was Vice Dean and, from 2011 to 2014, Dean of the Department of Business. In addition, he can look back on stays as a visiting professor in Australia and the USA as well as teaching positions in the Czech Republic, Turkey, Jordan, and Poland. Prof. Huth studied business administration at Goethe University in Frankfurt am Main and Southampton University (UK). After serving as a research assistant at Goethe

University, he initially worked as a self-employed management consultant and in 2003 founded a consulting company focusing on logistics and risk management before switching to academia in 2006.

George A. Zsidisin, Ph.D. (Arizona State University), CPSM, C.P.M., is the John W. Barriger III Professor and Director of the Supply Chain Risk and Resilience Research (SCR3) Institute at the University of Missouri—St. Louis, USA. Professor Zsidisin's research focuses on how firms assess and manage risk associated with supply disruptions and price volatility in their supply chains. He has published over 80 research and practitioner articles and seven books. His research on supply chain risk has been funded by the AT&T Foundation and IBM, and he has received numerous awards, such as from the Institute for Supply Management, Deutsche Post, the Council of Supply Chain Management Professionals, and the Decision Sciences Institute. Further, he is one of the founding members of the *International Supply Chain Risk Management* (ISCRiM) network, teaches and leads discussions on supply chain management and risk with various Executive Education Programs and numerous companies in the USA and Europe, is Co-Editor Emeritus of the *Journal of Purchasing & Supply Management* and serves on the Editorial Review Board for several academic supply chain journals.

Michael Henke is Director of Fraunhofer Institute for Material Flow and Logistics IML in Dortmund and holds the Chair in Enterprise Logistics (LFO) at the Faculty of Mechanical Engineering at TU Dortmund University, Germany. Furthermore, he is Adjunct Professor for Supply Chain Management at the School of Business and Management of Lappeenranta University of Technology in Finland. His research focuses inter alia on management of Industry 4.0 and platform economy, blockchain and smart contracts, financial supply chain management, supply chain risk management, procurement, logistics, and supply chain management. During and after his habilitation, he worked for the Supply Management Group SMG in St. Gallen, Switzerland. From 2007 until 2013, he was active in teaching and research as a professor at EBS European Business School.

Contributors

Saban Adana is Assistant Professor of Supply Chain Management at John Carroll University. His research interest includes supply chain resilience and risk management, supply chain learning, transportation management, and organizational factors that influence the performance of a supply chain. He received his undergraduate degree from United States Military Academy at West Point in 2002 in both system engineering and international relations. He earned his master's degree in National Security Affairs at Naval Postgraduate School in Monterey California and Turkish

Army War College. He earned his Ph.D. degree in Business-Logistics Systems at the University of North Texas in 2020. Saban Adana is the corresponding author and can be contacted at: sadana@jcu.edu.

Osaro Aigbogun, Ph.D., is a pharmacist and management specialist with a background in the pharmaceutical industry, academia, and management consulting. He is passionate about sharing his knowledge on pharmaceutical supply chain resilience, strategic management, and critical thinking. He has taught and led programs at the tertiary level for about a decade; and currently lectures students from diverse nationalities, directs a number of research projects, and sits on the examination board for doctoral candidates. He has spoken in a number of international conferences and delivered training and workshops on a wide range of subjects, including crisis management, pharmaceutical supply chain resilience, international business management, strategic management, and global issues in entrepreneurship. His current research focuses on developing innovative conceptual frameworks and analytical methods for supporting the operation of the global pharmaceutical supply chain in order to increase supply chain resilience.

Max Arnold is working as a Supplier Logistics Engineer at Schaeffler Automotive Buehl GmbH & Co. KG, based in Bühl, Germany. He has specialized in the optimization of automotive supply chains with regard to lean principles, resilience, and sustainability criteria. Max Arnold studied industrial engineering and management (MSc) at Karlsruhe Institute of Technology (KIT) and University of Massachusetts Amherst. Outside his professional life, he is a passionate chess player and holds the chess title FIDE Master.

Becem Bourbita is a Strategic Purchaser at DEMCON, a Dutch-based engineering company which is active as a high-end technology supplier in a wide range of markets. Becem earned an MBA—with a specific track in the field of purchasing and supply management—at the University of Twente. Becem has extensive experience in setting up new international supply chains for high-end technology projects. During the COVID-19 pandemic and the resulting supply chain disruptions, Becem played a significant role in scaling up the supply chain in order to increase the production of medical ventilators in the fight against COVID-19.

Hasan Celik is an Assistant Professor of Management at Robert Morris University, Moon Twp, PA, USA. His research interests include performance-based contracts, supply chain resilience, inter-organizational relations, relational contracts, and marketing strategy. He received his BS in System Engineering with a minor in Industrial Engineering in 2002 from Turkish Military Academy, his MS in Management (Manpower Systems Analysis) in 2011 from Naval Postgraduate School, Monterey, California, USA, and his MA in International Security Strategy Management and Leadership in Turkish Army War College in 2013. He earned his Ph.D. degree in Business-Logistics Systems at the University of North Texas in 2020.

Sedat Cevikparmak is Assistant Professor of Supply Chain Management at DeSales University, Center Valley, PA, USA. His research interests include effects of risk propensities on contracts, performance-based contracts, transaction cost economics theory and risk neutrality assumption, logistics infrastructure scorecard, and supply chain finance. He received his BS in Foreign Area Studies (Middle East) in 1997 at the United States Military Academy at West Point, NY, and his MS in National Security Affairs (Middle East) in 2002 at Naval Postgraduate School, Monterey, CA. He earned his Ph.D. degree in Business-Logistics sSystems at the University of North Texas in 2020.

Thomas Choi is the AT&T Professor of the W. P. Carey School of Business at Arizona State University. As a researcher of supply chain management, he has studied the upstream side of supply chains. He has published articles in *Decision Sciences*, *Harvard Business Review*, *Journal of Operations Management*, *Journal of Supply Chain Management*, *Production and Operations Management*, and others. He currently serves as co-director of the Complex Adaptive Supply Networks Research Accelerator (CASN-RA). He has co-authored three practitioner books including one on supply chain financing. More recently, he served as the lead editor of the *Oxford Handbook of Supply Chain Management*. From 2014 to 2019, he served as the Executive Director of CAPS Research. From 2011 to 2014, he served as co-editor-in-chief of the *Journal of Operations Management*. Since 2018, he has been listed as a Highly Cited Researcher by Clarivate's Web of Science.

Sascha Düerkop is Research Associate in the fields of supply chain management and logistics at Fulda University of Applied Sciences. He also works as researcher at the Fraunhofer Institute for Technological Trend Analysis. As a mathematician and economist by profession he tries to work on the edge of both disciplines by using quantitative methods to tackle economic challenges. Today, Mr. Düerkop is engaged in research on disaster and relief management, risk management, and supply chain resilience.

David Entrop, Customer Solutions Manager, Kuehne + Nagel Ltd., Canada, is a supply chain professional with a high level of competence in driving the adoption of digital solutions and optimizing supply chain processes. In the recent past, his focus has also been on closely monitoring current market developments in the logistics service provider industry and therewith helping to shape strategic directions. In his still young career, he has already gained extensive insights into the world of logistics and international freight forwarding through positions as a sea freight export coordinator at Kuehne+Nagel and in order management at Michelin. Currently, he is part of the Customer Solutions team within Kuehne+Nagel Canada and leads activities for the Canada central region. David Entrop holds a Master of Science degree in Supply Chain Management from Fulda University of Applied Sciences and a Bachelor of Science degree in International Management from the University of Applied Sciences Karlsruhe.

Pietro Evangelista is Research Director in Logistics and Supply Chain Management (SCM) at the Institute on Studies on the Mediterranean (ISMed) of the National Research Council (CNR), Italy. Pietro is a business economist by profession, and he was awarded a Ph.D. in logistics and SCM by Heriot-Watt University (UK). His current scientific interest focuses on the role of digitalization in the logistics service industry and decarbonization strategies in freight transport and logistics. Pietro is a member of the Research Committee of the European Logistics Association (ELA).

Barbara Gaudenzi, Ph.D., is Associate Professor in Supply Chain Management and Risk Management at the Department of Business Administration at the University of Verona, Italy (since 2011). She is Director of RiskMaster, Master's in Risk Management and is Director of LogiMaster, Master's in Supply Chain Management at the University of Verona. Her research interests are, in particular, supply chain management, supply chain risk management, resilience, and cyber risk in supply chains. She has published in several leading international journals, such as *Industrial Marketing Management*, *Journal of Purchasing and Supply Management*, *Supply Chain Management: an International Journal*, *International Journal of Production Economics*, *European Management Journal*, and others.

Jukka Hallikas is Professor of Supply Chain Management at LUT University, School of Business and Management (Finland). His current research interests focus on purchasing and supply operations, supply chain risk management, and digitalization of supply chains.

Erik Hofmann is the Director of the Institute of Supply Chain Management at the University of St. Gallen, Switzerland. He started his academic career at the Technical University of Darmstadt, Germany, where he also received his Ph.D. His primary research interest is innovations in purchasing, business logistics, supply chain financing, and operations management. He is a member of the board of the Supply Chain Finance Community (SCFC). Dr. Hofmann's research is published in, e.g., *Journal of Business Logistics*, *International Journal of Production Economics*, and *International Journal of Physical Distribution & Logistics Management*. He is the author of several awarded books like *Performance Measurement and Incentive Systems in Purchasing* and *Financing the End-to-End Supply Chain*.

Yavuz Idug is a second-year Ph.D. student in the logistics and supply chain management doctoral program at the University of North Texas. He received his Bachelor of Science degree in Management and International Relations from the Unites States Military Academy, West Point, NY, and his MBA in Financial Management from Naval Postgraduate School, Monterey, CA. His research interests include sharing economy, last-mile delivery, supply chain sustainability, and transparency.

Mika Immonen is Associate Professor at LUT University, School of Business and Management (Finland). He has worked in various projects focusing on healthcare technology and consumer behavior in health-related services. His accomplished academic works are services systems' structures, emerging business models, and customer value creation in multi-stakeholder environments.

Markus Johannsen, Senior Vice President Global Seafreight, Kuehne + Nagel (AG & Co) KG, has over 20 years of international transportation and logistics experience and currently has the global responsibility for the operation of the Seafreight business unit. In 2019, he was driving the new organizational, much more customer centric setup as well as utilizing technology to realize efficiency gains across the business. His focus during the last 3 years was on providing industry leading visibility, prediction of events, as well as making use of data to increase resilience of supply chains hand in hand with adjusting the operations to execute against the learnings and deliver the promised customer excellence. Previous to his current role, Mr. Johannsen was Senior Vice President Seafreight North Asia Pacific region from 2014 to 2018. He has a well-balanced perspective of Asia Pacific in particular China, having worked and lived in Shanghai since 2008 in various Seafreight Management positions.

Anni-Kaisa Kähkönen is Professor of Supply Management at LUT University, School of Business and Management (Finland). Her current research interests include sustainable purchasing and supply management, management of multi-tier sustainable supply chains, supply strategies, and value creation in purchasing and supply management.

Barno Kholikova is a graduate of the international Jacobs University Bremen. She has a BSc in Industrial Engineering and is currently employed at Zalando SE as Assistant Merchandise Planner. At the same time, she is completing a part-time master's degree at the Technical University of Berlin. Barno Kholikova is looking forward to diving into the academic world together with the industry and pursuing a scientific research project in one of the following topics: product design and development in the automotive industry, integrated and sustainable supply chain networks, advanced lean management principles, and associated supply chain disruption risks.

Johanna Kim Kippenberger is a research assistant at the Fraunhofer Institute for Material Flow and Logistics (IML) in Dortmund, Germany. The focus of her research is supply chain simulation using the OTD-NET simulation tool. While in the past the simulation tool was mainly used for bottleneck analyses and evaluations of actual and target concepts in the automotive industry, she identifies application cases in other sectors. Triggered by the COVID-19 pandemic, the use of simulation in crisis situations is of particular interest. In this context, she is primarily looking at the supply chains of crisis-relevant goods, such as medical goods. Her work includes researching the coupling simulation with artificial intelligence for the evaluation of effects of disruptive events and a quick parametrization of the supply chain.

Philipp Klink is simulation expert at the Department of Supply Chain Engineering at Fraunhofer Institute for Material Flow and Logistics. He gained his simulation expertise in various projects with the industry. With his additional proficiency in digitalization projects, he supports an extension and reshaping of the simulation software OTD-NET. By working with the supply chain simulation, Philipp Klink established major expertise in risk management solutions. Next to the simulation, he applied Crystal Ball® for predictive modeling of risk situations.

Maximilian Klöckner (MSc, Technical University of Darmstadt) is a doctoral researcher at the Chair of Logistics Management at the Swiss Federal Institute of Technology Zurich (ETH Zurich), Switzerland. His main research interests are at the interface of operations management and information systems, examining the financial implications of disruptive technologies for operations and supply chain management applications. He is also interested in supply chain risk management, particularly in the role of digital technologies for disruption resilience. Maximilian's work has been published in different operations and innovation management journals, such as *Production and Operations Management*, *Journal of Business Logistics*, and *Research-Technology Management*.

Carsten Knauer studied economics and business administration at the Bavarian Julius Maximilian University in Würzburg. The focus was on competition and economic policy as well as procurement market analyses. After a brief stint at the Chair of Industrial Management in Würzburg, he joined the BME as a consultant with a focus on service purchasing. Since 2016, he has been in charge of the logistics section and has focused on supply chain management issues, especially in the areas of digitalization, sustainability, and risk management.

Rohan Y. Korde is currently pursuing doctoral studies in supply chain management at the W. P. Carey School of Business at Arizona State University. He is interested in studying problems in the movement of physical goods in global supply networks as well as the financing mechanisms among the various intermediaries. He is also interested in coordination, competition, cooperation, and coopetition dynamics between organizations to improve supply chain efficiency and flexibility.

Rudolf Leuschner is Associate Professor in the Department of Supply Chain Management and the Program Director for the online Master of Science in Supply Chain Management program at Rutgers Business School. His research focuses on the end-to-end supply chain and the integration of its three primary flows: products, information, and finances. Specifically, in the new field of supply chain finance, he has been active in developing relevant insights for academic and practitioner audiences. He received his Ph.D. in Logistics and a minor in marketing from the Ohio State University. His work has appeared among others in the *Journal of Supply*

Chain Management, Journal of Business Logistics, Decision Sciences, the *Journal of Business Ethics, Harvard Business Review*, and *Rutgers Business Review*.

Katrina Lintukangas is Professor of Supply Management at LUT University, School of Business and Management (Finland). Her current research focuses on innovations, sustainable purchasing and supply management, risk management and supply chain resiliency, and value creation in public procurement.

Roberta Pellegrino is Associate Professor in Management Engineering at Politecnico di Bari (Italy). Her main research interests are in public–private partnership (PPP), supply chain risk management, real options theory, and other topics in the field of economic management engineering. She coordinates and is involved in research projects with companies and other private/public organizations. She is member of the ISCRIM network (Supply Chain Risk Management Network) and has been member of European project European Cooperation in the field of Scientific and Technical Research—COST—"Public Private Partnerships in Transport: Trends and Theory" since 2010. She has been teacher for several master's courses or Ph.D. lecturer on the themes as risk management, PPP, and real option theory. She has been a visiting scholar at Columbia University (New York, USA). She is author of more than 45 publications in international journals and books, and more than 60 papers presented at international and national conferences.

Dale Rogers is the ON Semiconductor Professor of Business at Arizona State University. He is also the Director of the Frontier Economies Logistics Lab and the Co-Director of the Internet edge Supply Chain Lab ASU. He is the Principal Investigator of the $15 million CARISCA Project at Kwame Nkrumah University of Science and Technology in Kumasi, Ghana, and also a visiting professor there. Dale is the Director of Global Projects for ILOS—Instituto de Logística e Supply Chain in Rio de Janeiro, Brazil. He is the 2021 CSCMP Distinguished Service Award winner.

Saskia Sardesai is deputy head of the Department of Supply Chain Engineering at Fraunhofer Institute for Material Flow and Logistics (IML) in Dortmund. In her function as Senior Scientist for SCM Research and Strategy, she focuses on topics of supply chain management concerning risk management, discrete event simulation, and interfacing application areas for artificial intelligence. She specializes in designs of logistics structures and processes with an emphasis on global supply chains and supplier management. Within her doctoral thesis she evaluated robustness and resilience of global supply chain networks. Saskia Sardesai gained international experience during her employment at Kuehne+Nagel India Pvt. Ltd. where she worked for several years in the Department of Contract Logistics. Having been in charge of continuous improvement at Indian warehouse facilities, she has profound knowledge about intralogistics processes.

Andreas Schick is Chief Operating Officer (COO) at Schaeffler AG, Herzogenaurach, Germany. In his function as Executive Board Member and COO he is responsible for production, supply chain management, and purchasing. Before this position he was responsible for the Schaeffler business in Asia Pacific located out of Singapore. Andreas Schick studied Automotive Engineering at the University of Applied Sciences in Munich, Germany. After his studies he held several positions as development engineer, production lead for a clutch plant, and plant manager for an iron casting foundry in Brazil. His professional career also included president of LuK North America and the lead of the business unit Transmission Applications at Schaeffler, Germany. Andreas is member of the supervisory board of SupplyOn AG, Germany (since 2018), advisory board member of the German Logistics Association (BVL), since 2019, and Deputy Chairman of VDA Produktionsausschuss (since 2019).

Christoph G. Schmidt (Ph.D., EBS University of Business and Law) is a postdoctoral researcher at the Chair of Logistics Management at the Swiss Federal Institute of Technology Zurich (ETH Zurich), Switzerland. His research interests in operations and supply chain management include supply chain risks and disruptions, sustainable practices and performance along the supply chain, and the intersection of social media technologies and supply chain management. His work has appeared in the *Journal of Operations Management, Production and Operations Management, Journal of Supply Chain Management, Journal of Business Logistics, Journal of Purchasing & Supply Management*, and other journals.

Florian Schupp works as Head of Purchasing & Supplier Management Automotive Technologies at Schaeffler Automotive Buehl GmbH & Co. KG, Germany. He completed his Ph.D. at the Technical University Berlin in the field of strategy development in purchasing and logistics and has more than 20 years of purchasing experience. He integrates practical purchasing and supply management work with academic research together with the Universities of Missouri—St. Louis (USA), Catania (Italy), Lappeenranta (Finland), and Savoie Mont Blanc (Chambéry, France). He teaches international purchasing and supply management and does research at the Technical University Berlin and at Jacobs University Bremen, where he is Adjunct Professor for Logistics. His main research interests are purchasing strategy, behavioral aspects in purchasing, purchasing in nature, and supplier innovation. Florian Schupp is a member of the Advisory Boards of BLG Logistics, Bremen, Germany; Xtronic GmbH, Böblingen, Germany; and SupplyOn AG, Hallbergmoos, Germany.

ManMohan S. Sodhi (Ph.D., UCLA) is professor in operations and supply chain management at the Business School (formerly Cass) at City University of London. His interests lie in supply chain management broadly, with papers in risk, sustainability, finance, and technology. His current projects include (1) supply chain management in extreme conditions such as those caused by the pandemic; (2) supply chains for recovery after disasters and development; (3) modern slavery; (4) public–private supply chains; and (5) use of analytics and technologies in the supply chain including for finance.

Christopher S. Tang (Ph.D., Yale) is UCLA Distinguished Professor and Edward W. Carter Chair in Business Administration. His current research is focused on social innovation in developing countries, identifying how companies operate in the environment to do good while doing well at the same time. Exposure to real-life industry projects motivated his academic research. He has developed teaching cases on a variety of concerns such as micro-finance for the poor, mobile platforms for developing economies, creating shared values and direct procurement of agricultural products, response management in disasters, and new business models in the age of the Internet.

Simon Templar is a qualified management accountant and a visiting fellow at Cranfield University. Simon has over 20 years' industrial and managerial experience before joining Cranfield University. Simon completed his Ph.D. at Cranfield in 2013 and lectures on management accounting and supply chain costing. His research interests are related to supply chain finance and costing. Simon has authored and collaborated on journal, conference, and practitioner papers. Simon's work was recognized by the International Federation of Accountants Articles of Merit Award Program for Distinguished Contribution to Management Accounting in 2005. His recent books include *Supply Chain Management Accounting: Managing Profitability, Working Capital and Asset Utilization* (2019), and he co-authored *Financing the End-To-End Supply Chain: A Reference Guide to Supply Chain Finance* (2020). Simon is a founding member of the Supply Chain Finance Community, a non-for-profit association, which aims to share supply chain finance good practice and research.

Hasan Uvet is Assistant Professor of Logistics and Supply Chain Management at the Georgia Gwinnett College, Lawrenceville, Georgia, USA. His research interests include performance-based contracts, logistics service quality, and supply chain learning. He received his BS in System Engineering with a minor in Business Administration in 2003 from Turkish Military Academy, and his MA in International Security Strategy Management and Leadership in Turkish Army War College in 2013. He earned his Ph.D. degree in Business-Logistics Systems at the University of North Texas in 2015.

Stefan Viehmann Senior Vice President Global Customer Solutions, Kuehne + Nagel (AG & Co) KG, has long-standing experience in international logistics, IT management, and business consultancy. For more than 10 years, he is globally responsible for the Kuehne+Nagel Customer Solutions organization. The teams consult, integrate, and support customers with digital solutions, offering visibility and information services for air, sea, and road logistics. He joined Kuehne + Nagel Ltd. Canada in 2007 and served as Country Vice President IT until 2011. Before Kuehne+Nagel from 2001 until 2006, Stefan Viehmann worked for DHL in various IT management roles in the German country organization, developing and rolling out customer facing tools and technologies. He started his professional career as a business consultant at Andersen Consulting (now Accenture) in 1997. Viehmann holds an MBA degree from Marburg University, Germany.

Remko van Hoek is a full professor of practice in the Supply Chain Management Department of the Sam M. Walton College of Business at the University of Arkansas. He is also executive director of the CSCMP Supply Chain Hall of Fame which is hosted by the Walton College as a service to the supply chain profession and is an advisor to several companies. Prior to joining the Walton College, he worked in procurement and supply chain executive roles around the world for a number of companies, including Disney, Nike, and PwC, and he taught in the UK, the Netherlands, and Belgium.

Stephan M. Wagner (Ph.D., University of St. Gallen) is Professor of Supply Chain Management, holds the Chair of Logistics Management, and is Director of the HumOSCM Lab at the Swiss Federal Institute of Technology Zurich (ETH Zurich). His current research interests include the management of startups as suppliers, supplier innovation, digitalization, supply chain sustainability, and humanitarian operations and supply chain management. His work has been published in management journals, such as the *Academy of Management Journal*, *Journal of Management*, and *Journal of Business Research*, as well as operations management journals, such as *Journal of Operations Management*, *Production and Operations Management*, *Decision Sciences*, and *Journal of Supply Chain Management*.

Heiko Wöhner is Vice President Supply Management & Sustainability Automotive Technologies at Schaeffler Automotive Buehl GmbH & Co. KG, based in Bühl, Germany. He is an expert for the setup and management of international automotive supply chains with more than 10 years of experience. Together with the supplier base, third parties, and research institutions, he develops strategies for material and information flows in automotive supply chains—and puts them into practice. He studied industrial economics and management at the University of Bremen (Germany) and Mid Sweden University (Sweden). His doctoral theses at European Business School focused on supply chain integration. Before joining Schaeffler, Heiko Wöhner was a project manager at German Logistics Association (BVL).

Part I
Approaches, Methods and Models

One can never really know how exposed to risk one is until one is tested. The COVID-19 pandemic called into question the veracity of models and processes that had until 2020 been staples of the modern supply chain. Before then, the idea that lean and agile, or indeed Just-In-Time, might be the undoing of supply networks would have carried little weight. How times have changed!

In the face of such an uncertain and dynamic environment, almost every single industry was forced to re-examine how they managed their supply chains. In many ways this wake-up call was needed. The challenges firms encountered serve to underline the importance of resilience and risk management and the immediacy with which they should be dealt. The aftermath of the pandemic has provided a new lens in the way we view supply chain risk management and resilience.

Part I of this book, *Approaches, Method and Models*, examines the impact of the pandemic on supply chain theories, models and approaches through systematic literature reviews and the conceptual development of new models and frameworks. It provides an overview of how to create resilience and re-conceptualise supply chain risk management, and investigates measures and methods to plan, prepare, react and evaluate the supply chain disruptions.

Chapter 1, *How to manage impacts of disruptions during the COVID-19 pandemic*, provides a systematic literature review that investigates the impact of the pandemic on supply chain management areas and actors. It seeks to understand the resilience strategies companies can learn and apply, and also describes the key digital approaches that they can take to respond to COVID-19.

The authors argue that the stream of current research could benefit from qualitative and empirical studies examining how firms and supply chains were able to ensure resilience during the height of COVID-19. They add that while there are strategies for mitigating and controlling the effects of COVID-19 on supply chains, no studies measuring their effectiveness exist. They finally suggest that some of the different methods for resilience and risk mitigation—flexibility, visibility and agility—are combined and examined to find ways for companies to improve supply chain performance.

The authors also review the role of digitisation as a way of dealing with disruption, establishing that it improves supply chain resilience when combined with other strategies. They suggest that because there are no studies to provide guidelines to organisations on how to implement this in an organisation, companies need to have a structured model supporting the adoption of digital solutions if they are to improve supply chain resilience.

In Chap. 2, *Covid-19 Disruption impacts on Supply Chains*, the authors explore the effects of the pandemic on upstream and downstream supply chains, drawing on survey data from the medical device industry. The study examines the strategies used by Italian and Finnish medical companies in response to COVID-19 and looks into how they responded per disruption effect.

The authors identify managerial implications for companies that are resilient (low upstream and downstream impact), downstream resilient (those experiencing upstream COVID-19 effects, but low/no downstream effects) and unprepared (those experiencing upstream and downstream effects) and suggest practices and strategies for pursuing greater resilience in the future. While the pandemic highlights the vulnerability of global supply chains and their reliance on certain regions, it also reveals the need to ensure long-term viability. They state that, while the pandemic has highlighted the vulnerability of global supply chains, and their reliance on certain regions, it also revealed the need to ensure long-term viability. That can only happen through developing new competencies and capabilities.

The authors add that in order to do so, it is necessary to explore and understand impacts in real-terms—which is what the evaluation of upstream and downstream impacts demonstrates. Among the conclusions they draw, the most pressing is perhaps the need to carefully consider decisions to realign resources to better respond to customer demand.

Chapter 3, *An Exploration of Resilience in Medical Gloves Supply Chain during the COVID-19 Pandemic*, advances the discussion of downstream effects of the COVID-19 pandemic by examining how organisations in the medical glove supply chain Implemented various strategies for improving supply during a global health crisis. Using a qualitative study, the author identifies 20 main themes that are categorised into seven vulnerability drivers and 13 capability drivers, each representing indicators of supply chain resilience.

The challenge for businesses today is to devise strategies for building a resilient supply chain that is capable of mitigating vulnerabilities to disruption. Success therefore is partly dependent on the adaptive capability of a supply chain and its ability to prepare for and respond to disruptions to facilitate a timely and cost-effective recovery.

To that end, the author's findings highlight the need for the aforementioned capabilities to be viewed as essential internal resources that can be used to improve and foster competitive advantage. The drivers offer insight and clarity into weaknesses, strengths, and opportunities to improve resilience and mitigate risk; moreover, they provide a tested and proven means for dealing with disruption in medical supply chains.

Chapter 4, *Status Quo of Supply Chain Risk Management: Results of an Empirical Study in Germany*, discusses the need for supply chain risk management systems to have a certain level of maturity. The authors state that the maturity level is usually assessed qualitatively and not through other means such as empirical surveys. Their study assessed the maturity of companies in German speaking countries through a set of 40 questions in order to gain a detailed and quantified picture of participants' SCRM systems.

The approach led to insights that enable targeted improvements of SCRM systems. By establishing the current status quo of SCRM within in an organisation, the authors argue that measures to evolve and improve risk performance can be developed and, moreover, determine the extent to which greater visibility is called for in the future.

In that context, the authors suggest that it is relatively easy to establish a structured, systematic and lean process for identifying, analysing and managing risks. They state that established risk management methods can be used to support the process and that it should be anchored to the organisational structure.

It is well known that crisis creates opportunity and that necessity breeds innovation. If there is any "silver lining" emerging from the pandemic it is that the opportunities that lie ahead will help organizations shape a stronger, more resilient future. Innovation will be the driving force.

The chapters in this part offer a map of the territory, a collation of ideas and a platform for further discussion. They are the precursor from which to develop further theory and practical guidance. Of course, the solutions herein are a starting point—a launching pad for further experimentation for trial and error and for the development of best practice for supply chain risk management and resilience.

As we move from a bruising period into one of recovery and regrowth, risk and resilience will be pivotal in the development of supply chains. As technology develops further and as sustainability moves further up the corporate agenda, we should expect more disruption. Therein lies an opportunity. Change is the only constant, and with it comes the opportunity to test, to refine and to adapt– all of which are precursors to growth. With that in mind, resilience matters more now than at any other time in recent history.

Chapter 1
Impacts and Supply Chain Resilience Strategies to Cope with COVID-19 Pandemic: A Literature Review

Roberta Pellegrino and Barbara Gaudenzi

Abstract Coronavirus COVID-19 is an extraordinary event that can be categorized as a subcategory of Supply Chain (SC) disruptions. This pandemic has impacted supply chains differently, depending on the produced item, the industry, and the role of firms along the supply chains.

Several studies, that emerged during the last 2 years, have analyzed the impact of COVID-19 on supply chains and firms, and the strategies adopted to cope with the pandemic. In addition to several resilience strategies, papers also highlighted the key role of digitalization to support firms in building more effective resilience strategies. The literature on the topic is however still fragmented. To overcome this fragmentation, our chapter offers a Systematic Literature Review (SLR), which investigates, in particular, the impacts of COVID-19 on Supply Chain Management (SCM) areas and actors, the SC resilience strategies which can enable firms to cope with the pandemic, and the role of digitalization.

1 Introduction

Coronavirus COVID-19 represents one of the most challenging disruptive events over the last decades, causing extraordinary impacts on economy, people, and firms (Araz et al., 2020). It can be categorized as Supply Chain (SC) disruptions, having in particular three characteristics: "(a) long-term disruption existence with unpredictable scaling, (b) simultaneous disruption propagation in the SC (i.e., the ripple effect) and epidemic outbreak propagation (i.e., pandemic propagation), and (c) simultaneous disruptions in supply, demand, and logistics infrastructure" (Ivanov, 2020).

R. Pellegrino (✉)
Department of Mechanics, Mathematics and Management, Politecnico di Bari, Bari, Italy
e-mail: roberta.pellegrino@poliba.it

B. Gaudenzi
Department of Business Administration, University of Verona, Verona, Italy
e-mail: barbara.gaudenzi@univr.it

Since the SCs of many companies are increasingly lean and globalized in their structures, they are more exposed to disruptions (Shih, 2020). Fortune (2020) indicated that 94% of the companies listed in the Fortune 1000 list were facing SC disruptions due to COVID-19. The pandemic has impacted supply chains differently, depending on the produced item, the industry, and the role of firms along the supply chain.

Scholars have recently studied this topic and, consequently, several papers have been published so far. However, the literature is still highly fragmented (Deloitte, 2020). Some scholars studied challenges posed by COVID-19 for suppliers (Sodhi & Tang, 2021), for customers, and others for manufacturers (Belhadi et al., 2021; Handfield et al., 2020). To the best of the authors' knowledge, there is no state-of-art review of the literature focusing on COVID-19 challenges for firms, and responses developed by companies to deal with them, including the adoption of digital supply chain technologies to manage resilience during pandemic disruptions (Balakrishnan & Ramanathan, 2021; Ivanov, 2021).On the other hand, the World Economic Forum—WEF (2020a, 2020b) emphasized the need for firms and organizations to reengineer and adapt SCs to their future trade challenges. Firms are continuously facing exceptional challenges during COVID-19 that require them to design their SC operations to deliver quick and accurate goods and services at the highest degree of safety and security (Sharma et al., 2020a, 2020b). As a result, this chapter performs a systematic literature review (SLR) on COVID-19 impacts, mitigation strategies and role of digitalization with the ambition of identifying research gaps, thus shedding light on future research directions and providing some tangible guidelines that might be used by researchers and practitioners involved in this field.

The key research questions of this study are therefore the following ones:

RQ1. What is the impact of COVID-19 on key SCM areas and actors?
RQ2. How do SC resilience strategies enable firms to cope with the COVID-19 pandemic?
RQ3. How does digitalization help firms to respond to the COVID-19 pandemic?

2 Systematic Literature Review Methodology

In this study, we adopted a Systematic Literature Review (SLR) methodology based on the approach of Tranfield et al. (2003). This approach has been recently widely adopted in SC contexts (Chowdhury et al., 2021; Queiroz et al., 2019, 2020; Kamal & Irani, 2014).

We followed the three key phases for designing a SLR (Tranfield et al., 2003; Sawyerr & Harrison, 2019):

Identification of Studies
We selected studies published—from 2020 until May 2021—in Scopus, as a primary source, including other contributions from Wiley Online Library, Science Direct,

Emerald, Google Scholar, Taylor and Francis Online, SpringerLink, and others were supplementary (Datta, 2017).

Selection and Evaluation of Studies
According to the key research questions, we selected the keywords and search parameters:

TITLE-ABS-KEY (impact AND covid-19 AND supply AND chain AND strateg* OR resilien* OR digital* OR innovation) AND (EXCLUDE (SRCTYPE, "p")) AND (LIMIT-TO OR LIMIT-TO) AND (LIMIT TO (LANGUAGE, "English")).

We excluded documents deriving from conferences and not-coherent articles, including other few documents that we found relevant. The final database is composed of 92 articles.

The SLR procedure is illustrated in Fig. 1.1, while Table 1.1 reports the results of the papers selected in each database.

Analysis and Synthesis
Each article was in-depth read by analyzing the content with regard to the key focuses of the research. The selected articles were therefore classified according to the three key focuses: Impacts (73 papers), Mitigation Strategies (58 papers), and Digitization (53 papers) (Fig. 1.2).

The methodologies adopted in the articles have been grouped as indicated in Fig. 1.3.

3 Results

This section discusses the key results of the SLR, in particular the impacts of COVID-19 on supply chain management key areas and actors, also analyzing the role of resilience strategies, and digitalization.

3.1 Impacts of COVID-19 on Key SCM Areas

73 articles describe the impacts of COVID-19 on supply chains, that have been linked to the following key SCM areas: demand management impacts, supply management impacts, production management impacts, transportation and logistics management impacts, relationship management and supply chain-wide impacts, and financial management impacts. Regarding the key impacts related to the *demand management* area, researchers reported fluctuating demand and panic buying, which reflect a change in consumer buying behavior (Shen et al., 2020). COVID-19 has led to a drastic drop in demand in the HORECA sector (Rivera-Ferre et al., 2021; Borsellino et al., 2020), and unexpected picks in FMCGs (Deconinck et al., 2020),

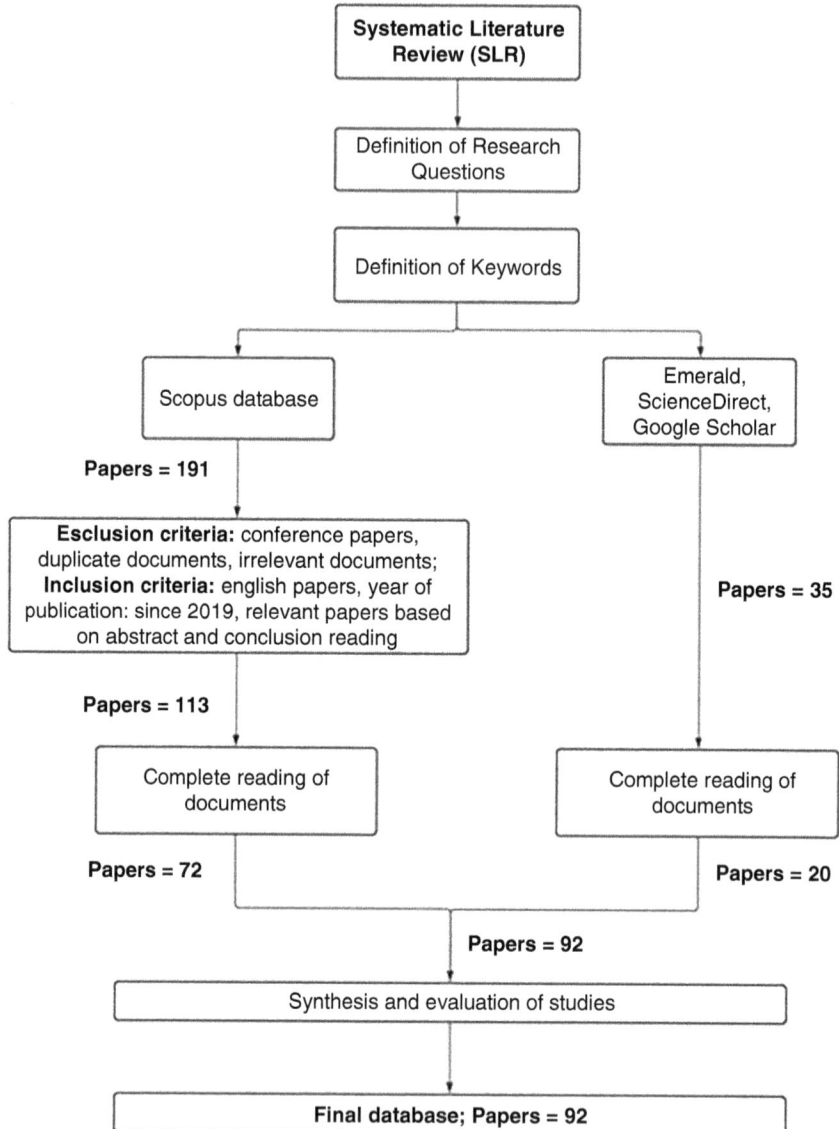

Fig. 1.1 SLR procedure description

especially for preservable foods (Coluccia et al., 2021; Marchant-Forde & Boyle, 2020). A commonly reported example is the considerable increase in the toilet paper demand at the beginning of the pandemic (Paul & Chowdhury, 2020b). Some studies highlight the link between panic purchases and the decrease in raw materials availability (Paul & Chowdhury, 2020a). Online demand increased strongly (Magableh, 2021). The COVID-19 pandemic generated therefore demand shocks

Table 1.1 Selected articles by database

Accademic databases	Number of papers
Scopus	75
Wiley Online Library	2
Science Direct	3
Emerald	2
NCBI	1
Google Scholar	1
Taylor and Francis Online	2
SpringerLink	1
IEEE Xplore	1
PubMed	2
PrePrints	1
Elsevier	1
Totale	92

Fig. 1.2 Number of selected articles grouped by topic

Mitigation strategies (5.8)

COVID-19 impacts (73)

Digitalization (53)

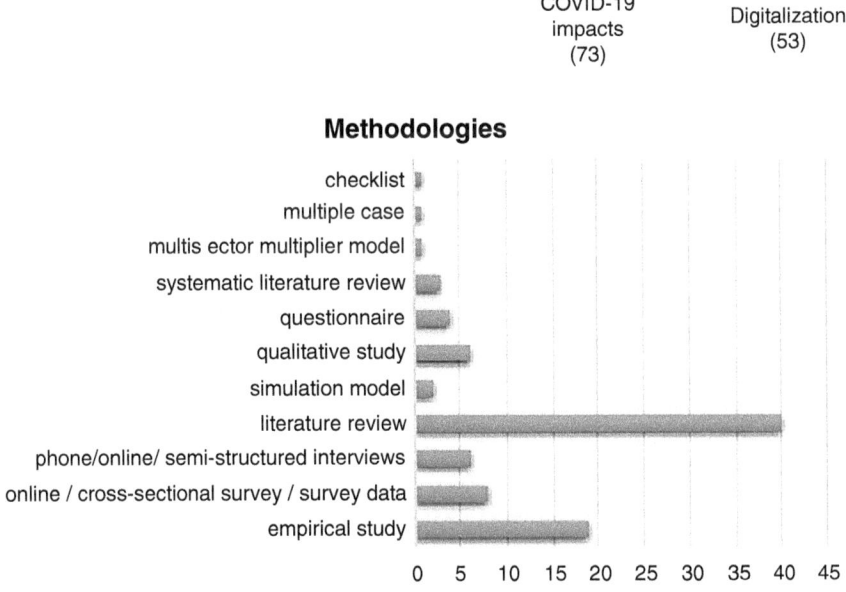

Methodologies

Fig. 1.3 Methodologies used in the analyzed papers

in both the directions, with peaks and drastic decreases (Butt, 2021). In this scenario, the purchasing bargaining power has also changed (Farrell et al., 2020; Cai & Luo, 2020), as reported particularly in industries such as fashion (Castañeda-Navarrete et al., 2020; Brydges et al., 2021), seafood (Waiho et al., 2020; Love et al., 2021; Belton et al., 2021) and food (Farrell et al., 2020; Brydges et al., 2021; Barcaccia et al., 2020).

Regarding the key impacts related to the *supply management* area, COVID-19 pandemics generated a significant reduction in supply, forcing many companies to close their plants, with cascading effects on supply chain continuity (Chowdhury et al., 2020).

The most affected countries and supply chains are those which experienced higher prices due to the materials shortage and logistics service cost increase (Končar et al., 2020; García-Villagrán et al., 2020), for example, in the food sector (Barcaccia et al., 2020), impacting downstream supply chain continuity (Liu et al., 2020; Paul & Chowdhury, 2020a; Notteboom et al., 2021; Ibn-Mohammed et al., 2021). The shocks in supply and demand impacted final product price increase (Coluccia et al., 2021; Whelan et al., 2021).

Regarding the key impacts related to the *production management* area, many companies have decreased or stopped production due to the lack of raw materials (Wannaprasert & Choenkwan, 2021; Taqi et al., 2020; Mor et al., 2020), particularly in those sectors where home-working was not applicable (Ali et al., 2021; Chitrakar et al., 2021; Yadav et al., 2021), such as in the agricultural and food industry (Butt, 2021; Cai & Luo, 2020), and in sectors characterized by short-term stocks (Mohd Helmi Ali et al., 2021; Hobbs, 2021; Pérez Vergara et al., 2021).

Regarding the key impacts related to the *transportation and logistics management* area, the governments' decisions during the lockdown dramatically impacted transport and logistics services (Magableh, 2021; Chitrakar et al., 2021), with direct impacts in terms of delays in the distribution of raw materials (Magableh, 2021; Waiho et al., 2020; Končar et al., 2020) and final goods (Taqi et al., 2020; Končar et al., 2020; Gray, 2020), and also with impacts in terms of job losses (Zhang et al., 2020). Authors highlighted that the impacts were more relevant for sectors with high levels of exports (Coluccia et al., 2021; Whelan et al., 2021; Xu et al., 2021). For example, the Chinese export decline of manufacturing components has gradually affected downstream supply chains globally (Cai & Luo, 2020).

Regarding the key impacts related to the *relationship management* area, authors highlighted an increased difficulty in information sharing and coordination among supply chain partners (Magableh, 2021; Chen & Huang, 2020).

Regarding the key impacts related to the *financial management* area, articles reported general reductions in income and profit (Dube et al., 2021), limited credit availability (Abu Hatab et al., 2021a, 2021b; Chopra et al., 2021; Sharma et al., 2020a, 2020b; Qingbin et al., 2020), higher incidence of fixed costs (Ibn-Mohammed et al., 2021; Abu Hatab et al., 2021a, 2021b; García-Villagrán et al., 2020) and production costs (Wannaprasert & Choenkwan, 2021; Butt, 2021; Qingbin et al., 2020; Belton et al., 2021; Abu Hatab et al., 2021a, 2021b) and labor (Tougeron & Hance, 2021; Abu Hatab et al., 2021a, 2021b; Wannaprasert &

Choenkwan, 2021). In addition, the above-mentioned changes in bargaining power between customers and suppliers influenced the purchasing policies (Çakır et al., 2021; Waiho et al., 2020; Wannaprasert & Choenkwan, 2021; Borsellino et al., 2020) causing—in several sectors—price drops and lower profits, especially for supply chains with less developed distribution channels (Bassett et al., 2021) and labor availability (Han et al., 2021).

3.2 Impacts of COVID-19 on SC Actors

As already cited, with regard to the analysis of the key SCM areas, COVID-19 differently affected the four main players along the supply chain: manufacturers, retailers, wholesalers/distributors, and consumers.

Our results, in particular show that *manufacturers* have been typically affected by the shortage of labor force (Rivera-Ferre et al., 2021; Zhang et al., 2020), which typically led to the interruption of production, especially in some sectors, like agricultural and food (Wannaprasert & Choenkwan, 2021). *Retailers* faced particular difficulties in demand management (García-Villagrán et al., 2020). *Distributors*, due to the restrictions introduced during the pandemic period, suffered difficulties in the management of transport and logistics processes (Rivera-Ferre et al., 2021), and on-time deliveries (Waiho et al., 2020).

Finally, *consumers* were characterized by large changes in their purchasing behavior, which caused severe problems throughout supply chains (Coopmans et al., 2021; Qingbin et al., 2020; Borsellino et al., 2020).

3.3 SC Resilience Strategies to Cope with the COVID-19 Pandemic

The results of our SLR highlighted 58 studies focused on resilience strategies to cope with COVID-19 impacts.

Supply Chain *flexibility* is the most discussed strategy to cope with pandemic interruptions (Deconinck et al., 2020), particularly with the pandemic-derived short- and medium-term capacity shortages. Geographically diversification of suppliers and multiple sourcing (García-Villagrán et al., 2020; Zhang et al., 2020), nearshoring or reshoring, volumes and production flexibility (Xu et al., 2021) are largely reported.

Few papers also report the strategy of production diversification (Althaf & Babbitt, 2021; Montoya & Flores, 2021).

Inventory management is also reported as a strategy to cope with COVID-19 but is typically linked to the need to assure efficiency, for example, by improving logistics management efficiency.

Supply chain *visibility* allows companies to take more effective decisions to mitigate disruptions such as the COVID-19 pandemic, mainly through communication and information sharing (Yang et al., 2021). Visibility allows, in particular, service level improvements (Paul & Chowdhury, 2020b), bullwhip effect reduction (Pérez Vergara et al., 2021), raw materials purchasing optimization (Paul & Chowdhury, 2020a), and hence a more resilient supply chain (Shen et al., 2020).

Reactivity is also considered a strategy that allows companies to mitigate COVID-19 impacts, for example, by reconfiguring quickly (more local) distribution networks or by shortening (too) complex supply chains (Bassett et al., 2021; Montoya & Flores, 2021). Reactivity is also linked to the capability to redesigning B2B contractual clauses and logistics and service agreements (Caballero-Morales, 2021), and reengineering products with *agility*. Reactivity and agility have been also described in terms of adoption of remote working mode, especially in nonproductive departments (Cai & Luo, 2020; Končar et al., 2020; Magableh, 2021).

Government incentives are also reported as short-term and temporary incentives to minimize the damages caused by the pandemic (Waiho et al., 2020; Taqi et al., 2020) and hence to protect industries and organizations (Brydges et al., 2021).

3.4 The Role of Digitalization to Respond to the COVID-19 Pandemic

Our SLR shows, in 52 articles, a various range of technologies, that are reported as useful tools for managing supply chains during (and after) the COVID-19 pandemic. *Internet of Things* is recognized as a key principle to gradually guide supply chain toward internal digitization (in operations) and external digitization including end consumers and supply chains (Končar et al., 2020).

Blockchain technology appears to be the most discussed. According to various studies, it can play a key role to improve supply chain resilience (Sharma et al., 2020a, 2020b), particularly for the purposes to improve information sharing and visibility (Cai & Luo, 2020), to reduce the intermediation among the actors, for example, in the omni-channel distribution (Grinberga-Zalite et al., 2021; Love et al., 2021; Bassett et al., 2021), and to increase efficiency (Xu et al., 2021).

Other technologies, such as *big data analytics* and the use of *artificial intelligence*, allow for further develop the visibility of the supply chain (Taqi et al., 2020). These, in particular, played an important role during the pandemic, allowing firms to revise the demand forecasts, anticipate customer needs, mitigate uncertainties, and redesign operations during the crisis (Cai & Luo, 2020). The findings also show that big data can be used as predictive applications in post-COVID-19 to address future demands through customer behavior analysis, trend analysis, and long-term demand forecasting.

Another technology that emerged from our SLR is, for example, the use of *Digital Twins*, which can allow a deeper understanding of SC processes by using virtual representations, hence improving the real-time monitoring of the key supply chain processes during the COVID-19 (Shen et al., 2020; Chen & Huang, 2020).

Other technologies reported are, for instance, *Robotics* (Ivanov & Das, 2020), which help reduce the likelihood of contagions (Sharma et al., 2020a, 2020b), *Additive Manufacturing* or *3D printing* which—for example—allowed to manage additional demand (Chowdhury et al., 2021; Paul & Chowdhury, 2020a), Augmented reality, which is able to assure visibility and efficiency (Dube et al., 2021), and the use of Drones to ensure last-miles deliveries (Chowdhury et al., 2021; Shen et al., 2020).

4 Conclusion

In this chapter, we analyzed the most relevant impacts that the COVID-19 pandemic produced on key SCM areas and actors. We particularly addressed the key impacts on demand, supply, production, transportation, distribution, relationships, and finance, with respect to the different positions of the actors along the supply chains, particularly distinguishing among manufacturers, retailers, distributors, and customers. In addition, we described how the literature presents the key SC resilience strategies that enable firms to cope with the COVID-19 pandemic, which have been grouped into the categories of flexibility, visibility, inventory management, reactivity and agility, and government incentives. Finally, we described the key digitalization approaches which can help firms to respond to the COVID-19 pandemic.

The SLR reveals some important gaps that can be investigated by further scholars.

First, this stream of research could benefit from some empirical and quantitative studies, to measure how epidemic outbreak disruptions impact on firms with a global supply chain, considering a multistage SC with suppliers, factory, distribution centers, and customers located in different places in the world. Thirty-eight percent of the selected papers focusing on impacts report some cases of specific supply chains or firms, but in most cases, it is quite difficult to derive general insights about the relationship between supply chain characteristics and epidemic outbreak disruptions' impacts.

This gap in the existing literature calls for quantitative studies exploring how and whether configurations of supply chain-related factors, including the actors, the number of stages, etc., influence epidemic outbreak disruptions' impacts and, therefore, are linked to the SC resilience.

Second, there seems to be a substantial gap on analyzing how different strategies impact on firms' performance and how they can be combined to ensure SC resilience.

This gap requires empirical studies to analyze how SC resilience practices exploiting different mitigation capabilities (flexibility, visibility, agility, etc.) are used, also in a combined way, to deal with disruption and the effect of adopting different combinations of SC strategies on firms' performance. This investigation will support decision makers of firms operating in different industries, with a global supply chain, to understand how SC operations policy may be used and combined to build viable recovery plans against epidemic outbreak disruptions.

Third, although we find that some strategies are more recurrent for mitigation of some SC impacts, there are no studies investigating the relationship between SC strategies and continuity at a demand, production, logistic, and other SC areas level. This gap can be filled by developing simulation models, grounded to real cases, which permits studying the effect of SC strategies on demand, production, and logistics continuity.

Fourth, several strategies have been founded as actions for mitigating and controlling the effect of COVID-19, which are built on different mitigation capabilities, coming at different costs and bringing different benefits for firms. There are however no studies analyzing the impact of their adoption in economic terms, exploring the tradeoff between benefits and costs and, hence, their impact on firms' financial performance. This gap calls for quantitative investigations of the effects that SC practices adopted for mitigating epidemic outbreak disruptions have on firms' cash flows, with the aim of optimizing them and enhancing the profitability as well as the competitive position of firms.

Finally, the digitalization has been widely reported as a way of dealing with disruptions. It emerged to be a booster of resilience if also applied in combination with other SC strategies, but no studies provided guidelines to firms on how and when investing in digitalization to improve SC resilience. This calls for a structured model supporting the decision-making about digitalization adoption to mitigate effect of disruption and hence improve SC resilience.

Acknowledgments This work was developed within the "SCREAM" project, supported by the Italian Ministry of University and Research (MUR) in the Special Supplementary Fund Program for research ("Fondo Integrativo Speciale per la Ricerca (FISR)").

References

Abu Hatab, A., Lagerkvist, C. J., & Esmat, A. (2021a). Risk perception and determinants in small- and medium-sized agri-food enterprises amidst the COVID-19 pandemic: Evidence from Egypt. *Agribusiness, 37*(1), 187–212.

Abu Hatab, A., Liu, Z., Nasser, A., & Esmat, A. (2021b). Determinants of SARS-CoV-2 impacts on small-scale commercial broiler production systems in Egypt: Implications for mitigation strategies. *Animals, 11*(5), 1354.

Ali, M. H., Suleiman, N., Khalid, N., Tan, K. H., Tseng, M. L., & Kumar, M. (2021). Supply chain resilience reactive strategies for food SMEs in coping to COVID-19 crisis. *Trends in Food Science and Technology, 109*, 94–102.

Althaf, S., & Babbitt, C. W. (2021). Disruption risks to material supply chains in the electronics sector. *Resources, Conservation and Recycling, 167*, 105248.

Araz, O. M., Choi, T. M., Olson, D. L., & Salman, F. S. (2020). Data analytics for operational risk management. *Decision Science, 51*(6), 1316–1319.

Balakrishnan, A. S., & Ramanathan, U. (2021). The role of digital technologies in supply chain resilience for emerging markets' automotive sector. *Supply Chain Management: An International Journal, 26*(6), 654–671. https://doi.org/10.1108/SCM-07-2020-0342

Barcaccia, G., D'Agostino, V., Zotti, A., & Cozzi, B. (2020). Impact of the SARS-CoV-2 on the Italian agri-food sector: An analysis of the quarter of pandemic lockdown and clues for a socio-economic and territorial restart. *Sustainability, 12*(14), 5651.

Bassett, H. R., Lau, J., Giordano, C., Suri, S. K., Advani, S., & Sharan, S. (2021). Preliminary lessons from COVID-19 disruptions of small-scale fishery supply chains. *World Development, 143*, 105473.

Belhadi, A., Kamble, S., Jabbour, C. J. C., Gunasekaran, A., Ndubisi, N. O., & Venkatesh, M. (2021). Manufacturing and service supply chain resilience to the COVID-19 outbreak: Lessons learned from the automobile and airline industries. *Technological Forecasting and Social Change, 163*, 120447.

Belton, B., Rosen, L., Middleton, L., Ghazali, S. B., Mamun, A., Shieh, J., et al. (2021). *COVID-19 impacts and adaptations in Asia and Africa's aquatic food value chains*. Working Paper: FISH-2021-02. COVID-19 impacts and adaptations in Asia and Africa's aquatic food value chains, 2021. ii+27 pp. many ref.

Borsellino, V., Kaliji, S. A., & Schimmenti, E. (2020). COVID-19 drives consumer behaviour and agro-food markets towards healthier and more sustainable patterns. (Special Issue: Agri-food markets towards sustainable patterns: Trends, drivers and challenges.). *Sustainability, 12*(20), 8366.

Brydges, T., Heinze, L., & Retamal, M. (2021). Changing geographies of fashion during Covid-19: The Australian case. *Geographical Research, 59*(2), 206–216.

Butt, A. S. (2021). Strategies to mitigate the impact of COVID-19 on supply chain disruptions: A multiple case analysis of buyers and distributors. *The International Journal of Logistics Management*. https://doi.org/10.1108/IJLM-11-2020-0455

Caballero-Morales, S. O. (2021). Innovation as recovery strategy for SMEs in emerging economies during the COVID-19 pandemic. *Research in International Business and Finance, 57*, 101396.

Cai, M., & Luo, J. (2020). Influence of COVID-19 on manufacturing industry and corresponding countermeasures from supply chain perspective. *Journal of Shanghai Jiaotong University (Science), 25*(4), 409–416.

Çakır, M., Li, Q., & Yang, X. (2021). COVID-19 and fresh produce markets in the United States and China. *Applied Economic Perspectives and Policy, 43*(1), 341–354.

Castañeda-Navarrete, J., Hauge, J., & López-Gómez, C. (2020). COVID-19's impacts on global value chains, as seen in the apparel industry. *Development Policy Review, 39*, 953–970.

Chen, Z., & Huang, L. (2020). Digital twins for information-sharing in remanufacturing supply chain: A review. *Energy, 220*, 119712.

Chitrakar, B., Zhang, M., & Bhandari, B. (2021). Improvement strategies of food supply chain through novel food processing technologies during COVID-19 pandemic. *Food Control, 125*, 108010.

Chopra, S., Sodhi, M., & Lücker, F. (2021). Achieving supply chain efficiency and resilience by using multi-level commons. *Decision Sciences, 52*, 817–832.

Chowdhury, M. T., Sarkar, A., Paul, S. K., & Moktadir, M. A. (2020). A case study on strategies to deal with the impacts of COVID-19 pandemic in the food and beverage industry. *Operations Management Research*, 1–13. https://doi.org/10.1007/s12063-020-00166-9

Chowdhury, P., Paul, S. K., Kaisar, S., & Moktadir, M. A. (2021). COVID-19 pandemic related supply chain studies: A systematic review. *Transportation Research Part E: Logistics and Transportation Review, 148*, 102271.

Coluccia, B., Agnusdei, G. P., Miglietta, P. P., & De Leo, F. (2021). Effects of COVID-19 on the Italian agri-food supply and value chains. *Food Control, 123*, 107839.

Coopmans, I., Bijttebier, J., Marchand, F., Mathijs, E., Messely, L., Rogge, E., et al. (2021). COVID-19 impacts on Flemish food supply chains and lessons for agri-food system resilience. *Agricultural Systems, 190*, 103136.

Datta, P. (2017). Supply network resilience: A systematic literature review and future research. *The International Journal of Logistics Management, 28,* 1387–1424.

Deconinck, K., Avery, E., & Jackson, L. A. (2020). Food supply chains and Covid-19: Impacts and policy lessons. *EuroChoices, 19*(3), 34–39.

Deloitte. (2020). *COVID-19: Managing supply chain risk and disruption.* Retrieved March 30, 2020, from https://www2.deloitte.com/global/en/pages/risk/articles/covid-19-managing-supply-chain-risk-and-disruption.html

Dube, K., Nhamo, G., & Chikodzi, D. (2021). COVID-19 pandemic and prospects for recovery of the global aviation industry. *Journal of Air Transport Management, 92,* 102022.

Farrell, P., Thow, A. M., Wate, J. T., Nonga, N., Vatucawaqa, P., Brewer, T., et al. (2020). COVID-19 and Pacific food system resilience: Opportunities to build a robust response. *Food Security, 12*(4), 783–791.

Fortune. (2020). Retrieved June 15, 2020, from https://fortune.com/2020/02/21/fortune-1000-coronavirus-china-supply-chain-impact/

García-Villagrán, A., Cano-Olivos, P., Martínez-Flores, J. L., & Sánchez-Partida, D. (2020). The COVID-19 effect in mexican SMEs. *Advances in Science, Technology and Engineering Systems, 5,* 63–71.

Gray, R. S. (2020). Agriculture, transportation, and the COVID-19 crisis. *Canadian Journal of Agricultural Economics/Revue canadienne d'agroeconomie, 68*(2), 239–243.

Grinberga-Zalite, G., Pilvere, I., Muska, A., & Kruzmetra, Z. (2021). Resilience of meat supply chains during and after COVID-19 crisis. *Emerging Science Journal, 5,* 57–66.

Han, S., et al. (2021). COVID-19 pandemic crisis and food safety: Implications and inactivation strategies. *Trends in Food Science and Technology, 109,* 25–36.

Handfield, R. B., Graham, G., & Burns, L. (2020). Corona virus, tariffs, trade wars and supply chain evolutionary design. *International Journal of Operations and Production Management, 40*(10), 1649–1660. https://doi.org/10.1108/IJOPM-03-2020-0171

Hobbs, J. E. (2021). The Covid-19 pandemic and meat supply chains. *Meat Science, 181,* 108459.

Ibn-Mohammed, T., Mustapha, K. B., Godsell, J., Adamu, Z., Babatunde, K. A., Akintade, D. D., et al. (2021). A critical analysis of the impacts of COVID-19 on the global economy and ecosystems and opportunities for circular economy strategies. *Resources, Conservation and Recycling, 164,* 105169.

Ivanov, D. (2020). Predicting the impacts of epidemic outbreaks on global supply chains: A simulation-based analysis on the coronavirus outbreak (COVID-19/SARS-CoV-2) case. *Transportation Research Part E: Logistics and Transportation Review, 136,* 101922.

Ivanov, D. (2021). Digital supply chain management and technology to enhance resilience by building and using end-to-end visibility during the COVID-19 pandemic. *IEEE Transactions on Engineering Management.* https://doi.org/10.1109/TEM.2021.3095193

Ivanov, D., & Das, A. (2020). Coronavirus (COVID-19/SARS-CoV-2) and supply chain resilience: A research note. *International Journal of Integrated Supply Management, 13*(1), 90–102.

Kamal, M. M., & Irani, Z. (2014). Analysing supply chain integration through a systematic literature review: A normative perspective. *Supply Chain Management: An International Journal, 19,* 523–557.

Končar, J., Grubor, A., Marić, R., Vučenović, S., & Vukmirović, G. (2020). Setbacks to IoT implementation in the function of FMCG supply chain sustainability during COVID-19 pandemic. *Sustainability, 12*(18), 7391.

Liu, Y., Lee, J. M., & Lee, C. (2020). The challenges and opportunities of a global health crisis: The management and business implications of COVID-19 from an Asian perspective. *Asian Business and Management, 19*(3), 277–297.

Love, D. C., Allison, E. H., Asche, F., Belton, B., Cottrell, R. S., Froehlich, H. E., et al. (2021). Emerging COVID-19 impacts, responses, and lessons for building resilience in the seafood system. *Global Food Security, 28,* 100494.

Magableh, G. M. (2021). Supply chains and the COVID-19 pandemic: A comprehensive framework. *European Management Review, 18,* 363–382.

Marchant-Forde, J. N., & Boyle, L. A. (2020). COVID-19 effects on livestock production: A One Welfare issue. *Frontiers in veterinary science, 7,* 734.

Montoya & Flores. (2021). Contingency plan in the supply chain of companies in the retail industry in the face of the impacts of COVID-19. *Advances in Science, Technology and Engineering Systems, 6,* 819–832.

Mor, R. S., Srivastava, P. P., Jain, R., Varshney, S., & Goyal, V. (2020). Managing food supply chains post COVID-19: A perspective. *International Journal of Supply and Operations Management, 7*(3), 295–298.

Notteboom, T., Pallis, T., & Rodrigue, J. P. (2021). Disruptions and resilience in global container shipping and ports: The COVID-19 pandemic versus the 2008–2009 financial crisis. *Maritime Economics and Logistics, 23*(2), 179–210.

Paul, S. K., & Chowdhury, P. (2020a). A production recovery plan in manufacturing supply chains for a high-demand item during COVID-19. *International Journal of Physical Distribution and Logistics Management, 51,* 104–125.

Paul, S. K., & Chowdhury, P. (2020b). Strategies for managing the impacts of disruptions during COVID-19: An example of toilet paper. *Global Journal of Flexible Systems Management, 21*(3), 283–293.

Pérez Vergara, I. G., et al. (2021). Strategies for the preservation of service levels in the inventory management during COVID-19: A case study in a company of biosafety products. *Global Journal of Flexible Systems Management, 22,* 65–80.

Qingbin, W. A. N. G., Liu, C. Q., Zhao, Y. F., Kitsos, A., Cannella, M., Wang, S. K., & Lei, H. A. N. (2020). Impacts of the COVID-19 pandemic on the dairy industry: Lessons from China and the United States and policy implications. *Journal of Integrative Agriculture, 19*(12), 2903–2915.

Queiroz, M. M., Telles, R., & Bonilla, S. H. (2019). Blockchain and supply chain management integration: A systematic review of the literature. *Supply Chain Management: An International Journal, 25,* 241–254.

Queiroz, M. M., Ivanov, D., Dolgui, A., & Wamba, S. F. (2020). Impacts of epidemic outbreaks on supply chains: Mapping a research agenda amid the COVID-19 pandemic through a structured literature review. *Annals of Operations Research,* 1–38. https://doi.org/10.1007/s10479-020-03685-7

Rivera-Ferre, M. G., López-i-Gelats, F., Ravera, F., Oteros-Rozas, E., di Masso, M., Binimelis, R., & El Bilali, H. (2021). The relation of food systems with the COVID19 pandemic: Causes and consequences. *Agricultural Systems, 191,* 103134.

Sawyerr, E., & Harrison, C. (2019). Developing resilient supply chains: Lessons from high-reliability organisations. *Supply Chain Management: An International Journal, 25,* 77–100.

Sharma, A., Adhikary, A., & Borah, S. B. (2020a). Covid-19's impact on supply chain decisions: Strategic insights from NASDAQ 100 firms using Twitter data. *Journal of Business Research, 117,* 443–449.

Sharma, R., Shishodia, A., Kamble, S., Gunasekaran, A., & Belhadi, A. (2020b). Agriculture supply chain risks and COVID-19: Mitigation strategies and implications for the practitioners. *International Journal of Logistics Research and Applications,* 1–27. https://doi.org/10.1080/13675567.2020.1830049

Shen, W., Yang, C., & Gao, L. (2020). Address business crisis caused by COVID-19 with collaborative intelligent manufacturing technologies. *IET Collaborative Intelligent Manufacturing, 2*(2), 96–99.

Shih, W. (2020). Is it time to rethink globalized supply chains?. *MIT Sloan Management Review, 61*(4), 1–3.

Sodhi, M. S., & Tang, C. S. (2021). Supply chain management for extreme conditions: Research opportunities. *Journal of Supply Chain Management, 57*(1), 7–16.

Taqi, H. M., Ahmed, H. N., Paul, S., Garshasbi, M., Ali, S. M., Kabir, G., & Paul, S. K. (2020). Strategies to manage the impacts of the COVID-19 pandemic in the supply chain: Implications for improving economic and social sustainability. *Sustainability, 12*(22), 9483.

Tougeron, K., & Hance, T. (2021). Impact of the COVID-19 pandemic on apple orchards in Europe. *Agricultural Systems, 190*, 103097.

Tranfield, D., Denyer, D., & Smart, P. (2003). Towards a methodology for developing evidence-informed management knowledge by means of systematic review. *British Journal of Management, 14*(3), 207–222.

Waiho, K., Fazhan, H., Ishak, S. D., Kasan, N. A., Liew, H. J., Norainy, M. H., & Ikhwanuddin, M. (2020). Potential impacts of COVID-19 on the aquaculture sector of Malaysia and its coping strategies. *Aquaculture Reports, 18*, 100450.

Wannaprasert, P., & Choenkwan, S. (2021). Impacts of the COVID-19 pandemic on ginger production: Supply chains, labor, and food security in Northeast Thailand. *Forest and Society, 5*, 120–135.

Whelan, J., Brown, A. D., Coller, L., Strugnell, C., Allender, S., Alston, L., et al. (2021). The impact of COVID-19 on rural food supply and demand in Australia: Utilising group model building to Identify Retailer and Customer Perspectives. *Nutrients, 13*(2), 417.

World Economic Forum—WEF. (2020a). *How China can rebuild global supply chain resilience after COVID-19*. Retrieved April 5, 2020, from https://www.weforum.org/agenda/2020/03/coronavirus-and-global-supply-chains/

World Economic Forum—WEF. (2020b). *What past disruptions can teach us about reviving supply chains after COVID-19*. Retrieved March 30, 2020, from https://www.weforum.org/agenda/2020/03/covid-19-coronavirus-lessons-past-supply-chain-disruptions/

Xu, Z., Elomri, A., El Omri, A., Kerbache, L., & Liu, H. (2021). The compounded effects of COVID-19 pandemic and desert locust outbreak on food security and food supply chain. *Sustainability, 13*(3), 1063.

Yadav, S., Luthra, S., & Garg, D. (2021). Modelling Internet of things (IoT)-driven global sustainability in multi-tier agri-food supply chain under natural epidemic outbreaks. *Environmental Science and Pollution Research, 28*(13), 16633–16654.

Yang, J., Xie, H., Yu, G., & Liu, M. (2021). Antecedents and consequences of supply chain risk management capabilities: An investigation in the post-coronavirus crisis. *International Journal of Production Research, 59*(5), 1573–1585.

Zhang, Y., et al. (2020). Impact of COVID-19 on China's macroeconomy and agri-food system—An economy-wide multiplier model analysis. *China Agricultural Economic Review, 12*, 387–407.

Chapter 2
COVID-19 Disruption Impacts on Supply Chains: An Empirical Exploration on Disruptions, Resiliency, and Risk Management Strategies

Jukka Hallikas, Pietro Evangelista, Katrina Lintukangas,
Anni-Kaisa Kähkönen, and Mika Immonen

Abstract COVID-19 pandemic, which has spread to every country around the world, is causing major economic and social disruptions with far-reaching impacts on global supply chains. While the pandemic has highlighted the vulnerability of global supply chains and the dependence on certain geographical areas and purchasing categories, it also revealed the importance to manage supply chains in a way that ensures long-term resiliency and building new competencies and capabilities. The crisis created by the pandemic revealed the significance of having strong risk management practices in place. For building recovery abilities and resiliency for possible similar future events, it is important to explore and understand the real impacts of the pandemic on the supply chains. In this chapter, the impacts of COVID-19 on upstream and downstream supply chains are studied by using a survey data from the medical device industry which has been one of the critical industries during the pandemic era.

1 Introduction

Supply chains and supply chain management have been under critical investigation since the first impacts of COVID-19 hit the world at the beginning of the year 2020. Consequently, supply chain management has become the most famous function of companies, because the effects of COVID-19 were very visible in supply chains.

J. Hallikas (✉) · K. Lintukangas · A.-K. Kähkönen · M. Immonen
LUT University, Lappeenranta, Finland
e-mail: Jukka.hallikas@lut.fi; Katrina.Lintukangas@lut.fi; Anni-Kaisa.Kahkonen@lut.fi;
Mika.Immonen@lut.fi

P. Evangelista
Institute on Studies on the Mediterranean (ISMed) of the National Research Council (CNR),
Naples, Italy
e-mail: p.evangelista@iriss.cnr.it

Forbes (2021) announced that supply chain-related knowledge, competences, and talent are now more important than ever, and Bloomberg Businessweek (2021) wrote that supply chain management is the must-have degree of the pandemic era. COVID-19 hit the world with such massive effects that existing management models and operation practices did not work anymore. It caused supply chain vulnerabilities, disruptions, and risks at a level that the current business environment had never confronted before (Craighead et al., 2020; van Hoek, 2020) and thus, companies were required to create new ways for mitigating and managing supply chain disruptions and risks.

COVID-19 is a pandemic and pandemics, in general, create uncommon supply chain risks resulting in disruptions that spread quickly both upstream and downstream supply chains causing problems both in supply and demand (Ivanov, 2020). During the first phases of COVID-19, disruptions and problems in the upstream supply chain, garnered much public attention, because supply delays and raw material shortages of, for example, different medical devices and personal protection equipment or microchips in car manufacturing, were visible to the consumers as well. Rapidly increased demand for hand sanitizer, masks, and gowns combined with raw material shortages and supply delays of those products, paralyzed medical devices supply chains around the world and had a huge impact on operations in hospitals, countries, and societies. The disruptions in the upstream supply chain were reflected and cascaded downstream causing a ripple effect (Dolgui & Ivanov, 2021). In downstream supply chains, in addition to medical products, some unexpected disruptions were also noticed, for example, people started to buy a lot of toilet paper and other hygiene products, and at the same time garments and other similar products experienced reduced demand which led to postponed production and downstream disruptions (Paul & Chowdhury, 2020; Ali et al., 2021).

The significance of medical equipment and medical devices industry was highly emphasized during the global pandemic. To explore the supply chain disruptions and challenges as well as the overall impact of COVID-19 on this critical industry sector, we collected a quantitative data from a survey conducted in the medical devices industry in Italy and Finland in the summer of 2020. At that time, medical devices companies were under two different pressures. On the one hand, many companies in the sector faced a dramatic increase in the demand for personal protective products and other medical devices. On the other hand, there was a lack of availability of these products due to disruptions in the supply chain caused by the block of factories in China and other Southeast Asian countries. In addition, the distribution of products on the domestic market became more complicated due to the mobility restrictions introduced by the government to stop the contagion. In this scenario, many companies show considerable vulnerability due to a failure in predicting and managing risks and a lack of visibility in their supply chain. The supply chain resilience and the lack of appropriate capabilities can be considered highly significant for the future and thus, these were the key topics of the survey. Thus, the aim of this book chapter is to explore the impacts of COVID-19 on the firms' upstream and downstream supply chains and the practices and strategies that companies have used when trying to respond to these impacts. The empirical research context is the medical device industry which has been one of the critical industries during the COVID-19 pandemic.

This chapter is organized as follows. In the next section, the theoretical background of the study has been outlined. In the third section, the empirical study has been presented together with the methodological approach used and the results achieved. In the concluding section, the results of the empirical survey have been discussed and relevant managerial and research implications have been drawn.

2 Supply Chain Disruptions, Resiliency, and Risk Management

Before we can start looking at risk preparedness and management, we need to think a little bit about supply chain disruptions and, in particular, the impact of external disruptions on supply chains, as in the case of the COVID-19 pandemic. Sources of supply chain disruptions can arise from direct or indirect sources and often address vulnerabilities in inbound supply chain activities (Svensson, 2000). It is also important to realize that the supply chain is structured of multiple layers and external large-scale disruptions, like COVID-19 pandemic, can affect all these layers. The supply chain is attached to a company's organizational, informational, technological, financial, and process-functional structures (Ivanov, 2020). The organizational structure includes alternative suppliers and subcontractors, employees, and facilities. Informational structure covers traceability and visibility of the supply chain (e.g., blockchain and digital twins), analytics, and supplier portals. Technological structure relates to interfaces of production (industry 4.0, robotics, additive manufacturing, warehousing). Financial structure refers to liquidity and revenue and process-functional structure capacity flexibility, omni-channel logistics, inventory, and product diversification or substitution. The disruption event can have an impact on all these layers, and thus, to maintain viability of supply chain it must have risk management capabilities and an agile approach to supply chain operations and management (Ivanov, 2020).

According to Craighead et al. (2007), supply chain disruption risks can be considered as unintended and unplanned events that disrupt the normal flow of materials in the up- and downstream of the supply chain. Disruption can thus be seen as events that cause negative (or positive) effects related to typical supply chain risks, such as supply disruptions, prices, inventories, and demand. While the effects are often negative and their impact damages supply chain operations, the effects can also be positive for some supply chain actors. For example, as a result of a pandemic, there may be great uncertainties in the availability of products or in the delivery times of suppliers, it means that some companies will not receive the products in the desired quantity or at the desired price, thus losing sales. Some companies, on the other hand, may come up with alternative purchasing channels and for example, may be able to replace products with other solutions, which may have a positive effect on the company's competitive advantage in the end. There is, however, relatively little support for the positive aspects of supply chain disruptions and clearing strategies, as the risk management literature focuses much on the vulnerability dimension of risks (Craigshead et al., 2007).

Building resiliency, which according to Ponomarov and Holcomb (2009) means the ability to respond to and recover from unpredicted disruptions, has been highlighted in several studies (e.g., Ivanov, 2020; Paul & Chowdhury, 2020) as a key to surviving from the COVID-19 and the disruptions caused by it. Scholten et al. (2019) pointed out that building supply chain resilience capabilities necessitates mitigation processes that reduce the vulnerability of the supply chain. These further enable preventive solutions and performance of the essential processes during preparedness, response, and recovery stages (Scholten et al., 2019). Mitigation capabilities are related to regular organizational processes that help to recover from disruptions and additionally assist to create awareness of disruptions across organizations (Hallikas et al., 2004).

Supply chain disruptions are often linked to vulnerabilities that activate risk management and disruption preparedness in companies. Research suggests that resilience can be significantly increased by improving a company's capability to detect and therefore also respond to disruptions quickly (Sheffi & Rice, 2005). Chowdhury and Quaddus (2016) have pointed out that measuring resiliency of a supply chain should be based on the firm's readiness to respond to and recover from disruptions. Moreover, supplier orientation and development of risk management culture in the company improve supply chain resiliency significantly.

Supply chain risk management process is consisted of preventing, detecting, responding, and recovering from operational risks. It is a structured process including risk assessment, and mitigation and contingency plans (Tummala & Schoenherr, 2011). In addition to that, to maintain resiliency in the supply chain a firm must have the ability to cope with changes brought by disruption and adapt to the disruption, can respond quickly to the disruption, and maintain high awareness of external and internal changes that might impact on its supply chain in the future. Hence, in order to meet the challenges born from disruptive events, both exploration and exploitation strategies have to be considered. According to March (1991, p. 71) exploitation means "refinement, choice, production, efficiency, selection, implementation and execution," and exploration "search, variation, risk-taking, experimentation, play, flexibility, discovery, and innovation." In supply chain risk management, the goals of exploitation strategy are reducing operational redundancies in the existing supply chain processes and improvement and leveraging existing technologies and competence development whereas exploration strategies aim for proactivity and experiments to pursue new supply chain solutions, exploring new opportunities, and seeking novel approaches. Moreover, as Ojha et al. (2018) have demonstrated organizational learning fosters exploration and exploitation practices and strategy development. The impact of disruptions caused by COVID-19 was serious both on upstream and downstream supply chains. Hence, exploitation and exploration risk management strategies of a focal company should cover the whole supply chain.

Thus, the aim of this book chapter is to explore the impacts of COVID-19 on the firms' upstream and downstream supply chains and the practices and strategies that companies have used when trying to respond to these impacts Next, we will empirically investigate the impacts that COVID-19 pandemic had on upstream and downstream supply chains in the medical device industry.

3   Empirical Study

3.1   Sample

A questionnaire survey was conducted in Italy and Finland during the year 2020 to investigate the impact of the COVID-19 pandemic on supply chains with specific reference to disruptions, risk management, resilience, and eventual adaptive measures implemented in the supply chain of medical devices. Italy and Finland were chosen for different reasons. Both countries belong to the European Union but Italy is located in the South of the Union, while Finland is located in the very North part of the continent. From the demographic point of view, Italy has a much higher number of inhabitants living in a smaller territory in comparison to Finland where there are far fewer inhabitants than in Italy. Italy and Finland are two countries that were hit very differently by the COVID-19 pandemic, but both countries faced a very critical emergency, especially at the early stages of the pandemic. In both countries, the medical device companies were put under pressure as their business model is based on a strong reliance on companies operating in Southeast Asia to which production activities have been outsourced. This lengthens the supply chain managed by these companies and makes it difficult to control not only production but also logistics and transport cycles with inevitable disruptions when the lockdown came into force.

The survey instrument and the questions included were defined taking into account the earlier research experiences of the authors and the extant literature. The questionnaire was tested through a number of pilot interviews with the staff of the research office of the Italian medical devices association that provided feedback on the appropriateness of the objectives of the study and the clarity and readability of questions. The scope of the survey questions ranged from how COVID-19 affects (both directly and indirectly) different company business areas and its supply chain to the influence on resiliency and related supply chain disruptions caused by COVID-19 and risk management. The specific objectives of the survey were in particular:

- Measure supply chain disruptions as a result of the coronavirus pandemic.
- Assess the current state of risk management practices and actions to face extreme events.
- Identify the capabilities for recovering from supply chain disruption.

The data contains responses from 109 companies from a sample of 466 companies, 384 of which operated in Italy and 82 of which operated in Finland (response

Table 2.1 Respondents by company industry segments

Industry	n	%
Medical devices	22	20.2
Biomedical technology	4	3.7
Laboratory testing and in vitro diagnostics	13	11.9
Services and software	7	6.4
Other	32	29.3
N/A	31	28.4
Total	**109**	**100**

rate 24%). The respondents were companies of different sizes belonging to different industry segments. From the company size point of view, 59% of the surveyed companies were micro, small, and medium-sized companies. From the industry segment perspective, 35.8% were medical devices manufacturing companies and providers of biomedical technology and diagnostics, 6.4% were services and software companies, and 30 % were active in unspecified medical industry segment. However, the survey was organized in collaboration with the Italian medical devices association, thus making the Italian companies tightly connected to the industry in question by being the members of the association. Also, the Finnish companies were identified based on the fact that their industry was medical devices industry. Thus, we can assume that also the respondents whose industry segment was not specified in their response, belong to the medical devices sector. The industry profiles of firms investigated are shown in Table 2.1.

3.2 Disruption Profile Based on the Segmentation and Comparison of Segments

The results of the questionnaire surveys allowed to map out how companies have experienced the impact of COVID-19 on their supply chains at a general level. In addition, it is particularly interesting from the perspective of different management practices to see whether the COVID-19 disruption experienced by companies has an impact on their operations, particularly through risk management, resilience, improvement, and renewal of existing supply chain processes. In order to look at companies through different segments, we looked at disturbances through upstream and downstream COVID-19 impacts. Disruptions were measured through certain surveyed metrics as shown in Fig. 2.1. Upstream and downstream disruption indicators were defined using the mean value of the measured items.

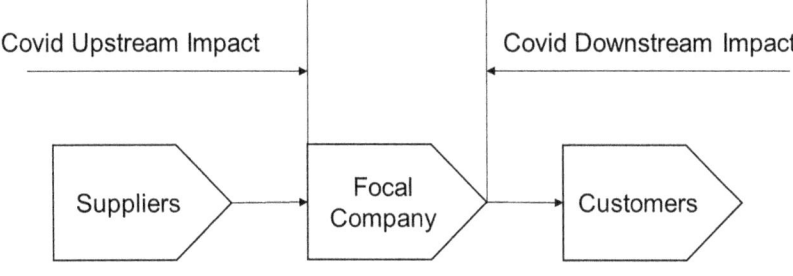

Covid Upstream Impact

Covid Downstream Impact

Suppliers → Focal Company → Customers

Covid Supply Chain Impact
- Product availability
- Risks related to product availability
- Delivery reliability (on-time delivery)
- Overall Impact on your supply chain

Covid ´Business Impact
- Costs/prices for the purchased items
- Responsiveness to customer demands
- Sales
- Customer satisfaction

Fig. 2.1 Upstream and downstream supply chain disruptions caused by COVID-19

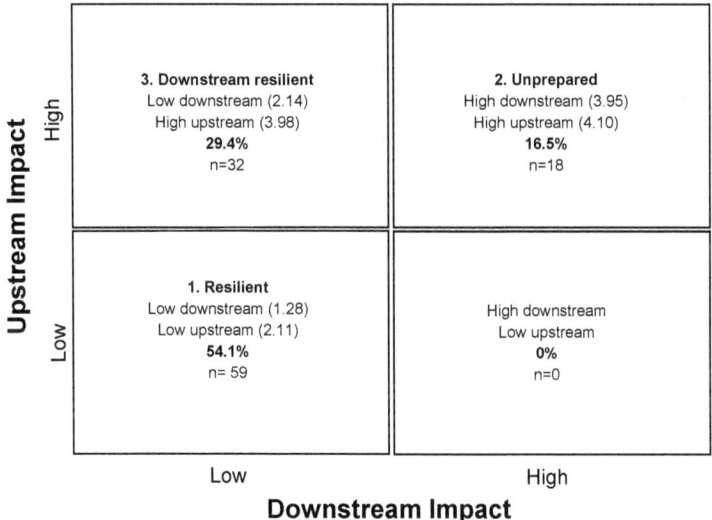

3. Downstream resilient
Low downstream (2.14)
High upstream (3.98)
29.4%
n=32

2. Unprepared
High downstream (3.95)
High upstream (4.10)
16.5%
n=18

1. Resilient
Low downstream (1.28)
Low upstream (2.11)
54.1%
n= 59

High downstream
Low upstream
0%
n=0

Upstream Impact — High / Low

Downstream Impact — Low / High

Fig. 2.2 Company segments based on the impact of COVID disruptions

Segments were formed by classifying companies through the upstream and downstream COVID-19 disruption effect. The two steps clustering algorithm was used to form the segments, which automatically groups the respondents using the given input variables (upstream and downstream impacts). These metrics were used to classify firms into three groups based on their COVID-19 effect as shown in Fig. 2.2.

The segmentation of the companies was obtained using company's responses regarding overall changes within the supply chain, the perceived shifts relating to

Table 2.2 Summary of company profiles by segment

Segment	1 Resilient	2 Unprepared	3 Downstream resilient	ANOVA	
Share in data	54.1 %	16.5 %	29.4 %		
		Mean(sd)		p	diff[a]
Downstream Impact	1.28(0.73)	3.95(0.6)	2.14(0.69)	.000	all
Upstream Impact	2.11(0.59)	4.1(2.8)	3.98(0.72)	.000	1 to rest
Employees (class)		Share within segment (%)			
1-9	27.1	38.9	25.0		
10-49	30.5	11.1	18.8		
50-249	27.1	16.7	28.1		
more than 250	15.3	33.3	28.1		
	100	100	100		

a) statistically significant difference between groups observed

customer demands, and the perceptions particularly related to operations in upstream and downstream activities of the supply chain. The clustering of data revealed three segments where different scopes and scales of supply chain disruptions can be recognized.

Analysis of variance ("ANOVA") is applied to test statistical differences in mean values between groups. In this case, the independent variable in the ANOVA was the created segments, and dependent variables were Downstream Impact and Upstream Impacts. Table 2.2 presents the summary of the company profiles by segment including mean values of the summed scales, results of the ANOVA test, and distribution of companies by size in each segment considered. The class representing the number of employees in the company is an indicator of size. Comparison of the mean values of the summed scales using ANOVA indicates that groups have statistically significant differences. As the four-field profiles in Fig. 2.2 clearly indicate, companies in the target sample have faced the impact of COVID-19 in different ways.

The first segment represents a group of companies where COVID-19 has the mildest impact in overall. For this reason, this segment has been labelled "Resilient." In fact, this group represents companies where the effects of both upstream and downstream are relatively low. These companies account for 54.1% of the target population. In the second segment, the companies have faced the most significant effects in the sample, and ratings regarding all features of shifts are clearly higher when compared with the "Resilient" segment. This segment is located in the upper right quadrant of the map drawing 16.5% of the sample where both the upstream and the downstream effects from the supply chain have been stronger in comparison with the other two segments. These companies have faced the impact of COVID-19 holistically and for this reason have been called "Unprepared." For companies

Table 2.3 Resiliency—Differences between segments (mean values and statistical tests, ANOVA test results)—Asses how well your company has adapted to the supply chain disruptions caused by COVID-19?

Mean values	Total	Segment 1 Resilient	Segment 2 Unprepared	Segment 3 Downstream resilient	P-value	Post Hoc[a]
Cope with changes brought by disruption	3.81	3.69	4.67	3.54	0.100	
Adapt to the disruption	3.24	3.27	2.97	3.34	0.705	
Provide a quick response to the disruption	3.51	3.55	4.18	3.04	0.057*	2–3**
Maintain high situational awareness	3.21	3.34	3.02	3.09	0.817	

** Significant at the 0.05 level; *Significant at the 0.1 level
[a] Statistically differentiated segments

1 = strongly disagree and 5 = strongly agree

belonging to the segment located in the upper left part of the map, COVID's effects have been strong in the upstream supply chain, but more moderate in the downstream business (called "Downstream resilient"). These companies accounts for 29.4% of the sample firm. This segment differs from previous segments in relation to all dimensions considered except upstream impact, which was rated similarly as in segment 2. A profile where the company has a low upstream impact on the supply chain, but a high downstream business impact did not stand out as a separate entity in the segmentation analyzed.

Comparison of distribution of firm sizes in the segments shows that the strongest impact of COVID-19 occurs among very small companies and large enterprises. In turn, medium size businesses have the largest share in the "Resilient" segment where disruptions have rated rather low.

The segmentation categories formed are intended to explain in a little more detail in the following how companies that have faced COVID-19 risks have changed differently and, in general, how different segments have responded to the supply chain disruptions caused by COVID-19. The analysis of the comparison between segments was performed using the ANOVA mean test, which aims to compare the means between several groups to be analyzed and their statistical differences. In addition, ANOVA's post hoc tests have analyzed in more detail which segments have differences between the measured survey variables. If we look at the differences between the segments through the variables measuring the resiliency of the supply chain (see Table 2.3), we see that the variables measuring the resiliency do not differ statistically between the different segments.

However, segment 2 Unprepared (High upstream impact, High downstream impact) has a slightly higher average in adapting to the supply chain disruptions and providing a quick response to the COVID-19 disruption in the variables. In the post hoc analysis, the only statistically significant difference is between segments

Table 2.4 Risk Management—Differences between segments (mean values and statistical tests, ANOVA test results)—Asses how much COVID-19 has affected the management of the following risks in your company?

Mean values	Total	Segment 1 Resilient	Segment 2 Unprepared	Segment 3 Downstream resilient	P-value	Post Hoc[a]
Preventing operations risks	2.30	1.78	2.81	2.96	0.001**	1 – 2 1 – 3
Detecting operations risks	2.21	1.57	2.73	3.11	0.004**	1 – 2 1 – 3
Responding to operations risks	2.76	2.05	3.98	3.39	0.000**	1 – 2 2 – 3
Recovering from operations risks	2.88	2.17	3.91	3.63	0.000**	1 – 2 1 – 3

* Significant at the 0.05 level; **Significant at the 0.01 level

[a] Statistically differentiated segments

1 = no effects at all and 5 = extremely strong effects

2 and 3 for the variable "Provide a quick response to the disruption." It can be said that companies that have faced COVID-19 disruptions both upstream and downstream at the same time have had to invest more in rapid response than other companies. The disruption profile thus seems to have an effect on building resiliency in firms.

Next, we take a closer look at supply chain risk management between different segments. The results in Table 2.4 related to the mean test show that the means of the variables differ significantly from the statistical point of view. Operations risk preventing, detecting, and recovering is clearly lower for segment 1 (Resilient) compared to segments 2 (Unprepared) and 3 (Downstream resilient). For the variable "Responding to operations risks," there is a significant difference between segments 1 and 2 but also between segments 2 and 3. This indicates the need to respond to operational risks more intensively if a company has encountered disruptions caused by COVID-19 from both upstream and downstream.

If we look at how COVID-19 has influenced the development of existing supply chain assets and processes in the surveyed companies (see Table 2.5), it can be concluded that companies have invested in the development of existing processes and technologies. Segment 2 has, on average, invested slightly more than other segments in improving asset processes, but statistically the difference is only visible in terms of developing strong competencies in the existing supply chain processes between segments 1 and 2. Thus, exploitation strategies do not appear to be strongly involved in the management of COVID-19 disruptions, nor do the different disruption profiles differ much here.

Finally, we measured corporate exploration strategies between different segments, i.e., how much COVID-19 has driven companies to develop supply chains and seek new solutions in the longer term. Based on the results (see Table 2.6), it is possible to conclude that all items measuring exploration receive a high value in

Table 2.5 Exploitation strategies - Differences between segments (mean values and statistical tests, ANOVA test results) Asses how much COVID-19 has influenced on development of existing supply chain assets and processes in your company

Mean values	Total	Segment 1 Resilient	Segment 2 Unprepared	Segment 3 Downstream resilient	P-value	Post Hoc[a]
Reducing operational redundancies in our existing processes	3.22	2.99	3.60	3.46	0.518	
Focus on improving our existing technologies	3.05	2.96	3.71	2.82	0.197	
Leveraging our current supply chain technologies	3.33	3.18	3.78	3.35	0.655	
Developing strong competencies in our existing SC processes	3.04	2.83	3.89	2.92	0.106	1–2*

* Significant at the 0.05 level; **Significant at the 0.01 level
[a] Statistically differentiated segments

1 = strongly disagree and 5 = strongly agree

Table 2.6 Exploration strategies—Differences between segments (mean values and statistical tests, ANOVA test results) Asses how COVID-19 has influenced supply chain development for prospects in your company

Mean values	Total	Segment 1 Resilient	Segment 2 Unprepared	Segment 3 Downstream resilient	P-value	Post Hoc[a]
Proactively pursue new supply chain solutions	2.98	2.77	4.17	2.69	0.180	
Experiment to find new solutions that will improve our supply chain	3.31	3.03	4.34	2.80	0.030**	1–2** 2–3**
Explore new opportunities to improve our SC	3.51	3.18	4.75	3.50	0.000**	1–2** 2–3**
Seeking novel approaches in order to solve SC problems	3.59	3.18	4.16	3.46	0.113	1–2*

* Significant at the 0.05 level; **Significant at the 0.01 level
[a] Statistically differentiated segments

segment 2. Segment 2 also differs statistically significantly from the actual segments, especially in terms of "Experiment to find new solutions that will improve our supply chain" and "Explore new opportunities to improve our SC." It can therefore be said that companies that have been strongly influenced by COVID-19 have clearly sought to explore new practices and develop new solutions to develop their supply chains over a longer period of time.

4 Discussion and Conclusion

The medical devices industry has been one of the critical industries during the COVID-19 pandemic and thus, we used the medical device industry as an empirical research context for our study. We collected a survey data from medical device companies in Italy and Finland. Italy and Finland were chosen for different reasons. Both countries belong to the European Union but Italy is located in the South of the Union, while Finland is located in the very North part of the continent. From the demographic point of view, Italy has a much higher number of inhabitants living in a smaller territory in comparison to Finland where there are far fewer inhabitants than Italy. Italy and Finland are two countries that were hit very differently by the COVID-19 pandemic, but both countries faced a very critical emergency, especially at the early stages of the pandemic. In both countries, the medical device companies were put under pressure as their business model is based on a strong reliance on companies operating in Southeast Asia to which production activities have been outsourced. This lengthens the supply chain managed by these companies and makes it difficult to control not only production but also logistics and transport cycles with inevitable disruptions when the lockdown came into force.

This book chapter focused to explore the impacts of COVID-19 on the firms' upstream and downstream supply chains and the practices and strategies that companies have used when trying to respond to these impacts. In our analysis, we have segmented the respondent companies of our survey based on the disruption effect and investigated how companies in different segments have adopted risk management and supply chain strategies for the perceived disruptions caused by COVID-19. As a result of COVID-19 pandemic, companies have faced various disruptions and changes that have affected their supply chains and operations.

Supply chain risks can be considered to rise on both upstream and downstream sides of the supply chain. Upstream risks are related to purchasing and supplier deliveries. As a result of COVID-19, companies experienced supply disruptions, especially through material shortages and delivery delays. In the downstream supply chain, demand and prices had a significant impact on companies. The medical devices companies surveyed in this study experienced the effects of COVID-19 in the upstream supply chain (supply side) clearly higher (avg. 2.99) than the effects of downstream (demand) (avg. 1.97).

When the medical devices companies in the survey were segmented according to their disruption effects, three types of firm groups were identified from which the "Unprepared" cluster had experienced both upstream and downstream effects as significant. This group had clearly activated more different risk management and supply chain development practices. The cluster of "Downstream resilient," meaning companies that have experienced upstream COVID-19 effects as significant but downstream effects as low, had also activated significantly more measures than the cluster of "Resilient," where both upstream and downstream COVID-19 effects were perceived as low. This clearly highlights the need to implement practices and strategies to manage upstream impacts in particular, but also, especially when impacts of disruption affect both directions of the supply chain.

An interesting finding is also that there was no significant difference in supply chain resiliency between the different segments. Instead, firms seem to activate risk management practices triggered by the disruption effect and thus seek to balance effects and resiliency through these means. The more a company experiences disruption, the more they seem to have activated different ways to manage COVID-19-related risk and resilience, and vice versa.

Interestingly, there were no statistical differences between the segments regarding the use of exploitation strategies. Segment 2 "Unprepared" had the highest mean values which are logical as companies in this segment faced the highest impact of COVID-19 both upstream and downstream supply chains. For the exploration strategies, it was discovered that the companies belonging to this segment, the exploration strategies were used clearly more than in other segments. In the "Unprepared" segment experiments regarding new solutions to improving the supply chain and exploring the opportunities for improvement were more often used.

Because understanding the disruption effects helps to implement management tools, companies should strive to monitor and share information about disruptions as effectively as possible. Here, various solutions for measuring disruptions and resiliency in real time have a great potential, as they can be used to maintain situational awareness of disturbances in the supply chains and their potential effects in real time. Information can also be shared quickly between supply chain parties to respond to critical situations as effectively as possible.

On the basis of the above results, it is possible to identify some interesting managerial implications for each of the segments identified in this study. In relation to the companies belonging to segment 1 (Resilient), it seems that these companies have coped better with the impact of COVID-19 than companies belonging to the other two groups. In fact, for these companies the overall impact of the pandemic on supply chain resiliency was perceived low. Nevertheless, the ability to predict changes in the business environment is limited and risk management is generally underestimated. For this reason, decisions related to the realignment of resources to better respond to customer demand needs to be carefully reconsidered and involve decisions concerning several areas. From the downstream supply chain perspective, logistics is an area where it may be crucial to evaluate alternative outbound logistics arrangements. In addition, forming partnerships with logistics service providers who can complement existing network-related capabilities will be a strategic necessity in a future crisis. Looking at the upstream part of the supply chain, inventory management appears as another critical area where the pandemic resulted in an inventory shortage. In this case, communication with key suppliers is necessary to find out alternative supply arrangements to secure product flows and supplies.

As far as segment 2 (Unprepared), the companies belonging to this group suffered the strongest impact on both upstream and downstream sides of their supply chain. In the upstream side of the supply chain, sourcing and securing volumes was a significant pain point. In particular, the dependence on supplies from overseas, especially from China, requires a rapid connection with qualified local suppliers.

Fragmented supply and networks of contract manufacturers exacerbated the sourcing challenge and attempt to quickly ramp up short-term production had a negative impact on product quality. In the downstream side of the supply chain, investment to improve the control of the logistics and delivery systems should become a priority for these companies to prevent future setbacks and disruptions seen in the COVID-19 outbreak. In addition, an emergency risk plan is necessary to reduce their vulnerability. A strategic response plan, established in advance, can determine which activities along the entire supply chain should be ad hoc (e.g., gathering real-time demand data) and which should be pre-planned (e.g., setting up decision-making).

Finally, the companies belonging to segment 3 (Downstream resilient) suffered the impact of COVID-19 mostly on the upstream side of the supply chain. For these companies, re-shoring/near-shoring strategies need to be carefully considered. In fact, the effect of the pandemic should accelerate companies' decisions to relocate production (or part of it) to Europe as a consequence of disruptions caused by the pandemic in China. In addition, to build up strong relationships with key suppliers through investment in supply chain planning systems supported by digital technologies that are able to provide visibility across the entire supplier network not just to the first tier is a mandatory strategy to avoid the negative consequences of a future catastrophic event of this kind.

From the research point of view, further studies are required to investigate larger sample firms in order to generalize results. In addition, the development of case study analyses could provide further insight into how medical devices companies reacted to COVID-19. Finally, carrying out studies of this kind in more countries and comparing results may allow to identify best practices that may improve the level of preparedness of medical devices companies to face future similar catastrophic events. This chapter contributes to a better understanding of recent disruptions caused by COVID-19 in the medical devices supply chain and the related strategies to cope with these disruptions. The aim is that it can help medical devices companies to be prepared for future emergencies.

References

Ali, M., Rahman, S. M., & Frederico, G. F. (2021). Capability components of supply chain resilience for readymade garments (RMG) sector in Bangladesh during COVID-19. *Modern Supply Chain Research and Applications, 3*, 127–144. https://doi.org/10.1108/MSCRA-06-2020-0015

Bloomberg Businessweek. (2021). *Forget finance: Supply-chain management is the pandemic era's must-have MBA degree*. Retrieved October 22, 2021, from https://www.bloomberg.com/news/articles/2021-09-03/business-school-mba-students-forgo-finance-for-supply-chain-management-degree

Chowdhury, M. M. H., & Quaddus, M. (2016). Supply chain readiness, response and recovery for resilience. *Supply Chain Management: An International Journal, 21*(6), 709–731.

Craighead, C., Blackhurst, J., Rungtusanatham, M. J., & Handfield, R. B. (2007). The severity of supply chain disruptions: Design characteristics and mitigation capabilities. *Decision Sciences, 38*(1), 131–156.

Craighead, C., Ketchen, D. J., & Darby, J. L. (2020). Pandemics and supply chain management research: Toward a theoretical toolbox. *Decision Sciences, 51*(4), 838–866.

Dolgui, A., & Ivanov, D. (2021). Ripple effect and supply chain disruption management: New trends and research directions. *International Journal of Production Research, 59*(1), 102–109.

Forbes. (2021). *Supply chain talent is more important than ever*. Retrieved October 22, 2021, from https://www.forbes.com/sites/stevebanker/2021/03/10/supply-chain-talent-is-more-important-than-ever/?sh=173d123e5e19

Hallikas, J., Karvonen, I., Pulkkinen, U., Virolainen, V.-M., & Tuominen, M. (2004). Risk management processes in supplier networks. *International Journal of Production Economics, 90*(1), 47–58.

Ivanov, D. (2020). Viable supply chain model: Integrating agility, resilience and sustainability perspectives—Lessons from and thinking beyond the COVID-19 pandemic. *Annals of Operation Research*. https://doi.org/10.1007/s10479-020-03640-6

March, J. G. (1991). Exploration and exploitation in organizational learning. *Organization Science, 2*(1), 71–87.

Ojha, D., Struckell, E., Acharya, C., & Patel, P. C. (2018). Supply chain organizational learning, exploration, exploitation, and firm performance: A creation-dispersive perspective. *International Journal of Production Economics, 204*, 70–82. https://doi.org/10.1016/j.ijpe.2018.07.025

Paul, S. K., & Chowdhury, P. (2020). A production recovery plan in manufacturing supply chains for a high-demand item during COVID-19. *International Journal of Physical Distribution & Logistics Management, 51*(2), 104–125.

Ponomarov, S. Y., & Holcomb, M. D. (2009). Understanding the concept of supply chain resilience. *The International Journal of Logistics Management, 20*(1), 124–143.

Scholten, K., Scott, P. S., & Fynes, B. (2019). Building routines for non-routine events: Supply chain resilience learning mechanisms and their antecedents. *Supply Chain Management: An International Journal, 24*(3), 430–442.

Sheffi, Y., & Rice, J. (2005). A supply chain view of the resilient enterprise. *MIT Sloan Management Review, 47*(1), 41–48.

Svensson, G. (2000). A conceptual framework for the analysis of vulnerability in supply chains. *International Journal of Physical Distribution and Logistics Management, 30*(9), 731–749.

Tummala, R., & Schoenherr, T. (2011). Assessing and managing risks using the Supply Chain Risk Management Process (SCRMP). *Supply Chain Management, 16*(6), 474–483.

van Hoek, R. (2020). Research opportunities for a more resilient post-COVID-19 supply chain—Closing the gap between research findings and industry practice. *International Journal of Operations and Production Management, 40*(4), 341–355.

Chapter 3
An Exploration of Resilience in Medical Gloves Supply Chain During COVID-19 Pandemic

Osaro Aigbogun

Abstract Given the impact of the COVID-19 pandemic on the global supply of medical gloves, this chapter describes an exploration of resilience in the downstream sector of medical gloves supply chain with the aim of identifying practical strategies for improving supply during global health crisis. A qualitative study using an exploratory and phenomenological design was carried out in 2021 using a web-based open-ended questionnaire. The results led to the identification of 20 main themes which were categorized into 7 vulnerability drivers and 13 capability drivers representing vital indicators of supply chain resilience. The findings of this study will assist managers at the supply chain level to take decisions on strategies for developing capabilities to mitigate the vulnerabilities in the medical gloves supply chain during a crisis.

1 Introduction

Safety concerns for health personnel and a surge in end-user demand have led to a sharp increase in global requirements for medical gloves, which is an indispensable Personal Protective Equipment (PPE) amidst the COVID-19 pandemic. Although this spike in demand has created a boom in sales, with global market projections expected to reach USD70 billion by 2027 (Globe Newswire, 2020), vulnerability to supply chain disruptions have forced companies in the industry to devise risk mitigating strategies.

The Food and Drug Administration has expressed concerns about the possibility of medical gloves supply chain disruptions leading to shortages (FDA, 2020). Disruptions created by risky supply chains mount pressure on manufacturers to deliver as they struggle to meet the demand surge. This calls for closer scrutiny and the need to mitigate the threat of disruptions that can pose a risk to global health security. A resilient supply chain is thus required to sustain an optimum health system performance in the midst of this pandemic.

O. Aigbogun (✉)
Faculty of Business, Curtin University Malaysia, Miri, Sarawak, Malaysia

© The Author(s), under exclusive license to Springer Nature Switzerland AG 2023
O. Khan et al. (eds.), *Supply Chain Resilience*, Springer Series in Supply Chain Management 21, https://doi.org/10.1007/978-3-031-16489-7_3

In an increasingly uncertain global environment, the concept of supply chain resilience transcends recovery from disruptive events. Although extensive discussions on resilience are available in the supply chain literature, specific focus on the supply chain of medical gloves has been given only limited attention. This raises a concern that goes beyond revenue and market share losses, to a threat to health safety. Strategies required may be different from other supply networks, especially with the involvement of regulatory authorities which may affect the applicability of conventional strategies on supply chain resilience.

With a global market share of 65%, and an estimated annual production of 240 billion units in 2020, Malaysia's leading role as the "world's medical gloves factory" suggests that any major disruption in its production puts global supply chains at risk. As a result, medical glove manufacturers in Malaysia are working overdrive in the forefront to meet up with global demand during the pandemic (Campbell & Raghu, 2020). The continued uncertainty and vulnerability of supply chains to disruptions during this pandemic underscores the need to understand supply chain resilience in this all-important industry. This chapter describes an exploratory evaluation of resilience of the medical gloves supply chain in the midst of COVID-19 pandemic. The scope of this investigation is limited to the identification of supply chain vulnerabilities and capabilities in the intermediate and downstream sectors of the industry, comprising the manufacturers, distributors, and wholesalers located in Malaysia.

2   Literature Review

2.1   Supply Chain Vulnerabilities, Risk, and Disruptions

Vulnerabilities are the properties of a system that weakens its ability to endure threats and survive accidental events that originate both from within and outside the system boundaries (Waters, 2011). The presence of vulnerabilities in a supply chain makes it risky. Supply chain risk has been conceptualized as an event that adversely affects supply chain operations and its desired performance measures (Zsidisin, 2003; Tummala & Schoenherr, 2011). Like the risks facing individual businesses, supply chain risks have been categorized in different ways and from varying perspectives. According to Mason-Jones and Towill (1998), they are either process risks, which are those associated with interruptions in the processes of creating value within the business; or control risks that are connected with a breakdown in or misapplication of the systems and standards that are used to control the processes. Mandal (2011) suggests two types of risks in a supply chain—operation risks, arising from uncertainties in demand, supply, and cost factors; and disruption risks which arise from natural disasters such as weather disruptions, economic crises, or pandemics such as COVID-19. Leat and Revoredo-Giha (2013) view supply chain risks as either demand risks, which involves a breakdown in the flow of product, information, and revenues between an enterprise and its customers; or supply risk which is a breakdown in material and service supplies, information, and monetary flows between an enterprise and its suppliers. Supply chain risks are important determinants for disruptions.

Disruptions are unplanned and unanticipated events that interrupt the normal flow of goods and materials within a supply chain. Regardless of the way risk is interpreted, it is certain that disruption is somewhat associated with supply chain risk. Supply chain disruption has been argued as having no clear difference from supply chain risk; rather, it is viewed as a consequence of risk (Yaroson et al., 2021). Given the scale and scope of today's global supply chains, there is no way for a company to predict and prepare for every possible risk. As supply chains inevitably become more global, so does their vulnerability also increase, however, companies can withstand this by designing resilient supply chains (Christopher & Peck, 2004). Vulnerabilities are at the heart of our understanding of disruptions and risks in the supply chain. In recent years, supply chain researchers/practitioners have struggled with the issue of vulnerable supply chains, and a considerable amount of literature has been published on supply chain vulnerabilities. The large volume of published studies on supply chain resilience describes the role of vulnerabilities in supply chain risk and disruption management. The challenge to business today is to devise strategies for building a resilient supply chain that is capable of mitigating vulnerabilities to disruptions.

2.2 Supply Chain Resilience

In the supply chain domain, several definitions have been proposed for resilience, however, the key concept taken from all the definitions is that resilience confers on the supply chain the adaptive ability/capacity to side-step risks or revert quickly to its original or perhaps better performance under emergency disruptions. Li et al. (2015) suggest that resilient supply chains are better positioned relative to their competitors in dealing with High-Impact-Low-Probability (HILP) supply chain risks, thus achieving a sustainable competitive edge. In line with the assertion that resilient supply chains are better positioned to deal with HILP events, Tukamuhabwa et al. (2015) define resilience as the adaptive ability of a supply chain to prepare, respond, and recover to an ideal state from a disruptive event in a timely and cost-effective manner. As such, one can infer an association between resilience, enhanced supply chain risk management, and reduction in disruption frequency (Zsidisin & Wagner, 2010).

Recent developments in global supply chain risks, occasioned by the COVID-19 pandemic, have heightened the need for increased understanding of resilience as a supply chain risk management strategy. Although the end game and key motivation for companies to achieve supply chain resilience are to see improvement in their bottom line, a typical medical gloves manufacturer, as with similar complex supply chains (e.g., pharmaceutical supply chain) is subject to ethical responsibilities in terms of product and process development, manufacture, and distribution under highly regulated settings (Hongpiriyakul et al., 2014; Aigbogun et al., 2016). The challenge here is that population health is reliant on these complexities, hence more robust solutions for improving supply chain resilience under highly regulated conditions are required. Ignoring these peculiarities may inflict threatening risks to the whole supply chain (Sabouhi et al., 2018). It is a matter of concern that there are not many studies that employed empirical methods to address the main supply chain disruptions issues in this industry. Many previous studies on supply chain resilience have proffered solutions without considering peculiarities per industry. The generalizability of the findings is rather problematic and barriers exist to the widespread application of these knowledge. Hence, some industries, such as medical glove manufacturing, may not be subjected to traditional business-as-usual solutions.

2.3 Supporting Theories

A number of theories have been employed in supply chain resilience research. Resource-based view and complex adaptive systems theory, are some that have been commonly used. These theories fit into the context of this study in an industry where supply chain relationships are in a somewhat complex matrix-like structure, combining both vertical and horizontal relationships in real time under strict regulation. This study adopts the definition of supply chain resilience suggested by Tukamuhabwa et al. (2015, p. 5599) as "The adaptive capability of a supply chain to prepare for and/or respond to disruptions, to make a timely and cost-effective recovery, and therefore progress to a post-disruption state of operations—ideally, a better state than prior to the disruption." This definition incorporates the essential elements of what a resilient supply chain entails.

2.3.1 Resource-Based View

Resource-Based View (RBV) contends that the capability, capacity, and competitive advantage of a firm is anchored on its internal resources (physical, human, and organizational) which must be valuable, scarce, and irreplaceable (Barney, 1991). Proponents of the RBV argue that performance at the organizational level is primarily dependent on internal resources which are significant to implementing strategies that improve efficiency and effectiveness, and lead to a sustainable competitive advantage.

Some studies on supply chain resilience that have employed RBV are Ponomarov and Holcomb (2009), Brandon Jones et al. (2014), and Dubey et al. (2017). They argue that supply chain resilience is a firm's capital or a resource that forms the essential elements of its capabilities which it uses to gain competitive advantage and put it ahead of its competitors. Pettit et al. (2013) contend that capabilities are an essential dimension of supply chain resilience. An increase in the capabilities of a supply chain positively influences the resilience of that supply chain. Therefore, in a volatile and unstable environment, firms need to continually prepare, integrate and reallocate resources in response to external events in order to enhance their capabilities and improve their supply chain resilience.

2.3.2 Complex Adaptive Systems Theory

Complex Adaptive Systems (CAS) theory is defined as the dynamic capability of systems to adapt and evolve to environmental changes (Nair & Reed Tsochas, 2019). A Complex Adaptive System possesses three distinct features (internal mechanisms, external mechanisms, and coevolution), which on the one hand, interact with each other and work collectively as a whole, and on the other hand, interact with the evolving and changing environment (Yaroson et al., 2021).

With more attention given to the complexity of modern global supply chains, the CAS theory is increasingly being used to explain supply chain resilience in a volatile, uncertain, and complex environment. Some recent studies that have employed the CAS theory in supply chain resilience research include Novak and Eppinger (2001) and Yaroson et al. (2021). The complex dynamics of the medical gloves supply chain has been illustrated by Hongpiriyakul et al. (2014) to consist of the upstream sector (rubber grower, minor collector, major collector, supplier of chemicals, suppliers of packaging, suppliers of fuel, suppliers of glove former); intermediate sector (manufacturers); and downstream sector (warehousing, distributors, and all levels of customers). With uncertainties such as that presented by the COVID-19 pandemic, the medical gloves supply chain, which is an open system, interacts with environmental dynamics to develop resilience strategies.

Yaroson et al. (2021) in their study on pharmaceutical supply chain resilience argue that the CAS theory allows for better comprehension of practical methods for building resilience into the pharmaceutical supply chain. They suggest that this approach can be generalized to other complex supply chains such as the medical gloves supply chain.

3 Methods

This qualitative study, using an exploratory and phenomenological design, was conducted between May and July of 2021. Due to the exploratory nature of this study, qualitative data were collected using a web-based/online open-ended questionnaire. Compared to closed-ended questions, and other survey forms, open-ended questions in web/online surveys are richer and produce more diverse responses; also, it helps to avoid the bias associated with limiting respondents to predetermined response alternatives (Reja et al., 2003).

Purposive and snowball sampling methods were used to select experts and supply chain decision makers from the intermediate and downstream sectors comprising the manufacturers, distributors, and wholesalers located in Malaysia (Table 3.1).

Table 3.1 Characteristics of respondents

Respondents	Description of Company	Respondent Roles	Respondents' Experience in Supply chain operations
RESP1	Manufacturer of gloves	Production manager	13 years
RESP2	Manufacturer of gloves	Supply chain manager	23 years
RESP3	Distributor of medical gloves and medical equipment	Joint owner	25 years
RESP4	Manufacturer of gloves	General manager	22 years
RESP5	Logistics provider	Procurement manager	17 years
RESP6	Distributor of medical gloves and other personal protective equipment	Regional head of supply chain	20 years
RESP7	Distributor of gloves and other personal protective equipment	Operations manager	19 years
RESP8	Wholesaler of personal protective equipment	General manager	17 years
RESP9	Manufacturer of a wide range of gloves	Supply chain manager	40 years
RESP10	Manufacturer of gloves and other personal protective equipment	Supply chain executive	11 years
RESP11	Manufacturer of gloves	Supply chain manager	21 years
RESP12	Distributor of personal protective equipment	Purchasing manager	18 years
RESP13	Manufacturer of gloves	Financial controller	32 years
RESP14	Third party logistics service provider	General manager	19 years

Initially, the web surveys were sent to supply chain managers of medical gloves manufacturing companies. This is because they occupy a vital position in the supply chain and have a comprehensive understanding of how supply chain design affects performance (Dubey et al., 2017). Subsequently, they were asked to introduce other well-informed individuals in the downstream sector of the industry who were willing to participate in this study. Due to the type of information required, the participants' experiences surrounding the phenomenon of investigation were important. The phenomenological design provided the freedom for the experts to demonstrate their knowledge and experience in medical gloves supply chain.

The beginning of the open-ended questionnaire contained information about the purpose of the study as well as assurance of confidentiality of information and the voluntary nature of participation. Trustworthiness and rigor of the study were executed using four-dimension criteria of credibility, transferability, dependability, and confirmability (Lincoln & Guba, 1985). Prolonged engagement was used to establish credibility of the study. Adequate time was spent studying various aspects of the medical gloves supply chain and developing rapport with experts in this industry. This ensured appreciation of the context, in-depth understanding of how they are integrated into the literature, the design of the open-ended questionnaire. The transferability of the study was assured by providing a thick description of the phenomenon and context in sufficient detail. Also, by selecting the participants according to defined inclusion criteria in line with the study's aim. The dependability of the study was improved by external audits. The data content was subjected to peer debriefing in which two other researchers who are experts in qualitative methods reviewed the coded data and findings. In doing this, the codes were finalized. Confirmability of the study was ensured by providing a clear description of the research process and ensuring the deductions made were well grounded on the primary data.

The primary data were analyzed in five steps using MAXQDA 2020 for data coding and classification. In the first step, the survey data in spreadsheet format was imported into the MAXQDA 2020 software. Secondly, meaningful units were identified and categorized to make sense of the data. The third step involved the recording of the individual responses. In the fourth step, the categories were organized into thematic codes. The analyzed data were then visually represented in charts in the fifth step.

4   Results and Findings

The codes and subthemes generated led to the identification of 20 main themes which have been categorized into 7 vulnerability drivers and 13 capability drivers. Vulnerabilities and capabilities are vital indicators of supply chain resilience (Pettit et al., 2013).

4.1   Vulnerability Drivers

Vulnerabilities are fundamental factors that make an enterprise susceptible to disruptions (Pettit et al., 2013). In line with this definition, two questions were asked: (1) Describe the type of issues your company faced during the COVID-19 pandemic;

and (2) Describe the nature of supply chain disruptions faced during the COVID-19 pandemic. From the responses, seven main themes emerged: Demand outweighs supply, Movement restrictions, COVID-19 outbreak in factory, Order fulfillment delay, Transport disruptions, and Raw material (supply) delays.

From the findings, some of the respondents indicated that the resilience of medical gloves supply chain during the COVID-19 pandemic has been affected by a global surge in demand which exceeded the supply and/or capacity of their companies to meet this demand. In line with this fact, one of the respondents stated that:

> This challenge put pressure on us and other similar manufacturers who have been faced with issues like missed deadlines etc. We are most times working round-the-clock and over stretching facilities to meet the demand which may not be sustainable. [RESP4]

Movement restrictions were also implicated by many of the respondents. The argument was that the government imposed restriction of movement causing a delay in workers coming to the factory and in the movement of supplies. In regards to this, one of the respondents said the following:

> Obtaining permits for our workers to come to the factory slowed down operations. And we encountered difficulty in moving our goods around due to numerous bureaucracies. [RESP10]

A few of the respondents noted that there were instances of COVID-19 outbreak in their facility leading to a compulsory shutdown of operations. This event created a disruption in scheduled productions. One of the respondents had the following to say:

> There were sudden cases of COVID-19 among our foreign workers. We had to follow government SOPs leading to shut down of the factory for some days to disinfect and trace contacts. This led to interruption in our operations and we fell behind in our production and delivery. [RESP9]

Several respondents also highlighted the delay in fulfilling customer orders due to a multiplicity of reasons. One of the more recurring reasons was the increased requirements on company logistics and material handling capabilities due to the excess production output and numerous demands to be fulfilled. One of the respondents had the following to say:

> We were short of lorry transporters and enough holding capacity for the production increase and this affected our fulfillment of customer order. [RESP2]

Some respondents implicated transport disruptions as a major hindrance to their operations. This created challenges in material handling. In regard to this problem, one of the respondents had the following to say:

> We had issues with our lorry drivers particularly those who hold permits to cross over to other states. Also issue with road blocks, area closures, and numerous rules for transportation causing chaos. [RESP14]

Regarding delays in the receipt of raw material/supplies for production, some respondents attributed this to some occasional disruption in production. Regarding this, one respondent noted that:

> Our business was interrupted because we got late supplies from our usual suppliers and this affected our ability to continue with rapid productions. I think they too were affected with the many COVID-19 Country lockdown & restrictions. [RESP1]

4.2   Capability Drivers

Capabilities are attributes that enable an enterprise to anticipate and overcome disruptions (Pettit et al., 2013). In line with this definition, three questions were asked: (1) Describe how your company resolved the major issues discussed in question 1; (2) Describe what your company did to handle or mitigate disruptions in production and supply during COVID-19; and (3) How can your company be better prepared for future disruptions such as COVID-19? From the responses, 13 main themes emerged: Ramp-up production lines, Engage more third-party logistics (3PL), Alternative distribution channels, Source alternative suppliers, Update customers regularly, Source local suppliers, Increase redundancy, New product variation, Improve supplier collaboration, Crisis management, Enterprise resource planning, Business continuity planning, and Improve supply chain collaboration.

In response to how the companies responded to the issues they faced during the COVID-19 pandemic, several respondents who worked in medical gloves manufacturing companies said that their immediate response was to ramp up their production capacities. One of the respondents said the following:

> We took immediate measures to expand our lines of production and even considered opening new factory. I know of some other companies which were previously not making gloves but have diversified to make gloves because of the current huge profits in this business. [RESP1]

Some of the respondents also stated that, in order to improve their capabilities, more logistics partners were employed to handle the spike in production output and customer demand. For example, one of the respondents said the following:

> It cost us a higher price, but we had no choice than to engage more 3rd parties in our delivery which cut into our profit margin. [RESP2]

Due to the movement restrictions and transport demands placed on the company's distribution systems, alternative distribution channels were evaluated and employed in order to meet up with demand. With regard to this, one of the respondents said the following:

> We sought alternative channels for distributing the products and this meant that sometimes we had to collaborate with our competitors. [RESP7]

In response to what their companies did to handle or mitigate disruptions in production and supply during COVID-19, many of the respondents stated that they kept their customers informed and up-to-date about their order status. In line with this, one of the respondents said the following:

> We updated our customers regularly on their shipment status, also activities in the supply chain for more informed response of the customers. This helped us to negotiate new deadlines. [RESP2]

Moreover, for those further downstream who were reliant on supplies from overseas, delays in receiving inputs were encountered and this led to their sourcing for inputs from local suppliers. This was a way to stay in competition by mitigating the fallout from numerous restrictions and bureaucracies for inbound products. In this regard one of the respondents had this to say:

> Alternatively to source for local substitution instead of overseas supply. [RESP12]

Some respondents stated that increasing their raw material reserve capacity was a strategy they used to manage occasional shortages in raw material supplies that had come to typify the pandemic period due to the demand increase. This strategy can be employed to deal with the potential shortages of raw materials or finished products as a consequence. With regard to increasing redundancy, one of the respondents said the following:

> We had to stock up our inventory and manage safety stock levels with the aid of software. [RESP11]

A few of the manufacturing companies introduced new product variations for their usual products as a way of maximizing the raw material supplies available in the market. This helped them to stay competitive. In this regard one of the respondents had this to say:

> We increased the internal variety of our raw material components and semi-finished products that we offer to our customers in the market. [RESP9]

Many of the respondents stated that improvement in their supplier collaboration was a major influence on their business performance during the pandemic. They had to improve their joint working relationships with their suppliers in a manner that ensured cost effective, timely, and reliable availability and movement of products. In this regard one of the respondents had this to say:

> In this time we engaged more with our suppliers and cooperated in sharing information to help us track and monitor the things that were happening with products. [RESP12]

In response to how companies can be better prepared for future disruptions such as COVID-19, many of the respondents were of the opinion that in the future companies should improve their ability to correctly predict and identify crisis signals in the external business environment. Although the external business environment is beyond the control of managers, they can, however, reorganized their internal environment to make them better prepared to handle the fallout of such a crisis. In line with this, one of the respondents said the following:

Managers should take crisis management strategies more serious in the future because this will be important for their survival. More efforts should concentrate on risk management systems to identify and prevent negative effect on running a business. [RESP8]

Some respondents were of the opinion that companies should invest more in Enterprise Resource Planning (ERP) IT solutions that provide more effective methods in managing procurement and product supply across the supply chain. They reckon that ERP improves supply chain relationships and confers visibility in the supply chain. One of the respondents said the following:

Better prepared to leverage ERP software with systematic procedures that will handle day-to-day challenges during such issues. [RESP5]

Most of the respondents opined that, resulting from the lessons learned in this pandemic, business continuity planning is key to business survival; as a result, in the future, organizations should empower themselves and build their capacities to ensure operations, as well as core business functions, are not severely disrupted by a disaster or events that compromise their critical systems. One of the respondents said the following:

When similar circumstances repeat itself in the future, companies that will compete better and not close shop are those that already have survival plans for their business operations to survive. [RESP3]

Some of the respondents were of the opinion that in the future companies should collaborate more with supply chain partners through symbolic, trust-based relationships in order to avoid disruptions and achieve common goals. One of the respondents said the following:

Companies should improve their performance by creating more platforms for cooperation by entering and cementing their relationships with suppliers and customers. [RESP9]

5   Discussion

The findings indicate potential vulnerability and capability drivers of the medical gloves supply chain during crisis. In line with the reasoning of Pettit et al. (2013), these capability drivers could act as strategies to address the vulnerability challenges and improve supply chain resilience.

As stated earlier, the findings of this study established the presence of the following vulnerability drivers in the supply chain of medical gloves during the COVID-19 pandemic: Demand exceeding supply, Movement restrictions, COVID-19 outbreak in factory, Order fulfillment delay, Transport disruptions, and Raw material (supply) delays. Vulnerability drivers have the potential to weaken/limit the ability of the medical gloves supply chain to endure threats and survive accidental events, making it susceptible to disruptions. Research scholars (e.g., Svensson, 2002; Wagner & Bode, 2006; Blos et al., 2009) argue that by addressing these vulnerabilities, the supply chain risks are mitigated, and resilience is improved.

The study findings also identified certain capability drivers which have been used by companies to address supply chain vulnerabilities due to COVID-19. These capability drivers are Ramp-up production lines, Engage more third-party logistics (3PL), Alternative distribution channels, Source alternative suppliers, Update customers regularly, Source local suppliers, Increase redundancy, New product variation, Improve supplier collaboration, Crisis management, Enterprise resource planning, Business continuity planning, and Improve supply chain collaboration. Fundamentally, drawing from the resource-based view theory, capabilities can be viewed as essential internal resources that can be deployed to improve resilience, thus, offering a superior business position and competitive advantage among competing firms (Barney, 1991). Strategies to mitigate vulnerability would improve resilience (Waters, 2011). As a result, the key business goals for supply chain managers should be channeled toward investing in these capabilities.

In this study a recurring pattern among the drivers of capability was collaboration. Collaboration among members of the supply chain has been viewed to be a key enabler of supply chain resilience during crisis (Le & Koh, 2002). When considering the set-up of the medical gloves supply chain, each member tends to be independent of the others and is guided principally by their own goals, hence to limit the occurrence of disruptions, there is a need for more collaboration during crisis. For example, the findings of Yaroson et al. (2021) in the UK pharmaceutical supply chain show conflicting goals of major supply chain actors. The goal of the NHS is quality and cost-oriented, the goal of the community pharmacy is service-oriented while the aim of the manufacturing companies is to make profits. This divergence of goals creates conflicts which make the supply chain more vulnerable to disruptions. It stands to reason that an increase in collaboration among the supply chain actors will improve the congruence of their goals, thus enhancing their resilience.

6 Conclusion

The objective of this study was to evaluate the resilience of the medical gloves supply chain during the COVID-19 pandemic. To this end, an open-ended web questionnaire survey was used to gather qualitative data that led to the identification of the vulnerability drivers that increased the susceptibility to disruptions, and the capability drivers that acted as strategies to overcome/mitigate disruptions in the medical gloves supply chain. Managers and key decision makers need to be aware of potential vulnerabilities that can exist in the supply chain during uncertainties. The capability drivers are strategies that could enable the medical gloves supply chain to be more resilient.

References

Aigbogun, O., Ghazali, Z., & Razali, R. (2016). The mediating impact of halal logistics on supply chain resilience: An agency perspective. *International Review of Management and Marketing, 6*(4S), 209–216.

Barney, J. (1991). Firm resources and sustained competitive advantage. *Journal of Management, 17*(1), 99–120.

Blos, M. F., Quaddus, M., Wee, H. M., & Watanabe, K. (2009). Supply chain risk management (SCRM): A case study on the automotive and electronic industries in Brazil. *Supply Chain Management: An International Journal, 14*(4), 247–252.

Brandon Jones, E., Squire, B., Autry, C. W., & Petersen, K. J. (2014). A contingent resource based perspective of supply chain resilience and robustness. *Journal of Supply Chain Management, 50*(3), 55–73.

Campbell, M., & Raghu, A. (2020, August 21). The pandemic is a bonanza for Malaysia's medical glove industry. *Bloomberg Business Week.* Retrieved from https://www.bloomberg.com/news/articles/2020-04-21/the-pandemic-is-a-bonanza-for-malaysia-s-medical-glove-industry

Christopher, M., & Peck, H. (2004). Building the resilient supply chain. *The International Journal of Logistics Management, 15*(2), 1–14.

Dubey, R., Gunasekaran, A., Childe, S. J., Papadopoulos, T., Blome, C., & Luo, Z. (2017). Antecedents of resilient supply chains: An empirical study. *IEEE Transactions on Engineering Management, 66*(1), 8–19.

Food and Drug Administration. (2020). *Medical gloves for COVID-19.* Retrieved from https://www.fda.gov/medical-devices/coronavirus-covid-19-and-medical-devices/medical-gloves-covid-19

Globe Newswire. (2020). *Global medical gloves industry.* Retrieved from https://www.reportlinker.com/p05896703/?utm_source=GNW

Hongpiriyakul, S., Sirivongpaisal, N., Suthummanon, S., Kongkaew, W., & Penchamrat, P. (2014). Reduction of cost employing lean supply chain in rubber glove industry. In: *Advanced materials research* (Vol. 844, pp. 421–424). Trans Tech.

Le, T. T., & Koh, A. C. (2002). A managerial perspective on electronic commerce development in Malaysia. *Electronic Commerce Research, 2*(1), 7–29.

Leat, P., & Revoredo-Giha, C. (2013). Risk and resilience in agri-food supply chains: The case of the ASDA PorkLink supply chain in Scotland. *Supply Chain Management: An International Journal, 18*(2), 219–231.

Li, G., Fan, H., Lee, P. K., & Cheng, T. C. E. (2015). Joint supply chain risk management: An Agency and collaboration perspective. *International Journal of Production Economics, 164*, 83–94.

Lincoln, Y. S., & Guba, E. G. (1985). *Naturalistic inquiry.* Sage.

Mandal, S. (2011). Supply chain risk identification and elimination: A theoretical perspective. *The IUP Journal of Supply Chain Management, 8*(1), 68–86.

Mason-Jones, R., & Towill, D. (1998). Shrinking the supply chain uncertainty cycle. *IOM Control, 27*(4), 17–22.

Nair, A., & Reed Tsochas, F. (2019). Revisiting the complex adaptive systems paradigm: Leading perspectives for researching operations and supply chain management issues. *Journal of Operations Management, 65*(2), 80–92.

Novak, S., & Eppinger, S. D. (2001). Sourcing by design: Product complexity and the supply chain. *Management Science, 47*(1), 189–204.

Pettit, T. J., Croxton, K. L., & Fiksel, J. (2013). Ensuring supply chain resilience: Development and implementation of an assessment tool. *Journal of Business Logistics, 34*(1), 46–76.

Ponomarov, S. Y., & Holcomb, M. C. (2009). Understanding the concept of supply chain resilience. *The International Journal of Logistics Management, 20*(1), 124–143.

Reja, U., Manfreda, K. L., Hlebec, V., & Vehovar, V. (2003). Open-ended vs. close-ended questions in web questionnaires. *Developments in Applied Statistics, 19*(1), 159–177.

Sabouhi, F., Pishvaee, M. S., & Jabalameli, M. S. (2018). Resilient supply chain design under operational and disruption risks considering quantity discount: A case study of pharmaceutical supply chain. *Computers and Industrial Engineering, 126*, 657–672.

Svensson, G. (2002). A conceptual framework of vulnerability in firms' in-bound and out-bound logistics flows. *International Journal of Physical Distribution and Logistics Management, 32*(2), 110–113.

Tukamuhabwa, B. R., Stevenson, M., Busby, J., & Zorzini, M. (2015). Supply chain resilience: Definition, review and theoretical foundations for further study. *International Journal of Production Research, 53*(18), 5592–5623.

Tummala, R., & Schoenherr, T. (2011). Assessing and managing risk using the Supply Chain Risk Management Process (SCRMP). *Supply Chain Management: An International Journal, 16*(6), 474–483.

Wagner, S., & Bode, C. (2006). An empirical investigation into supply chain vulnerability. *Journal of Purchasing and Supply Management, 12*(6), 301–312.

Waters, D. (2011). *Supply chain risk management: Vulnerability and resilience in logistics.* Kogan Page.

Yaroson, E. V., Breen, L., Hou, J., & Sowter, J. (2021). Advancing the understanding of pharmaceutical supply chain resilience using complex adaptive system (CAS) theory. *Supply Chain Management: An International Journal., 26*, 323–340.

Zsidisin, G. A. (2003). A grounded definition of supply risk. *Journal of Purchasing and Supply Management, 9*(5), 217–224.

Zsidisin, G. A., & Wagner, S. M. (2010). Do perceptions become reality? The moderating role of supply chain resiliency on disruption occurrence. *Journal of Business Logistics, 31*(2), 1–20.

Chapter 4
Status Quo of Supply Chain Risk Management: Results of an Empirical Study in Germany

Michael Huth and Carsten Knauer

Abstract Two of the main objectives of having a supply chain risk management (SCRM) implemented include once to be prepared for risks threatening the supply chain and second to have set up a resilient supply chain. To be able to reach those objectives requires the SCRM system to have a certain maturity level. The maturity level measures the degree of professionalism of an SCRM system. Often the maturity level is both described and assessed in a qualitative way for the SCRM system as a whole. Additionally, the maturity level of an SCRM system is hardly ever assessed in empirical surveys. However, the survey conducted by the authors in German-speaking countries in 2020 used a set of 40 questions to derive a both detailed and quantified look at the maturity level of the participants' SCRM system. This new approach leads to insights that enable targeted improvement of the SCRM system.

1 Introduction

The Corona pandemic has been, and continues to be, one of several causes of the current supply chain disruptions that have been increasingly reported since the spring of 2020; an overview of disruptions in supply chains in 2021 can be found at Zimmerman (2021). Other causes of such disruptions include the blockage of the Suez Canal in spring 2021 (for example, Schiffling & Kanellos, 2021) as well as supply bottlenecks for semiconductors and their raw materials (for example, Vakil & Linton, 2021). The consequences of these interruptions can be significant: The average reduction in enterprise value, based on supply chain risks studied in the

M. Huth (✉)
Fulda University of Applied Sciences, Fulda, Germany
e-mail: michael.huth@w.hs-fulda.de

C. Knauer
BME e.V., Association for Supply Chain Management, Procurement and Logistics, Eschborn, Germany
e-mail: carsten.knauer@bme.de

1989–2001 period, was more than 10% (Hendricks & Singhal, 2008). As a result of these supply chain risks and the consequences demonstrated, the topics of risk management and resilience in supply chains have received much greater attention since the onset of the Corona pandemic. Of course, there have also been previous events that have caused major disruptions in supply chains and have led to an increased focus on risk management and resilience in supply chains. Examples include the eruption of the Eyjafjallajökull volcano in 2010, which led to significant restrictions on air traffic, and the Fukushima disaster in 2011, which caused disruptions in supply chains worldwide (Manners-Bell, 2018). Nevertheless, the Corona pandemic has taken on a special significance in the recent past, mainly due to its temporal, but also geographical extent and, in conjunction with other supply chain risks, the consequences for supply chains in almost all industries.

Despite its particular importance in the Corona pandemic, the concept of supply chain risk management is not new: scholars began to explore SCRM in the late 1990s and even more so in the early 2000s (for example, Khan & Zsidisin, 2012; Zsidisin & Henke, 2019). Publications on SCRM continue to increase: From 2010 to 2019 alone, publications in ABCD journals nearly quadrupled (Gurtu & Johny, 2021). The increasing number of articles and books not only demonstrates the importance attached to this subject area, but above all represents a substantial body of knowledge, especially methodological knowledge. In this context—in the period from 2003 to 2013—articles focusing on quantitative, analytical methods represented the clear majority: They account for more than 71% of the publications, whereas articles focusing on qualitative methods represent only just under 24% of all publications; negligible are quantitative-empirical publications, which are covered in only about 5% of the publications (Ho et al., 2015). Accordingly, the knowledge exists to manage supply chain risks. It should therefore not be difficult for companies to establish effective supply chain risk management that contributes to high resilience to supply chain risks. However, studies by Huth and Lohre, which examined the status quo of risk management at logistics companies, already revealed an overall low level of implementation: in various studies from 2008, 2011, and 2013, for example, between 54 and 67% of logistics companies said they had established a risk management system, between 7 and 24% planned to introduce it within the next 2 years, between 4 and 10% planned to introduce it at a later date, and between 16 and 17% did not plan to introduce any (Huth & Lohre, 2014). These studies showed that the degree of implementation of risk management among logistics companies was still manageable; the authors summarized, among other things: "[...] the application of methods in the context of risk identification and risk assessment is currently still comparatively low" (Huth & Lohre, 2015).

While the studies by Huth and Lohre focused on the logistics service provider sector, the fundamental question is to what extent companies from industry, trade, and the service sector practice risk management of their supply chains. However, empirical surveys on the status quo of supply chain management are only available in small numbers. The "BME Logistics Survey 2020: Supply Chain Risk Management" on which this chapter is based, conducted by the Association Supply Chain Management, Procurement and Logistics (BME) and Fulda University of Applied

Sciences (Huth et al., 2020), aims to fill this gap. The objective of the study was to empirically record and document the status quo of SCRM in German-speaking countries. This chapter presents and discusses selected results of this study, some of which have not yet been published in this form, and derives recommendations for action for companies. The following section first explains the framework data for the empirical survey. The most important results of the study are then presented and discussed. The focus is initially on the maturity of SCRM at companies, followed by topics such as the anchoring of SCRM in the organizational structure and transparency across the entire supply chain. The chapter concludes with recommendations for action derived from the study results.

2   Framework Data for the Empirical Survey

The purpose of the underlying "BME Logistics Survey 2020: Supply Chain Risk Management" was to record and document the status quo of SCRM—above all the degree of maturity, but also strengths and weaknesses—in German-speaking countries and to derive recommendations for action that will lead to effective and efficient SCRM. It was initiated before the start of the coronavirus pandemic; its focus was therefore not on corona-related aspects. However, in response to the rapidly changing circumstances in the first half of 2020, questions on the contribution of SCRM to the management of the COVID-19 crisis were added.

An initial and standardized collection of primary data on the status quo of SCRM was carried out as part of an online survey. Subsequently, expert interviews were conducted by telephone with selected participants of the online survey to discuss individual aspects of SCRM in more detail. The online survey was conducted between May 19, 2020, and June 30, 2020. Two hundred fourteen people participated in the survey. One hundred sixteen of the participants answered the questionnaire completely. An additional 98 people dropped out of answering the questionnaire at various points within the survey; however, their responses were saved at the time of dropout and were also included in the analysis. The expert interviews were conducted between July 1 and July 31, 2020. In the process, 12 experts were interviewed on the basis of non-standardized interviews.

One-third of the participants come from the mechanical engineering, pharmaceutical and chemical, and warehousing and transport sectors. These three industries represent the largest proportion of participants. In total, companies from 11 industries took part. In addition to the industry origin of the participants, the company size is also of interest. This was represented in the survey by annual sales. This shows that large companies with sales of more than 1 billion euros were the strongest group of participants; the shares of the other company sizes were between 7 and 22%. Around two-thirds of the participants come from supply chain management or related functions such as logistics or purchasing. One in six participants comes from risk management or a related function such as controlling or quality management. A good 10% of the participants are managing directors or belong to the board of directors.

3   Results of the Empirical Survey

3.1   *Procedure for Eliciting the SCRM Maturity Level*

One possible way to evaluate a risk management system in general, but also a risk management system for supply chains in particular, is to use a maturity model. The basic purpose of such maturity models is to describe different levels of maturity as well as the path from one to the next maturity level (Pöppelbuss & Röglinger, 2011). From an application point of view, descriptive, prescriptive, and comparative purposes can be distinguished (Pöppelbuss & Röglinger, 2011): If descriptive purposes are pursued, the maturity model can be used as a diagnostic tool by reporting the current state to internal or external stakeholders. If, on the other hand, the maturity model is used to define necessary actions based on a targeted maturity level, prescriptive purposes are pursued. Ultimately, a maturity model can also pursue comparative purposes in the sense of benchmarking. A maturity model for SCRM can also support the three purposes described. In the context of the empirical study presented, the first purpose was in the foreground, i.e., the description of the status quo.

While there are no maturity models for SCRM, such models do exist for risk management at the enterprise level, i.e., for enterprise risk management: Among others, the following older models can be named (Government Centre for Information Systems, 1993; Hillson, 1997; Hopkinson, 2000). Approaches of the past decade include the contributions of Chapman (2011) and Oliva (2016) and Proença et al. (2017). The OECD has also developed a maturity model which—in contrast to some of the previously mentioned models—is surprisingly detailed: in addition to five maturity levels, it distinguishes between a total of nine criteria, some of which relate to the risk management process, and others to further aspects of risk management: Indicative attributes, strategy, governance, culture, risk identification, risk analysis and evaluation, risk treatment, review and revision, information, communication, and reporting (OECD, 2021). Not all of these maturity models can be operationalized without restriction: although the most important criteria are defined, the criteria characteristics are not always delineated. In such cases, the application of the maturity model is limited.

For the survey on which this chapter is based, we used a maturity model developed by RiskNet GmbH, which was not specifically developed for supply chain risk management but for enterprise risk management, and which was adapted for the SCRM-related survey (Details can be found at Romeike, 2018). The maturity model used defines five maturity levels (Initial, Basic, Evolved, Advanced, and Leading). Furthermore, four categories are defined as core elements of effective risk management; these are risk management culture, risk management organization,

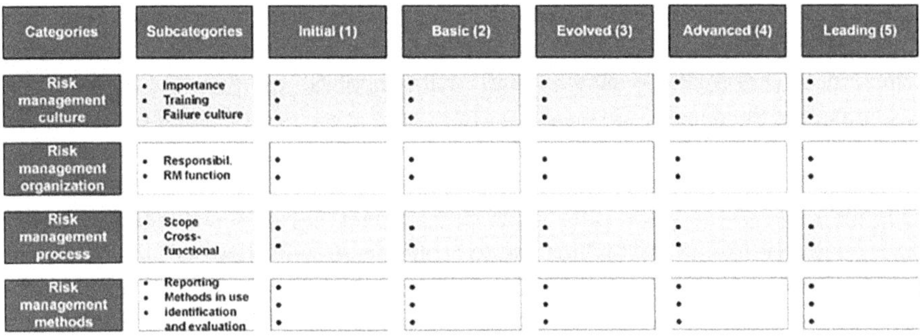

Categories	Subcategories	Initial (1)	Basic (2)	Evolved (3)	Advanced (4)	Leading (5)
Risk management culture	• Importance • Training • Failure culture	• • •	• • •	• • •	• • •	• • •
Risk management organization	• Responsibil. • RM function	• •	• •	• •	• •	• •
Risk management process	• Scope • Cross-functional	• •	• •	• •	• •	• •
Risk management methods	• Reporting • Methods in use • Identification and evaluation	• • •	• • •	• • •	• • •	• • •

Fig. 4.1 Basic concept of the maturity model used [own representation, based on Romeike (2018)]

risk management process, and risk management methods (Romeike & Hager, 2020). Within each category, there are either two or three subcategories (ten subcategories in total across all categories); for example, the "risk management culture" category is about the added value of risk management, risk management training, and error culture.

The maturity levels and the categories including subcategories thus span a matrix consisting of five columns and ten rows (see Fig. 4.1). Within this matrix, the maturity model provides descriptions about the status to the company. For example, in the category of risk management culture, the maturity level "Initial" is marked, among other things, by the description "no risk management training," and the maturity level "Leading" is marked by the description "constant risk management culture transformation program to maintain good risk management culture." In the risk management process category, the description in the "Initial" maturity level is "comprehensive RM process in place, imposed by top management; (almost) no acceptance"; in the "Leading" maturity level, it is "RM process is effectively integrated into all supply chain processes; full acceptance."

In order to use the maturity model for an online survey, it must be operationalized. First, the descriptions within the matrix were adjusted where a focus on supply chain risk management was necessary. For example, "good common understanding of enterprise risk management" was changed to "good common understanding of supply chain risk management."

There are two basic approaches for querying the (perceived) maturity levels of the participating companies; both are based on the subcategories of the model. The first approach is based on a survey participant receiving all responses for a subcategory and estimating their own maturity level in this subcategory based on the complete responses. This corresponds to querying the maturity level using a Likert scale and can be implemented in the online survey, for example, using sliders or radio buttons. The advantage of the approach is a clear decision for one of the five maturity levels, related to the subcategory, based on all descriptions of the five maturity levels. The disadvantage, however, is that assessing one's own maturity level may be difficult due to the verbal descriptions, which are often extensive. In order to make it easier for the survey participants, who were asked to answer a large number of questions in addition to the maturity level questions, a second approach was chosen: Here, the respondents were presented with one statement for each of the ten subcategories, which they were asked to answer purely with "applies" or "does not apply." The assignment of the maturity levels of the statements was based on a random principle, so that statements were not made only for the maturity level "Initial" at the beginning. The order of the ten subcategories was also determined at random. In the next step, the respondents were again assigned statements for all ten categories, which were randomly selected and which had to be answered with "applies" and "does not apply." Based on the response behavior for the previous statements, certain subcategories could be excluded depending on the response. In total, this resulted in a maximum number of 40 statements covering all subcategories and maturity levels. Within a subcategory, the maturity level was determined by the highest level at which a respondent answered "applies." The advantage of this approach is that it is easy to answer, in that only one decision had to be made about whether it was true or not. At the same time, by selecting the highest level with an applicable answer, the procedure can lead to higher maturity levels being shown than with the first procedure using Likert scales.

The maturity level within a category results from the mean value of the maturity levels for each assigned subcategory. The maturity level of the SCRM results from the mean value of the maturity levels of all subcategories.

3.2   Maturity of SCRM: Results of the Empirical Survey

The following section describes selected results of the empirical survey. It focuses on the maturity level concept explained above. Instead of verbal terms, the maturity levels are numbered from 1 (= Basic) to 5 (Leading).

The results of the empirical survey show that companies have a high level of maturity above all in the area of SCRM processes: 60% of companies have a maturity level of 4 or 5. Risk management culture, on the other hand, is the element in SCRM with the lowest maturity level. The SCRM organization is also an element that has some catching up to do in terms of maturity. Figure 4.2 shows the proportion of companies surveyed per category and maturity level and—in the lowest bar—the distribution of maturity levels overall.

First, the results are examined with regard to the low maturity levels 1 (Initial) and 2 (Basic). This shows that the SCRM organization is the category in which the largest proportion of companies with a low maturity level exists: just under 38% of companies have a maturity level of 1 or 2. SCRM culture also has a large proportion of companies that have low maturity levels (just under 36% with a maturity level of 1 or 2). In the other two categories (SCRM process and SCRM methods), on the other hand, there is a significantly lower proportion of companies with a low maturity level: in the case of methods, just under 26% of companies have a maturity level of 1 or 2, and in the case of the SCRM process only around 17%.

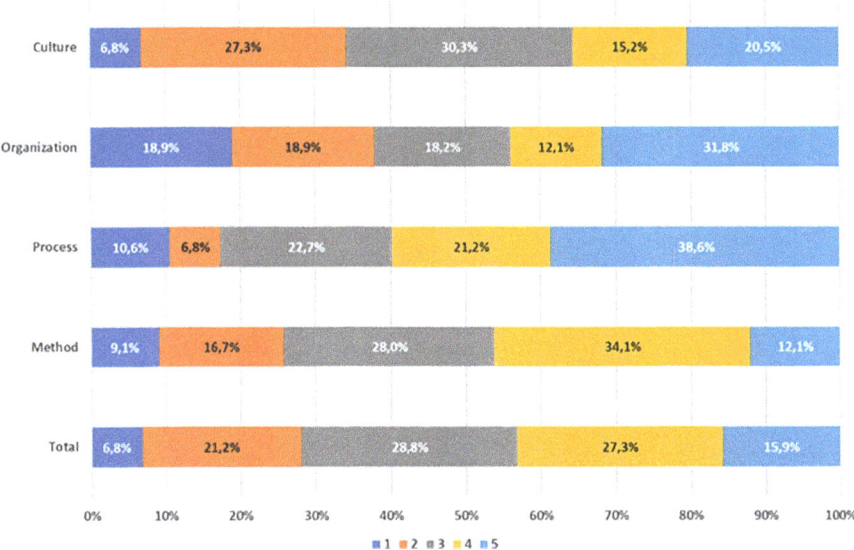

Fig. 4.2 Maturity levels of the SCRM in different categories ($n = 132$)

The results can also be analyzed with a focus on the high maturity levels 4 (Advanced) and 5 (Leading). Although the picture is not identical, it is similar: around 6 out of 10 companies have a high maturity level of 4 or 5 for the SCRM process. Lower percentages for mature SCRM can be seen for methods (46%) and organization (44%). Only around one in three companies shows a high level of maturity for the SCRM culture.

The basic finding that the maturity level of the SCRM organization, in particular, is low and that of the SCRM process is high seems plausible: Defining and implementing a process—and thus designing the process organization—is significantly easier than changing the organizational structure with its assignments and responsibilities. Structures have often grown historically, but they also manifest spheres of influence and areas of power that are reluctantly relinquished. Adjusting the organizational structure is therefore often a strategic decision that is rarely made in the short term.

The relatively low level of maturity in the use of methods is surprising, given that—as mentioned above—a wide range of methods are available, often supported by software applications. However, observations by the authors and discussions with experts as part of the underlying study show that methods are often used at a low level: Preference is given to methods such as brainstorming and checklists. These results were also obtained in earlier empirical surveys of logistics service providers: For example, between two-thirds and three-quarters of the companies used brainstorming, checklists, and expert or employee discussions; only 3 out of 10 companies used a Failure Mode and Effect Analysis (FMEA), only one in five companies used a risk map, and other methods were mentioned even less frequently (Huth & Lohre,

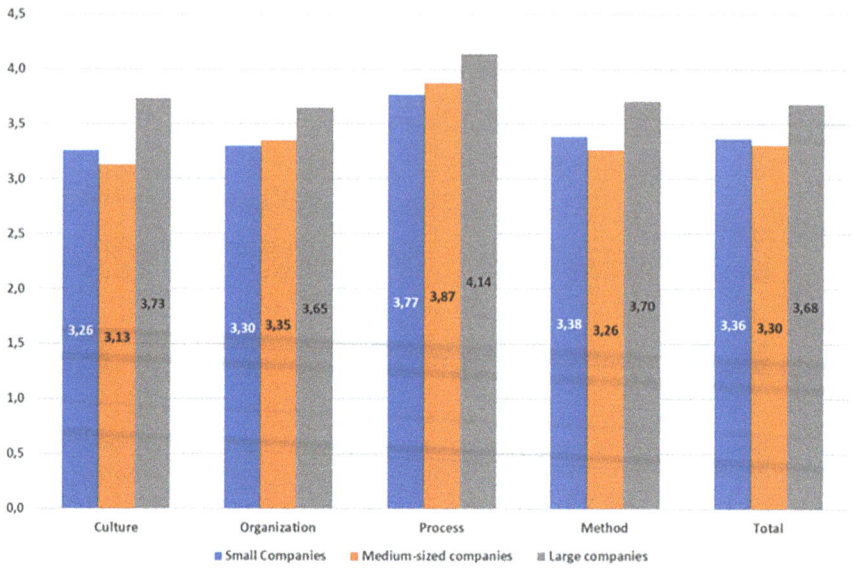

Fig. 4.3 Maturity levels of SCRM in different categories by company size ($n = 107$)

2014). The reasons for low use of methods are manifold: partly the necessary method knowledge is missing, partly the data required for a method use is missing. These two deficiencies are often coupled with the need to achieve the highest possible level of acceptance in the company through methods that are easy to use, which seems to be in danger when more sophisticated methods are used.

As shown in Fig. 4.3, large companies with sales of 1 billion euros and more have higher maturity levels. This applies both to the maturity of SCRM as a whole and to the individual categories.

For the results shown in Fig. 4.3, the individual results for different sales sizes were combined: Small companies have sales of up to 250 million euros (47 companies), medium-sized companies have sales of up to 1 billion euros (23 companies) and large companies have sales of more than 1 billion euros (37 companies).[1] The difference in maturity between large and all other companies is visible in all categories. Differences between small and medium-sized companies, on the other hand, are negligible. Large companies thus exhibit more mature risk management and thus a higher degree of professionalization. If this level of professionalization leads to greater effectiveness of risk management in the sense that risks are identified earlier, preventive measures are developed and implemented in a more targeted manner, and a company and its supply chains are thus more resilient. Competitive

---

[1] The number of responses in this evaluation is lower than the number of responses in Fig. 4.2. This is due to the fact that the company size (here as sales) was only recorded at the end of the survey and some participants had already left the survey at this point. Not all responses from Fig. 4.1 could therefore be assigned to a company size.

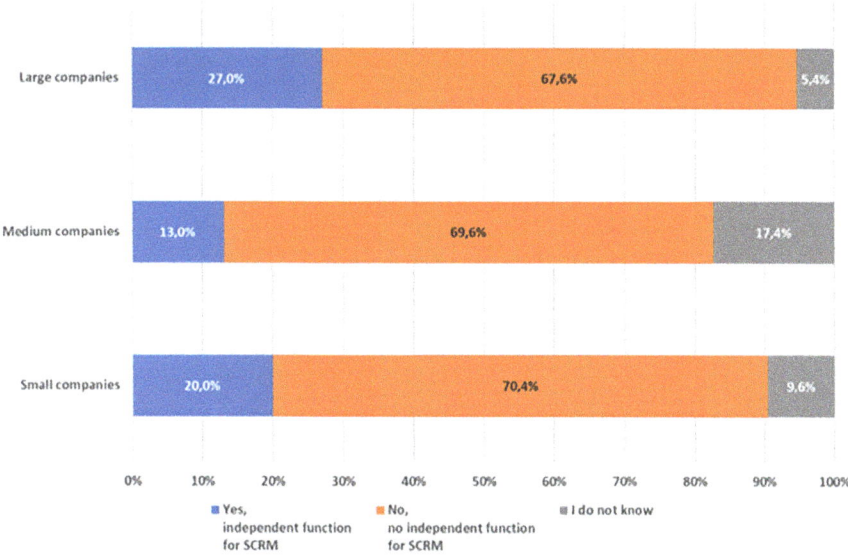

Fig. 4.4 Stand-alone function for the SCRM ($n = 175$)

advantages can be achieved because risks are either not realized or risks that have occurred can be mitigated more effectively.

3.3   Further Results of the Empirical Survey

One sign of how significant SCRM is considered to be is the establishment of a function in the company that deals with risks in supply chains. Based on past risks, but especially the coronavirus pandemic, there is likely to be a push for SCRM and the establishment of an SCRM function as companies then assign specific responsibility for managing supply chain risks. However, the results of the study show a different picture: The anchoring of SCRM in companies is currently at a limited level. Figure 4.4 shows that only a small proportion of companies have set up an independent function responsible for SCRM.

In large companies, this proportion is—as expected—larger than in small and medium-sized companies. Nevertheless, the differences are not great. Depending on size, between 68% and 70% of companies have not yet set up such a function. This may be an indicator that the topic of SCRM is currently still assigned a low level of importance.

Companies that have not established a separate function for SCRM distribute the responsibility for managing supply chain risks among one or more different functions: Supply chain management (including logistics, purchasing, and materials management) is solely or jointly responsible for 77% of companies, management

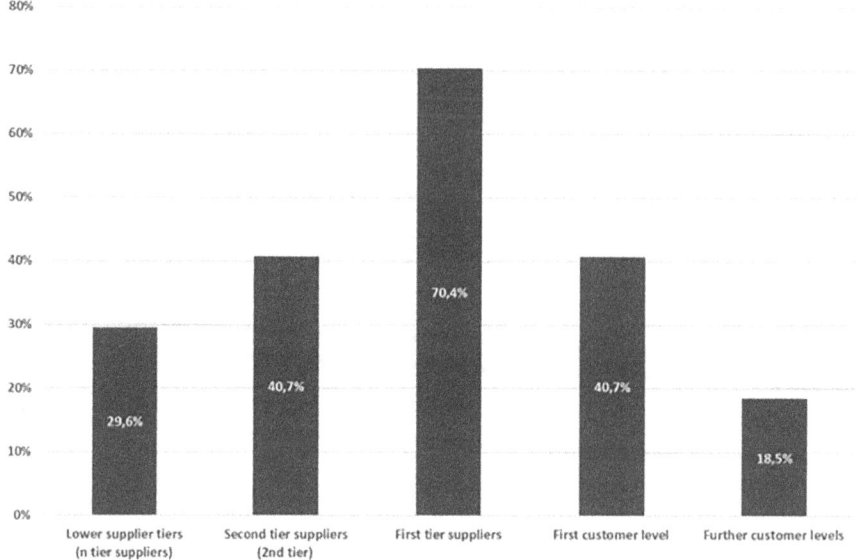

Fig. 4.5 Coverage of the stages of a supply chain by SCRM ($n = 27$) (Only those companies that had implemented a standalone function for SCRM were included. This results in the low number of 27 responses.)

(executive management, board of directors) at 49% of companies, and risk management (including controlling, internal auditing, and quality management) at 28% of companies.

Some of the chapters in this book focus explicitly on the need for transparency in supply chains. Visibility is often mentioned in this context. Against this background, we were interested in the extent to which such visibility is already available in order to be able to detect risks in supply chains at an early stage.

Figure 4.5 illustrates that SCRM is still far from expected visibility. Only the first supplier level is reasonably well covered: a good 70% of companies cover these suppliers through their SCRM. On the other hand, this also means that even at this level, 30% of companies do not have a deep insight. The visibility of the further upstream stages of the supply chain is significantly lower. These findings are consistent with statements in the "Supply Chain Resilience Report 2021" that companies continue to have problems understanding the business continuity arrangements at suppliers below the first tier (Elliott, 2021). A survey by McKinsey also shows that there is still considerable room for improvement in supply chain visibility: However, in this study, which only looks at a specific industry, the results are even more dramatic: only 2% of companies have visibility beyond the second supplier level (Alicke et al., 2021). On the other hand, at least 30% of supply chain disruptions (excluding COVID-19-related risks) result from levels below the direct supplier (Elliott, 2021). Visibility of these levels is therefore of high importance to strengthen resilience in supply chains. In addition, customer stages should not be

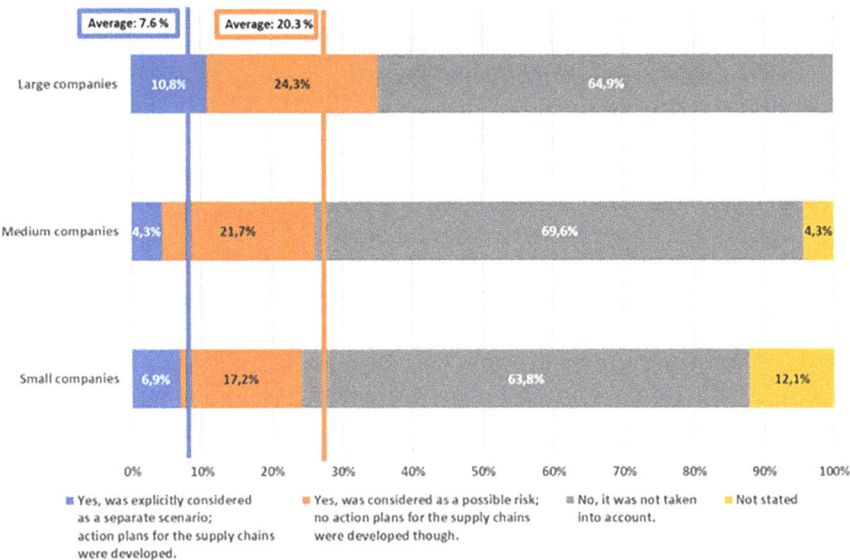

Fig. 4.6 Consideration of a pandemic as a risk scenario ($n = 118$)

neglected in order to be able to identify and manage risks that arise through customers or on the way to customers [zu den verschiedenen Risikokategorien siehe Götze and Mikus (2015)]. Such customer- and market-related risks arise, among other things, from attributes of the market described as "VUCA", i.e., volatile, uncertain, complex, and ambiguous (Christopher, 2018).

Ultimately, the question always arises of identifying risks as early as possible so that proactive action can then be taken. The current question is: How was the Corona crisis recognized and handled against this background? Figure 4.6 shows the extent to which a pandemic was considered as a basic risk scenario.

It became clear that—regardless of the size of the company—such a scenario was not taken into account by a large proportion of the companies (65% on average). Only a small proportion of companies have considered a pandemic as a risk scenario (27% of all companies, regardless of company size). Of these companies, again only 27% (and thus around 7.6% of all companies) have developed concrete action plans to secure their supply chains. It is clear from Fig. 4.6 that large companies had acted more proactively: around 35% considered a pandemic to be a risk scenario; and still just under 11% of companies had developed concrete action plans.

The realization that effective identification of relevant risks only occurs to a limited extent can also be seen in the results of the Allianz Risk Barometer. Even during the survey for the Allianz Risk Barometer 2020 in October and November 2019, only 3% of the more than 2700 respondents considered a pandemic to be an important risk scenario; a pandemic was thus listed as the 17th most important risk (Allianz Global Corporate & Specialty SE, 2020). By contrast, in the subsequent survey in 2021, a pandemic was seen as the second most important risk scenario

(Allianz Global Corporate & Specialty SE, 2021). At the time of this survey, however, the Corona pandemic had already been a reality for more than half a year, so it is difficult to speak of a (future) risk. On the other hand, it is surprising that before the outbreak of the COVID-19 pandemic, only a vanishingly small proportion of experts considered a pandemic outbreak to be relevant. Even though—also in this book—the opinion can certainly be expressed that the Corona pandemic is a so-called black swan, it can also be argued that at least the probability of a pandemic is not low, so that there can be no talk of a black swan. There have been several pandemics since 2000, even if they did not have the significant consequences of the Covid19 pandemic: SARS, swine flu, Ebola, and MERS, among others (World Economic Forum, 2022). In addition, risk analyses for a possible pandemic outbreak already existed years ago: for example, the "Report on Risk Analysis in Population Protection 2012" of the German Federal Government shows the results of a risk analysis for the outbreak of a hypothetical pathogen "Modi-SARS" (Deutscher Bundestag, 2013). Qualitative statements on probabilities and effects were made. Thus, it can be summarized: Information on the threat of a pandemic outbreak was available, so that a pandemic is not unlikely, at least as a risk scenario. The risk analysis commissioned by the German government states that such a pandemic is "conditionally probable," i.e., that it occurs statistically once in a period of 100–1000 years (Deutscher Bundestag, 2013). With such a high estimate, the results shown in the empirical study that companies were not sufficiently prepared were surprising.

4   Final Discussion

The results of the empirical survey presented here, some of which have not been published before, provide insight into the status quo of risk management. In particular, the survey of the maturity level, differentiated according to the four categories, makes it possible not only to show the current status, but also to develop targeted measures to achieve a higher maturity level and thus greater effectiveness of SCRM; in this case, the maturity level also serves prescriptive purposes. The results can therefore be used as a starting point for (further) development of the SCRM. They can also be used to determine, in the sense of a longitudinal analysis, the extent to which the greater visibility called for—also in this book—will be implemented in future years; specifically, this involves transparency across the various supplier and customer levels.

At the same time, the limitations associated with the results must be seen. The geographical restriction of the survey to the German-speaking area limits the number of participating companies and disregards possible country-specific differences. The number of companies that participated in the survey is acceptable; at the same time, it reflects only a small portion of the companies operating in the region studied. Furthermore, the individuals who participated in the survey, especially their function and function-specific knowledge may influence the results. Even though the survey was addressed to persons not only from the area of supply chain management but also from the area of risk management, a large proportion of the participants came from the SCM environment (and here again many from the areas of purchasing or procurement). Given the number of participating companies, the results may well have been different if more other functionaries with specific knowledge, especially from risk management, had taken part. Ultimately, the determination of the maturity level is also subject to uncertainties and inaccuracies. This starts with the chosen methodology of answering by means of "applies" and "does not apply," which should make it easier for the respondents to answer. At the same time, inconsistencies may arise—in connection with the adopted and, if necessary, adjusted statements on the individual maturity levels—which are not recognized during the evaluation.

Despite these limitations, the survey collected primary data that should contribute to further shaping and professionalizing SCRM. Several recommendations for action can be derived. If it can be assumed that a high level of maturity also leads to more effective SCRM, it is worthwhile for companies to increase their level of maturity. This is particularly true for small and medium-sized companies, whose maturity level is significantly lower than that of large companies. There are two areas in particular where low-hanging fruit can be harvested: First, it is (relatively) easy to establish a structured and systematic, but at the same time lean, process for identifying, analyzing, and managing risks. This process should be run through on a regular basis without being overly bureaucratic. Furthermore, established risk management methods can be used to support this process. Even though brainstorming, checklists, and employee or expert discussions are frequently mentioned in previous studies, higher-quality methods can also be used for this purpose, which lead to a more systematic approach. In addition to these two easy-to-implement measures, it is also worthwhile to address the medium- to long-term approaches: This involves anchoring SCRM in the organizational structure, which will certainly entail intensive discussion within the company. It is also important to establish a risk management culture in which the focus is not on fear of risks (and responsibility for them), but on thinking in terms of and with risks. If such measures are implemented and greater transparency is achieved across the entire supply chain (i.e., across several customer and supplier levels), the identification, analysis and control, and thus the management, of even rare risks should not pose a problem, so that the resilience of supply chains can be increased.

References

Alicke, K., Barriball, E. D., & Trautwein, V. (2021). *How COVID-19 is reshaping supply chains*. Retrieved from https://www.mckinsey.com/business-functions/operations/our-insights/how-covid-19-is-reshaping-supply-chains#. Updated on November 23, 2021, checked on February 18, 2022.

Allianz Global Corporate & Specialty SE (Ed.). (2020). *Allianz risk barometer. Results appendix 2020*. Retrieved from https://www.agcs.allianz.com/content/dam/onemarketing/agcs/agcs/reports/Allianz-Risk-Barometer-2020-Appendix.pdf. Checked on February 18, 2022.

Allianz Global Corporate & Specialty SE (Ed.). (2021). *Allianz risk barometer. Identifying the major business risks for 2021.* Retrieved from https://www.agcs.allianz.com/content/dam/onemarketing/agcs/agcs/reports/Allianz-Risk-Barometer-2021.pdf. Checked on February 18, 2022.

Chapman, R. J. (2011). *Simple tools and techniques for enterprise risk management* (2nd ed.). Wiley. Retrieved from https://onlinelibrary.wiley.com/doi/book/10.1002/9781118467206. Checked on February 1, 2022

Christopher, M. (2018). *The mitigation of risk in resilient supply chains.* International Transport Forum (International Transport Forum Discussion Papers, 2018/19). Retrieved https://www.oecd-ilibrary.org/content/paper/db34fa22-en. Checked on February 23, 2022.

Deutscher Bundestag (Ed.). (2013). *Bericht zur Risikoanalyse im Bevölkerungsschutz 2012 (Drucksache, 17/12051).* Retrieved from https://www.google.com/url?sa=t&rct=j&q=&esrc=s&source=web&cd=&ved=2ahUKEwjx2eGkgon2AhVkgv0HHSDCCpgQFnoECAUQAQ&url=https%3A%2F%2Fdserver.bundestag.de%2Fbtd%2F17%2F120%2F1712051.pdf&usg=AOvVaw3YVcQ09zx8nFTEC3TSLk2S. Checked on February 18, 2022.

Elliott, R. (2021). *Supply chain resilience report 2021.* Edited by Business Continuity, Everstream Analytics. Retrieved from https://www.google.com/url?sa=t&rct=j&q=&esrc=s&source=web&cd=&cad=rja&uact=8&ved=2ahUKEwjRjI2o3pH2AhVpRvEDHdarDhIQFnoECAcQAQ&url=https%3A%2F%2Fwww.thebci.org%2Fstatic%2Fe02a3e5f-82e5-4ff1-b8bc61de9657e9c8%2FBCI-0007h-Supply-Chain-Resilience-ReportLow-Singles.pdf&usg=AOvVaw2AcV22poUCEXBm84zoKfJC. Checked on February 18, 2022.

Götze, U., & Mikus, B. (2015). Der Prozess des Risikomanagements in supply chains. In C. Siepermann, R. Vahrenkamp, & M. Siepermann (Eds.), *Risikomanagement in Supply Chains. Gefahren abwehren, Chancen nutzen, Erfolg generieren. With assistance of Markus Amann. 2., neu bearbeitete Auflage* (pp. 29–59). Erich Schmidt Verlag.

Government Centre for Information Systems. (1993). *Introduction to the management of risk.* Norwich (HMSO).

Gurtu, A., & Johny, J. (2021). Supply chain risk management: Literature review. *Risks, 9*(1), 16. https://doi.org/10.3390/risks9010016

Hendricks, K. B., & Singhal, V. R. (2008). The effect of supply chain disruptions on shareholder value. *Total Quality Management and Business Excellence, 19*(7–8), 777–791. https://doi.org/10.1080/14783360802159444

Hillson, D. (1997). Towards a risk maturity model. *International Journal of Project and Business Risk Management, 1*, 35–45.

Ho, W., Zheng, T., Yildiz, H., & Talluri, S. (2015). Supply chain risk management: A Literature review. *In International Journal of Production Research, 53*(16), 5031–5069. https://doi.org/10.1080/00207543.2015.1030467

Hopkinson, M. (2000). Risk maturity models in practice. *Risk Management Bulletin, 5*(4).

Huth, M., & Lohre, D. (2014). Risk management in logistics enterprises. Findings from the 2013 empirical study. *Logistics and Transport, 22*, 5–12. Retrieved from https://bibliotekanauki.pl/api/full-texts/2020/12/13/f35aaa4c-86fc-489c-8ee1-f77f54d2f558.pdf. Checked on January 31, 2022

Huth, M., & Lohre, D. (2015). In Hochschule Fulda (Ed.), *Risikomanagement in der Speditions- und Logistikbranche. Bestandsaufnahme zu Verbreitung und Reifegrad.* Discussion Papers in Business and Economics, 17. Retrieved from https://fuldok.hs-fulda.de/opus4/files/349/Discussion+Paper+No+17+%282015-10-23%29+Huth.pdf. Checked on January 31, 2022.

Huth, M., Knauer, C., & Prang, J. (2020). *BME-Logistikumfrage 2020. Supply chain risk management.* Bundesverband Materialwirtschaft, Einkauf und Logistik e.V. (BME) (Eds). Retrieved from https://a.storyblok.com/f/104752/x/e368482abd/bme-logistikumfrage-2020_supply-chain-risk-management.pdf. Checked on September 13, 2022.

Khan, O., & Zsidisin, G. A. (Eds.). (2012). *Handbook for supply chain risk management. Case studies, effective practices and emerging trends. With assistance of Omera Khan* (1st ed.). J. Ross. https://ebookcentral.proquest.com/lib/kxp/detail.action?docID=3319464.

Manners-Bell, J. (2018). *Supply chain risk management. Understanding emerging threats to global supply chains* (2nd ed.). Kogan Page. Retrieved https://ebs-patron.eb20.com/AccessTitle/ISBN/9780749480165

OECD. (2021). *Enterprise risk management maturity model maturity model* (OECD Tax Administration Maturity Model Series). Retrieved from https://www.oecd.org/tax/forum-on-tax-administration/publications-and-products/enterprise-risk-management-maturity-model.htm. Checked on February 1, 2022.

Oliva, F. L. (2016). A maturity model for enterprise risk management. *International Journal of Production Economics, 173*, 66–79. https://doi.org/10.1016/j.ijpe.2015.12.007

Pöppelbuss, J., & Röglinger, M. (2011). What makes a useful maturity model? A framework of general design principles for maturity models and its demonstration in business process management. In *ECIS 2011 Proceedings, 28*. Retrieved from https://aisel.aisnet.org/ecis2011/28. Checked on February 1, 2022.

Proenca, D., Estevens, J., Vieira, R., & Borbinha, J. (2017). *Risk management. A maturity model based on ISO 31000*. In 2017 IEEE 19th Conference on Business Informatics (CBI). Thessaloniki, July 24, 2017–July 27, 2017: IEEE, pp. 99–108.

Romeike, F. (2018). Reifegrade definieren Methoden. *GRC aktuell, 1*(1), 41–45.

Romeike, F., & Hager, P. (2020). *Erfolgsfaktor Risiko-Management 4. 0. Methoden, Beispiele, Checklisten Praxishandbuch Für Industrie und Handel* (4th ed.). Springer Gabler. In Springer Fachmedien Wiesbaden GmbH.

Schiffling, S., & Kanellos, N. V. (2021). *How the ever given exposed the fragility of global supply chains*. Retrieved https://www.rte.ie/brainstorm/2021/0406/1208101-ever-given-suez-canal-blockage/. Updated on April 9, 2021, checked on February 21, 2022.

Vakil, B., & Linton, T. (2021). *Why we're in the midst of a global semiconductor shortage*. Retrieved from https://hbr.org/2021/02/why-were-in-the-midst-of-a-global-semiconductor-shortage. Updated on February 26, 2021, checked on February 21, 2022.

World Economic Forum. (2022). *A visual history of pandemics*. Retrieved from https://www.weforum.org/agenda/2020/03/a-visual-history-of-pandemics. Checked on February 18, 2022.

Zimmerman, S. (2021). *10 disruptions that rocked supply chains in 2021*. Retrieved December 15, 2021, from https://www.supplychaindive.com/news/top-supply-chain-disruptions-2021/611513/. Checked on February 21, 2022.

Zsidisin, G. A., & Henke, M. (Eds.). (2019). *Revisiting supply chain risk. With assistance of Michael Henke* (Supply Chain Management Series) (Vol. 7). Springer. Retrieved from https://ebookcentral.proquest.com/lib/kxp/detail.action?docID=5622179

Part II
Industry Insights and Technology Applications

The extent to which global supply chains were able to cope with the pandemic was down in no small part to the technology at their disposal; that is also true of the recovery period which gives companies the opportunity to leverage both technology and insight to their advantage.

In that light, it is fair to say that we are at an inflection point where the necessity and opportunity for change are matched by the knowledge and tools available. So much of what we knew about supply chains has been challenged since 2020, and much of what we now know applies universally. That we are equipped with the technology to effect radical change means we are at a crucial point in history.

This part presents insight and learnings from the pandemic and discusses industrial and technological solutions in a number of key supply chain areas. The chapters explore a range of different industry approaches and the applications of technologies to transform supply chain risk management in the post-pandemic era. They also highlight the contagion and cascading effect of supply chain risk management caused by COVID-19, such as new financing arrangements, re-sourcing and re-distribution of logistics, technologies, and innovation.

Chapter 5, *How international logistics service providers counter supply chain disruptions through increased visibility and mitigate risk through technology*, addresses the growing need and demand for visibility in the supply chain. As a result of growing complexity, vulnerability to disruptions and high currency of operational efficiency, transparency is at a premium. It is a problem that has become a priority for businesses and their logistics providers to solve.

As a result, the authors argue that logistics companies must develop technologies for risk mitigation and for highly resilient supply chains. Yet, despite technological advances, they argue that the standard is not easy to achieve given the many different parties involved in global supply chains.

Using a real-world example, this chapter outlines recent developments in customers' expectations for real-time visibility and predictive analytics capabilities from their logistics providers. Using data and information from internal sources, the chapter examines two of Kuehne+Nagel's tools for enhancing resilience of its customers' supply chains. The focus of consideration is a digital planning platform for sea freight operations on the one hand and a real-time exception monitoring solution that enables proactive container management on the other.

Chapter 6, *Rapid reconfiguration of supply chains with simulation as a support to public-private partnerships during pandemics*, examines how small and medium enterprises (SMEs) can avoid disruptions such as those caused by the COVID-19 pandemic through the use of a simulation approach. The service component developed and analyzed by the authors allows users to quickly identify bottlenecks in supplier capacity and evaluate fluctuating lead times—enabling them to reduce the impact of disruptions on production.

To ensure applicability to real-world scenarios, the authors model the challenges created by COVID-19 and resolve it to create a standardized service. The underlying simulation evaluates the supply chain reconfiguration within a few minutes. The authors demonstrate that the simulation generated to identify bottlenecks, evaluate capacity and lead time allows supply chains to be reconfigured. Furthermore, they serve as a starting point for discussion between public and private entities to identify major pain points, allowing private partners to find solutions and enhance competencies during periods of major disruption.

Chapter 7, *Supply chain planning and the pandemic*, looks at supply chain financing options open to companies. Against a backdrop of interrupted value networks, lockdowns, and the resulting supply and demand issues, companies throughout the world are suffering from economic chaos and in turn major business disruptions. As a result, the authors say, companies are turning to supply chain financing solutions to stabilize liquidity and their net working capital to maintain solvency and ensure continuity of supply through their supply networks. This chapter examines several different types of supply chain financing solutions and the impact they have on companies and their value-creation partners during unstable trading periods.

The authors suggest that the pandemic should be seen as an opportunity to address supply chain financing options. They add that companies should prioritize net working capital (NWC) (current assets—current liabilities), which focuses on elements such as liquidity, accounts payable and receivable, inventory and planning.

Chapter 8, *Connecting Decision Making to Resilience*, argues that the capacity to address high-impact disruptions is becoming essential for businesses. The authors state that coping with increasing complexities and uncertainties requires a systemic view of supply chains as well as the ability to make rapid decisions. The chapter outlines the impact of the pandemic on global supply and from that position outlines two strategies for creating resilience in the post-pandemic era.

The authors highlight the weaknesses of JIT style approaches and extended global supply chains, arguing that they need to be addressed through a systematic understanding of how supply chains work. Doing otherwise they say, will lead to further bottlenecks. They add that the speed of decision-making should be able to match the speed of fast-moving and evolving crises, as demonstrated by the urgent action required during the pandemic.

Chapter 9, *Supplier Risk Tower: The vigilant eye on supply chains*, provides an action research approach to examine supply chain risk management at a tier-1 automotive supplier. They focus on this particular industry because it is reliant on a broad and global supply base, and is therefore vulnerable to supply disruptions. To that end, the authors focus on the bridge between risk assessment and risk mitigation for rare-but-severe events such as the COVID-19 pandemic.

In addition, the research looks at the inbound supply risk by introducing a new Supplier Risk Tower assessment. The Supplier Risk Tower assessment combines vulnerability indices specific to the supply chain, supplier feedback on the current risk situation and impact assessment from tier-1's perspective.

The approach is novel in that it calculates an absolute number that provides guidance for rare but severe disruptions. The approach also expands the understanding of lean management and the importance of buffer stocks in supply chains.

In the modern business environment, insight and technology go hand in hand—indeed gaining insight now is more often than not a case of having the right technology in place. Getting the best from it is a matter of asking the right questions in order to gain the understanding we need.

The lessons learned from the pandemic ask serious questions of the supply chain—questions that these chapters seek to provide answers to. They demonstrate that our ability to use technology to model and identify risk, run scenarios, and flag problems is dependent on the data we have available.

To that end, it is important that we view the pandemic as a rich source of data from which we can draw to solve problems, both now and in the future. In combination with increasingly sophisticated applications, the data and insight we have from the disruptions COVID-19 created in many supply chains can help us to develop new models for dealing with risk and ensuring supply chain continuity.

Chapter 5
How International Logistics Service Providers Counter Supply Chain Disruptions Through Increased Visibility and Mitigate Risk Through Technology

Stefan Viehmann, Markus Johannsen, and David Entrop

Abstract Supply chain visibility is an aspired ideal that has been gaining a lot of attention in times of globalization and digitalization. When digital capabilities were lacking in the past, the complexity and operational inefficiencies of supply chains led to a lack of visibility and a high vulnerability to supply chain disruptions. The world's logistics service providers as intermediates between carriers and shippers find themselves at the forefront of responding to arising needs in the supply chain space. At the latest since the COVID-19 crisis—and the resulting volatile environments with dwindling reliability of carriers and their schedules—lack of visibility has become a top priority to solve for businesses and their logistics partners. In response to the current tense situation in global trade—especially for sea freight operations—logistics providers must come up with technology solutions for risk mitigation and highly resilient supply chains. In spite of technological advances, supply chain visibility is not a standard to achieve easily, given the many different parties involved in global supply chains. Using a real-world example, this chapter outlines recent developments in customers' expectations for real-time visibility and predictive analytics capabilities from their logistics providers. Utilizing data and information from internal sources, we analyze two of Kuehne+Nagel's tools for enhancing resilience of its customers' supply chains with a particular focus on sea freight operations. The focus of consideration is a digital planning platform for sea freight operations on the one hand and a real-time exception monitoring solution that enables proactive container management on the other. We will use these tools to illuminate how one of the leading logistics service providers responds to customers' visibility needs and how this contributes to increased supply chain resilience.

S. Viehmann (✉) · M. Johannsen
Kuehne+Nagel (AG & Co.) KG, Hamburg, Germany
e-mail: stefan.viehmann@kuehne-nagel.com; markus.johannsen@kuehne-nagel.com

D. Entrop
Kuehne+Nagel Ltd., Mississauga, ON, Canada
e-mail: david.entrop@kuehne-nagel.com

O. Khan et al. (eds.), *Supply Chain Resilience*, Springer Series in Supply Chain Management 21, https://doi.org/10.1007/978-3-031-16489-7_5

1 Introduction

The long and complex supply chains that have emerged from globalization are subject to disruptions that are becoming more frequent and more severe. At the latest, the COVID-19 pandemic, accompanied by Brexit and trade tensions between the United States and China, forced companies to urgently focus on building resilience in their supply chains. When the COVID-19 pandemic struck, supply chain and logistics operations were at the forefront of the response (Danelia, 2021). Throughout the logistics sector, companies are using innovative solutions to overcome difficulties and maintain operations under challenging conditions. The pandemic acted as a catalyst that highlighted the increased need for supply chain visibility through real-time and risk-relevant data. COVID-19 has affected all modes of transportation in different ways. Since air cargo is often carried as supplemental freight on passenger aircrafts, the drastic slump in air traffic caused air cargo capacities to become scarce. Overland transportation had to deal with goods being held up at borders, while the sea freight industry faced a global container shortage and congested ports. Economic shocks, such as those caused by COVID-19, test the resilience and adaptability of the shipping industry and container ports. Sudden changes in consumer demand have an immediate impact on shipping and port operations and can change business strategies or even market structures. While this is not new to the industry, the COVID-19 pandemic poses new and unprecedented impacts on global supply chains and shipping industries (Notteboom et al., 2021). Clearly, each crisis has different characteristics and triggers different ramifications in the ocean freight market. However, smart, data-driven solutions have the potential to make the different types of impacts more manageable. Logistics service providers have a vital role to play in this respect: acting as intermediates between shippers and carriers, businesses expect their logistics service providers to guide them through challenges created by severe operational issues. In today's world, this includes the need for service providers to supply their customers with digital tools that support them in creating resilient supply chains.

With container shipping considered the backbone of global trade and Kuehne +Nagel a leading ocean freight forwarder, the following sections take a closer look at two of Kuehne+Nagel's digital tools to support sea freight operations. To demonstrate the need for these tools, a rough overview of the sea freight market characteristics at the time of mid-2021 is shown for this purpose. The main implications of the COVID-19 crisis on sea freight operations are highlighted and supported by practical examples. Building on this, the role of logistics service providers in relation to creating more resilient supply chains will be briefly outlined. While the information up to this point is presented in an abbreviated form, the final subsection discusses two of Kuehne+Nagel's digital tools and how they help businesses to establish resilience in their sea freight supply chains.

2 Disruptions in Global Container Shipping: How COVID-19 Affected the Maritime Transportation Market?

With the outbreak of COVID-19 at the beginning of 2020, governments around the world began to take measures that severely restricted commercial activities and affected both the demand and the supply of goods. Early in 2020, lockdown first started in China, then in Europe, the United States, and then in almost all countries. Travel and transportation restrictions came into effect. Sales dropped drastically, and so did global trade. In June of 2020, global cargo volumes began to increase sharply. Firstly between Asia and the United States, followed by Asia and South America and between Asia and Oceania. In response, carriers quickly reinstated capacity in some trade lanes, supporting the large increase in demand. However, as more trade lanes started to recover, the situation became difficult to handle. As of August 2021, the ocean freight market showed the following characteristics, in large part resulting from the COVID-19 pandemic (Kuehne+Nagel Global Sea Logistics Market Update, 2021):

- Unexpected volume increase: Following the initial dip in volumes at the start of the pandemic, export and import volumes have risen during the first half of 2021. This unexpected growth, coupled with the lingering effect of the COVID-19 pandemic, has severely impacted ports and led to unprecedented and rippling congestions across the entire industry.
- Port congestions and disruptions: Severe operational challenges and volume growth resulted in severe congestion in terminals across the globe. Vessel delays, postponed departures, lost sailings and schedule unreliability have become the reality in ocean shipping. Dwell times at ports[1] have increased from an average of about 6–12 days. Long turnaround times for vessels and equipment cause unprecedented delays in the asset cycle.
- Low schedule reliability and longer transit times: Carriers' schedule reliability reached its all-time low of 34.8% in January 2021 and improved only slightly in the subsequent months. Prior to COVID-19, schedule reliability averaged about 80%. In other words, at the most unfavorable times, only about a third of the vessels were on time, making it very difficult to ensure smooth port operations or, for example, to plan the allocation of equipment and drivers.
- Lack of equipment and container imbalance: The unexpectedly rapid increase in volumes has created serious equipment and container repositioning problems. Especially in Asia, this has led to a significant deterioration in the availability of equipment. Newly built containers can only be purchased at horrendous prices and with slow deliveries. Due to the trade imbalance and the sharp increase in volume, equipment procurement is expected to remain a problem.

---

[1] Time that cargo or vessels spend in a port.

Among other factors, these circumstances resulted in a four to fivefold increase in the price of a 40-ft container for shipping lanes from East Asia to the North American West Coast between late 2020 and August 2021 alone (Drewry Shipping Consultants Limited, 2021). In particular, for the lacking equipment and container shortage, it is valuable to understand the reasons behind it: as mentioned, at the beginning of 2020, global freight volumes declined before increasing significantly in the second half of the year. This sudden increase in volume resulted in serious problems with the repositioning of empty containers, causing a sharp decrease in the global availability of equipment. When the sea freight ecosystem is out of balance, there are simply not enough resources available to allow the smooth movement of cargo. In sea freight, the container shortage, which persisted throughout the year 2021, had many causes, mostly related to the pandemic. In the following, some of the most important reasons that have thrown the container ecosystem out of balance are highlighted (Kuehne+Nagel Global Sea Logistics Market Update, 2021):

- *Reduced number of available containers*: The unprecedented decline in world trade during the first 2 months of the pandemic disrupted the normal flow of containers.
- *Congested ports*: Reduced workforce affected many ports both within terminals and in support functions such as truck drivers. This led to severe delays in unloading and loading of vessels, shippers missing departures, and constraints on the volumes that could be loaded.
- *Reduced number of operational vessels*: When the world trade slowed down, some vessels went for refurbishment. With fewer vessels in the market, some vessels even had their voyages interrupted due to COVID-19 cases onboard.
- *A changed flow of goods*: Changes in consumers' buying behavior and the unpredictable development of COVID-19 have caused many irregularities in global trade. In particular, in the year-over-year comparison from 2020 to 2021, imports to the United States from Asia rose at a much higher rate than exports out of the United States. A development that further increased the imbalance in the global container market.

In order to give the description of the market a more practical character, two events that have arisen from the COVID-19 disorder, serve as an illustration: the port congestions in Los Angeles and the port congestions in Southern China. Throughout 2021, US ports have been experiencing record cargo volumes—mainly imports from Asia, but also from other origins. No historical disruption in the past two decades has seen a rebound in volumes as much as it could be observed at these times in Los Angeles and Long Beach. The resulting port congestion and vessel delays are further stressing the existing capacity shortage, which—along with the high demand—have resulted in soaring freight rates and a major strain on the container drayage[2] and trucking market across the United States, leading to high demand for drivers and

---

[2]Process of transporting containerized cargo over short distances, mainly within the same metropolitan area.

chassis[3] that is outpacing the availability of these resources. The pandemic has severely affected the availability of labor as well. Terminals in Los Angeles and Long Beach for example are unable to secure enough dock labor to manage vessel operations within normal time. The availability of chassis in relation to container volumes is at an all-time low. This is caused by loaded containers on chassis not being unloaded as quickly as usual, also due to extremely tight inventory levels in warehouses around the nation. Mainly due to high demand and massive volume shifts to transpacific trades, equipment and container shortages are also occurring in other parts of the world. For example, nearly all trades from and to Northern Europe face low vessel capacities. The situation with empty equipment and available vessel capacities on the one hand and port authorities worldwide reporting record cargo volumes moving through their facilities for consecutive months on the other hand, leads to an imbalance in offer and demand, which is constantly increasing the level of freight rates.

For another practical illustration of COVID-19 effects on sea freight operations, it is worth looking at Shenzhen in China. While the consequences of the Suez crisis were yet to be overcome, and the demand boom in the United States had only just begun, the sudden problems at the Chinese port of Yantian added another layer of challenges to already highly disrupted global supply chains. At the end of May 2021, the port of Yantian was temporarily closed as a measure to contain an outbreak of COVID-19. Due to the high volume of cargo handled through Yantian, this resulted in an immediate backlog of cargo and congestion outside the port of Yantian. In response to the closure of the Yantian port, many shippers decided to switch to the surrounding ports of Nansha, Shekou, and Hong Kong, which logically also experienced long delays due to congestion shortly after Yantian port closed. Two months after the port closure, around 60 vessels were still waiting in front of the mentioned ports. These vessels, and the containers loaded on them, are then missing elsewhere in the world, further reducing available capacity. In the current tense situation in container shipping, aftershocks of such events are still well felt around the globe months later. While the situation in Yantian and other South China ports has improved throughout June and July of 2021, it shows that recurring disruptions due to COVID-19 are possible at any time, and even if short-lived, will have additional ripple effects on global sea freight operations.

The examples given at this point practically illustrate the long and recurring impacts caused by the enduring pandemic. It becomes clear that the container shipping industry is a global and intertwined network in which disruptions at one point also affect other parts of the network. The examples will be reiterated later to illustrate how the functionalities of the presented tools can help to better manage disruptions.

---

[3] A special trailer or undercarriage to transport ocean containers by truck.

3   Acceleration of Supply Chain Visibility Requirements Due to COVID-19

The disruptions caused by COVID-19 have exposed the vulnerabilities in global supply chains and underscored an imperative need to make them more resilient. In comparison to external shocks of the past, the COVID-19 pandemic presented new and unprecedented impacts on global supply chains and on the port and shipping industry. The reason for this is that COVID-19 was an external shock that affected all elements of the supply chain rapidly and at approximately the same time (Notteboom et al., 2021): closed borders, transportation delays, reduced labor, fluctuating commodity flows, lockdowns, and ever-changing restrictions all complicated where shipments were and when they would arrive. At least since the beginning of the COVID-19 crisis, businesses have faced two major challenges: a lack of visibility into supply chain operations and a lack of actionable data. Not surprisingly, the pandemic acted as a catalyst for already rapidly evolving technologies in a transparency lacking industry. In the face of the aforementioned disruptions such as port congestions and container shortages, it can be observed that businesses are investing more time and money in accelerating digital business and end-to-end visibility.

The pandemic proved that many businesses were unaware of the vulnerability of their supply chains to global disruptions. For decades, the focus in supply chain management has been on optimizing costs, inventories and utilization. In many cases, this has resulted in insufficient safety buffers and low flexibility to absorb disruptions. In addition, the handling of exceptions in supply chains has often been reactive and ad hoc in the past. A potentially more effective long-term strategy than absorbing supply chain disruptions through increased safety stocks is to increase visibility into the supply chain network to respond to disruptions. Supply chain participants today need tools for proactive exception handling and show an increased need for visibility to handle disrupted supply chains. A key component of real-time visibility is providing accurate estimated arrival times (ETA) for shipments. Businesses want to know when a shipment will be picked up, when it will be shipped, and whether it will arrive on time or late, allowing them to accurately plan the delivery and availability of the respective goods (Elbert & Gleser, 2019). With real-time visibility data, all parties are always fully up to date, allowing potential bottlenecks to be identified earlier and resolved quickly. As a result, the involved parties can then react accordingly on their end to ensure that they can also make the best possible decisions. As highlighted in the previous section, in times of the pandemic, the industry faced heavy reliability issues of carrier services. Outdated market and service information made the monitoring of carriers' performances and cargo locations very cumbersome, and supply chain disruptions hard to handle. Decreasing reliability and time-consuming information sourcing reinforced the need for optimized monitoring. When disruptions occur, time-consuming data sourcing is valuable time lost. Supply chain participants want to focus on managing exceptions as opposed to permanently checking the status of carrier services, container locations, or possible disruptions. Businesses are looking to reduce manual work such as emails and calls to truck drivers or their logistics providers. Better accessibility of valuable information has been a major need reinforced by the pandemic. To maximize supply chain resilience, businesses need to improve the agility of their supply chain. To achieve this, they need real-time access to data about the current state of their supply chain network (Zdziarska & Marhita, 2020). Higher degrees of agility enables supply chain participants to react rapidly to unexpected situations and thereby minimize their impact. Businesses with a high level of supply chain visibility are better informed and in a better position to take action when disruptions occur. As businesses seek to transform their supply chains into intelligent, digital ecosystems with greater visibility, logistics service providers have a critical role to play.

4 The Role of Logistics Service Providers in Creating Resilient Supply Chains

In the environment that has been shaped by COVID-19, the choice of the right logistics partner has gained importance. The greater demand for actionable data and higher visibility that accompanied the COVID-19 crisis also meant an increased demand for the services of LSPs. Businesses expect their logistics partners to help them improve their operational efficiency and customer satisfaction on their end, and increase their agility, flexibility, and resilience. The higher the complexity of a supply chain, the more attractive it is to outsource related activities to an LSP. Supply chain participants can compensate for unreliability in global freight forwarding by accessing their LSP's global service network, combined with their local expertise and fully integrated technology. With fully integrated systems and processes, data-driven insights, and innovative technology solutions, LSPs ensure that their customers' inventories arrive on time and with minimal unplanned costs. Businesses benefit from complete visibility into their entire supply chain, from milestone tracking to supplier or order monitoring. Supply chains generate a vast amount of data that can help businesses to identify patterns, gain insights and build a resilient supply chain. However, making sense of this data is a complex task without the right tools and expertise. The right LSP can optimally support their customers in finding the best possible routes with the optimal mode of transport. LSPs provide a higher degree of flexibility and reliability thanks to their ability to contract space and equipment allocation on many carrier networks. Especially large LSPs with a global network of carriers across modes of transport represent the most important client partners for all global carriers across trade lanes and regions. As a response to COVID-19, some carriers have even implemented premium products, which offer certain advantages, such as priority for equipment and space availability, in order to provide a more stable level of service. While these services come at a higher price, they are particularly suited for important and more time-sensitive shipments. If timely delivery is essential, in these times businesses must consider using premium products, which an LSP can arrange for its customers.

In terms of COVID-19 disruptions, businesses with a logistics partner found themselves better positioned since it gave them a higher degree of flexibility and responsiveness. In the case of congested ports, for example, LSPs have the ability and the tools to develop alternative routes, or to change to a better suitable mode of transport. With the goal to enhance resilience in supply chains, businesses increasingly demand digital capabilities from their logistics partners. In particular, this means eliminating the requirement to retrieve information from multiple sources, thus avoiding inefficiencies, high costs, poor data quality, and delays. In this context, two essential, value-adding capabilities of LSPs are worth mentioning: data integration and business intelligence. While data integration addresses higher automation of the data flow between supply chain participants such as carriers, LSPs, and shippers, business intelligence addresses the interpretation and visualization of this data. By connecting involved parties and transforming large amount of data into actionable information, LSPs help businesses to access real-time information and predict patterns. Data integration and business intelligence complement each other and have become key capabilities of LSP.

With their technology portfolio, LSPs play a key role in their customers' overall efficiency and keeping operations running by giving them greater control over their cargo. For a long time, businesses had to rely on carriers and their LSPs to send EDI messages or make manual system updates to gain visibility into the status of their shipment and potential disruptions (Klappich et al., 2016). As real-time visibility into complex supply chains remains a major challenge, the industry has seen technology startups entering the logistics space to complement—and potentially challenge—services provided by traditional logistics companies in recent years. By the latest with the entry of these new players into the market, logistics incumbents have recognized the need for offering user-friendly platforms, to provide real-time and predictive visibility (Klappich et al., 2017). In recent years the industry has observed the rise of platform models that aim at maximizing operational efficiency through network visibility (Hausmann et al., 2020). By increasing visibility and thus the knowledge about the status of every shipment, these platforms empower businesses to act immediately and effectively.

5 How Kuehne+Nagel Responds to Intensified Needs Toward More Resilient Supply Chains?

In the following, two digital solutions of Kuehne+Nagel are used to illustrate how a digital planning platform and real-time exception monitoring solution contribute to minimizing and better handling risks in global supply chains. Founded in 1890, Kuehne+Nagel is a global logistics provider with services in sea freight, airfreight, road freight, contract, and integrated logistics. The company provides market-leading supply chain services that help its customers achieve a competitive advantage by leveraging people, processes, and technology to create highly efficient

Fig. 5.1 Routing results for port rotation Hamburg–Los Angeles (Kuehne+Nagel seaexplorer)

supply chains. Within the sea logistics business unit, Kuehne+Nagel's services provide global, end to end, and highly innovative solutions to companies in virtually all industries. Throughout 2020, Kuehne+Nagel continued to lead as the largest global non-vessel operating common carrier and the market leader across all regions for sea logistics. As such, Kuehne+Nagel must always be at the forefront of providing innovative solutions to its customers and provide state-of-the-art technologies and digital solutions. Two of these are presented in the following subsections.

5.1   Digital Planning Platform for Sea Freight Supply Chains

With its digital platform called *seaexplorer*, Kuehne+Nagel is able to provide its customers full visibility on global routing options across container shipping lines. Through comparative data, *seaexplorer* enables users to optimize their ocean freight operations according to their priorities. The platform aims at making time-consuming data sourcing obsolete, and enables data-driven in-depth service and routing insights in one single application. Before referring to the customer value of this digital platform, the next paragraph will first look at the features, and link them to the current challenges described in the previous sections.

With the help of *seaexplorer*, users can retrieve details of the voyage route, including live vessel positions and announced port-to-port transit times. Section 2 highlighted the dwindling reliabilities of ocean carrier services since the beginning of COVID-19. For this purpose, *seaexplorer* offers its users a rating system for carrier service reliability and sailing schedules. The service reliability is measured by aggregating the delay in days for all arrival events within a port rotation. Figure 5.1 shows an example of the port rotation between Hamburg and Los Angeles. As can be seen in this figure, the tool provides the predicted transit time, a reliability score, and the CO_2 emission per 20-ft equivalent unit container for the voyage. Reliability scores range from A to F, with A being the services with the highest reliability. The provided routing options can be sorted by the fastest, the most reliable, or the most ecologically friendly service.

In the case of above extract, *seaexplorer* shows three services with transit times ranging from 26 to 51 days. If transit times are marked with an anchor, they take into

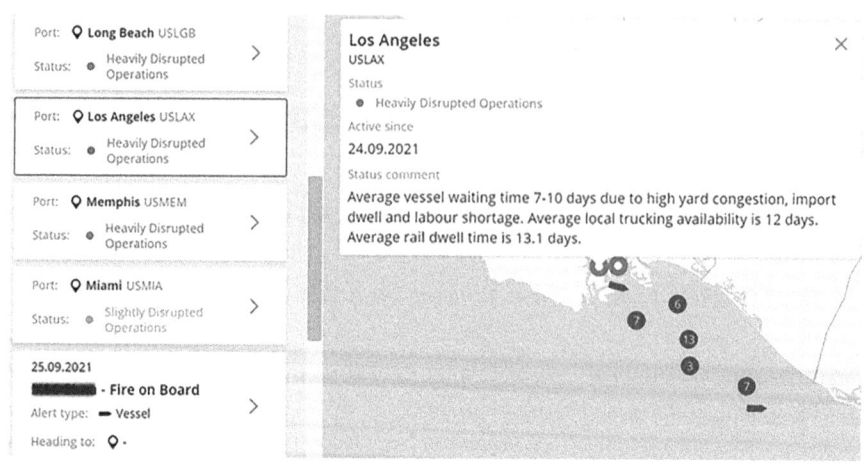

Fig. 5.2 Status information on port of Los Angeles, September 2021 (Kuehne+Nagel seaex-plorer)

account actual performances of the recent past using a best-of-the-industry algorithm. In order to provide realistic transit times, *seaexplorer* determines the sum of
the announced transit time by the carrier and the average arrival delay for this port
rotation in the past. The number between the two ports represents the amount of
transshipments included in the routing. In the case of the first option, there is one
transshipment for the voyage from Hamburg to Los Angeles. Clicking on this
service provides more information, such as details that this routing is from Hamburg
to Houston by sea, and then from Houston to Los Angeles by rail. Compared to route
options two and three, the first routing seems to be the fastest option at first glance.
However, one can also see that this route option does not include the average delay
in the transit time due to missing data for rail transportation. Despite the longer
transit time and lower reliability, the second routing option should be considered a
serious alternative for two reasons: As one can see from the anchor symbol, the
average arrival delay is already included in the provided transit time. In addition, the
CO_2 emissions for this option are significantly lower than for option one.

The features shown so far provide in-depth service and routing insights for sea
freight transports. For the presentation of the next two features, we refer back to the
two practical examples given on congested ports in Sect. 2. This previous section
highlighted the major reasons for the port congestions in Los Angeles and southern
China in mid-2021. On the *seaexplorer* platform, customers find a map showing all
port congestions including information about vessels waiting outside the ports. For
each service, it lists disruptions that might have an effect on the performance of the
vessels deployed in this service. To allow users to plan accordingly, each vessel's
predictive ETA is updated every 10 min based on its current position, distance to the
next port, and the average speed that vessels normally travel on the respective route.
Figure 5.2 shows an extract from the *seaexplorer* on the heavily disrupted operations
at the port of Los Angeles as of September 2021. Users can see a status and a status
comment on each port as well as the number of vessels waiting to enter the twin ports

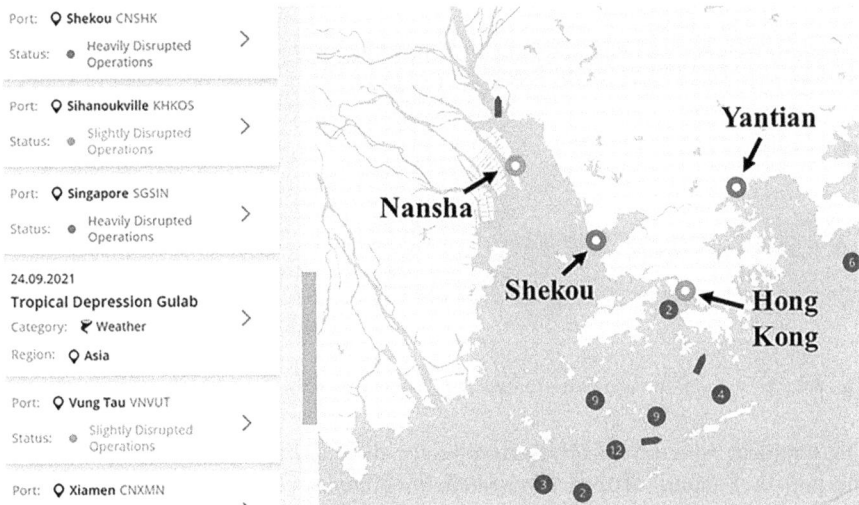

Fig. 5.3   Port congestion in Southern China, September 2021 (Kuehne+Nagel seaexplorer)

of Los Angeles and Long Beach. In the example, *seaexplorer* indicates the waiting time for unloading at the port of Los Angeles with an average of 7–10 days. Zooming in closer to the red circles shows the individual vessels with further information about which port the vessel is heading to and since when it is waiting for berth space.

When operations at ports are heavily disrupted, as in the case of Los Angeles and Long Beach, it is of particular interest for users to have easy access to information about alternative routing options. Using the example of congested ports in southern China (see Sect. 2), it will be highlighted how *seaexplorer* supports its users' decision on possible alternative routings for their cargo. As mentioned before, closures and congestion at one port—as happened in Yantian—can lead to more congested ports throughout a whole region. With the tool, it is possible to get greater visibility into this highly interconnected global network of the container shipping industry. This becomes clear when looking at Fig. 5.3. Heavily disrupted operations at the port of Yantian have caused disruptions at the surrounding ports of Hong Kong, Shekou, and Nansha. In this example, users can avoid these ports when choosing a service, if possible. This applies not only to sea freight shipments with these ports as their port of destination, but also to services that call these ports in the course of their route. For this reason, *seaexplorer* shows an alert and update overview for each service in the detail view. The overview shows clearly which disruptions may occur along the route, which means, for example, that all congested ports—which the service calls—are displayed.

The question that arises is how users can leverage this information and find a better routing option if they want to ship goods to a region with congested ports. Again, the example of Yantian serves as an illustration. For this purpose, Fig. 5.4 depicts two related views of the tool. When searching for Yantian as the destination

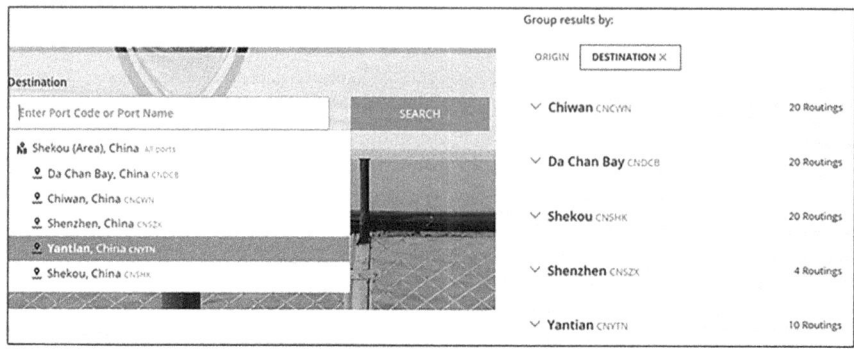

Fig. 5.4 Area search for alternative routing options (Kuehne+Nagel seaexplorer)

of a shipment, *seaexplorer* offers two options: either users can search specifically for the port in Yantian, or they can search for a connection to the region in which Yantian is located. In the following example (Fig. 5.4), the Shekou area was chosen as the region of destination. As opposed to searching connections to one specific port that might be congested, the search engine provides routing options to all ports in the region. This allows users to verify which route option offers the shortest transit times with the highest reliability scores, for instance.

In addition to port disruptions, the tool provides alerts on other issue types as well: through an alert overview, *seaexplorer* provides information on incidents that may affect supply chains such as severe weather conditions or vessel problems. As an example, this includes fire[4] or COVID-19 outbreaks on vessels, or weather conditions[5] that have the power to disrupt sea freight operations in certain areas.

Kuehne+Nagel's digital planning platform offers many benefits for users. Overall, the tool helps to minimize potential risks and therewith to increase resilience of sea freight supply chains. Considering that over 80% of goods are transported by sea, greater resilience in sea freight supply chains equates to greater supply chain resilience in general. To be more specific, the following list highlights some of the key aspects of how *seaexplorer* is helping to make supply chains more resilient:

- Comprehensive real-time information and alerts about changes in service rotations enable fast and fact-based decision-making. This fact-based decision-making is enhanced by data-driven insights through a path-finding algorithm and big data technology that connects various data sources. This allows avoiding services with low on-time performances, or services that are calling congested ports, for instance.
- Businesses can integrate realistic lead times into their supply chain planning, giving them more planning certainty.

---

[4]See Fig. 5.2.
[5]See Fig. 5.3.

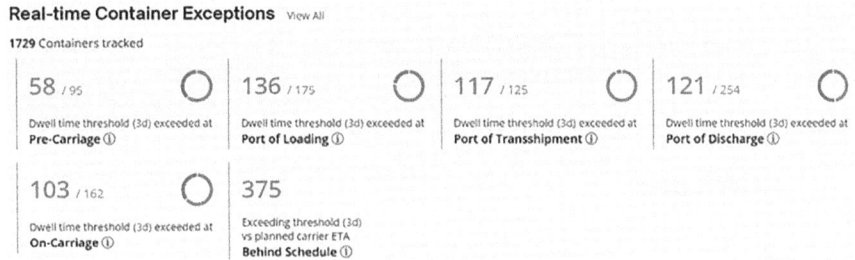

Fig. 5.5 Container exception issues (Kuehne+Nagel Container Dashboard)

- The platform supports users in examining alternative routing options if needed. The high level of integration and partnerships with all major carriers contributes to offering the best possible routing option and to decreasing inefficiencies and risks for supply chain participants.

5.2 Real-Time Exception Monitoring on Container Level in Sea Freight

The Kuehne+Nagel Container Dashboard evolved from the customers' need for an extension to *seaexplorer*. Customers requested a simple dashboard to recognize potential service disruptions at the earliest possible stage. While the *seaexplorer* is mainly informing about carrier services and vessels, the Container Dashboard is tracking containers in real time. The system is able to receive data from multiple sources and make sense of all information for optimized detection of significant events such as milestones, deviations, and inconsistencies. The tool responds to challenges that occur from lacking container visibility, such as:

- Planning errors due to out-of-date ETA.
- Incorrect information about product availability and therewith dissatisfied customers.
- Out-of-stock situations leading to lost orders or production shutdowns.
- Great expenditure of time to detect disruptions and exceptions.
- High costs for demurrage[6] and detention[7] due to lack of visibility.

Customers showed the need for more up-to-date and accurate ETAs at port of discharge, the possibility to monitor port transshipment arrivals and departures, and proactive, customizable exception management. Figure 5.5 shows the overview

---

[6] Surcharges demanded by carriers when containers are not moved out of the port or terminal within an agreed period.

[7] Surcharges demanded by carriers for holding a container or equipment beyond an agreed period (outside of terminal).

dashboard on all existing exception issues at the time of the screen capture. The tool classifies exceptions into different types and shows the number of containers affected by the respective exception.

The screen capture shows a total number of 1729 containers tracked. The tool allows modifying threshold settings as desired and was set to 3 days for all exception types in this example. For a better understanding, the different exception types are briefly explained below:

- *Pre-Carriage*: The gate-in of 58 out of 95 containers is delayed at the port of loading. These containers show a "gate-out empty" or "pick-up" status, but have not yet been returned full at the port of loading for more than 3 days.
- *Port of Loading*: The loading of 136 out of 175 containers onto the vessel is delayed by more than 3 days at the port of loading.
- *Port of Transshipment*: The loading of 117 out of 125 containers onto the connecting vessel is delayed by more than 3 days at the port of transshipment.
- *Port of Discharge*: The pickup of 121 out of 254 containers is delayed by more than 3 days at the port of discharge.
- *On-Carriage*: 103 out of 162 containers were picked up at the port of discharge (gate-out full status) or delivered to consignee, but have not yet been returned empty to port.
- *Behind Schedule*: For 375 containers the expected arrival date is later than the initially scheduled arrival at port of discharge and exceeds the dwell time threshold of 3 days. In other words, the planned carrier ETA is not as accurate as desired.

The tool makes use of carrier data, route maps, vessel tracking, and data science to combine information and predict the arrival time at the port of transshipment or discharge. The Container Dashboard compares the information from carriers to its own predictive ETA once per hour. If it detects a non-realistic carrier ETA, then Kuehne+Nagel's predictive arrival time is shown next to the carrier's ETA. For the calculations, it uses for instance historical data, vessel speed, and weather information. The many sources for raw data include Internet of Things and tracking devices, carrier data, or weather and news information. Figure 5.6 shows an example of a particular container for which the carrier's departure and arrival times do not match the Container Dashboard calculations. According to these calculations, the predicted time of departure (PTD) from the port of loading is expected to be significantly later than the carrier's original estimated time of departure (ETD). The same applies to the ETA specified by the carrier. In this case, the predicted time of arrival (PTA)—determined by Kuehne+Nagel—is indicated 10 days later than the originally communicated ETA.

Using and combining knowledge from different sources makes it possible to identify issues and alert operators. Every consuming party—whether on the customer side or on the logistics service provider side—can understand the situation in near real time, and have access to consistent data. The Container Dashboard predicts situations in real time and automatically alerts customers and Kuehne+Nagel logistics operations employees without them having to search for the information

Fig. 5.6 Container routing details Los Angeles to Kobe (Kuehne+Nagel Container Dashboard)

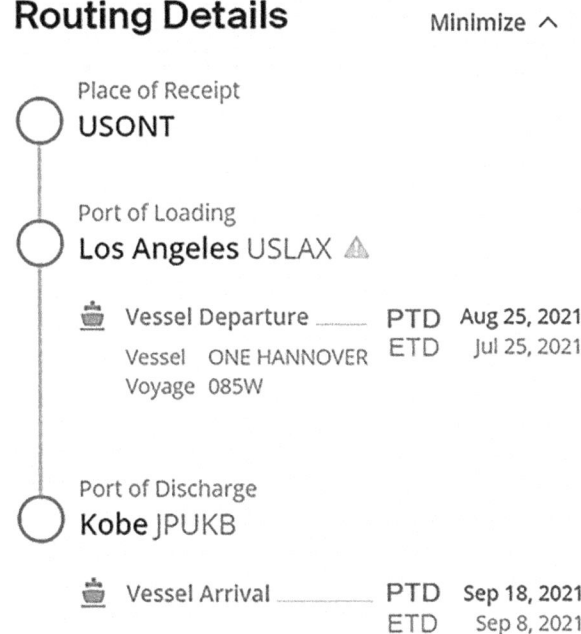

manually. This enables customers and the Kuehne+Nagel expert teams to react faster and reschedule the booking in case of route plan deviations or delays. Whenever a container enters or exits a certain milestone, the Container Dashboard creates a virtual status event and triggers live notifications. Therewith, the Container Dashboard facilitates the process of discovering important milestones and provides users with easy access to their affected containers and orders. Instead of trying to find deviations manually, the tool enables early identification of disruptions and timely and effective reactions. This means a reduced manual effort, increased accuracy, and productivity, as well as overall higher customer satisfaction. Furthermore, this dashboard solution benefits customers as follows:

- Improves efficiency by reducing time and effort spent on checking timeliness of transshipment port arrivals and departures.
- Reduces losses caused by lost orders and customers through more accurate delivery promises.
- Reduces risk of out-of-stock situations and production shutdowns through earliest possible corrective measures.
- Saves working capital by reducing the need for inventory safety buffers. Companies that do not trust their supply chain due to a lack of visibility, tend to increase their inventories during times of disruption. If this can be avoided, companies benefit from the reduced likelihood of bullwhip effects in global supply chains, as observed during COVID-19.

- Using the monitoring options, the Container Dashboard can help avoid unnecessary charges for demurrage and detention.
- Helps to improve and automate decision-making across the full end-to-end process.

6   Conclusion

In the volatile market environment formed by COVID-19, transparency is crucial. Resilient supply chains require real-time data and end-to-end visibility. While this is difficult to achieve in global, multitiered supply chains at the best of times, the pandemic has exposed supply chain vulnerabilities and their impact on the world economy. The importance of supply chain visibility and resiliency has never been clearer. The previous subsections have touched on some aspects of how COVID-19 has affected the sea freight market. It has become clear that lack of visibility is still a major issue for many supply chain participants. Real-time visibility is essential to reduce costs, save working capital and improve efficiency by better understanding and managing inventory accuracy, exception control, delivery speed, and on-time delivery. Building resilience is not a one-time exercise, but a continuous process and it is not established when a disruption occurs, but before. It is important to mention, that an unforeseen shock like the COVID-19 crisis does not turn strong supply chains into weak ones, but exposes vulnerabilities that existed all along. With fully integrated systems and processes, data-driven insights, and innovative technology solutions, LSPs have the power to ensure that their partners' inventories arrive on time and with minimal unplanned expenses. Improving the data flow between parties as well as providing actionable data and thus increasing visibility is one of the major challenges and capabilities that businesses expect from their LSPs. Digital logistics solutions, such as those presented in this section, allow businesses to be more productive, lower their costs and solve problems more efficiently. However, establishing supply chain resilience requires technology and people alike. Data is only actionable when logistics operators are equipped with the right technology and can draw the right conclusions. The highest level of resilience in supply chains can be achieved by orchestrating the right technology, people, and harmonized processes.

References

Danelia, I. (2021). Impact of COVID-19 on global container shipping industry. *European Scientific Journal, 17*(27), 5.

Drewry Shipping Consultants Limited. (2021). *World container index.* https://www.drewry.co.uk/supply-chain-advisors/supply-chain-expertise/world-container-index-assessed-by-drewry

Elbert, R., & Gleser, M. (2019). Digital forwarders. In *Logistics management: Strategies and instruments for digitalizinsg and decarbonizing supply chains* (pp. 19–32). Springer.

Hausmann, L., Wölfel, T., Stoffels, J., & Fleck, O. (2020). *Startup funding in logistics: New money for an old industry?* McKinsey.

Klappich, D. C., Stevens, A., de Muynck, B., & Salley, A. (2016). *Cool vendors in supply chain execution technologies.* Gartner.

Klappich, D. C., O'Daffer, E., Stevens, A., Gonzalez, D., de Muynck, B., & Salley, A. (2017). *Cool vendors in supply chain execution technologies.* Gartner.

Kuehne+Nagel. (2021). *Global sea logistics market update.* Kuehne+Nagel (AG & Co.) KG.

Notteboom, T., Pallis, T., & Rodrigue, J. (2021). Disruptions and resilience in global container shipping and ports: The COVID-19 pandemic versus the 2008–2009 financial crisis. *Maritime Economics and Logistics, 23*(2), 179–210.

Zdziarska, M., & Marhita, N. (2020). Supply chain digital collaboration. In A. Kolinski, D. Dujak, & P. Golinska-Dawson (Eds.), *Ecoproduction, environmental issues in logistics and manufacturing. Integration of information flow for greening supply chain management* (1st ed., pp. 63–76). Springer International.

Chapter 6
Rapid Reconfiguration of Supply Chains with Simulation as a Support to Public–Private Partnerships during Pandemics

Saskia Sardesai, Philipp Klink, Becem Bourbita, Johanna Kim Kippenberger, and Michael Henke

Abstract During the COVID-19 pandemic, many medical device manufacturers faced a significant and unexpected increase in demand. To handle this sudden spike in demand, a ramp-up of production and inbound material flow had to be organized. At the same time, the pandemic caused issues in the supply of materials for their medical products. Due to disruptions in global transportation, local unavailability of parts, and the urgency of the demand, companies established public–private partnerships to allow the organization of sufficient part supply for the production of medical products. In order to engage in the public–private partnership and to specify the necessary support, it is required to identify bottlenecks within the supply chain and options to address them. One of the methods commonly used to specify bottlenecks in a dynamic environment is event discrete simulation. To support the sudden simulation requirement by companies, a generalized simulation model is set up as a service to support, in particular, small and medium enterprises. The service allows to identify part bottlenecks and evaluate options in a rapid mode. The resulting service enables companies to address supply chain bottlenecks to ensure a fast ramp-up of production.

1 Motivation

Under normal circumstances, medical equipment manufacturers are able to forecast annual demand for medical products. As such, medical equipment manufacturers design their supply chains based on the predicted annual production quantities,

S. Sardesai (✉) · P. Klink · J. K. Kippenberger · M. Henke
Fraunhofer Institute for Material Flow and Logistics, Dortmund, Germany
e-mail: saskia.sardesai@iml.fraunhofer.de; johanna.kim.kippenberger@iml.fraunhofer.de; michael.henke@iml.fraunhofer.de

B. Bourbita
Demcon, Enschede, The Netherlands
e-mail: becem.bourbita@demcon.com

which are subject to a forecastable annual growth rate. However, because of the global COVID-19 pandemic and sudden increase in demand for medical equipment, many medical equipment manufacturers and their suppliers have faced major supply chain challenges (Iyengar et al., 2020). These challenges are twofold. First, the pre-pandemic production capacities of medical equipment manufacturers and their suppliers were well defined and therefore limited to meet the exceeding demand requests from healthcare organizations. This resulted in delays as it took time for companies to adjust and expand their production capacities. Second, because of the increasing infection rates among citizens and local lockdowns that affected workforce availability and cross-border movement of people and goods, the supply chains were exposed to the risk that companies fail to produce and deliver parts in time (Velayutham et al., 2021). Both incidences lead to an unavailability of parts required for production, and have an instant effect on production planning, which causes various issues for the ramp-up of production (Klink et al., 2020).

In order to allow for a stable ramp-up, capacity revamping, staff scheduling, and inventory availability are crucial factors, which need to be considered for internal ramp-up management (Glock & Grosse, 2015). In addition, a strong coordination with suppliers is required to ensure parts availability. This is especially critical since the pandemic caused several risk factors, like closed borders or unavailability of containers for the transfer of goods (Chowdhury et al., 2021). Hence, it is important to find adequate measures to achieve supply chain resilience.

Public–private partnerships can play a significant role in building supply chain resilience (Papadopoulos et al., 2017). During a disruptive event as experienced during the COVID-19 pandemic, an intense collaboration of private and public entities can stimulate supply chain resilience and provide the necessary support to ensure the material supply (Gabler et al., 2017). Because public–private partnerships can serve a prominent role when confronting these supply chain challenges, we focus on how a support can be generated by public–private partnerships and the opportunities they offer to better manage supply chains during future pandemics.

In this context, the chapter discusses options to support supply chain reconfiguration with public–private partnerships while focusing on the identification of relevant bottlenecks to cover parts availability. The remainder of this chapter is divided into five sections. Section 2 presents an overview of risk management and drivers of supply chain resilience, describing their role in setting up supply chain resilience via public–private partnerships. This is followed by an introduction of methods and tools that assist reconfiguration of supply chains in Sect. 3. Based on the selection of a method, Sect. 4 of the chapter introduces a conceptual model for a tool that allows to identify bottlenecks and options to reconfigure supply chain settings to overcome those bottlenecks. Thus, this tool is used to identify a set of measures to be taken through collaboration within public–private partnership. In Sect. 5, to verify the suitability of the tool, the model is applied to a use case from Demcon—a European manufacturer of medical ventilator modules and respiratory systems based in the Netherlands. Section 6 concludes the chapter with a summary of the findings and an outlook on further topics for research.

2   Supply Chain Resilience via Public–Private Partnerships

2.1   Supply Chain Risk Management and Supply Chain Resilience

The supply chain risk management includes strategies, measures, information, and processes to identify and assess risks within a supply chain and thus generates a basis for future decisions (Wagner et al., 2010). More specifically, its objective is to monitor the risks identified and assessed and to develop possible responses to risks if they cannot be prevented in advance. In contrast to the risk management of an individual company, the cross-network risk management of a supply chain is characterized by complex interrelationships in the risk analysis and the delayed and sustained negative consequences in a supply chain when risks occur (Shi, 2004).

   Within a supply chain, there are various risks that occur at different levels due to a large number of participants. These risks can therefore be grouped into different risk categories (see Fig. 6.1). Internal supply chain risks include risks inside a company (process and control risks) and risks that occur at or emanate from supply chain partners (supply and demand risks). Furthermore, sustainability risks and cyber risks must be distinguished, which affect all supply chain partners upstream (in supply direction) and downstream (in demand direction). In addition, external supply chain risks (environmental risks) include natural disasters, political, or social risks (Brindley, 2004; Kersten et al., 2017). A disturbance at an upstream or downstream point in the supply chain can have a direct impact on the entire supply chain due to the close links between material, financial, and information flows.

   In summary, supply chain risks are understood as disturbances or impairments, assessed in terms of their probability of occurrence, which affect not only an individual company but the entire supply chain (Kersten et al., 2009). Furthermore, supply chain risks can be both strategic and operational in nature. While operational risks refer to the endangerment of short- to medium-term goals (e.g., breakdown due to missing components/materials as well as obstacles within the delivery processes), strategic risks affect long-term goals (e.g., loss of know-how to suppliers/

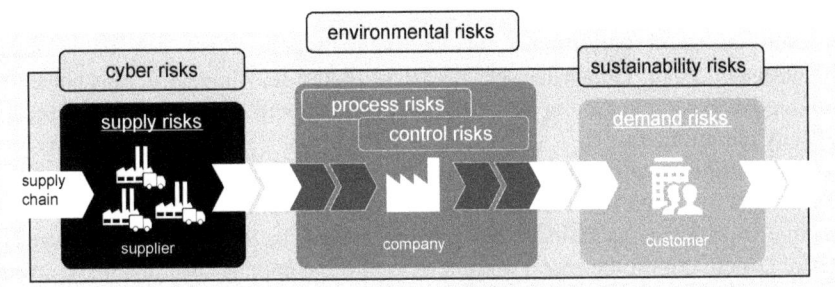

Fig. 6.1 Supply chain risk categories [own representation based on Schreckenberg et al. (2021)]

competitors or increasing dependence on one member of the supply chain) and should therefore be seen as a threat to the entire company (Pfohl & Aberle, 2002).

As a consequence of the various trends, the environment of global supply chains evolves to become less deterministic, increasingly unpredictable and thus unplannable (ten Hompel & Henke, 2017), which can be summarized by the acronym VUCA (Volatility, Uncertainty, Complexity, and Ambiguity). The combination of volatility, uncertainty, complexity, and ambiguity (Worley & Jules, 2020) necessitates a further expansion of conventional risk management instruments. In this context, the focus is on disruptive events, which are characterized by strong damage in the event of occurrence and by low probabilities of occurrence. Supply chains are particularly vulnerable to disruptive events due to the increased division of labor in global and tightly synchronized supply networks that focus on lean processes and inventories. When disruptive events occur, it can result in strong supply chain interruptions (Zitzmann, 2018). Concurrently, the prediction, identification, and preparation for the risk response are more difficult than for more expectable operational risks. Disruptive events can be events that occur from internally in the supply chain (bankruptcies, fire or explosion-related failures) or that are external to the supply chain (environmental disasters, man-made disasters, political shocks).

The capability for managing disruptions within a supply chain can be divided into four different phases. In the first phase of readiness, the relatively undisturbed supply chain can be proactively prepared for future disruptions. With these disruptions, there is often a variable, short advance warning time at least for parts of the supply chain, which could be used for short-term preparations (Zitzmann, 2018). Disruptive events cover both expected risks (the expected unexpected) such as earthquakes in vulnerable regions or hurricanes during the Atlantic hurricane season, as well as unexpected risks (the unexpected) like global pandemics, cyberattacks, or terrorist attacks (Dailey, 2021; Wagner & Bode, 2009). While proactive preparation for fundamentally expected disruptive disturbances is possible, the preparation for unexpected disruptions is not instantly feasible. Once a disruption has happened, the second phase of response begins, in which control is (re-)gained and further damage should be prevented, if possible. After the supply chain has overcome the initial disruption and its consequences, the third phase of recovery begins, which is intended to make up and compensate for the accumulated backlogs or consequences in the best possible way. Ideally, in the fourth phase (the growth phase), the original or even increased performance of the entire supply chain can be achieved (Biedermann, 2018; Hohenstein et al., 2015). Figure 6.2 shows the four phases of a disruptive event and the impact on the supply chain with differentiated timing and capacity requirements.

The instruments currently used for risk management can be divided into proactive instruments for preparing a supply chain for disruptions in the readiness phase and reactive instruments specifically for gaining control in the reaction and recovery phase. Depending on the sector and the size of the company, instruments used can vary considerably. The proactive measures in the readiness phase should ensure a general increase in the resilience of a supply chain, the earliest possible identification

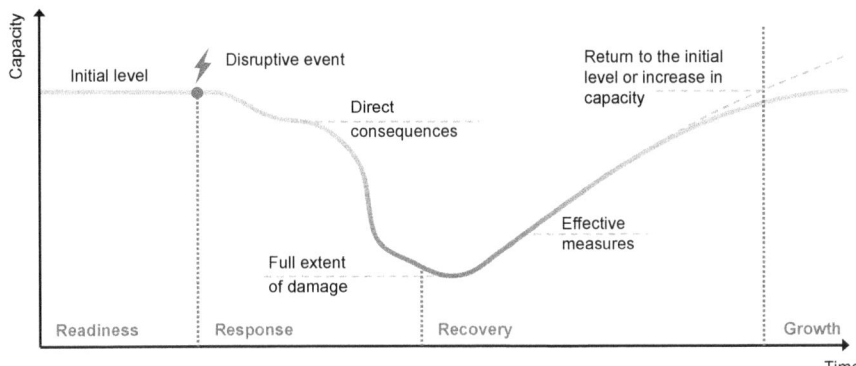

Fig. 6.2 Phases of a disruptive event and its impact on a supply chain [own representation based on Biedermann (2018), Zitzmann (2018), and Sheffi and Rice (2005)]

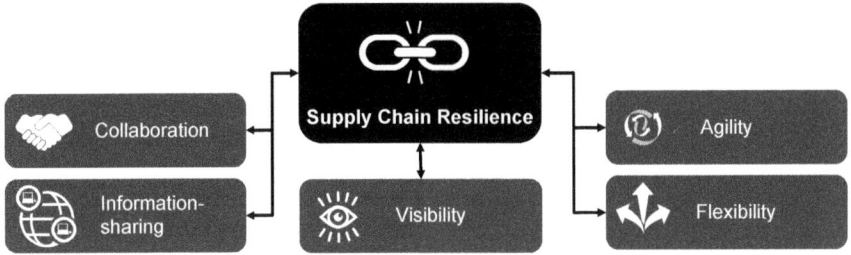

Fig. 6.3 Drivers of supply chain resilience [own representation based on Hosseini et al. (2019)]

of risks and the preparation of a rapid and targeted risk response in the event of damage. Thereby, supply chain resilience is "the adaptive capability of the supply chain to prepare for unexpected events, respond to disruptions and recover from them by maintaining continuity of operations at the desired level of connectedness and control over structure and function" (Ponomarov & Holcomb, 2009: p. 131). Hosseini et al. highlighted the five drivers of supply chain resilience as presented in Fig. 6.3. In addition to the flexibility and agility of the participating companies, the visibility, the sharing of required and current information, and the collaboration of the participants are the key drivers for resilience within supply chains (Hosseini et al., 2019).

- *Agility*
  The agility of a company stands for the ability to quickly, smoothly, and cost-effectively respond to sudden changes (Wieland & Marcus Wallenburg, 2013), react to unexpected market changes and convert them into business opportunities (Jain et al., 2008).
- *Flexibility and Redundancy*
  Flexibility is defined as the ability of all members of a supply chain to adapt to changing environments and stakeholders with minimal effort, cost, and time

(Manders et al., 2016). Redundancy represents a strategic availability of additional resources (incl. capacities) within the supply chain (Kiebler et al., 2020).

- *Visibility*

    Visibility reflects the ability to have a transparent view of inventories, demand, and supply conditions as well as production and purchasing schedules in both directions; upstream and downstream (Christopher & Peck, 2004).

- *Collaboration*

    Collaboration within a supply chain refers to the ability of two or more autonomous companies to work effectively together and target common goals (Cao et al., 2010).

- *Information Sharing*

    Information sharing, in combination with backups and storage possibilities, enables the drivers above and thus leads to a more robust and less vulnerable supply chain (Saghafian & van Oyen, 2012).

In addition to the collaboration between companies directly involved within a supply chain, the establishment of public–private partnerships can add value to allow for a resilient supply chain. In this chapter, we argue that public–private partnerships can be leveraged to strengthen other drivers of supply chain resilience next to collaboration, especially agility and flexibility. Moreover, initiatives derived from public–private partnerships can support and help to facilitate the development of additional drivers of supply chain resilience.

2.2   Collaboration via Public–Private Partnerships

One of the factors supporting supply chain resilience is determined by the way how actors in a supply chain network collaborate in order to reconfigure and restore the supply chain (Boin et al., 2010; Ivanov et al., 2014; World Economic Forum, 2015). In this context, Papadopoulos et al. showed that trust, swift information sharing, and public–private partnerships are critical enablers of resilience in supply chain networks (Papadopoulos et al., 2017). Public–private partnerships can be characterized by collaboration between public and private partners that aim to pursue common goals, while leveraging joint resources and capitalizing on each other's competences and strengths (Nijkamp et al., 2002; Pongsiri, 2002). For example, as part of EU's Coronavirus Global Response, European Commission mobilized funding and programs that were made available to support innovation projects, start-ups, and SMEs during COVID-19. The support instruments include financing, technical support, and networking assistance (EIT, 2020; Spinant & Pisonero-Hernandez, 2020).

The European Commission distinguishes two traditional forms of public–private partnerships:

1. Institutional public–private partnership: Public and private sectors establish a partnership for the fulfillment of a specific task.

2. Contract public–private partnership: Public entity contracts a private entity to fulfill a specific task (European Commission, 2004).

Originally, "public-private partnerships [...] are long-term contracts between two units, whereby one unit acquires or builds an asset or set of assets, operates it for a period and then hands the asset over to a second unit. Such arrangements are usually between a private enterprise and government [...]" (Article 15.41 European Union, 2013). Within this paper, we extend this definition to short-term contracts that enable to fulfill a required task for the public entity.

Collaboration between public and private entities shows several mutual benefits in the context of management of disruptive events, especially with regard to unexpected risks. First, the establishment of a collective responsibility facilitates the fulfillment of the goals from the public as well as from the private partner. Second, solutions that stimulate resilience are created by aligning private and public entities (Gabler et al., 2017). Third, collaboration leads to improved flexibility and performance (Fiksel et al., 2015; Scholten et al., 2014). Fourth, it gives public and private entities the opportunity to learn from each other (Singh et al., 2019). And fifth, interpersonal relations and social capability may benefit post-disruption supply chains (Li et al., 2017) by building trust and engaging in co-creation processes (Jain et al., 2017).

In most disruptive, unexpected events, the response action, as the second phase of a disruptive event, is reactive. Taking this into account, measures that are introduced by private and public entities are a reaction to a disruptive event. Due to additional social capability and interpersonal relations, public-private partnerships can specifically support post-disruption (Li et al., 2017), which is essential for unexpected events. The reactive nature of these actions may not lead to optimal outcomes during a pandemic crisis. A disruptive situation often results in so-called short-term collaboration between public and private entities, which can be defined as "intense yet temporary collaborations between organizations created in direct response to an unforeseen disruptive event" (Gabler et al., 2017). Public and private entities are incentivized for engaging in public–private partnerships as they can share risks, have mutual learning opportunities and are able to benefit from economies of scale and scope (Bovaird, 2004). A public entity can take the role of a facilitator to find ways to increase flexibility, visibility, and other indicators of supply chain resilience. To enable the public entity to take the role of a facilitator, the private entity needs to define the issues caused by the unexpected risk. This requires extended supply chain visibility and transparency about the required support. When private firms are empowered with tools that increase their supply chain visibility—which expresses the ability to follow the actual status of material, capacities, and planning (Christopher & Peck, 2004)—they are able to identify supply chain bottlenecks better and faster. This gives companies valuable time to take actions and limit negative supply chain effects (Tang, 2006). In this regard, it is considered important to develop and institutionalize public–private partnerships before the disruptive event strikes, so they can be activated immediately upon requirement.

In summary, public–private partnerships under pandemic circumstances are set up upon actual requirements and are characterized by reactive elements of supply chain resilience. Approaching public–private partnerships in a reactive way may not result in the optimal outcome in terms of supply chain resilience during a pandemic hit. In order to effectively leverage public-private partnerships and build supply chain resilience during pandemic times, these initiatives should have a more proactive approach. Next to the initiation of a private–public partnership it is important to deploy the proactiveness within those partnerships, which requires an early identification of pain points and bottlenecks. Those can then be communicated by the private partner to the public partner as a political facilitator to identify reconfiguration options. With regard to technological means this is assisted by decision-support methods and tools.

3 Decision-Support Methods and Tools for a Reconfiguration of Supply Chains

3.1 Approaches for a Reconfiguration of Supply Chains

To establish a resilient supply network, it requires a frequent reconfiguration of supply chains (Ivanov, 2018, 2020). This is especially true as supply chains act in a dynamic and changing environment; hence changes are the only constant in a supply chain (Rice, 2020). This is particularly valid in the case of the unexpected spike in demand for medical equipment as it has happened during the COVID-19 pandemic. A reconfiguration has to involve all stakeholders of a supply chain and hence requires proper methods.

The literature states several methods on how to reconfigure supply chains. Supporting methods for a reconfiguration of supply chain processes and structures are procedure models. They provide a successive procedure on how to plan and implement changes in a supply chain. A procedure model describes the activities to be performed and the sequence of the workflow (Seidel, 2008). The literature states procedure models from Reiner and Schodl (2003), Seidel (2008), Klingebiel (2009), and Kuhn et al. (2010).

The procedure model from Kuhn et al. (2010) builds upon the findings of the above-mentioned authors and integrates their concepts into a procedure model that allows for a dynamic, frequent analysis of supply chains and adaption of their processes and their design. This procedure model subdivides into eight steps. The first two steps state the strategic orientation of the supply chain and the relevant criteria against which the performance of a supply chain shall be measured. The third step serves to identify bottlenecks and further potential in the existing setting of a supply chain. This is followed by the analysis of the supply chain toward potential adjustment options and the identification of most suitable options. Step five refines the most suitable options that represent potential to-be scenarios of the supply chain.

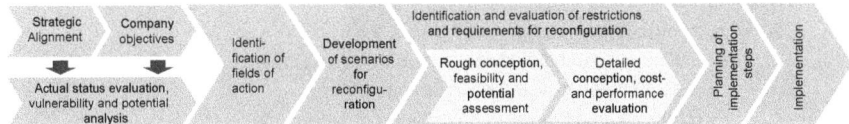

Fig. 6.4   Different steps and overall concept of the procedure model (Kuhn et al., 2010)

The subsequent step six supports the identification and evaluation of restrictions and requirements to implement the potential to-be scenarios. This step is subdivided into a draft concept and is accomplished by a general feasibility check. Then, it integrates a detailed appraisal of the concept and evaluation of costs and performance of the to-be scenarios and results in a decision on a specific to-be scenario. Step seven refines the necessary actions to implement the to-be scenario before step eight takes care of the final execution of the implementation stage into the supply chain setting. Figure 6.4 shows the different steps and the overall concept of the procedure model according to Kuhn et al. (2010).

In a similar manner, Pettersen et al. (2018) present an approach that combines a design procedure model with methods from risk assessment. The original flowchart from Petterson et al. has been adapted for the reconfiguration of supply chains. The flowchart consists of four major blocks; first, the "operation and systems definition" that includes a description of the underlying supply chain and defines a trade space for possible supply chain reconfigurations. The second step, "risk investigation," integrates an analysis of risks within the supply chain while identifying and quantifying relevant risks. Within the third step, "reconfiguration proposal," optional fields of actions are proposed, and the feasibility is determined. Those fields of action require evaluation to recommend the best suitable supply chain reconfiguration via performance assessment in step four, "reconfiguration evaluation" (Pettersen et al., 2018). Figure 6.5 shows the flowchart for the setup of a reconfiguration of a supply chain.

The flowchart in Fig. 6.5 reflects the procedure model of Kuhn et al. (2010), as the steps "operation and system definition" and "risk investigation" integrate the strategic orientation of the supply chain and evaluate the underlying supply chain configuration, for which a reconfiguration is required due to evolving risks (steps one, two, and three in the procedure model). The step "reconfiguration proposal" of the flowchart reflects the steps four and five of the procedure model as design actions are identified and a reconfiguration of the supply chain configuration is proposed in these steps. The procedure model then combines the feasibility check of the "reconfiguration proposal" with the "reconfiguration evaluation." Hence there are parallels between both approaches.

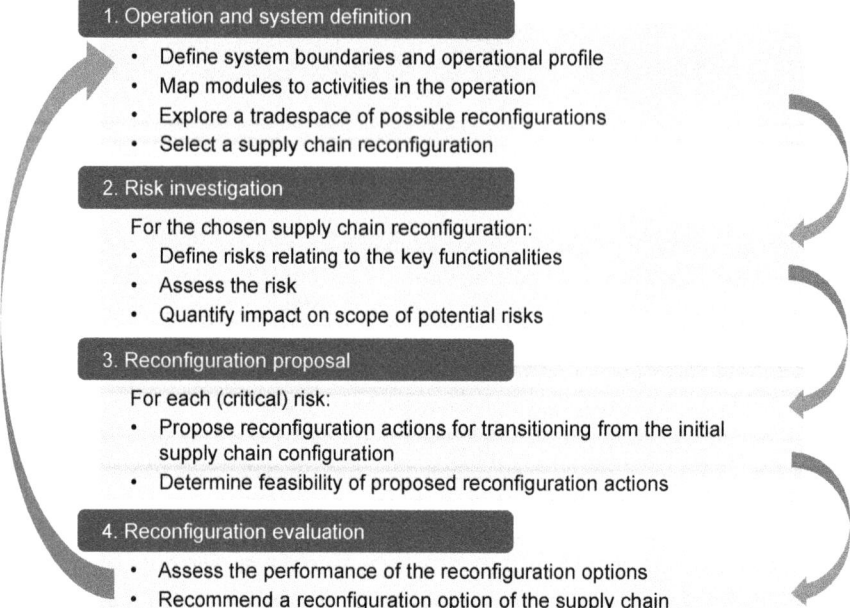

1. Operation and system definition
- Define system boundaries and operational profile
- Map modules to activities in the operation
- Explore a tradespace of possible reconfigurations
- Select a supply chain reconfiguration

2. Risk investigation
For the chosen supply chain reconfiguration:
- Define risks relating to the key functionalities
- Assess the risk
- Quantify impact on scope of potential risks

3. Reconfiguration proposal
For each (critical) risk:
- Propose reconfiguration actions for transitioning from the initial supply chain configuration
- Determine feasibility of proposed reconfiguration actions

4. Reconfiguration evaluation
- Assess the performance of the reconfiguration options
- Recommend a reconfiguration option of the supply chain

Fig. 6.5 Flowchart of a supply chain reconfiguration supply chain methodology [own representation based on Pettersen et al. (2018)]

3.2 Analytical Methods for Reconfiguration of Supply Chains

Analytical methods can be applied for the evaluation of a supply chain reconfiguration before its implementation. Several analytical methods exist to assess the performance of a reconfiguration of the supply chain, among them mathematical optimization and simulation.

In the context of a dynamic evaluation, a simulation acts as a suitable method. Simulation describes a high-performance, widely used analytical tool (Kolonko, 2008) in which a model represents a complex system (Gutenschwager et al., 2017). Typically, a simulation approach is used whenever an effective mathematical optimization approach is not feasible or is difficult to perform. Simulation methods require less restrictive assumptions than optimization models and allow great flexibility in the representation and analysis of real systems (Gutenschwager et al., 2017). In many cases, simulation supports a decision-making process in which several system variants are analyzed that differ in structure or behavior (März et al., 2011).

Simulation for the field of production and logistics is defined as "the reproduction of a system with its dynamic processes in a model that can be experimented with in order to arrive at findings that can be transferred to reality" (VDI 3633 Blatt 1, 2014). The simulation model contains an abstracted image, e.g., of a machine, a production process, or a supply chain, which either already exists or will be created in the future.

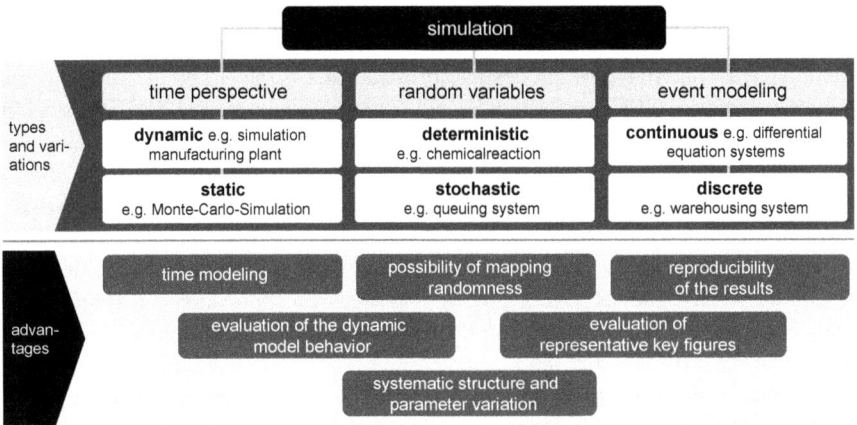

Fig. 6.6 Simulation variants and advantages [own representation based on Eley (2012) and Rabe et al. (2008)]

The abstraction supports the description of the structure or behavior of the system with a lower level of detail than in reality (März et al., 2011). The level of detail depends in each case on the object of analysis and the research question.

Three characteristic properties distinguish a simulation. First, the behavior of a system can be represented at a point in time or over time, allowing an evaluation of the static and dynamic model behavior. Second, most simulation tools represent randomness and include deterministic and stochastic behavior, which is particularly valuable in the case of risk management. Third, simulation models distinguish between continuous and discrete simulation with respect to the periodic updating of events (März et al., 2011). Figure 6.6 illustrates the various simulation properties as well as exemplary fields of application and discusses the advantages of simulation, where the dynamic and stochastic behavior of the model and the presentation of key results over time are particularly noteworthy.

In supply chains, there are various planning problems that are predestined for the use of simulations due to their complexity (Eley, 2012). In addition to supply chain design and planning, risk analysis in the supply chain is one of the main areas of application. Event-discrete simulation has proven to be a suitable tool for gaining insights into the behavior and dynamics of a supply chain (Güller et al., 2015; Yüzgülec & Kuhn, 2015). Stress tests can be mapped well-using simulations. Furthermore, simulation is often used to identify flexibility potentials and to propose corrective measures. In this way, simulation provides decision support, both for the supply chain manager and for the coordination of supply chains (Güller et al., 2015), and allows coordinated and pretested start-up management.

The execution of simulations can be supported by special software. The Order-To-Delivery-Network Simulator (OTD-NET) developed by the Fraunhofer Institute for Material Flow and Logistics is an event-discrete simulation tool that can be used to map supply chain processes and their planning sequences (Henke & Motta, 2014). It has a module-oriented structure and allows a complete, multi-level representation of the supply chain (Liebler et al., 2013). The detailed representation of comprehensive planning processes represents a special unique selling point of OTD-NET. Planning and material flow processes are made assessable from the order to the delivery regarding costs, performance, and ecology (Fruhner et al., 2020). In addition to a graphical modelling environment, the simulation software has interfaces for the automated integration of enterprise resource planning data into the model environment. From the extensive simulation results, the simulation tool summarizes information in a comprehensible way and enables an evaluation of individual relevant key performance indicators such as service level, required capacities, and throughput times (Liebler et al., 2013). The areas of application are diverse and include, among others, weak point and bottleneck analysis. Considering the complex bill of materials (BOM) and the associated number of suppliers and corresponding transportation relationships as well as strong interdependencies between the participants within a supply chain, the significance of systematic bottleneck identification and the derivation of relevant measures for the reconfiguration of supply chains becomes apparent.

With the additional possibility to integrate and aggregate risks by including stochastic events, the evaluation of risk management is included. Different supply risk scenarios can be represented via risk occurrence and impact. This demonstrates the stochastic dependencies between the supply chain partners (Cottin & Döhler, 2013). Thereby, interactions between different risks as well as their effects on the supply chain partners can be represented. The systematic use of supply chain simulation provides decision support and enables scenario-based evaluation.

4   Creation of a Service Component for Reconfiguration of a Supply Chain

4.1   Requirements for a Service Component in a Pandemic Situation

Disruptive risk events like the COVID-19 pandemic require a reconfiguration and adaptation of the supply chain settings. Based on the procedure model of Kuhn et al. (2010) and the flowchart of Pettersen et al. (2018), it is important to analyze first the current supply chain setting and to evaluate the risk effects caused by the disruptive event. In some cases, the disruptive event might only trigger a single risk, in other cases—a bundle of various risk factors. This has been the case in the COVID-19 pandemic when a number of different risks, such as border closure or the unavailability of production capacity, influenced the supply chain (Chowdhury et al., 2021).

As reasoned above, in such emergency situations, public–private partnerships can actively influence the available reconfiguration options to set up a resilient supply chain and thus help to reduce the response and recovery time of a private partner. To enable the cooperation between the private and public partners, the private partner has to identify relevant bottlenecks that have been caused by the disruptive event. In the case of a sudden demand increase, the private partner has to ensure that the production capacities in its own production facility are ready and that all parts for the product in demand are available. Using a service component for lead time and capacity evaluation can help companies as a private partner to identify and evaluate bottlenecks due to capacity restrictions of a supplier or bottlenecks in parts availability. Once volume and time constraints for necessary parts are identified, this facilitates communication within a public–private partnership and enables the private partner to discuss options wherein the public partner can support. This support can either be monetary, as it is usual for private–public partnerships, or, especially in the case of contract public–private partnership, the public partner involves its network and political influence to apply its respective competences. In the case of a pandemic situation, the public partner can even enable and enhance the competences of the private partner such as to overcome issues caused due to border closures or limited transportation capacities. Similar public–private partnerships were formed for the development of vaccines as public entities financially supported and prioritized the release of vaccines (Le et al., 2020). During the COVID-19 pandemic, public–private partnerships also have been formed to ensure security of supply for medical products.

In the following it is assumed that the private partner is able to ramp up and provide the relevant production capacity for producing medical equipment. But it is necessary to ensure parts availability to feed the production. This includes an evaluation of the capacity availability at the suppliers and to ensure a timely transport of parts from the supplier to the production facility. Considering adaptions in capacity availability and lead time requirements due to the disruptive risk event, the private partner necessitates a service that rapidly evaluates optional reconfigurations.

It is of relevance for such a service that the evaluation of capacity and lead time changes can be provided within several minutes as the situation might change quickly in a disruptive scenario. In addition, the generated service needs to be applicable to different industries. To integrate both requests, the service requires a model setting that is abstract enough to enable a quick evaluation and a transfer between different industrial sectors, and yet is detailed enough to offer the required solutions.

To sum up, the problem to be solved by the service lies in the evaluation of increasing demand or irregularly fluctuating demand coupled with supplier risks that cause issues for parts availability. The purpose of the service shall result in:

- An identification of suppliers with major bottlenecks.
- An identification of bottlenecks that are caused by transport time alterations.
- A quick recheck and evaluation of bottlenecks.
- A tool for the private partner to communicate support requirements to the public partner.

The service is constructed in such a manner that it focuses on supporting small and medium enterprises (SMEs) who generally do not have a simulation service in hand at the time a disruptive event occurs.

4.2 Conceptual Model with Data Requirements

The evaluation of a supply chain reconfiguration is part of the "reconfiguration evaluation" of the flowchart by Pettersen et al. (2018) or the "identification and evaluation of restrictions and requirements for reconfiguration" of the procedure model by Kuhn et al. (2010). The setup of a conceptual simulation model supports the generalization of the reconfiguration models. Each reconfiguration is evaluated in terms of cost, performance, and general company objectives. Out of the requirements to the service, the generalization of the model constitutes the main difficulty in setting up the conceptual model as simulation models are typically specified for an individual company (Brahmadeep & Thomassey, 2014).

The conceptual model analyses a single product of the private partner. To include forecasted orders, the conceptual simulation model contains customer orders distributed over time. This includes the expected demand peak at the production plant due to unexpected demand peaks. The plant adjusts its capacities to be able to cover the demand peak and is connected to its suppliers. A distribution channel that connects suppliers to the plant and the plant with end customers represents necessary transport and lead times. As lead time deviations have to be considered, the conceptual model considers two distribution channels from the suppliers, one with the "usual" lead time (general lead time) and another with lead time deviations. The darker shaded part in Fig. 6.7 depicts this setting.

In addition, it needs to be considered that the private partner (the plant) does not only require parts from the suppliers for the product with the demand peak, but for additional products, too. This is solved by integrating a "fictional plant," which orders parts from the suppliers that are required for all other products of the private partner. Thus, the overall demand of the private partner from the suppliers can be ascertained. Distribution channels connect the suppliers with the fictional plant. This constellation is represented in gray in Fig. 6.7.

The general conceptual model is specified to the requirements of the private partner by a set of data. Starting from the customer order toward the supplier, the private partner provides the following data. The order quantity for the customer order is included as ordered pieces per product per month. At the production plant, the working days per week and the respective output per day in pieces are defined. This information needs to be provided before and during the capacity adjustment at the plant. The service component provides a possibility to define the timeframe for the necessary capacity deviation. In addition, the private partner states the BOM for the product.

For the relation between the plant and the supplier, it is necessary to determine the lead time. The service will automatically adjust the transportation time in case it is

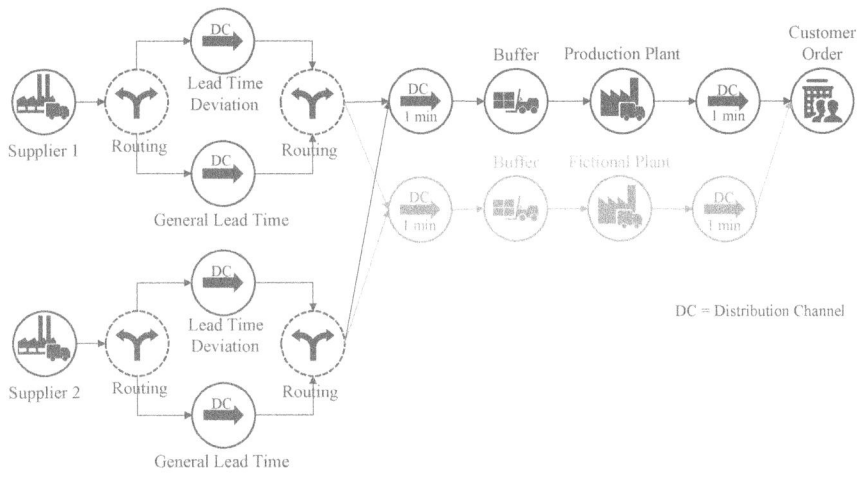

Fig. 6.7 Conceptual model for the supplier capacity evaluation

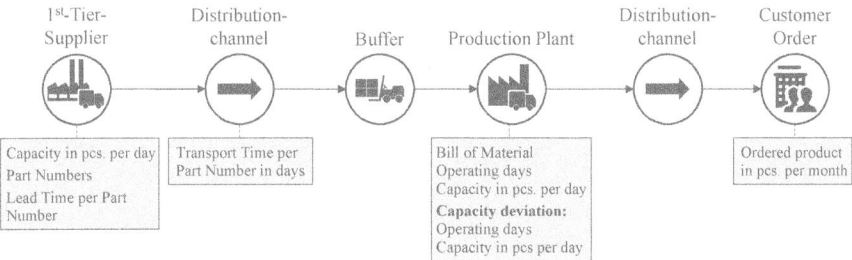

Fig. 6.8 Data requirement for the supplier capacity evaluation in a simplified conceptual model

not specifically known. For the suppliers, it is required to set the information of the part numbers supplied and the capacities provided.

Figure 6.8 summarizes the data required in a simplified conceptual model to provide clarity on the data requirement. The data is transferred into the simulation by using a user interface to enable changes in the simulation model. This allows the quick evaluation of an adjusted model in terms of transport time or capacity amendments.

The following figures display the fields for the data entry. First, general information is required, including the name and the start of the simulation. The timeline for the service is configured to represent a period of 2 years. This is followed by general information about the plant, such as working days on weekends, capacity in output per day and the time period for the capacity deviation including the expected number of pieces the production can produce on a day. Furthermore, information about the type of product is required. The basic setting of the service allows the evaluation of one specific product. The monthly demand for the product can be provided within

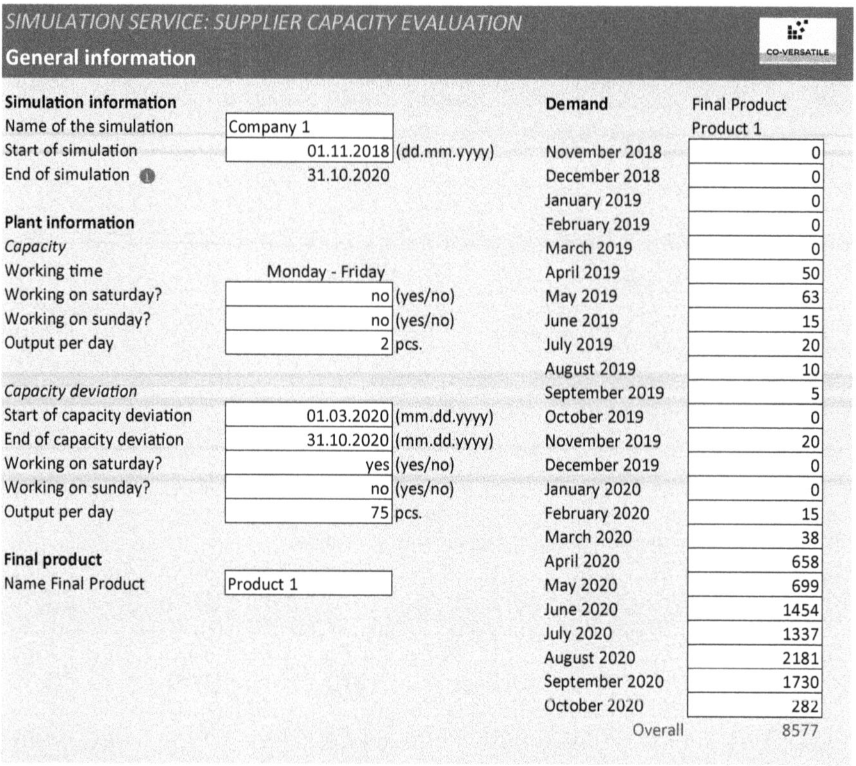

SIMULATION SERVICE: SUPPLIER CAPACITY EVALUATION

General information

CO-VERSATILE

Simulation information

Name of the simulation	Company 1	
Start of simulation	01.11.2018	(dd.mm.yyyy)
End of simulation	31.10.2020	

Plant information

Capacity

Working time	Monday - Friday	
Working on saturday?	no	(yes/no)
Working on sunday?	no	(yes/no)
Output per day	2	pcs.

Capacity deviation

Start of capacity deviation	01.03.2020	(mm.dd.yyyy)
End of capacity deviation	31.10.2020	(mm.dd.yyyy)
Working on saturday?	yes	(yes/no)
Working on sunday?	no	(yes/no)
Output per day	75	pcs.

Final product

Name Final Product	Product 1

Demand	Final Product Product 1
November 2018	0
December 2018	0
January 2019	0
February 2019	0
March 2019	0
April 2019	50
May 2019	63
June 2019	15
July 2019	20
August 2019	10
September 2019	5
October 2019	0
November 2019	20
December 2019	0
January 2020	0
February 2020	15
March 2020	38
April 2020	658
May 2020	699
June 2020	1454
July 2020	1337
August 2020	2181
September 2020	1730
October 2020	282
Overall	8577

Fig. 6.9 Input requirement by the company for general information

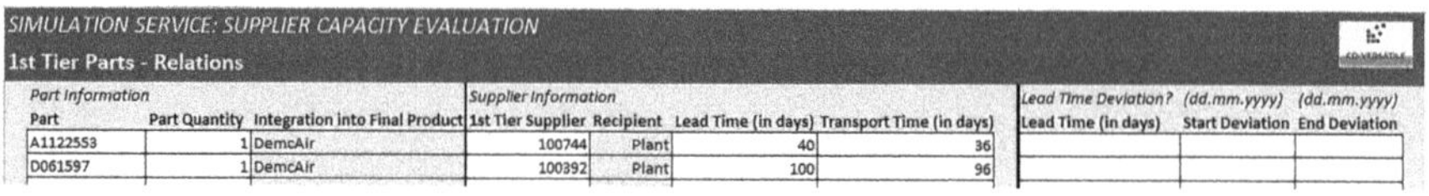

SIMULATION SERVICE: SUPPLIER CAPACITY EVALUATION

1st Tier Parts - Relations

Part Information			*Supplier Information*				*Lead Time Deviation?*	(dd.mm.yyyy)	(dd.mm.yyyy)
Part	Part Quantity	Integration into Final Product	1st Tier Supplier	Recipient	Lead Time (in days)	Transport Time (in days)	Lead Time (in days)	Start Deviation	End Deviation
A1122553	1	DemcAir	100744	Plant	40	36			
D061597	1	DemcAir	100392	Plant	100	96			

Fig. 6.10 Necessary input requirements for the supplier relations

the right columns of the overview. Figure 6.9 gives an overview of the required entries:

In addition to the general information, the private partner needs to provide input for the supply relations. Figure 6.10 states the header for necessary input on the user interface. The first section deals with the part information, where part number, the required part quantity for the product and the respective product ("Integration into final product") are provided. The second section integrates the respective supplier information for each part. Thus, the information of the respective supplier number and the recipient can be provided. For each part, the lead time and the transport time can be defined separately. In case of changes in lead time, the generalized model allows to specify the lead time deviation per part for a specific time period.

In addition to this, the data set is enhanced by an input about the supplier capacity and demand of parts for additional products. Along with this data, the supply chain model is set up and is getting transferred into the simulation model. In case of amendments on supply relations or with regard to the demand, the information is adjusted accordingly in the simulation model. A run of the simulation provides the required output about the possibility to produce the requested demand and discloses bottlenecks within the supply chain. An overview of these bottlenecks serves to discuss possible options with the public partner in case no immediate solution is available for the private partner.

5   Application of the Model for a Manufacturer of Medical Equipment

5.1   The Use Case of Demcon

As Demcon and its supply chain had to deal with a sudden demand increase paired with the supply chain challenges caused by the pandemic, Demcon had to respond and take immediate action in order to secure parts that were sourced globally. However, bottlenecks in the supply chain were initially not known or visible. They became visible when Demcon and other medical equipment manufacturers started to increase their orders at their (in many cases the same) suppliers. This eventually resulted in bottlenecks in the supply chain. In addition, the seriousness of the bottlenecks increased when (1st, 2nd, or 3rd tier) suppliers were affected by growing infection rates and local lockdowns. In this dynamic setting, it became a full day-to-day operation for Demcon to identify and monitor the most significant supply chain bottlenecks. This was done in a static excel-based tool, where the results were difficult to interpret in a dynamic context where capacity levels and lead times at suppliers were changing on a daily basis and sometimes even on an hourly.

The changes at the suppliers were caused by several factors, primarily related to the limited supplier capacity levels. Some critical suppliers—which were also suppliers for other respiratory device manufacturers—only allocated a part of their capacity to Demcon. Capacity levels at the suppliers were constantly changing due to (1) fluctuations (mainly increases) in demand, (2) efforts to increase production capacity, (3) hiccups in scheduled ramp-up planning, (4) partial deliveries from 2nd tier suppliers, and even (5) complete supply chain disruptions caused by local lockdowns or infection rates at supplier plants. As the factors above also had a significant impact on the lead time of suppliers, Demcon needed to reconfigure its production input from day to day. As lead times were changing, Demcon had difficulties in evaluating the implications of the constantly fluctuating lead times and the horizontal interplay between changing lead times of different suppliers. The focus constantly shifted from one supplier to another, depending on the seriousness of the bottleneck.

With the tool available at that time, Demcon experienced a lot of issues in keeping track of the implications of changes in capacity and lead times at the supplier. Also, the interplay between fluctuating lead times had to be taken into account as it was not sufficient to speed up the lead time of one part when other parts were not available. This means that Demcon constantly had to monitor the horizontal alignment of all parts of which many were subject to fluctuating lead times. Thus, Demcon was not able to effectively determine where and when new supply chain bottlenecks emerged and how that would impact the production continuity at Demcon's production plant.

As the supply chain was characterized by a highly dynamic and uncertain environment during the pandemic, it became extremely difficult to keep track of all moving parts and react to delays accordingly. One of the most critical suppliers for a part of a ventilator module—a supplier which produced unique die-casting molds—was limited to a maximum production output per week. In order to keep up with the production quantities at Demcon, a weekly transportation from China to the Netherlands was necessary. Even with airfreight, the parts would reach the Demcon plant too late because of the congestion at the airport of Ningbo and the extreme scarcity of cargo/freight aircrafts.

Since the die-casting molds became a major bottleneck, Demcon (private partner) asked the Dutch government (public partner) to support on this matter. The Dutch government acted accordingly by setting up an air bridge between China and the Netherlands that helped Demcon to reduce the lead time from several weeks to several days. When the air bridge became available, Demcon increased the transportation frequency to a weekly transport in order to keep up with Demcon's production level. It showed that public–private partnerships can play a significant role as public entities could enable private entities to improve supply chain flexibility and visibility.

It is presumed that outcomes might have been even better if Demcon (1) would have known about the possible (short term) public–private partnerships, (2) if (emerging) supply chain bottlenecks could be identified quicker and (3) if it would have been possible to facilitate communication between private and public entities by pointing out the actual requirements and possible solutions. A service component to enable the identification of bottlenecks and the impact of a rapid reconfiguration of the supplier relations can serve to enhance this new cooperation and helps to define the steps to be taken by all parties. As such, a proactive approach is necessary for public–private partnerships to ensure supply chain resiliency and preparedness for challenges triggered by future pandemics or other disruptive events.

5.2 Application of the Service Component to reconfigure Lead Time and Capacity Constraints in the Supply Chain

The service component for the supply chain reconfiguration is applied to the use case of Demcon. The supply chain with the increased demand and capacity adjustment is simulated with the underlying supply chain model to identify bottlenecks. The service component identifies existing bottlenecks at the supplier either due to capacity constraints, due to extensions of the lead time or simply since the peak in demand does not fit with the capacity availability at the supplier. In a second step, suggested reconfiguration scenarios are evaluated. Upon discussion within a public-private partnership, several options to reconfigure the supply chain are discussed under the consideration of the current scenario. In case of Demcon, this included a suggestion from the public entity to arrange an airfreight shipment for a supplier where the lead time increased considerably and led to a major bottleneck.

The templates for the supplier capacity evaluation are used to provide the required information for the supply chain model. The given time period covers 2 years in order to be able to reflect on the situation before the disruption as well as during and after the disruption period. This allows to reflect the complete disruption cycle as shown in Fig. 6.2. It enables to evaluate the situation before the disruption and to measure the impact of the disruptive event. The simulation integrates a pre- and after-simulation time of a year before and 3 months after in order to ensure lead time considerations for the first order or delays in producing the last order. The original allotted capacity at the plant for the product under consideration is extended from the period of March 01, 2020, to October 31, 2020. The supply chain for the considered product has got 28 first-tier suppliers who deliver a total of 56 different parts. The requirement of each part is stated in the template according to the BOM.

The data from the use case of Demcon is transferred into the template as shown in Figs. 6.9 and 6.10. For confidentiality reasons, the data applied in the use case has been adapted but reflects the original situation faced by Demcon. Within the use case, the service component analyses a specific product of Demcon that was ordered by Dutch hospitals. This product faced a major bottleneck with parts using specific die-casting molds coming from China. Due to the congestion of harbors, parts were available but could not be transferred to Demcon, hence the lead time increased considerably. Alternative suppliers of this part within Europe could not be contacted, mainly as the required molds for the parts had very specific features that are time consuming to replicate and were at this time only available with the supplier in China. When Demcon faced a sudden demand peak, flight transports were not available and the lead time from the Chinese supplier had to be adjusted to 80 days from March 16, 2020, to March 25, 2020. Having integrated all necessary data and lead times for the other parts, the service component starts the simulation. The event-discrete simulation simulates the required parts from the suppliers based on the final customer order from the Dutch hospital considering the production of the parts according to the supplier's capacity and their transhipments via road, rail, or ship. Whenever all parts for the final product are available at the facility at Demcon, the plant produces according to the production schedule. The simulation saves each transaction within a SQL Database. The model is simulated with computational power of 32 RAM and a six core Intel Core Processor i7, 2.7 GHz. As intended, the simulation runtime stays below 1 min and therefore serves as a quick rapid evaluation in case changes are required.

Bottleneck part	Supplier	Month	Amount of missing parts
A1127574	101505	2020-04	616
D297633	100702	2020-05	281
A1125230	100747	2020-04	154

Fig. 6.11 Resulting overview on the parts that cause a bottleneck

For the underlying use case, the simulation provides several bottlenecks for the production of the final products. Figure 6.11 shows an overview of parts that cause a bottleneck at the time of planned production of the final products. The bottlenecks are sorted by the number of missing parts in a month. For each bottleneck, the name of the part, the related supplier, the month in which the bottleneck occurs, and the number of missing parts are displayed.

As shown in Fig. 6.11, the major bottleneck part is "A1127574" from supplier "101505" with 616 missing parts in April 2020. Further bottleneck parts are "D297633" and "A1125230."

The overview in Fig. 6.11 can be used to contact the suppliers with bottleneck parts. The suppliers on the top of the list should ideally be contacted first. Next to this overview, an additional graphic allows for a time-related view on the bottleneck of a specific supplier. Figure 6.12 shows the detailed analysis of the delivered and demanded parts of supplier "101505" for the part "A1127574." The last delivery of the part occurs on March 31. As stock is still available with Demcon, the first bottleneck arises on April 06. The first parts are then delivered by April 11 again, while the bottleneck can then only be resolved by a high volume delivery by June 08.

Once these bottlenecks are identified, changes in capacity level or transport time can be analyzed with a second run of the service component. In the underlying use case, Demcon realized its major bottleneck and discussed with the government as the public partner about options to enable transportation from China via airfreight. This reduced the lead time from the original extension of 80 days considerably to 8 days. Upon integration of the new lead time, the service component now shows two further bottlenecks by suppliers within Europe, which were due to constraints in capacity allotted to Demcon. Demcon could solve these capacity issues upon direct discussion with the supplier by communicating the necessary amount and the specific timeline of requirement (see Fig. 6.13).

To summarize, the service component enables a quick evaluation of demand peaks and of changed circumstances in terms of capacity availability and lead time requirements. It allows to identify the most relevant supplier to be contacted, to discuss the changed capacity requirements with the supplier, or to find alternative sources of supply. As the runtime of the service component only takes a few minutes,

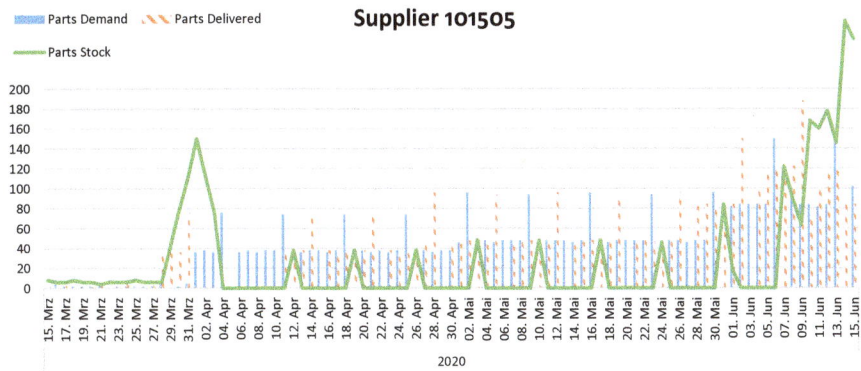

Fig. 6.12 Overview on delivered and demanded parts from a specific supplier

CO-VERSATILE MS5: Bottlenecks

Bottleneck part	Supplier	Month	Amount of missing parts
D297633	100702	2020-05	281
A1125230	100747	2020-04	154

Fig. 6.13 Overview on remaining bottlenecks after the major bottleneck had been solved

the re-evaluation can happen instantly upon confirmation with the supplier. In addition, it enables to test suggested options by the supplier instantly. Another option to use the service component remains with the test of alternative handling options to test feasible options for a discussion with the public entity.

6   Conclusion

The COVID-19 pandemic caused several disruptions within the supply chain. Companies in the medical sector experienced a sudden increase in demand for specific products. At the same time, they had to deal with a decreased supply reliability. As this unforeseen event caused additional risks, companies had to ensure parts availability. As circumstances changed quickly during the pandemic, especially SMEs faced issues in coordinating the supply chain as dedicated planning tools that allow a quick evaluation of changes were missing.

In order to avoid this shortcoming for SMEs in the future, the chapter describes a service component that can support SMEs during such disruptive events by stabilizing their supply chains. The service component allows to quickly identify bottlenecks upon the supplier's capacity development and evaluate changes in lead times.

The service component contains an event-discrete simulation that gives insights on the capacity levels of the suppliers and the interplay between suppliers fluctuating lead times. It enables to take action effectively to reduce the impact of bottlenecks on the production continuity. To ensure applicability of the service to any SME, the challenge was resolved by modelling the underlying simulation in such a manner that it allows a standardized service. The underlying simulation evaluates the supply chain reconfiguration within a few minutes.

The generated simulation service for the identification of bottlenecks and evaluation of capacity and lead time changes facilitates the reconfiguration of supply chains. In addition, it assists discussions within a public–private partnership by identifying major pain points. This enables to evaluate tasks and options that the public partner can address in order to combine and enhance competences during pandemic times.

Acknowledgment Special thanks for her advice and comments are addressed to Elena Leinemann from EIT Manufacturing. In addition, the authors are grateful to Janine Gehring from Fraunhofer IML for her support in editing the paper. The research on reconfiguration of supply chains has been made possible by the work conducted within CO-VERSATILE. CO-VERSATILE has received funding from the European Union's Horizon 2020 research and innovation program under grant agreement No. 101016070.

References

Biedermann, L. (2018). *Supply Chain Resilienz* (Dissertation). Springer Fachmedien Wiesbaden GmbH.

Boin, A., Kelle, P., & Clay Whybark, D. (2010). Resilient supply chains for extreme situations: Outlining a new field of study. *International Journal of Production Economics, 126*, 1–6. https://doi.org/10.1016/j.ijpe.2010.01.020

Bovaird, T. (2004). Public–private partnerships: From contested concepts to prevalent practice. *International Review of Administrative Sciences, 70*, 199–215. https://doi.org/10.1177/0020852304044250

Brahmadeep, & Thomassey, S. (2014). A simulation based comparison: Manual and automatic distribution setup in a textile yarn rewinding unit of a yarn dyeing factory. *Simulation Modelling Practice and Theory, 45*, 80–90. https://doi.org/10.1016/j.simpat.2014.04.002

Brindley, C. (2004). *Supply chain risk.* Taylor and Francis.

Cao, M., Vonderembse, M. A., Zhang, Q., & Ragu-Nathan, T. S. (2010). Supply chain collaboration: Conceptualisation and instrument development. *International Journal of Production Research, 48*, 6613–6635. https://doi.org/10.1080/00207540903349039

Chowdhury, P., Paul, S. K., Kaisar, S., & Moktadir, M. A. (2021). COVID-19 pandemic related supply chain studies: A systematic review. *Transportation Research Part E: Logistics and Transportation Review, 148*, 102271. https://doi.org/10.1016/j.tre.2021.102271

Christopher, M., & Peck, H. (2004). Building the resilient supply chain. *The International Journal of Logistics Management, 15*, 1–14. https://doi.org/10.1108/09574090410700275

Cottin, C., & Döhler, S. (2013). *Risikoanalyse: Modellierung, Beurteilung und Management von Risiken mit Praxisbeispielen* (Studienbücher Wirtschaftsmathematik) (2nd ed.). Springer.

Dailey, N. (2021). *A bad hurricane season could be the next headache for businesses already facing a supply shortage.* Retrieved February 22, 2022, from https://www.businessinsider.com/a-bad-hurricane-season-could-be-the-next-supply-chain-problem-2021-5?r=DE & IR=T

EIT. (2020). *€60 million crisis response initiative for Europe's innovators.* Retrieved June 7, 2021, from https://eit.europa.eu/news-events/news/eit-announces-eur-60-million-crisis-response-initiative

Eley, M. (2012). *Simulation in der Logistik: Einführung in die Erstellung ereignisdiskreter Modelle unter Verwendung des Werk-zeuges "Plant Simulation" Springer-Lehrbuch.* Springer.

European Commission. (2004). *Green Paper on public-private partnerships and Community law on public contracts and concessions.* Publications Office of the EU. https://op.europa.eu/en/publication-detail/-/publication/94a3f02f-ab6a-47ed-b6b2-7de60830625e/language-en

Fiksel, J., Polyviou, M., Croxton, K. L., & Pettit, T. J. (2015). From risk to resilience: Learning to deal with disruption. *MIT Sloan Management Review, 56,* 79–86.

Fruhner, D., Grimm, D., Sardesai, S., Wagenitz, A., Vennemann, A., & Hegmanns, T. (2020). *A tool-independent generalized description for sustainable supply chain design.* In: Proceedings of the 19th International Conference on Modeling & Applied Simulation (MAS 2020). CAL-TEK srl, pp. 99–106

Gabler, C. B., Richey, R. G., & Stewart, G. T. (2017). Disaster resilience through public-private short-term collaboration. *Journal of Business Logistics, 38,* 130–144. https://doi.org/10.1111/jbl.12152

Glock, C. H., & Grosse, E. H. (2015). Decision support models for production ramp-up: A systematic literature review. *International Journal of Production Research, 53,* 6637–6651. https://doi.org/10.1080/00207543.2015.1064185

Güller, M., Koc, E., Hegmanns, T., Henke, M., & Noche, B. (2015). A simulation-based decision support framework for real-time supply chain risk management. *International Journal of Advanced Logistics, 4,* 17–26. https://doi.org/10.1080/2287108X.2015.1008948

Gutenschwager, K., Rabe, M., Spieckermann, S., & Wenzel, S. (2017). *Simulation in Produktion und Logistik: Grundlagen und Anwen-dungen.* Springer Vieweg.

Henke, M., & Motta, M. (2014). IT im Supply Chain Management: Simulationsgestützte logistische Assistenzsysteme als Ansatz zur Steigerung der Supply Chain Agilität. In C. Kille (Ed.), *Navigation durch die komplexe Welt der Logistik: Texte aus Wissenschaft und Praxis zum Schaffenswerk von Wolf-Rüdiger Bretzke; [...Festschrift zum 70. Geburtstag]* (pp. 153–169). Springer Gabler.

Hohenstein, N.-O., Feisel, E., Hartmann, E., & Giunipero, L. (2015). Research on the phenomenon of supply chain resilience. *International Journal of Physical Distribution and Logistics Management, 45,* 90–117. https://doi.org/10.1108/IJPDLM-05-2013-0128

Hosseini, S., Ivanov, D., & Dolgui, A. (2019). Review of quantitative methods for supply chain resilience analysis. *Transportation Re-search Part E: Logistics and Transportation Review, 125,* 285–307. https://doi.org/10.1016/j.tre.2019.03.001

Ivanov, D. (2018). *Structural dynamics and resilience in supply chain risk management* (International Series in Operations Research & Management Science) (Vol. 265). Springer International.

Ivanov, D. (2020). Viable supply chain model: Integrating agility, resilience and sustainability perspectives-lessons from and thinking beyond the COVID-19 pandemic. *Annals of Operations Research,* 1–21. https://doi.org/10.1007/s10479-020-03640-6

Ivanov, D., Sokolov, B., & Dolgui, A. (2014). The Ripple effect in supply chains: Trade-off 'efficiency-flexibility-resilience' in disruption management. *International Journal of Production Research, 52,* 2154–2172. https://doi.org/10.1080/00207543.2013.858836

Iyengar, K. P., Vaishya, R., Bahl, S., & Vaish, A. (2020). Impact of the coronavirus pandemic on the supply chain in healthcare. *British Journal of Healthcare Management, 26,* 1–4. https://doi.org/10.12968/bjhc.2020.0047

Jain, V., Benyoucef, L., & Deshmukh, S. G. (2008). A new approach for evaluating agility in supply chains using Fuzzy Association Rules Mining. *Engineering Applications of Artificial Intelligence, 21,* 367–385. https://doi.org/10.1016/j.engappai.2007.07.004

Jain, V., Kumar, S., Soni, U., & Chandra, C. (2017). Supply chain resilience: Model development and empirical analysis. *International Journal of Production Research, 55*, 6779–6800. https://doi.org/10.1080/00207543.2017.1349947

Kersten, W., Böger, M., Hohrath, P., Singer, C., & Kemmerling, R. (2009). *Schlussbericht zum Projekt "Supply Chain Risk Management Navigator".* Schlussbericht eines Projektes, Technische Universität Hamburg-Harburg.

Kersten, W., Schröder, M., & Indorf, M. (2017). Potenziale der Digitalisierung für das Supply Chain Risikomanagement: Eine empirische Analyse. In M. Seiter, L. Grünert, & S. Berlin (Eds.), *Betriebswirtschaftliche Aspekte von Industrie 4.0: Arbeitskreis "Integrationsmanagement für neue Produkte" der Schmalenbach-Gesellschaft für Betriebswirtschaftslehre e. V.* (pp. 47–74). Springer Gabler.

Klingebiel, K. (2009). *Entwurf eines Referenzmodells für Built-to-order-Konzepte in Logistiknetzwerken der Automobilindustrie. Zugl.* Dortmund University, Dissertation, 2008. Unternehmenslogistik. Verl. Praxiswissen, Dortmund.

Klink, P., Sardesai, S., Gehring, J., & Görtz, M. D. (2020). FAST RAMP-UP: Anlaufmanagement nach disruptiven pandemischen Ereignissen. https://doi.org/10.24406/iml-n-599453

Kiebler, L., Ebel, D., Klink, P., & Sardesai, S. (2020). Risikomanagement disruptiver Ereignisse in Supply Chains. https://doi.org/10.24406/iml-n-599788

Kolonko, M. (2008). *Stochastische Simulation: Grundlagen, Algorithmen und Anwendungen* (1st ed.). Vieweg+Teubner Verlag/GWV Fachverlage GmbH Wiesbaden.

Kuhn, A., Wagenitz, A., & Klingebiel, K. (2010). *Praxis Materialflusssimulation: Antworten, zu oft zu spät?* (pp. 206–211). Jahrbuch der Logistik.

Le, T. T., Andreadakis, Z., Kumar, A., Román, R. G., Tollefsen, S., Saville, M., & Mayhew, S. (2020). The COVID-19 vaccine development landscape. *Nature Reviews Drug Discovery, 19*, 305–306.

Li, X., Wu, Q., Holsapple, C. W., & Goldsby, T. (2017). An empirical examination of firm financial performance along dimensions of supply chain resilience. *Management Research Review, 40*, 254–269. https://doi.org/10.1108/MRR-02-2016-0030

Liebler, K., Beissert, U., Motta, M., & Wagenitz, A. (2013). *Introduction OTD-NET and LAS: Order-to-delivery network simulation and decision support systems in complex production and logistics networks.* In: 2013 Winter Simulations Conference (WSC), pp. 439–451.

Manders, J. H. M., Caniëls, M. C. J., & Ghijsen, P. W. T. (2016). Exploring supply chain flexibility in a FMCG food supply chain. *Journal of Purchasing and Supply Management, 22*, 181–195. https://doi.org/10.1016/j.pursup.2016.06.001

März, L., Krug, W., Rose, O., & Weigert, G. (2011). *Simulation und Optimierung in Produktion und Logistik: Praxisorientierter Leitfaden mit Fallbeispielen. VDI-Buch* (Vol. 130). Springer.

Nijkamp, P., van der Burch, M., & Vindigni, G. (2002). A comparative institutional evaluation of public-private partnerships in Dutch urban land-use and revitalisation projects. *Urban Studies, 39*, 1865–1880. https://doi.org/10.1080/0042098022000002993

Papadopoulos, T., Gunasekaran, A., Dubey, R., Altay, N., Childe, S. J., & Fosso-Wamba, S. (2017). The role of Big Data in explaining disaster resilience in supply chains for sustainability. *Journal of Cleaner Production, 142*, 1108–1118. https://doi.org/10.1016/j.jclepro.2016.03.059

Parliament Office. (2013). *Regulation (EU) No 549/2013 of the European Parliament and of the Council.*

Pettersen, S. S., Asbjørnslett, B. E., & Erikstad, S. O. (2018). Designing resilience into service supply chains: A conceptual methodology. In Y. Khojasteh (Ed.), *Supply chain risk management: Advanced tools, models, and developments* (pp. 253–268). Springer Singapore.

Pfohl, H.-C., & Aberle, G. (Eds.). (2002). *Risiko- und Chancenmanagement in der Supply Chain: Proaktiv – ganzheitlich – nachhaltig; 17. Fachtagung, Institut für Logistik, 4. Juni 2002, Darmstadt. Unternehmensführung und Logistik* (Vol. 20). Schmidt.

Pongsiri, N. (2002). Regulation and public-private partnerships. *International Journal of Public Sector Management, 15*, 487–495. https://doi.org/10.1108/09513550210439634

Ponomarov, S. Y., & Holcomb, M. C. (2009). Understanding the concept of supply chain resilience. *The International Journal of Logistics Management, 20*, 124–143. https://doi.org/10.1108/09574090910954873

Rabe, M., Spiekermann, S., & Wenzel, S. (2008). *Verifikation und Validierung für die Simulation in Produktion und Logistik: Vorge-hensmodelle und Techniken*. VDI-Buch.

Reiner, G., & Schodl, R. (2003). A model for the support and evaluation of strategic supply chain design. In *Strategy and Organization in Supply Chains, Physica* (pp. 305–320). Heidelberg. ISBN: 978-3-7908-2451-3.

Rice, J. B. (2020). Prepare your supply chain for Coronavirus. *Harvard Business Review, 27*.

Saghafian, S., & van Oyen, M. P. (2012). The value of flexible backup suppliers and disruption risk information: Newsvendor analysis with recourse. *IIE Transactions, 44*, 834–867. https://doi.org/10.1080/0740817X.2012.654846

Scholten, K., Sharkey Scott, P., & Fynes, B. (2014). Mitigation processes—Antecedents for building supply chain resilience. *Supply Chain Management: An International Journal, 19*, 211–228. https://doi.org/10.1108/SCM-06-2013-0191

Schreckenberg, F., Motta, M., Sardesai, S., Klink, P., & Kamphues, J. (2021). ACES - Eine Revolution auch für das Risikomanagement in der Automobilbranche? https://doi.org/10.24406/IML-N-635040

Seidel, T. (2008). *Ein Vorgehensmodell des softwareunterstützten Supply Chain Design* (Dissertationsschrift). Technische Universität Dortmund.

Sheffi, Y., & Rice, J. B. (2005). A supply chain view of the resilient enterprise. *MIT Sloan Management Review, 47*, 41.

Shi, D. (2004). A review of enterprise supply chain risk management. *Journal of Systems Science and Systems Engineering, 13*, 219–244. https://doi.org/10.1007/s11518-006-0162-2

Singh, C. S., Soni, G., & Badhotiya, G. K. (2019). Performance indicators for supply chain resilience: Review and conceptual framework. *Journal of Industrial Engineering International, 15*, 105–117. https://doi.org/10.1007/s40092-019-00322-2

Spinant, D., & Pisonero-Hernandez, A. (2020). *Coronavirus Global Response: €7.4 billion raised*. Retrieved June 7, 2021, from https://ec.europa.eu/commission/presscorner/detail/en/ip_20_797

Tang, C. S. (2006). Robust strategies for mitigating supply chain disruptions. *International Journal of Logistics, 9*, 33–45. https://doi.org/10.1080/13675560500405584

ten Hompel, M., & Henke, M. (2017). Logistik 4.0 – Ein Ausblick auf die Planung und das Management der zukünftigen Logistik vor dem Hintergrund der vierten industriellen Revolution. In B. Vogel-Heuser, T. Bauernhansl, & M. ten Hompel (Eds.), *Handbuch Industrie 4.0: Bd. 4: Allgemeine Grundlagen* (2nd ed., pp. 249–259). Springer Vieweg.

VDI 3633 Blatt 1. (2014). *Simulation von Logistik-, Materialfluss- und Produktionssystemen – Grundlagen*. Verein Deutscher In-genieure e.V., Düsseldorf.

Velayutham, A., Rahman, A. R., Narayan, A., & Wang, M. (2021). Pandemic turned into pande-monium: The effect on supply chains and the role of accounting information. *AAAJ, 34*, 1404–1415. https://doi.org/10.1108/AAAJ-08-2020-4800

Wagner, S. M., & Bode, C. (2009). Dominant risks and risk management practices in supply chains. In F. S. Hillier, G. A. Zsidisin, & B. Ritchie (Eds.), *Supply chain risk* (Vol. 124, pp. 271–290). Springer.

Wagner, S. M., Kemmerling, R., Kersten, W., & Böger, M. (2010). Supply Chain Risikomanagement: Besonderheiten und Herausforderungen für kleine und mittlere Unternehmen. In C. Engelhardt-Nowitzki, O. Nowitzki, & H. Zsifkovits (Eds.), *Supply Chain Network Management: Gestaltungskonzepte und Stand der praktischen Anwendung* (pp. 97–116). Gabler Verlag/GWV Fachverlage GmbH Wiesbaden.

Wieland, A., & Marcus Wallenburg, C. (2013). The influence of relational competencies on supply chain resilience: A relational view. *International Journal of Physical Distribution and Logistics Management, 43*, 300–320. https://doi.org/10.1108/IJPDLM-08-2012-0243

World Economic Forum. (2015). *Building resilience in Nepal through public-private partnerships.* https://www.weforum.org/reports/building-resilience-nepal-through-public-private-partnerships

Worley, C. G., & Jules, C. (2020). COVID-19's uncomfortable revelations about agile and sustainable organizations in a VUCA world. *The Journal of Applied Behavioral Science, 56,* 279–283. https://doi.org/10.1177/0021886320936263

Yüzgülec, G., & Kuhn, A. (2015). *Aggregierte Bewertung von Risikoursachen in Supply Chains der Automobilindustrie* (Dissertationen. Unternehmenslogistik). Verlag Praxiswissen.

Zitzmann, I. (2018). *Supply Chain-Flexibilität zur Bewältigung von Unsicherheiten – Taktisch-operative Potenzialplanung zur Schaffung von Robustheit, Resilienz und Agilität.*

Chapter 7
Supply Chain Financing and Pandemic: Managing Cash Flows to Keep Firms and Their Value Networks Healthy

Erik Hofmann, Simon Templar, Dale S. Rogers, Thomas Y. Choi, Rudolf Leuschner, and Rohan Y. Korde

Abstract The COVID-19 pandemic has interrupted firms and their value networks. The lockdown measures taken by governments around the globe have triggered a massive supply and demand shock. The ensuing crisis has created economic chaos that resulted in massive business disruptions for companies, their customers, their suppliers, and their affiliated service providers (banks and logistics providers). Firms are turning to supply chain financing solutions to stabilize liquidity and their net working capital to maintain solvency and ensure continuity of supply through their supply chains. This paper discloses several different types of supply chain financing solutions and how these can impact firms and their value creation partners struggling through the uncertain business environment caused by a global pandemic.

This paper is a reprint of Hofmann, Erik; Templar, Simon; Rogers, Dale S.; Choi, Thomas Y.; Leuschner, Rudi &Korde, Rohan Y. (2021) Supply Chain Financing and Pandemic: Managing Cash Flows to Keep Firms and Their Value Networks Healthy. Rutgers Business Review, 6 (1). 1–23. ISSN 2474-2376.

E. Hofmann (✉)
University of St. Gallen, St.Gallen, Switzerland
e-mail: erik.hofmann@unisg.ch

S. Templar
Cranfield University, Cranfield, UK
e-mail: simon.templar@cranfield.ac.uk

D. S. Rogers · T. Y. Choi · R. Y. Korde
Arizona State University, Tempe, AZ, USA
e-mail: dale.rogers@asu.edu; thomas.choi@asu.edu; rykorde@asu.edu

R. Leuschner
Rutgers University, Newark, NJ, USA
e-mail: rudi@business.rutgers.edu

1   Introduction

The COVID-19 pandemic has resulted in millions of people infected and hundreds of thousands killed during 2020. It has created economic chaos and caused great damage to firms, their customers, and their suppliers. A critical need for firms is to maintain their financial liquidity to facilitate demand and supply challenges.

Across the supply chain, organizations have been forced to reduce staffing to cut costs. These cuts resulted in a dramatic fall in demand for goods and services. For some industrial sectors such as hospitality, tourism, and airlines, most revenues were wiped out. Managers had to take drastic decisions to maintain liquidity to survive which resulted in eroding cash reserves, further headcount reductions, reduced expenditures, and postponing capital investments. Late customer payments increase in bad debt, and restrictive bank lending practices compounded cash flow problems and decreased liquidity. These problems led to an increased risk of insolvency and resulted in more employee layoffs. Firms found themselves in a downward spiral.

A key strategic priority for companies is ensuring that they can meet their net working capital (NWC) needs, where NWC = current assets—current liabilities. Supply chain financing (SCF) is an approach that builds on traditional trade finance solutions to help organizations manage its net working capital more flexibly and at a lower rate of interest than is normally available to a supplier. Suppliers are able to sell their approved invoices to a bank or financial technology (fintech) firm. From a buyer perspective, SCF provides an opportunity to finance suppliers on favorable terms increasing their business resilience and overall health. From a supplier perspective, SCF enables opportunities to reduce receivables risks of customers and continue to be financially viable.

SCF is not a "silver bullet," but it has been increasingly used since the financial crisis in 2008/2009 to stabilize the liquidity of a supplier organization and interrupt the vicious circle (Jia et al., 2020). SCF has been incorporated into an organization's supply chains including customers on the demand side and suppliers on the supply side to assist the organization with its cash flows by securing enough liquidity to ensure supply continuity (Hofmann & Wetzel, 2020). SCF can help mitigate the impact of the pandemic and can also enable an organization and its suppliers to position themselves for a post-pandemic upturn.

Over the previous decade practitioners and academics have referred to SCF solutions as a win, win, win for buyers, suppliers, and financial service providers (FSPs) (Hofmann & Zumsteg, 2015) However, the pandemic has revealed some negative aspects of SCF too (Cowton & San-Jose, 2017). For instance, SCF has been accused of aiding buying companies to force cash discounts on their suppliers. Therefore, decision makers want to know what SCF is about and how this approach might help to manage cash flows to keep firms healthy. We raise the following question: *How can supply chain financing (SCF) mitigate the disruptive impact of the COVID-19 pandemic on an organization's ability to finance and protect their supply chains?*

To understand the financial impact of the COVID-19 crisis on organizations and its supply chains, a group of researchers studied the emerging practitioner literature and interviewed leading experts in SCF. As a group, we recently published two books in SCF and numerous articles on this subject and in related areas. In this paper, we address the management of NWC by considering the impact of the crisis on the organization and the affiliated supply chain partners, the measures taken to mitigate the impact, and the future for SCF after the crisis passes. Our analysis provides decision makers with a powerful set of options for action in the SCF field to respond adequately to the current crisis and future pandemics.

2   Concept of Supply Chain Financing

SCF can assist firms and their supply chains by increasing the velocity of cash flow and making those flows more consistent. Implemented properly, the firm and its supply chains can enjoy a symbiotic relationship. Rogers et al. (2020) define SCF as follows (Rogers et al., 2020): *"Supply chain financing is using the supply chain to fund the organization and using the organization to fund the supply chain"*.

In a simplistic sense, SCF has been mistakenly equated with approved financing approaches (i.e., reverse factoring). This understanding does not go far enough—SCF is more. In its broadest interpretation, SCF covers not only the financing of all the transactions being done in the end-to-end upstream and downstream supply chain, but also the long-term financing of all resources and capacities required for operating activities (Templar et al., 2020).

Banks and other financial service providers have moved away from the term "reverse factoring". Supply chain finance (not supply chain financing which encompasses all solutions related to using the supply chain to fund the organization and vice versa) Includes all solutions that utilize helping the supplier deal with buyer extended payment terms. Additionally, in this era reverse factoring typically takes place at lower interest rates than it did several years ago. Because of its bad reputation as being close to usury, banks and other financial service providers are using supply chain finance because what factoring and reverse factoring used to mean.

SCF encompasses a broader class of solutions that provide NWC and trade financing to firms and their supply chains. These can be grouped around the following supply chain activities: inbound supply chain and accounts payable (AP) solutions, company focus and inventory solutions, and outbound-supply chain and accounts receivable (AR) solutions. Over recent years a variety of SCF instruments have been made available to firms, to mitigate the impact of a supply chain disruption on their cash flow. See Fig. 7.1 for an overview.

Typical SCF solutions with NWC reference point accounts payable are:

- *Purchasing cards* is a type of commercial card that allows organizations to take advantage of the existing credit card infrastructure to make electronic payments

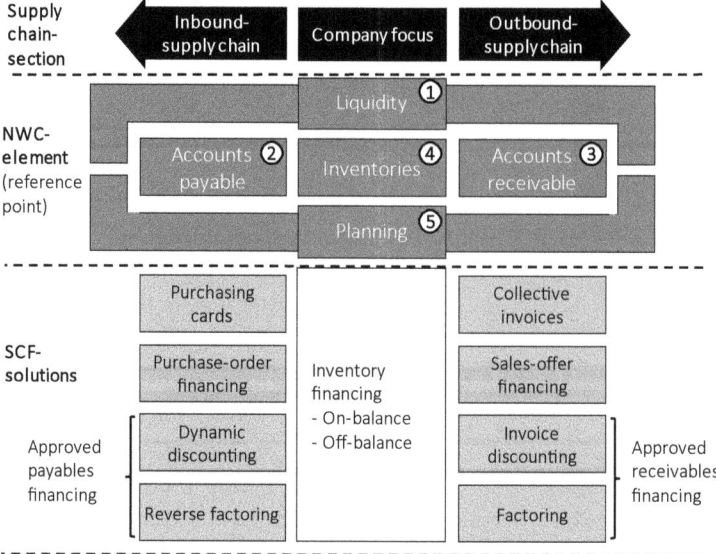

Fig. 7.1 Overview of SCF instruments [adapted from Templar et al. (2020)]

and enable goods and services to be purchased from predefined suppliers without a traditional procurement process. Purchasing cards are used for smaller purchases.

- *Purchase order financing* is an SCF financing solution agreed between buying companies and suppliers to achieve financing at an early stage (i.e., at the time of the order). It is a kind of advance payment.
- *Dynamic discounting* is an SCF solution where the purchasing company offers the supplier earlier payment of the invoice at a discounted rate based on a negotiation between buyer and supplier. In contrast to conventional discounting, dynamic discounting uses adjustable payment terms and is generally conducted via a dynamic SCF platform. The earlier an invoice is settled, the higher the discount.
- *Reverse factoring* is an SCF solution that essentially enables a buyer to obtain pre-financing of liabilities from their supplier via an approved invoice. A financial service provider can help suppliers obtain early payment with a discount typically computed using the interest rate of the financially stronger buying firm.

These SCF solutions with NWC reference point inventory can include:

- *On-balance sheet inventory financing* is an instrument for financing inventories. In contrast to the off-balance solution, the inventories remain on the buying company's balance sheet with the on-balance solution and serve only as a guarantee for a credit agreement. These solutions encompass an asset-based lending approach.

- *Off-balance sheet inventory financing* refers to the financing of inventories where operational goods logistics and ownership are transferred to an external logistics service provider. This method results in reduced costs due to lower storage and logistics costs and an increase in liquidity through a reduction in the capital tied up in inventories.

SCF solutions that are related to the management of accounts receivable are:

- *Collective invoices* are a form of billing where a cumulative invoice is sent to a customer for several deliveries per period.
- *Sales offer financing* refers to financing solutions that suppliers use to promote the sales of their products and to create financial flexibility for customers through the use of payment by instalments.
- *Invoice discounting* uses invoices for accounts receivable as collateral for short-term financing (asset-based lending approach). The use of digital invoice discounting platforms provides companies with flexible access to liquidity while reducing the risk for external financial service providers through increased transparency.
- *Factoring* refers to the commercial, revolving transfer of a company's accounts receivable to a financial service provider or a factoring company. Factoring as an SCF solution provides companies with an increase in liquidity while at the same time reducing financing costs and unpaid invoices.

Suppliers have always offered discounts to their buying companies to get paid early. For instance, we often talk about phrases like 2/10 net 30, which basically means, the supplier is willing to give the buyer a 2% discount if they pay in 10 days on an invoice due in 30 days. Dynamic discounting (DD) is a similar concept but more intricate. The supplier can review their approved invoices online using the buyer's platform which is likely operated by a fintech and can elect to be paid earlier. They can also leave the invoice to be settled on the agreed date. Whenever they decide to be paid, the system calculates the discount charged to the supplier for the early payment.

Traditional forms of financing focus on funding the corporation through traditional means. In supply chain financing, the corporation is specifically using suppliers and customers (usually suppliers) to fund the organization or vice versa. Supply chain financing is a special form of financing that includes using external entities in the supply chain to fund the organization instead of traditional means that we would typically think of as financing.

Major players engaged in SCF practices are suppliers and buyers. Logistics service providers (3PL's, transportation companies, etc.) are mainly involved in the physical flow of goods and information. In addition, public authorities and regulatory bodies (central banks, professional organizations, etc.) also play a certain role by shaping the formal framework for SCF. The SCF service supply market is dominated by fintechs such as Taulia (https://taulia.com/), PrimeRevenue (https://primerevenue.com/), CRX Markets https://www.crxmarkets.com/, Orbian https://orbian.com/, C2FO (https://c2fo.com/), and TrustBills (https://www.trustbills.com/

en/) (Hofmann et al., 2017). Banks are also important players in SCF and usually support high volumes of transactions between buyers and their largest suppliers. They operate extensive SCF programs. Deutsche Bank maintains 600 SCF programs worldwide with 30,000 connected suppliers (Buchholz, 2020). There are now numerous instances of cooperation between fintechs and banks.

3 Five NWC Elements Affected by the COVID-19 Crisis

During the COVID-19 crisis, every firm was out to fend for its survival. Buying firms extended payment terms, while at the same time suppliers tried to shorten payment terms to stay viable. Buying companies reduced their inventories, often at the cost of other firms in their supply chains. These strategies may be sensible from the point of view of securing liquidity, but from the point of view of the supply chain they can be damaging. They tend to shift the problems to suppliers and weaken the resilience of the supply chain.

We describe below how SCF works in practice. One example comes from Apple. A New York Times (Desai, 2018) article explains how Apple no longer plays the profit maximization game. The article contends they now instead play the cash flow game. Apple puts suppliers on a 90–120 days term, but they receive payments from consumers immediately after buying phones and other products. Concurrently, Apple keeps the inventory at suppliers which results in a negative cash conversion cycles at around −70 days and cash reserves of over $200 billion.

Appropriate measures of SCF can be divided into five areas, which correspond to the key elements of NWC. For each of the elements, we address what happened during the pandemic and the challenges caused by the pandemic crisis.

3.1 NWC Element 1: Liquidity and the Interface to Financial Service Providers

During the COVID-19 crisis, a core priority for companies is preserving liquidity in the form of cash. With sales plummeting due to lockdowns and credit markets tightening, companies grapple with higher financing costs and more stringent borrowing structures. They are short on cash and find it difficult to meet all NWC requirements (Demmou et al., 2020). The expression "cash is king" has never been so important as many companies were no longer able to pay their suppliers and were not able to keep their own operations running. They had to consider alternative ways to fund their businesses and their supply chain as credit was getting tight.

In this regard, the pandemic has had significant implications for FSPs. It accelerated a trend that was well underway before it struck—higher private and public debt, lower interest rates, and shrinking fiscal and monetary room for policy maneuvers (Borio, 2020). In the crisis, a number of banks have also run into difficulties and had to adapt their lending practices, for instance, by reprioritizing credit lines. Banks (lenders) have begun to incorporate anti-cash hoarding provisions into their lending agreements (Lentz & Smith, 2020). However, massive public stimulus is masking the true magnitude of the economic impact of the COVID-19 crisis. Provisions being taken by major financial institutions indicate they believe that loss rates will exceed those from the Great Recession (McIntyre et al., 2020). These provisions are designed to preserve banks' liquidity by ensuring that borrowers only draw funds for specific needs and deploy them accordingly. Some banks have failed to serve as a facilitator for the liquidity needed within the supply chain. For instance, companies running a dynamic discounting solution were unable to supply these systems with sufficient cash. The consequence was that suppliers connected to such a SCF solution did not receive early payments (Ulbricht, 2020). Additionally, reverse factoring programs of some companies were not secured, and FSPs were not able to provide sufficient liquidity (Taube, 2020). One of our interviewees explained:

> In the early days (of the pandemic) we were reaching out to our financial industry to ensure credit lines were secured, just in case, if the worst case is happening.

Also, companies see potential covenant violations with their cash lending facilities, having no clear picture of how the pandemic will affect sales on the demand side of the supply chain. In addition, it is not clear whether they will be able to operate at all if their current production facilities are closed (Myrskog, 2020). However, if organizations can use their supply chain assets (whether inventory or receivables) as collateral, it may provide them with additional time to ride out the crisis.

When the global economy restarts, it may be that overall economic output will settle at a lower level than before the pandemic crisis. Improved incoming orders from customers will lead to increased material procurement with an increase in payment obligations to suppliers. A new challenge arises. FSPs will need to consider how to prepare for a sustained return in sales demand and checking that there is enough liquidity to support the ramping-up of supply chains.

3.2 NWC Element 2: Accounts Payable and the Interface to Suppliers

The value-added share attributable to suppliers is more than 60% for manufacturing companies (Kallstrom, 2020) and in some cases as high as 80 or 90%. In most countries, small and medium-sized enterprise (SME) suppliers account for the vast majority of the value-adding work. However, the negative impact of the COVID-19 crisis has been particularly acute for SMEs. For example, in Northern Italy where the significance of SMEs is critically important, SMEs have been particularly vulnerable to the disruption of supply chains (Cusmano & Raes, 2020).

Compared to MNEs with a larger resource base, SME suppliers are likely less resilient in dealing with the costs the pandemic shocks entail. Costs for prevention as well as requested changes in work processes, such as the shift to teleworking, are relatively higher for SMEs, with their low level of digitalization and difficulties in accessing technologies. If production is reduced, the costs of underutilized labor and capital weigh greater on SME suppliers. In the United States, 50% of SMEs are operating with fewer than 15 days in buffer cash and that even healthy SMEs have less than two-month cash reserves (JPMorgan Chase, 2020). There is a significant risk that even solvent suppliers, particularly SMEs, could go bankrupt (OECD, 2020).

Buying companies have generally extended payment terms with their suppliers. This is because such supplier credits can be enforced spontaneously, and such supplier credits are usually interest free. This trend of extending payables to suppliers during the crisis with an increasing number of SME suppliers claiming late payments by their customers (Taulia, 2020). Some companies were able to offset their increased accounts receivables from customers with longer accounts payables to their suppliers, as one of the interviewed companies points out:

> We were able to set off AR impact with AP for the first half year, which is good news.

Ultimately, extending payment terms with suppliers is a zero-sum game. The problems are passed on to the suppliers, who now must deal with the financing challenges, even though they may have worse refinancing conditions than the buyer. From an overarching supply chain perspective, not only does this not seem to be effective but such a practice may even be considered unethical, as the Australian Small Business and Family Enterprise Ombudsman pointed out in a recent report (Australian Government, 2020).

In countries like Germany, Austria, or Switzerland during the pandemic, companies are sheltered from filing legal insolvency. The Federal Ministry of Justice and Consumer Protection in Germany states: *"The suspension of the obligation to file for insolvency gives companies in distress the necessary scope to apply for state aid and to press ahead with restructuring efforts"* (Federal Ministry of Justice and Consumer Protection, 2020). However, this "well-intentioned" measure may lead to mistrust in the supply chain; in the absence of transparency, suppliers cannot estimate whether a customer is actually insolvent or not. In fact, suppliers would likely switch to advance payment, because if payment is not made and insolvency is filed, the managing directors and board members of the company that is left sitting on the damage suddenly find themselves confronted with personal liability risks. They could be accused of having delivered or paid without collateral in the wake of the crisis and thus acted in breach of due diligence (Isaksson, 2020).

Furthermore, it should be noted that the financial stability of the supply chain depends not only on the immediate suppliers at tier 1, but also on the sub-suppliers far upstream in the supply chain. The financial failure of a critical nexus supplier (Yan et al., 2015) at the n-th tier level due to insolvency can bring the entire supply chain to a standstill. Such interlinked relationships beyond direct business relations must also be considered in the context of a global pandemic crisis.

3.3 NWC Element 3: Accounts Receivable and the Interface to Customers

Throughout the global economy, lockdowns during the COVID-19 crisis have caused sales to collapse abruptly, except for a few product groups that were temporarily in high demand at the beginning of the crisis (e.g., healthcare equipment, food, medicines, consumer electronics for home office, and personal protective equipment). The lockdowns caused the stationary distribution channel to dry up, which in turn led to a massive drop in accounts receivable and a tightening of the liquidity situation. An interviewed representative from a pharmaceutical company makes this clear:

> (Cancer) patients were not showing up and/or infusion centers were not open and so this had an effect to our sales.

Before the crisis, the payment terms for supplier credits granted to customers ranged from just under 30 days in Switzerland to 90 days in Italy (Statista, 2020). When the outbreak began to spread outside China, late payments already affected 52% of the total value of business-to-business invoices issued in Asia (Cessford, 2020). These average figures skyrocketed during the COVID-19 crisis. Customers asked for a deferment of payment or were temporarily unable to pay at all. Large customers seemed to be no longer willing or able to pay their suppliers on time. The receivables collection periods of 60–90 days, which were increasingly being observed even in Switzerland, are tantamount to a unilaterally forced extension of the supplier credit by buying firms. In some cases, the changes were not explicit, as one interviewee clarifies:

> You're used to getting payments two to three times a month. Now you are receiving them once a month. So that's a significant difference.

With the suspension of the obligation to notify insolvencies make it difficult for companies to assess the liquidity situation of their customers and their willingness to pay, COVID-19 is creating an insolvency time bomb. Even as economies emerge from lockdowns, it is expected a bulk of insolvencies are still to come. The top increases will be recorded in the United States (+57% by 2021 from 2019), Brazil (+45%), China (+20%), the United Kingdom (+43%), Spain (+41%), Italy (+27%), Belgium (+26%), and France (+25%) (Lemerle, 2020).

Finally, trade credit insurance companies started to reduce their exposures and would no longer cover the trade risks caused by the COVID-19 crisis. For example, the trade credit insurer Euler Hermes has announced that insurance coverage for companies with a weak credit rating will expire at the end of 2020 (Buchholz & Dentz, 2020). Due to the rapidly deteriorating creditworthiness of customers, many suppliers no longer want to work on a payment term basis and require more expensive solutions such as payment in advance or letters of credit. This has led to a drying up of the trade flows and increased default risks in supply chains. As soon as the first dominoes fall, a chain reaction of bankruptcies is feared, as the insolvency of their customers puts suppliers in financial difficulties.

3.4 NWC Element 4: Inventory and the Interface to Logistics Service Providers

Due to the COVID-19 crisis, major manufacturing hubs in China were locked down such as Wuhan and Shenzhen and borders were temporarily closed. As result, buying firms around the world found themselves running out of inventories. Lockdowns in Europe and the United States followed relatively quickly, which further worsened the supply situation. These lockdowns initiated panic consumer buying behaviors that saw a rush and stockouts of different goods, from personal protective equipment (PPE) to certain basic foods and drugs. One of the SCF experts interviewed illustrates this as follows:

> We had such a backlog for the first two, three days when sales spiked, it took a month to get through that.

Organizations were unable to move inventory fast enough to replenish empty shelves. Their supply chains now became fragile, disclosing the potential danger of being "lean, leaner, too lean!"(Eroglu & Hofer, 2011) This was supported by one interviewee as follows:

> Inventory is at a record high. It is just because of risk mitigation inventory we established.

Reducing inventory levels over recent years has resulted in the associated inventory carrying costs, which can be between 20 and 30% of the value of the goods being held (Tuovila, 2020). Often, companies have outsourced the inventory management to logistics service providers (LSPs). It reduced assets and put the emphasis on the third party to continue managing the inventory and ensure the outsourcing company's just-in-time goals are met. Outsourced inventory had slowed down even in such companies looking to pivot quickly to counter the effects of the pandemic. Figure 7.2 illustrates that from January 2020 that inventory costs and levels are now rising with warehouse capacity decreasing and utilization increasing.

The inventory challenges during the pandemic were significant. Organizations did not have sufficient transparency regarding the inventories held by their suppliers and customers (Kemp, 2020). The lack of inventory visibility at a customer level is relevant for estimating the actual net demand. Inventory transparency at the suppliers is important for deriving production planning. Combined with a lack of trust and insufficient information, issues surrounding inventories and capacities are compounded further. During the COVID-19 crisis, sales and operations planning (S & OP) became imprecise due to the massive interruptions and uncertainties and made it impossible for firms to adequately plan demand and supply (Trepte et al., 2020). As a result, many companies continued to order from their suppliers despite the abrupt slump in demand from customers, leading to a massive bullwhip effect (Vuealta, 2020).

During normal times, companies with valuable assets could leverage them to get an asset-based loan. Usually, lenders would loan funds based on a percentage of the secured assets' value (i.e., 50% of the value of finished inventory). However, the

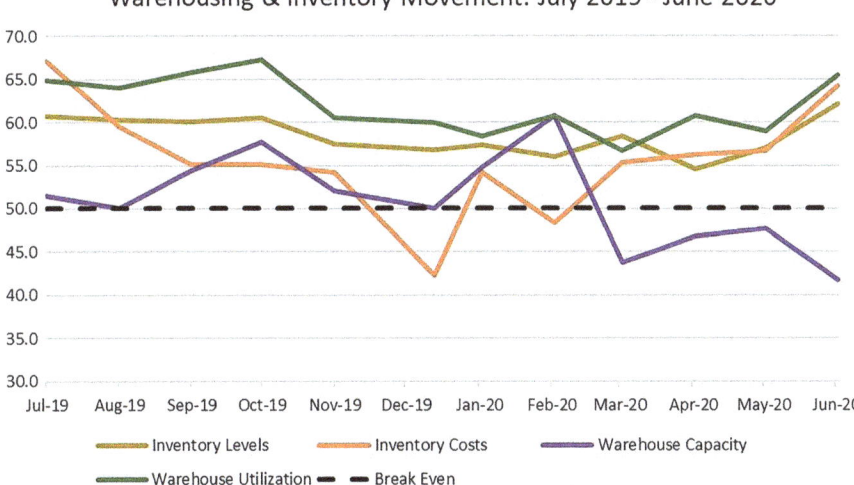

Fig. 7.2 Warehousing and inventory movements during the COVID-19 crisis (adapted from the Logistics Managers Index http://The-LMI.com)

physical and economic consequences of the pandemic made it difficult to conduct physical inventory appraisals. The pandemic crisis is tantamount to unsafe environment for loan collateral appraisers to perform physical assessments of inventory. Moreover, the liquidation market for inventories was disrupted because retail distribution channels were closed. There was also the question of timing: How should companies appraise merchandise meant to be sold during a given season if it needs to be replaced with inventory for a subsequent season when reopening for business? Interest rates on asset-based lending rose by 75–100 basis points since the COVID-19 outbreak to reflect the current liquidity environment and increased credit risk (Gately, 2020).

During the recovery phase of the pandemic crisis, it seems to be essential that organizations carefully consider before making inventory purchases whether they are proportionate to customer demand and sales. Such "uncovered" stocks are a risk of overextending credit to purchase inventory resulting in a negative borrowing cycle.

3.5 NWC Element 5: Planning and the Cross-Functional Interface

Planning relates to intra- and interorganizational interfaces between the various actors involved in managing liquidity and NWC. To manage NWC, several functions within the organization must be involved. Often, different tasks are linked to different reporting lines, and responsibilities are often not clearly defined. In manufacturing, for example, purchasing is usually responsible for negotiating payment terms with suppliers and is often under the supervision of the operations board. Treasury is responsible for cash management and reports to the CFO. This condition often leads to internal conflicts of interest. The primary goal of purchasing is to keep the price low. The terms of payment, which the finance department examines every month, are often neglected in negotiations with suppliers. The disconnect was compounded during the COVID-19 crisis, as cooperation became more difficult as employees and decision makers were either furloughed or working from home.

Even in companies that have already initiated a SCF program, there are always interface problems across the functions involved. The cooperation between treasury and purchasing is relatively well established in such companies. However, the severity of the COVID-19 crisis made it necessary to additionally involve the sales and operations departments in order to obtain a holistic view of NWC.

The pandemic generated significant planning challenges for organizations both internally and externally. In many companies, there was a lack of transparency to NWC. This could be attributed to the good economic situation of the past years, among other things, when liquidity was not the focus. Those who pursued growth targets also accepted that the NWC had become bloated. But with the COVID-19 crisis this changed. As one of our interviewees recognized:

> Our normal S & OP processes were inadequate because of the volatility and in some cases, you just can't make enough so you make all you can and you get as much as you can in the market and we're playing catch up on those products as we as we go forward.

Transparency is often lacking with regard to the partners in the supply chain. Especially SMEs often realize in the COVID-19 crisis that they do not have sufficient data to evaluate the liquidity situation of their suppliers and customers. Larger MNEs have more resources to establish good financial supply chain risk management. Especially in a phase of high uncertainty like a pandemic, the exchange with important suppliers and customers was not always sought in a timely manner.

4 Supply Chain Financing Measures to the COVID-19 Crisis

A broad variety of measures have been launched to mitigate the business impact of the pandemic on the organization's NWC including the affiliated supply chain and financial partners. Table 7.1 shows the recommended SCF measures along the five NWC elements.

With regard to the NWC element 1 liquidity, companies need to recognize the balancing act during the recovery phase of a pandemic crisis. The balancing act pertains to investing in growth versus cost control, as the costs are immediate, but the revenues are still uncertain. Considering the NWC elements 2 and 3 on accounts payables and accounts receivable, firms have to recognize that depending on the size

Table 7.1   Selected SCF mearsures

NWC element 1—Liquidity

• Hold regular meetings to assess your current cash and financing situation together with key FSPs, to be able to estimate the liquidity requirements in the short, medium, and long-term on a rolling basis
• Establish diversified SCF programs with several FSPs. We suggest a multibank model as it reduces dependence on a single bank
• Accept responsibly, if necessary, the governmental support (e.g., enabling banks to lend by providing liquidity via short-term credit lines), but note that this aid usually corresponds to a loan and must be repaid at a later date. Such government stimulus efforts include:
   – Paycheck protection programs, a loan dedicated to SMEs that helps businesses keep their workforce employed (U.S. Small Business Administration, 2002)
   – Non-repayable grants on application, which partially compensate for loss of revenue (Demmou et al., 2020)

NWC element 2—Accounts Payable
• Support suppliers with financing advice, as part of an overall supplier development program. Suppliers should benefit from the buyer's financial expertise • Pay suppliers voluntarily and on your own initiative with shortened payment terms. That will help SME suppliers get stabilized financially (see, for example, the Obama 2011 SupplierPay initiative) (The White House, 2014) • Establish a dynamic discounting program, in order to use the buyer's own liquidity. It should be noted that sufficient liquid funds must be available to ensure the long-term operation of such a program • Adopt a reverse factoring program, where a factoring company (factor) finances invoices from the suppliers. They usually benefit from the better creditworthiness of the buyer • Switch to purchase order financing, especially for very vulnerable suppliers. For them, this means early payment, even before the goods are delivered and the invoice is issued (Purchase Order Financing, 2009)
NWC element 3—Accounts Receivable
• Analyze and evaluate the financial health of your customers on a regular basis including receivable trends and customers' risk exposures • Examine payment deferrals closely, while non-negotiated payment arrears should be followed up with dunning procedures. Introduce clear rules for payment deferrals (e.g., per customer group, country, or severity of the pandemic) and ensure enforcement • Settle asset-backed finance instruments, most notably invoice discounting in the United States and factoring in Europe and rest of the world. The degree of disclosure to the debtor under this type of facility varies, ranging from full disclosure to no disclosure (Patel, 2020) • Use innovative trade receivable auctions platforms [e.g., TrusBills (DZ Bank, 2020)], on which a supplier can upload specific trade receivables and institutional investors can bid on them • Watch out for government safeguarding efforts that guarantee trade credit insurers, since it cannot be excluded that the credit protection for outstanding receivables could be reduced or, in the worst case, even cancelled completely
NWC element 4—Inventory
• Realign the just-in-time and lean management systems with a higher "minimum sliding stock," barring prohibitively high holding costs. This measure increases the resilience of the supply • Establish a single pool of inventory for the traditional and online distribution channels. This will increase flexibility, especially when one channel is suddenly in greater demand than the other • Ensure that suppliers, especially of critical goods, have an adequate safety stock. Optionally, diversification of the supplier base could help to increase the robustness of the supply chain • Increase, together with your key LSPs, transparency in the supply chain, both on the demand and the supply side. Ideally, this can enable an anticipatory reaction to emerging fluctuations or

(continued)

Table 7.1 (continued)

disturbances in the supply chain • Investigate with LSPs and FSPs the possibility of using on- and off-balance inventory financing solutions. For example, the instrument of asset-based lending (ABL) could be used to interim finance inventory (Buzacott & Zhang, 2004)
NWC element 5—Planning
• Establish a cross-functional team covering NWC, both strategically and operationally. Ensure that adequate governance is established, which includes incentives that are balanced with NWC objectives • Introduce zero-based planning principles, especially in phases of a lockdown and of recovery from a pandemic. In line with zero-based budgeting, no recourse is made to past values in supply chain planning until the "new normal" is reached • Include critical suppliers, customers, and service providers in regular NWC planning. Supply and demand network mapping with reference to NWC issues can help to identify critical suppliers and customers • Enforce the SCF performance measurement including access to internal and external parameters as this enables an overview of the current status of the NWC in the organization and the connected supply chain partners during a pandemic crisis and beyond • Link operational risk and disruption management systems with financial and liquidity planning in order to bridge the operations-finance divide

and complexity of their supply chains, it takes between 8 weeks and 4 months to set up an SCF program. One reason for this is the complex and time-consuming supplier onboarding process. For companies that are experiencing acute liquidity difficulties, this is probably too long. With regard to the NWC element 4 inventory, companies should expect an increase in average safety stocks during a pandemic crisis. This is primarily to cushion the distortions in the supply chain. However, the transition from crisis mode to the recovery phase and the post-pandemic crisis phase should not be overlooked. Finally, with regard to the NWC element 5 planning, companies must adapt their supply chain planning based on the experience of the pandemic. During a pandemic, speed is important. The speed enables organizations and their supply chain to react quickly to unforeseen events.

5 Looking Beyond the COVID-19 Crisis

Although the impact of the current pandemic on global economy is enormous, a proactive approach to this black swan event can be used as an opportunity to make lasting changes for the organization and supply chains. In the following, we show selected aspects of managing cash flows in supply chains to keep firms and their partners financially healthy beyond the pandemic. For structuring, we will again use the five NWC elements.

5.1 NWC Element 1: Liquidity

The COVID-19 crisis shows the relevance of managing cash flow. Based on the weakest link in the supply chain, liquidity needs to be reorganized in a way which ensures that supply chain financing does not only cover the top tier of the supply chain, but functions smoothly across every supply chain level. KPIs, based on liquidity factors including the cash conversion cycle (Theodore Farris, 2002), should be part of the repertoire of every supply chain manager. Of the three factors that affect cash conversion cycle (i.e., accounts payable, inventory, and accounts receivable), supply chain managers have traditionally been responsible for managing accounts payable and inventory. Now, with increasing pressure to integrate upstream activities with downstream demand, supply chain managers touch all aspects of the cash conversion cycle (including the use of SCF instruments).

The pandemic highlighted the important role that state institutions, including the rerouted aid and support programs, can play in supporting organization's liquidity and maintaining financially sustainable supply chain operations. However, organizations should be prepared to tap into the governmental support offered. FSPs and supporting fintechs play a vital role to maintain the financial health of supply chains. They are poised to become an integral part of operations and supply chain management.

5.2 NWC Element 2: Accounts Payable

It is essential that organizations in the future, not only focus on the financing of direct suppliers but also sub-tier suppliers must be considered. Deep-tier SCF programs should be established. Blockchain technology could be used in this form of financing the "long-tail supply chain" (Stolberg-Larsen, 2019). Traditional SCF models rarely reach beyond the first-tier suppliers of large corporates, and thus exclude the long tail and SME deeper tiers. Using an open blockchain protocol for supply chains, suppliers may be able to prove their creditworthiness, and this, in turn, helps to obtain financing. In addition, the trust and reputation of large companies ripple down the supply chain through interconnected business relations. Therefore, a funder provides financing for sub-suppliers for a rate based on the anchors' buyer's credit risk (Centrifuge, 2020). Above all SME suppliers would benefit from this.

Further, the pandemic may provide an opportunity to integrate supplier sustainability programs with SCF. The buyer can define certain sustainability criteria. The suppliers that score high on these criteria can receive preferential conditions as part of the SCF program. Choosing the right sustainability criteria is still a big obstacle to the further spread of sustainable supplier financing. The number-driven treasury departments are still struggling with the limited comparability of sustainability-based ratings. There is still a need for standardization in this area. Specialized rating agencies like EcoVadis (https://ecovadis.com/) could help to develop and establish such a standard. Treasurers and SCF program owners should therefore rely on the expertise of the sustainability department and the purchasing department when introducing such a program. In addition to lower reputation risks, studies indicate that sustainable suppliers are also more stable (Network for Business Sustainability, 2012). The food manufacturer Nestlé has securitized sustainable supplier financing, using CRX Markets' NWC financing marketplace. The securitization was a bundle of invoices from a certified coffee supplier participating in a Nestlé sustainability program (Kogler, 2020).

5.3   NWC Element 3: Accounts Receivable

Post-pandemic, an organization's key account managers and customer relationship management teams must focus on the financial stability of their customers, while developing and retaining sales revenue. An organization should enable their customers to achieve long-term sustainable growth, which also generates future customer lifetime revenues for the supplier.

Supplying organizations will decide whether they accept the SCF solutions of their customers (e.g., a reverse factoring program) or whether they want to establish their own solution for their account receivables. It is not yet clear how the clash between supplier-driven trade receivables financing programs and buyer-centered accounts payables programs will eventually pan out. It would be desirable if technology-based interaction between these two accesses were possible. The technological progress and the increasing interoperability of different SCF programs should reduce manual efforts to a minimum in the future. Moreover, the future efficiency of trade finance solutions could be increased by using digital solutions, which may be based on blockchain technology, especially for international transactions.

5.4   NWC Element 4: Inventory

Post the COVID-19 pandemic, organizations may take a joint approach to inventory management in their supply chain operations. Enhanced transparency in the supply chain requires reliable and independent data in real time, enabling informed decisions based on augmented intelligence and providing them with greater insights into their operations (Röck et al., 2020). In the future, it seems to be essential that organizations have the ability to acquire and analyze data in real time, from customers, suppliers, manufacturers, and transportation and warehousing providers. For instance, a combination of Internet of Things (IoT) sensors and cloud-based software allows companies and their supply chain partners to manage the moving bottlenecks that arise in inventory management. With greater insight, practitioners can make faster and evidence-based decisions, rather than leaning on assumptions. Supply transparency solutions, like the Swiss-based "real time cargo monitoring provider" Arviem (https://arviem.com/), are providing the data that allows suppliers and buyers to more accurately manage their risk, allowing each actor within the supply chain to optimize their finances and reduce costs.

Moreover, a future innovated solution referred to as "off-balance inventory finance" has the potential to be attractive for organizations. However, the establishment of such a solution on a broad scale is still pending as are challenges relating to the accounting treatment that need to be solved.

5.5   NWC Element 5: Planning

As a consequence of the pandemic, most companies have learned to work effectively without physical meetings. Remote and virtual interactions will be the new normal, which will also affect supply chain and NWC planning. In addition, we witnessed how the asymmetrical responses of governments and regulators, local shutdowns, workforce requisitions, and the lack of a coordinated regional or global political response were considered in S & OP in times of a pandemic. Conditions should be created to proactively address these critical factors.

Companies need to be aware that especially during a pandemic, with all the restrictions, local operations increase, and standard planning shifts from the short-term issues that threatened distributed operations for a period of days or weeks to long-term crisis-resistance scenarios. Moreover, the pandemic crisis highlights the fact that not everyone has the same level of NWC planning professionalism and access to the necessary technologies and digital tools. In the future, it must be ensured that customers and suppliers in the supply chain have access to appropriate planning capabilities, so that limits in NWC knowledge should not be used as an excuse.

The COVID-19 crisis has opened new avenues to combine financials with the value of data in supply chains. Cash flows among supply chain partners in return for the accomplishment of specific tasks and the exchange of comprehensive data sets. Thus, liquidity and NWC pair with data in a hitherto underexploited way. This helps to get data out of existing data silos, thereby significantly increasing transparency in the supply chain (Jäkel & Borchert, 2020).

Finally, the disruption of global supply chain networks and the following economic crisis caused by COVID-19 might trigger a wave of innovations. The liquidity and NWC issues provoked by the pandemic will lead to a shakeout in the FSP and other SCF companies, facilitating initiatives that promote clear long-term economic viability. Nevertheless, it is quite likely that this development will lead to a new landscape at the operations–finance interface with the emergence of SCF ecosystems, geared more to well-balanced cooperation and real win–win and less to a one-sided advantage at the expense of the supply chain partners.

References

Australian Government. (2020, February). *Supply chain finance review*. Retrieved September 2020, from https://www.asbfeo.gov.au/sites/default/files/documents/ASBFEO-SCF-position-paper.pdf

Borio, C. (2020, July 2). *The Covid-19 economic crisis: Dangerously unique*. Bank for International Settlements. Retrieved September 17, 2020, from https://www.bis.org/speeches/sp200722.pdf

Buchholz, D. (2020, July 24). Deutsche Bank steigt bei Fintech Traxpay ein. *Der Treasurer*. https://www.dertreasurer.de/news/finanzierung-corporate-finance/deutsche-bank-steigt-bei-fintech-traxpay-ein-2014641/

Buchholz, D., & Dentz, M. (2020, August 28). *Euler Hermes cuts insurance coverage*. DerTreasurer. Retrieved September 17, 2020, from https://www.dertreasurer.de/news/risiko-management/euler-hermes-kappt-versicherungsschutz-2014931/

Buzacott, J. A., & Zhang, R. Q. (2004). Inventory management with asset-based financing. *Management Science, 50*(9), 1274–1292.

Centrifuge. (2020). *What is deep tier finance?* Retrieved September 17, 2020, from https://centrifuge.io/products/deep-tier-finance/

Cessford, G. (2020, July 24). *Survey shows Asian businesses facing huge liquidity pressures*. Supply Chain Brain. Retrieved September 17, 2020, from https://www.supplychainbrain.com/blogs/1-think-tank/post/31648-survey-shows-asian-businesses-facing-huge-liquidity-pressures

Cowton, C. J., & San-Jose, L. (2017). On the ethics of trade credit: Understanding good payment practice in the supply chain. *Journal of Business Ethics, 140*(4), 673–685.

Eroglu, C., & Hofer, C. (2011). Lean, leaner, too lean? The inventory-performance link revisited. *Journal of Operations Management, 29*(4), 356–369.

Cusmano, L., & Raes, S. (2020, July 15). *Coronavirus (COVID-19): SME policy responses*. OECD. Retrieved September 17, 2020, from http://www.oecd.org/coronavirus/policy-responses/coronavirus-covid-19-sme-policy-responses-04440101/

Demmou, L., Franco, G., Calligaris, S., & Dlugosch, D. (2020, May 5). *Corporate sector vulnerabilities during the Covid-19 outbreak: Assessment and policy responses*. OECD. Retrieved September 17, 2020, from http://www.oecd.org/coronavirus/policy-responses/corporate-sector-vulnerabilities-during-the-covid-19-outbreak-a6e670ea/#endnotea0z16

Desai, M. A. (2018, August 6). Why Apple is the future of capitalism. *The New York Times*.

DZ Bank. (2020). *TrustBills – The digital auction platform*. Retrieved September 17, 2020, from https://www.dzbank.de/content/dzbank_com/en/home/products_services/corporate_customers/products_and_achievements/financing/classical_dept_financing/trustbills.html

Hofmann, E., & Zumsteg, S. (2015). Win-win and no-win situations in supply chain finance: The case of accounts receivable programs. *Supply Chain Forum: An International Journal, 16*(3), 30–50.

Federal Ministry of Justice and Consumer Protection. (2020, September 8). *Suspension of the obligation to file for insolvency should be extended*. Retrieved September 18, 2020. https://www.bmjv.de/DE/Themen/FokusThemen/Corona/Insolvenzantrag/Corona_Insolvenzantrag_node.html

Gately, E. (2020). *COVID-19 is popularizing asset-based lending. Here's why*. Retrieved September 17, 2020, from https://www.sfnet.com/home/industry-data-publications/the-secured-lender/magazine/tsl-article-detail/covid-19-is-popularizing-asset-based-lending-here-s-why

Hofmann, E., & Wetzel, P. (2020). *Working capital management study 2020—Supply chain finance in-n-out* (7th ed.). Zürich 2020. https://www.alexandria.unisg.ch/publications/260104. A recent study shows that companies with a SCF program not only have a capital tie-up period shorter by 28 days on average (–64%), approximated with the cash conversion cycle, but the financial performance, approximated with the ROCE (return on capital employed), is also higher by just under 40% (9 percentage points) on average.

Hofmann, E., Strewe, U. M., & Bosia, N. (2017). *Supply chain finance and blockchain technology: The case of reverse securitisation.* Springer.

Isaksson, M. (2020, May 27). *Supporting businesses in financial distress to avoid insolvency during the COVID-19 crisis.* OECS. Retrieved September 17, 2020, from http://www.oecd.org/coronavirus/policy-responses/supporting-businesses-in-financial-distress-to-avoid-insolvency-during-thecovid-19-crisis-b4154a8b/

Jäkel, C., & Borchert, H. (2020, June 16). *The European way: How to advance Europe's strategic autonomy.* Retrieved September 18, 2020, from https://www.ey.com/en_ch/supply-chain/the-european-way-how-to-advance-europes-strategic-autonomy

Jia, F., Blome, C., Sun, H., Yang, Y., & Zhi, B. (2020). Towards an integrated conceptual framework of supply chain finance: An information processing perspective. *International Journal of Production Economics, 219*, 18–30.

JPMorgan Chase. (2020, April). *Small business cash liquidity in 25 metro areas.* Retrieved September 17, 2020, from https://institute.jpmorganchase.com/institute/research/small-business/small-business-cash-liquidity-in-25-metro-areas

Kallstrom, H. (2020). *Suppliers' power is increasing in the automobile industry.* Market Realist. Retrieved September 17, 2020, from https://marketrealist.com/2015/02/suppliers-power-increasing-automobile-industry/

Kemp, L. (2020, June 19). *How supply chain transparency can help businesses make the right calls.* Retrieved September 17, 2020, from https://www.weforum.org/agenda/2020/06/supply-chain-transparency-can-pre-risk/

Kogler, A. (2020, July 15). *Novelty in sustainable supply chain finance.* Der Treasurer. Retrieved September 17, 2020, from https://www.dertreasurer.de/news/finanzierung-corporate-finance/novum-bei-sustainable-supply-chain-finance-2014431/

Lemerle, M. (2020, July 16). *Calm before the storm: COVID-19 and the business insolvency time bomb.* Allianz. Retrieved September 17, 2020, from https://www.allianz.com/content/dam/onemarketing/azcom/Allianz_com/economic-research/publications/specials/en/2020/july/2020_07_16_InsolvencyTimeBomb_V4.pdf

Lentz, K. L., & Smith, T. M. (2020, May 18). *Anti-cash hoarding provisions in reserve-based credit agreements.* Davis Graham & Stubbs. Retrieved September 17, 2020, from https://www.dgslaw.com/news-events/anti-cash-hoarding-provisions-in-reserve-based-credit-agreements

McIntyre, A., Spellacy, M., & Baraldi, D. (2020, July 29). *Banking as a force for good in navigating the COVID-driven credit crisis.* World Economic Forum. Retrieved September 17, 2020, from https://www.weforum.org/agenda/2020/07/banking-force-for-good-covid-driven-credit-crisis/

Myrskog, N. (2020). *When the covenants fall—The risk of recovery in covenant based lending.* DKCO. Retrieved September 17, 2020, from https://www.dkco-law.com/en/news/when-the-covenants-fall-the-risk-of-recovery-in-covenant-based-lending/

Network for Business Sustainability. (2012, May 8). *How sustainability can help strengthen your global supply chain.* Retrieved September 17, 2020, from https://www.nbs.net/articles/how-sustainability-can-help-strengthen-your-global-supply-chain

OECD. (2020). *OECD economic outlook, interim report March 2020.* OECD. Retrieved September 2020, from https://doi.org/10.1787/7969896b-en

Patel, D. (2020, September 3). *Trade finance guide 2020—Now launched.* Trade Finance Global. Retrieved September 17, 2020. https://www.tradefinanceglobal.com/posts/trade-finance-guide-2020-itfa-tfg/

Purchase Order Financing. (2009, May 27). *What is purchase order financing.* Retrieved September 17, 2020, from https://www.purchaseorderfinancing.com/po-finance/what-is-purchase-order-financing/#:~:text=Purchase%20order%20financing%20is%20a,because%20of%20cash%20flow%20challenges

Röck, D., Hofmann, E., & Rogers, D. (2020, April 5–8). *Determinants of transparency in supply chains: A frame to assess the influence of digital technologies on transparency.* In 29th IPSERA Conference proceedings: Procurement Innovation, Knoxville.

Rogers, D., Leuschner, R., & Choi, T. (2020). *Supply chain financing: Funding the supply chain and the organization*. World Scientific & CAPS Research.

Statista. (2020, January 17). *Average payment terms granted by companies from selected countries in Western Europe*. Retrieved September 18, 2020. https://de.statista.com/statistik/daten/studie/922547/umfrage/von-unternehmen-aus-laendern-in-westeuropa-gewaehrte-zahlungsziele/

Stolberg-Larsen, M. (2019, December 6). *Deep-tier financing: What is it and why should you care?* The Global Treasurer. Retrieved September 17, 2020, from https://www.theglobaltreasurer.com/2019/12/06/deep-tier-financing-what-is-it-and-why-should-you-care/

Taube, S. (2020, July 19). Reverse factoring: A ticking time bomb in corporate books? *Wealth Daily*. Retrieved September 17, 2020, from https://www.wealthdaily.com/articles/reverse-factoring-a-ticking-time-bomb-in-corporate-books-/96582

Taulia. (2020). *Supplier survey 2020*. Retrieved September 17, 2020, from https://466u538gkwa2slst8218cmm1-wpengine.netdna-ssl.com/wp-content/uploads/2020/04/Taulia-Supplier-Survey-2020.pdf

Templar, S., Hofmann, E., & Findlay, C. (2020). *Financing the end-to-end supply chain: A reference guide to supply chain finance* (2nd ed.). Kogan Page.

The White House. (2014, November 17). *FACT SHEET: President Obama's SupplierPay initiative expands; 21 additional companies pledge to strengthen America's small businesses*. Office of the Press Secretary. Retrieved September 17, 2020, from https://obamawhitehouse.archives.gov/the-press-office/2014/11/17/fact-sheet-president-obama-s-supplierpay-initiative-expands-21-additiona

Theodore Farris, M., II, & Hutchison, P. D. (2002). Cash-to-cash: The new supply chain management metric. *International Journal of Physical Distribution and Logistics Management, 32*(4), 288–298.

Trepte, K., Rice, J. B., & Klibi, W. (2020, May 14). *S & OP: A new frontier for supply chain resilience?* Retrieved September 17, 2020, from https://www.supplychainquarterly.com/articles/3443-sop-a-new-frontier-for-supply-chain-resilience

Tuovila, A. (2020, September 7). *Inventory carrying cost*. Investopedia. Retrieved September 17, 2020, from https://www.investopedia.com/terms/c/carryingcostofinventory.asp

U.S. Small Business Administration. (2002). *Paycheck protection program*. Retrieved September 17, 2020, from https://www.sba.gov/funding-programs/loans/coronavirus-relief-options/paycheck-protection-program#:~:text=The%20Paycheck%20Protection%20Program%20is,are%20used%20for%20eligible%20expenses

Ulbricht, J. (2020). *Why do so many supply chain finance programs fail?* Trustbills. Retrieved September 17, 2020, from https://www.trustbills.com/en/resource/insights/10/?utm_source=LinkedIn&utm_medium=link&utm_campaign=SCF

Vuealta. (2020). *5 Ways to achieve supply chain resilience*. Retrieved September 17, 2020, from https://www.vuealta.com/blog/covid-19-the-lessons-for-s-and-op/

Yan, T., Choi, T. Y., Kim, Y., & Yang, Y. (2015). A theory of the nexus supplier: A critical supplier from a network perspective. *Journal of Supply Chain Management, 51*(1), 52–66.

Chapter 8
Connecting Decision-Making to Resilience: The Importance of Decentralization and Supply Chain Orientation in a Post-COVID World

Saban Adana, Sedat Cevikparmak, Hasan Celik, Hasan Uvet, and Yavuz Idug

Abstract Global supply chains are increasingly moving toward being more prone to high-impact disruptions, which has been fairly evident with the COVID-19 pandemic. The capacity to address disruptions is essential for the survival of any organization. Coping with increasing complexity and uncertainties requires a systemic view of supply chains and rapid decision-making. This study outlines the impact of the COVID-19 pandemic on supply chains as well as provides two strategies for forming resilient supply chains in the post-pandemic environment. COVID-19 unraveled the weaknesses in decades-long JIT approaches and extended global supply chains. Moving forward, these weaknesses calls for a systemic understanding of the supply chains. Fixing and focusing on only part of a supply chain will only create other bottlenecks, therefore, necessitating a supply chain orientation approach. Furthermore, the need for urgent action in disruptions like COVID-19 calls for rapid decision-making and removing silos among firms and business functions. When crises are moving fast, so should decision-making.

S. Adana (✉)
Boler College of Business, John Carroll University, University Heights, OH, USA
e-mail: sadana@jcu.edu

S. Cevikparmak
Division of Business, DeSales University, Center Valley, PA, USA
e-mail: sedat.cevikparmak@desales.edu

H. Celik
School of Business, Robert Morris University, Moon Twp, PA, USA
e-mail: celik@rmu.edu

H. Uvet
School of Business, Georgia Gwinnett College, Lawrenceville, GA, USA
e-mail: huvet@ggc.edu

Y. Idug
G. Brint Ryan College of Business, University of North Texas, Denton, TX, USA
e-mail: yavuz.idug@unt.edu

© The Author(s), under exclusive license to Springer Nature Switzerland AG 2023
O. Khan et al. (eds.), *Supply Chain Resilience*, Springer Series in Supply Chain Management 21, https://doi.org/10.1007/978-3-031-16489-7_8

1   Introduction

The beginning of 2020 saw the advent of one of the most dramatic black swan events in supply chain history. The sudden supply shock that started in China rippled through every possible supply chain in every single industry we can think of. Elongated supply chains, trade restrictions, challenges of off-shoring, lean-based JIT approaches, and capacity constraints of critical part suppliers such as semiconductors have all together revealed the inherent weaknesses of the global supply chain quite clearly. It was not the first time that supply chains have witnessed a disruption, but with its magnitude and shock, the COVID-19 pandemic will continue to generate long-lasting lessons learned for both academicians and practitioners. With the COVID-19 pandemic, unlike other disruptions, we observed three specific shocks—demand, supply, and transportation shocks—at the same time within several supply chains. According to the Institute of Supply Management (ISM), about 94% of the Fortune 500 companies reported a supply chain disruption from COVID-19 (Lahyani, et al., 2021). According to Interos, each of those companies on average lost $184 million. Dun and Bradstreet data show that more than five million companies with tier 2 supplies were impacted by the COVID-19 pandemic. Altogether these developments are a wake-up call for supply chain management and we have to realize that with significant global economic interdependence, more serious disaster planning must become the standard, not the exception.

Over the last 20 years, researchers have underlined the importance of resilience in supply chains (Kochan & Nowicki, 2018), yet there are still numerous avenues of research that remain to unpack this complex phenomenon. The essential relationships between suppliers and buyers have witnessed significant strain and have resulted in supply and service shortages. Technology-enabled global connectivity invariably leads to highly complex supply chain networks that challenge responsiveness. Without agility, supply chains would become increasingly more vulnerable to economic, public health, technological, and other disruptive forces (Gligor et al., 2019). Along with the increased complexity and globalization, the frequency and types of disruptions have grown exponentially since the beginning of the 2000s (Christopher & Holweg, 2011; Richey, 2009). However, specifically in the last decade, the impact of these disruptions on the economy became even more disruptive with a high dependency level on globalization. The adoption of outsourcing strategies has further exacerbated the uncertainties in supply and demand (Resilinc, 2018) and has caused the loss of capabilities in the United States within critical industries, such as the semiconductor industry. The damaging effects of disruptions, such as natural disasters, transportation failures, cyberattacks, or supplier bankruptcies, can have long-lasting impacts if not addressed immediately and appropriately (Pettit et al., 2013). Whether man made or natural, a single disruptive event can impact the value of a company tremendously within a short period of time, especially when it hits the news. For instance, following the tsunami and the earthquake in Japan in 2011, which caused an extended power disruption, the value of Toyota diminished by 17% in a single day (Kachi & Takahashi, 2011). Most recently, we have observed the semiconductor chip shortage in the auto industry alone, causing a $110 billion loss globally (Forbes, 2021). The nature of dynamic and high-impact disruptive events has stimulated an increased interest in the topic of resilience in supply chains (Kochan & Nowicki, 2018; Machado et al., 2018). Extant research and anecdotal evidence suggest that companies should cultivate resilience practices in their supply chain activities to react to unanticipated disruptions (Jüttner & Maklan, 2011).

During any disruption, a resilient supply chain would react quickly and efficiently due to its capabilities and capacities. Sheffi and Rice (2005) contend that decisions, primarily the ones made before the disruption more so than during the disruption, will define resilience. Nonetheless, while it may be argued that resilience depends on both, there is little doubt that resilience must be ingrained into the supply chain structure to maintain a stable state (Christopher & Pseck, 2004). The decision-making process lies at the heart of all supply chain management activities (Manuj & Sahin, 2011; Haraguchi & Lall, 2015). Whether they are responding to an ongoing hurricane or a pandemic, such as COVID-19, organizations with appropriate and timely decision-making processes will always be one step ahead of others. Especially these types of crises require fast decision-making in a complex and uncertain environment.

The decision-making process of an organization is impacted by a multitude of factors (Davis-Sramek et al., 2015). One of the more pronounced factors, as evidenced by its impact on the agility to respond, is organizational structure (Gligor & Holcomb, 2012). The structure of an organization and the decision-making process are inextricably linked in normal and disrupting times (Treiblmaier, 2018). One organization can possess all the necessary resources, but if the managers tasked with decision-making are not involved in the process of decision-making in a centralized structure, then the disruption could create greater impacts compared with an organization with more empowered employees. Inferior decision-making could also make an organization more vulnerable to future disruptions (Cantor et al., 2014). Supply chain structure is derived from the structure of an organization (Stock et al., 2000), which is defined as "the design of the organization through which the enterprise is administered" (Chandler, 1969, p. 14). The structure is the means through which integration and interaction take place within the organization and among the members of the chain. This mechanism, depending on where it stands on the decentralization spectrum, would encourage interaction, cross-functional initiatives, information sharing, and collaboration within the organization and supply chain (Defee & Stank, 2005). In addition, the structure does not function in isolation. It starts within an organization but extends across the spectrum of multiple organizations (Chow et al., 1995). The structure has also a cultural dimension, demonstrating itself with organizational traditions, norms, procedures, and policies (McAfee et al., 2002). The literature on organizational structure can be categorized under three main constructs, namely, decentralization (centralization), formalization, and specialization. Decentralization denotes the level that the decision-making authority is given to lower echelons in an organization (Daugherty et al., 2011). Formalization refers to the extent of how many rules and processes are written down

(Jaworski & Kohli, 1993), whereas specialization is the degree of narrowness for the skill set that is required by an organization (Troy et al., 2001).

The remainder of this chapter is organized as follows. Sections 2–4 define the terms around the phenomenon of "supply chain resilience" and provides an overview of the relevant literature on supply chain orientation and decentralization in decision-making process. Section 5 outlines the frameworks between supply chain orientation, decentralization of decision-making, and supply chain resilience capabilities and provides examples of how it impacted supply chains and forced companies to adapt. Section 6 provides a more in-depth look to post-pandemic supply chains and illustrates the strategies in several company examples. Section 7 provides concluding remarks.

2 Supply Chain Orientation

Supply Chain Orientation (SCO) is described as the systemic awareness of the consequences of coordinating the flows of products, cash, services, and information within organizations and across supply chains shared by the organizations and employees (Patel et al., 2013; Davis-Sramek et al., 2015). Strategically managing the whole supply chain in the absence of a guiding philosophy such as SCO would be fairly difficult and inefficient (Esper et al., 2010). Accordingly, SCO offers the characteristics of structures to have a well-rounded picture of supply chains. In classifying the structural part of SCO, Trent (2004) provides the following four categories: human resources, organizational measurement, information technology, and organizational design. These characteristics apply within and across the supply chains. Consequently, the structures adopted by a supply chain-oriented organization necessitate trust, leadership support, and require information technology. As a result, this would lead to more information sharing, cross-functional thinking, and communication. Conversely, companies without an SCO approach may not generate similar structures and characteristics (Esper et al., 2010).

The literature categorizes SCO into two parts, namely, structural and strategic (Esper et al., 2010). The strategic part involves approaching supply chains comprehensively as opposed to focusing on individual components and searching for incorporating, blending, and synthesizing capabilities. The structural part emphasizes how the SCM philosophy is reflected in the decision-making of an organization, its coordinating mechanisms, and its formal and informal interactions (Patel et al., 2013). The organizational structure, which is influenced by the SCO of an organization, will cultivate an environment where integration, collaboration, and information sharing within the organization and across the supply chain would take place.

One of the key ways that SCO demonstrated itself during the COVID-19 crisis is to underline the necessity of a systemic view throughout the supply chain. According to a study by Resilinc Corporation (2020) immediately following the COVID-19 outbreak in China, more than 70% of the companies were still trying to identify which of their suppliers had a site in locked down parts of China around the March timeframe. Many companies talk about visibility over their supply chain but only a few were able to map their networks thoroughly before the pandemic and get an instant insight into where they stand and take appropriate action. If they had mapped their supply chain beyond their first tier, including second and third tiers, they would have reacted much faster during any disruption. Although this is a resource-intensive effort, for example, a Japanese semiconductor company allocated 100 personnel to map their network for a year, it did serve them immensely during the pandemic (Choi et al., 2020). Thus, it is critical for adaptation of this SCO philosophy, systemic view, and to increase resiliency of organizations.

3 Supply Chain Resilience

Resilience involves the ability to plan proactively for disruptions, address them without losing control over structure and function, and move to a better position before their occurrence (Ponis & Koronis, 2012). Supply chain disruptions can be defined as unexpected incidences that disturb the flow of products and services across supply chains (Kleindorfer & Saad, 2005). These disruptions can originate from natural catastrophes, such as earthquakes, or man-made disasters, such as a fire, an electrical breakdown, or a cyberattack (Wagner & Neshat, 2010). Given that SCRES is still a developing area, there are numerous definitions for it. There are two main differing views on Supply Chain Resilience (SCRES) in the literature. One view looks at SCRES as an ability to recover from unforeseen disruptive situations and to return to where they were before the disruptions (Christopher & Peck, 2004). The other view looks beyond recovery to involve the generation of additional capabilities and an improved ability to utilize new opportunities (Ponomarov, 2012).

4 Decentralization in Decision-Making

Academics and industry members have emphasized the importance of organizational structure in supply chain management and marketing over the years (Olson et al., 2005; Patel et al., 2013). The Marketing Science Institute has identified "organizational structure" as a crucial research area in its two biannual reports concentrating on the following essential question: "How do organizational structures influence business performance?" (Lee et al., 2015). An essential decision that must be made by an organization manager is the design of his or her organization. As soon as an organization hires employees and establishes rules and reporting relationships, some type of organizational structure develops. A design decision does not take place in a vacuum; it is a combination of external dynamics, its strategies to achieve organizational goals and specific choices in terms of work specialization, departmentalization, chain of command, decentralization, formalization, and span of control. In the end, the result would be the designation of responsibilities, boundaries, and coordination systems within the organization (Chaston, 1997).

The impact of the decentralization of decision-making can be illustrated in a supply chain disruption context by Nokia vs. Ericsson case (Norrman & Jansson, 2004). A thunderstorm caused a minor fire in a Philips plant on March 17, 2000. Nokia, one of Philips' customers, instantly recognized the problem and acted quickly. It also identified a second supplier and worked actively with Philips to obtain the remaining quantity of products from other locations. Because of its quick response, Nokia suffered only from minor shipping delays. For Ericsson, another Philips customer, it took approximately 4 weeks to realize the extent of the problem and not communicate the issue to their managers; thus, the company lost 400 million in sales and eventually decided to quit the phone business. The way Nokia structured its decision-making allowed it to be more responsive and ultimately gained a competitive advantage over Ericsson. The close monitoring of the critical parts and knowledge of the market for alternative suppliers with the decentralization of the organization in decision-making processes allowed Nokia to detect the problem early and facilitated the mitigation of risk.

Decentralization in decision-making processes does not automatically improve performance during and after disruptions. For the agility of organizations, decision-making is critical not only at the executive level but also is crucial at lower levels. The quality of decisions is directly linked to the abilities of employees at lower levels. Those in lower levels should be vetted and trained properly to make important decisions that must be made in times of disruption (Giannoccaro, 2018). Furthermore, local decisions can impact other functions in organizations and geographic areas, and there would be unintended consequences. Therefore, continuing information sharing is necessary to ensure that every stakeholder agrees (Davis-Sramek et al., 2015). The external conditions of an organization are significant in designating authority and power. Because, in uncertain and dynamic market conditions, the authority should be delegated to those in lower levels to respond quickly (Doll & Vonderembse, 1991). Centralization emphasizes improving efficiency, while decentralization highlights increasing agility and flexibility, which is more conducive to responding to crises (Treiblmaier, 2018).

5 Theoretical Framework for Supply Chain Resilience, Decentralization, and Supply Chain Orientation

This section will lay out the impact of COVID-19 through the lenses of the aforementioned concepts and provide relationships that could offer insights into minimizing the impact of future disruptions.

5.1   Supply Chain Orientation and Decentralization

COVID-19 has, once again, demonstrated that supply chains are system of systems. When one part is impacted, it is a matter of time to witness the ripple effect throughout the whole supply chain. In every supply chain, unless we adopt a systemic view, we will end up with the phenomenon called "bullwhip effect." Famous toilet paper crisis, meat shortages, or empty Clorox shelves at the beginning of 2020, all started with a trigger (a demand change ranging from 50 to 200%), panic buying, from the consumer side which resulted in a huge amplification at the manufacturer level. This is because each actor is doing what is rational for them by increasing demand without thinking about the systemic implications. In the end, this generates wasted resources for everyone. Conversely, when things started to settle, now no retailers were making new orders, while retailers were selling their current inventory. The macroeconomic impact of bullwhip effect showed itself in the later phases of COVID-19, where retail sales dropped 12%, whereas manufacturing sales declined 30%.

One way to minimize the impact of this is to establish supply chain orientation. In simple terms, an SCO approach views the whole supply chain as one system and considers the implications of internal integration, organizational design, and internal and external cooperation (Esper et al., 2010; Kotzab et al., 2011). This philosophy necessitates a flat, empowering, and continuous information sharing with a decentralized system. The extent of having SCO impacts several aspects not only within an organization but also in the management of relations with other organizations (Min et al., 2007). A shared vision and practice of how companies should approach their relations strategically within and outside supply chains generate faster responses and established behaviors that help to build more agile organizations (Koulikoff-Souviron & Harrison, 2008). Internal and external integration, collaboration, and information exchange within the supply chain will facilitate cross-functional and inter-organizational cooperation, the cross-pollination of ideas, and flexibility and may ultimately lead to organizational responsiveness and supply chain agility (Mentzer et al., 2008).

5.2   Decentralization and Agility

Traditional planning and scheduling processes in supply chains are unlikely to work well in these uncertain environments. For those companies that don't have the tools to support rapid replanning, rescheduling, and reconfiguring, a war room type of structure with the required empowerment, will not be able to respond effectively to disruptions. For example, COVID-19 reduced the demand for certain items but also increased demand for some such as cleaning supplies or exercise equipment forcing agility at all levels. Many companies had to align this shift to stay competitive. Auto industry, such as Ford teaming up with GE, transitioned to supplement the much-needed 60,000 ventilators. The experience of Swamp Distilling company is also a unique one. The company transitioned from whiskey to sanitizer very quickly. But the challenge was not always production. Georgia Pacific, a paper manufacturing company, started to ship directly to retailers passing distribution centers in order to eliminate certain bottleneck steps and reach customers directly. These are all successful applications of supply chain agility during the pandemic.

The impact of the COVID-19 pandemic on the global supply chain was observed more significantly locally than other disruptions. To manage fluctuating demand around the globe, companies need to act fast. Considering the highly dynamic, complex, and competitive markets and the potential for disruptions, employees need greater autonomy to respond to these challenges. Agility has been suggested as the capacity of a supply chain to quickly address variations in the industry and customer expectations (Sharp et al., 1999). Agility involves having a clear view of the whole supply chain (Christopher & Peck, 2004), which is instrumental in identifying indicators of potentially disruptive events and responding swiftly. Agility to react to disruptions depends on how organizations regulate their actions to cohesively and quickly work together in turbulent times (Gligor & Holcomb, 2012). Wieland and Marcus Wallenburg (2013) determined that communication is an influential antecedent of supply chain agility. Additionally, Scholten and Schilder (2015) argued that cooperative decision-making, sharing information and resource, and aligning incentives contribute to the capacity of a supply chain to address disruptive events. Visibility and velocity primarily comprise supply chain agility. The majority of the characteristics of agility necessitate a structure that is conducive to information sharing, empowering, and lateral coordination, which is a decentralized one.

Drucker (1992) validated that an organization should have a low degree of centralization in decision-making process to react faster and to find innovative solutions. Decentralization fosters communication and improves employee involvement and satisfaction. Because in decentralized settings, it is much easier to have 360° of communication, and empowered subject matter experts can influence decision-making as much as the top management (Burns & Stalker, 1961) and respond more efficiently to dynamic market conditions (Schminke et al., 2000). Polyviou et al. (2019) empirically verified that due to their less complex decision-making systems and smaller echelons in the hierarchy, decentralized firms can avoid and respond to disruptions more effectively. The reason why firms delegate decision-making is that lower echelons can duly evaluate and apply quickly their expertise (Inkpen & Tsang, 2005). It allows the empowered people to act without being limited by bureaucracies and provides speed, agility, and flexibility.

5.3   Decentralization and Collaboration

In the literature, collaboration is defined as cooperating with other supply chain units and sharing information and other critical resources to address disruptive events

(Jüttner & Maklan, 2011). Christopher and Peck (2004) affirmed that the sense of creating a community where companies can share information is essential in developing a collaborative environment. Mandal (2012) demonstrated that unless each employee receives the appropriate information, the collaboration will not happen effectively and efficiently. In addition, Datta and Christopher (2011) asserted that decentralized structure, monitoring, flexibility, and information sharing are the building blocks of SCRES. Christopher and Peck (2004) also highlighted the importance of communication by stating that supply chains are about the flow of information as much as the flow of goods. Therefore, the selection of a specific organizational structure will directly impact the decision-making process inside an organization and a supply chain. A decentralized organizational structure would be more conducive to communication and coordination between different entities.

5.4   Decentralization and Situational Awareness

The idea of situational awareness starts with mapping out the vulnerabilities of supply chains. The resulting critical elements detect potential negative events through early warning systems and interpret them while having plans in place for the continuity of operations (Datta & Christopher, 2011). Through the help of these actions, avoiding, containing, and controlling risks would be possible by identifying them in the system (Stecke & Kumar, 2009). Nevertheless, the common denominators for all these practices are information exchange among supply chain members, coordination, and initiative-taking approaches in predicting disruptive events (Vargo & Seville, 2011). Basically, if the detection of a supply chain disruption is done early and communicated to the right people, then, the supply chain would suffer much fewer negative effects (Craighead et al., 2007).

In an organizational setting, the greater the decentralization, the greater the information sharing because organizations that welcome participation cultivate alertness, awareness, and involvement (Germain, 1996). Facilitating risk awareness through seamless communication and information sharing before a potential disruption mitigates the vulnerability and the damage absorbed (Wieland & Marcus Wallenburg, 2013). Employees must be proactive and take the initiative to identify and monitor potential events. Therefore, in a decentralized structure, the furthest nodes will be warned by a potential disruption early, which will translate into swiftness and agility within the supply chain.

5.5   Agility and Supply Chain Resilience

Bullwhip effect was not the only problem supply chains faced during COVID-19. The problems on the ground required agility to react. First, companies needed to increase their scale agility, to keep up with the surging demand. Second, they needed to increase asset utility, by deploying unused or underused resources. Lastly, some companies have shown scope agility, in which they transformed their production line to produce new types of products (Sheffi, 2021). For example, Unilever was able to ramp up its sanitizer product with an incredible ratio, 600 times, by repurposing some factories to produce sanitizer rather than low-demand items like ice cream. Economic shutdowns in response to the COVID-19 pandemic restricted the movement of people and goods throughout the world. Regulatory changes impacted every mode of transportation. The volume of passenger flights dramatically declined, which carry 50% of air cargo, which forced the airline companies to reconfigure the airplanes to be all-cargo airplanes.

Supply chain agility is described as a higher-order dynamic capability that would facilitate resource configuration and enable sensing and leveraging of opportunities and threats (Li et al., 2009). Lee (2004) confirmed that the capacity to recover quickly from disruptions improves service and delivery performances. As mentioned earlier, visibility and speed comprise the core of the agility construct. Supply chain visibility is defined as the knowledge of the environment and the state of the processes and operations (Pettit et al., 2013). Kleindorfer and Saad (2005) contended that to execute a risk management process, possessing supply chain-wide visibility is critical. A company with a high degree of visibility over its supply chain has more control over supply operations and interactions (Swift et al., 2019). As long as decision makers can detect potential indicators for disruptions, they can come up with alternative plans and scenarios that can facilitate the recovery process. Soni et al. (2014) also identified 14 enablers for resilience, among which agility ranks the highest followed by collaboration, visibility, and risk management culture. In addition, Blackhurst et al. (2011) highlighted that in their study, quickly redesigning supply chains to minimize the effect of disruptions was noted by four out of seven companies.

5.6   Collaboration and Supply Chain Resilience

Collaboration involves divergent entities in supply chains undertaking collaborative actions together, such as joint creating knowledge, sharing resources and information, aligning objectives and incentives, and synchronizing decisions (Cao & Zhang, 2010; Uvet et al., 2021). Furthermore, collaboration is an approach where several units work in an integrated manner to achieve common objectives. Supply chain visibility, through exchanging information and communication, generates the required transparency to sense and interpret disruptions in supply chains. Coordinating procedures, processes, and operations of individual firms in a concerted way is essential to fully leverage the benefits of collaboration. Specifically, during a disruption, unless all companies in supply chains cooperate and respond harmoniously, resilience will not develop (Jüttner & Maklan, 2011). As managers at lower levels take ownership of the processes, managers get involved in collaboration within and outside their organization (Peck, 2005; Sheffi & Rice, 2005). These dependencies show that supply chain collaboration is a requirement for SCRES.

5.7   *Situational Awareness and Supply Chain Resilience*

Situational awareness requires a deep comprehension of weaknesses in supply chains, appropriate planning, and the capacity to recognize potential disruptions by timely identifying risks through detection systems (Sáenz & Revilla, 2014). This step is critical in having the time necessary to (re)configure the resources at hand. Hence, organizations should execute the contingency plan or the business continuity plan in due time and effectively respond to a disruption when there is an anticipation of potential disruption. Closs and McGarrell (2004) view resilient supply chains as proactive, that is, anticipating and establishing planned steps to prevent and respond to disruptions. Ambulkar et al. (2015) measured SCRES on the basis of four measurement items, one of which was situational awareness. In the same vein, Bode et al. (2011) argue that organizations emphasize that disruption orientation management is more resilient because it generates "awareness and seriousness" toward disruptions. In the comprehensive literature review of SCRES by Ali et al. (2017), anticipation comes out to be fifth in the list, which is conceptually and empirically linked to resilience outcomes in 14 papers.

COVID-19 has brought the situational awareness capability to the forefront. While it has several dimensions, mapping the supply chain is by far the most critical one. Firms generally evaluate their supply chain vulnerabilities solely based on cost, concentrating on the most expensive parts to which they pay the largest share of spending. However, a cost-only focus does not capture all the vulnerabilities in the supply chain. Network analysis can unravel some of the critical dependencies present within supply chains. According to a study by McKinsey, 75% of Dell's 20 most connected suppliers are common with Lenovo, and 70% of Lenovo's 20 most connected suppliers are common with Dell. Foxconn, IBM, and Microsoft are suppliers to both companies and are highly connected in both networks. If there is a disruption, like COVID-19, it will not only affect Dell and Lenovo's current operations but also limit their ability to find alternative suppliers. Companies need to execute a deeper network analysis and monitor those tiers regularly to sense potential future disruptions.

6   Post-COVID Supply Chains

The COVID-19 pandemic became a stress test that shocked many organizations. Companies have had to deal with sharp upturns and declines in demand, manufacturing downtime, and supply and transport delays. As the coronavirus swept around the world, supply chains still face unprecedented stress and attention. Situational awareness became even more significant due to the large-scale impact of COVID-19 on all supply chains and the desire to avoid similar disruptions in the future by anticipating them. This "pre-warning" will be even more crucial in aligning the resources and capabilities of organizations. As companies have experienced devastating impacts on their supply chain, they have immediately shifted their attention and focus to sensing disruption capability. If companies do not develop a habit of scanning the horizon, then being ready when a disruption hits will be fairly difficult for them. During the COVID-19 pandemic, this scanning included assessment of infection risks for certain suppliers in addition to financial status, layoffs, country shutdowns, etc. This can become quite challenging since an average company has hundreds or thousands of suppliers. The key to overcoming this challenge is to filter data that is important and prioritize those for risk mitigation.

Many scholars and practitioners point to the need for more flexibility and having more inventory for supply and demand shocks. This is true but there are other strategies moving forward. Having experienced the impact, many supply chains will diversify their sourcing, not relying on one geography or country. For example, Wistron Corp., one of Apple's manufacturing partners, announcing half of its capacity could reside outside China within a year. Foxconn is planning to move some operations to India and Vietnam. We will probably see creative designs in product developments, eliminating certain "problematic" materials in the first place. We have seen this innovative way of producing alternative raw materials from face masks producing companies. Another dimension of the impact of the pandemic is that it facilitated the increase in e-commerce whether it is electronics or grocery industries. This change will put even more strain on the current last-mile delivery challenges for the firms and require working collaboratively with different stakeholders in order to align brick and mortar and online channels.

For decades, companies have not placed the necessary emphasis on their employees and the cultural dimension of resilience is generally overlooked due to efficiency concerns. However, a common denominator in the successful companies that were able to respond and recover from the COVID-19 disruption is their investment in their employees. More specifically, those companies create an environment where every employee is valued, they establish a culture for conditioning to disruptions and cultivate distributive power in decision-making. These attributes create a commitment on the side of the employee and take ownership of the disruptions they encounter. Accordingly, supply chain executives should take care of their people, improve working conditions and develop an empowering culture. Otherwise, the result is quite unforgiving, dramatically reducing your capacity.

Several companies adopted these strategies quickly and minimized the impact of the disruption. New Balance, an athletic apparel manufacturer, highlights that practitioners were required to make rapid decisions on mostly imperfect data during the pandemic. Their investment in digitization and empowerment throughout the company has enabled them to tackle the challenge and handle the pandemic. Another example is 3M, which was able to rapidly adapt and provide the much-needed pandemic gear by breaking down silos and inclusive emergency planning. The company could quickly adapt its production line manufacturing hand sanitizer in

72 h because it merged supply chain and operations functions. Caterpillar utilized alternative sources and transportation modes (air freight), shifted orders to other distribution centers, and was able to mitigate the impact of the disruption by acting quickly and securing capacity (Sheffi, 2020).

In line with this idea of decentralization, leading companies like Johnson and Johnson appoint "Tiger teams" to sense, assess and act quickly on the disruption as it would be too late to go through up the chain to make a decision. These teams both collect data and take appropriate action (Sheffi, 2020). For example, the chief procurement and supply chain officer of Flex explains that, through these teams, they were able to understand the severity of the situation, and rather than going through the normal procurement channel, the tiger team immediately recommended securing PPE for 2 months, which was essential to continue their operations (Sheffi, 2020).

7 Conclusion

Decades-long efficiency practices have created low-cost products and services for global supply chains but created inherent interdependencies that need to be carefully leveraged. As supply chains get more global and complex due to the competitive nature of markets, they become much more susceptible to several types of disruptions. The scale and the results of contemporary disruptions, such as COVID-19, demonstrate that if an organization fails in mapping out its weaknesses and generating mitigation strategies, it could result in losing competitiveness and even impact its survival. At the heart of all these interdependencies lies decision-making. Disruptions will not wait for organizations to make a decision; therefore, speed is imperative in adapting and reconfiguring their resources. To enhance SCRES, managers must understand the impact of the decentralization of decision-making on the resilience of supply chains as shown empirically in this study.

Furthermore, supply chain managers should appreciate the philosophy of viewing a supply chain holistically as a system and its positive impact on increasing organizational capabilities as the competition is no more among the companies but rather than within supply chains. Adopting SCO will have to accompany decentralizing decision-making to realize higher resilience. Large companies, in particular, should adopt simpler and more agile internal structures by delegating authority and enabling their personnel with expertise to take charge despite their status in the reporting design during disruptions. Understanding how the origin of the decision-making authority inside an organization would contribute to performance will allow managers to make more informed decisions.

Post-pandemic supply chain issues will continue to be complex and place us in the realm of greater uncertainty and will require holistic solutions. Moving forward, many companies will try to remediate only single points in their supply chains, or try to optimize locally, which will work against the systemic view of the supply chain and simply create other bottlenecks and lead to bullwhip effect. On the other hand, companies, which adopt the supply chain orientation perspective will optimize the whole chain and will be much robust for the next "black swan" event.

References

Ali, A., Mahfouz, A., & Arisha, A. (2017). Analyzing supply chain resilience: Integrating the constructs in a concept mapping framework via a systematic literature review. *Supply Chain Management: An International Journal, 22*(1), 16–39.

Ambulkar, S., Blackhurst, J., & Grawe, S. (2015). Firm's resilience to supply chain disruptions: Scale development and empirical examination. *Journal of Operations Management, 33,* 111–122.

Blackhurst, J., Dunn, K. S., & Craighead, C. W. (2011). An empirically derived framework of global supply resiliency. *Journal of Business Logistics, 32*(4), 374–391.

Bode, C., Wagner, S. M., Petersen, K. J., & Ellram, L. M. (2011). Understanding responses to supply chain disruptions: Insights from information processing and resource dependence perspectives. *Academy of Management Journal, 54*(4), 833–856.

Burns, T., & Stalker, G. M. (1961). Mechanistic and organic systems. *Classics of organizational theory*, 209–214.

Cantor, D. E., Blackhurst, J., Pan, M., & Crum, M. (2014). Examining the role of stakeholder pressure and knowledge management on supply chain risk and demand responsiveness. *The International Journal of Logistics Management., 25*(1), 202.

Cao, M., & Zhang, Q. (2010). Supply chain collaborative advantage: An Organization's Perspective. *International Journal of Production Economics, 128*(1), 358–367.

Chandler, A. D., Jr. (1969). *Strategy and structure: Chapters in the history of the American industrial enterprise* (Vol. 120). MIT Press.

Chaston, I. (1997). Small firm performance; Assessing the interaction between entrepreneurial style and organizational structure. *European Journal of Marketing, 31*(11-12), 814–842.

Choi, T. Y., Rogers, D., & Vakil, B. (2020). Coronavirus is a wake-up call for supply chain management. *Harvard Business Review, 27,* 364–398.

Chow, G., Heaver, T. D., & Henriksson, L. E. (1995). Strategy, structure and performance: A framework for logistics research. *Logistics and Transportation Review, 31*(4), 285.

Christopher, M., & Holweg, M. (2011). Supply chain 2.0: Managing supply chains in the era of turbulence. *International Journal of Physical Distribution & Logistics Management, 41*(1), 63–82.

Christopher, M., & Peck, H. (2004). Building the resilient supply chain. *The International Journal of Logistics Management, 15*(2), 1–14.

Closs, D. J., & McGarrell, E. F. (2004). *Enhancing security throughout the supply chain* (pp. 10–12). IBM Center for the Business of Government.

Craighead, C. W., Blackhurst, J., Rungtusanatham, M. J., & Handfield, R. B. (2007). The severity of supply chain disruptions: Design characteristics and mitigation capabilities. *Decision Sciences, 38*(1), 131–156.

Datta, P. P., & Christopher, M. G. (2011). Information sharing and coordination mechanisms for managing uncertainty in supply chains: A simulation study. *International Journal of Production Research, 49*(3), 765–803.

Daugherty, P. J., Chen, H., & Ferrin, B. G. (2011). Organizational structure and logistics service innovation. *The International Journal of Logistics Management, 22*(1), 26–51.

Davis-Sramek, B., Germain, R., & Krotov, K. (2015). Examining the process R&D investment–performance chain in supply chain operations: The effect of centralization. *International Journal of Production Economics, 167,* 246–256.

Defee, C. C., & Stank, T. P. (2005). Applying the strategy-structure-performance paradigm to the supply chain environment. *The International Journal of Logistics Management.*

Doll, W. J., & Vonderembse, M. A. (1991). The evolution of manufacturing systems: towards the post-industrial enterprise. *Omega, 19*(5), 401–411.

Drucker, P. F. (1992). Organizations. *Harvard business review, 20*(7), 281–293.

Esper, T. L., Clifford Defee, C., & Mentzer, J. T. (2010). A framework of supply chain orientation. *The International Journal of Logistics Management, 21*(2), 161–179.

Forbes. (2021). *America needs to build our own chip plants for sake of auto industry.* Retrieved June 1, 2021, from https://www.forbes.com/sites/dalebuss/2021/05/31/america-needs-to-build-our-own-chip-plants-for-sake-of-auto-industry/?sh=3fa0c5d56802

Germain, R. (1996). The role of context and structure in radical and incremental logistics innovation adoption. *Journal of Business Research, 35*(2), 117–127.

Giannoccaro, I. (2018). Centralized vs. decentralized supply chains: The importance of decision maker's cognitive ability and resistance to change. *Industrial Marketing Management, 73*, 59–69.

Gligor, D. M., & Holcomb, M. C. (2012). Understanding the role of logistics capabilities in achieving supply chain agility: A systematic literature review. *Supply Chain Management: An International Journal, 17*(4), 438–453.

Gligor, D., Gligor, N., Holcomb, M., & Bozkurt, S. (2019). Distinguishing between the concepts of supply chain agility and resilience: A multidisciplinary literature review. *The International Journal of Logistics Management, 30*(2), 467–487.

Haraguchi, M., & Lall, U. (2015). Flood risks and impacts: A case study of Thailand's floods in 2011 and research questions for supply chain decision making. *International Journal of Disaster Risk Reduction, 14*, 256–272.

Inkpen, A. C., & Tsang, E. W. (2005). Social capital, networks, and knowledge transfer. *Academy of Management Review, 30*(1), 146–165.

Jaworski, B. J., & Kohli, A. K. (1993). Market orientation: Antecedents and consequences. *Journal of Marketing, 57*(3), 53–70.

Jüttner, U., & Maklan, S. (2011). Supply chain resilience in the global financial crisis: An empirical study. *Supply Chain Management: An International Journal, 16*(4), 246–259.

Kachi, H., & Takahashi, Y. (2011). Plant closures imperil global supplies. *The Wall Street Journal, March 14.*

Kleindorfer, P. R., & Saad, G. H. (2005). Managing disruption risks in supply chains. *Production and Operations Management, 14*(1), 53–68.

Kochan, C. G., & Nowicki, D. R. (2018). Supply chain resilience: A systematic literature review and typological framework. *International Journal of Physical Distribution and Logistics Management, 48*(8), 842–865.

Kotzab, H., Teller, C., Grant, D. B., & Sparks, L. (2011). Antecedents for the adoption and execution of supply chain management. *Supply Chain Management: An International Journal, 16*(4), 231–245.

Koulikoff-Souviron, M., & Harrison, A. (2008). Interdependent supply relationships as institutions: The role of HR practices. *International Journal of Operations and Production Management, 28*(5), 412.

Lahyani, R., AlSaad, F., Merdad, L., & Alzamel, M. (2021). Supply chain resilience vs. COVID-19 disruptions during the second wave. *Procedia Cirp, 103*, 42–48.

Lee, H. (2004). The triple-A supply chain. *Harvard Business Review, 82*, 102–112.

Lee, J. Y., Kozlenkova, I. V., & Palmatier, R. W. (2015). Structural marketing: Using organizational structure to achieve marketing objectives. *Journal of the Academy of Marketing Science, 43*(1), 73–99.

Li, X., Goldsby, T. J., & Holsapple, C. W. (2009). Supply chain agility: Scale development. *The International Journal of Logistics Management, 20*(3), 408–424.

Machado, S. M., Paiva, E. L., & da Silva, E. M. (2018). Counterfeiting: Addressing mitigation and resilience in supply chains. *International Journal of Physical Distribution and Logistics Management, 48*(2), 139–163.

Mandal, S. (2012). An empirical investigation into supply chain resilience. *IUP Journal of Supply Chain Management, 9*(4), 46.

Manuj, I., & Sahin, F. (2011). Emerald Article: A model of supply chain and supply chain decision-making complexity. *International Journal of Physical Distribution and Logistics Management, 41*(5), 511–549.

McAfee, R. B., Glassman, M., & Honeycutt, E. D., Jr. (2002). The effects of culture and human resource management policies on supply chain management strategy. *Journal of Business Logistics, 23*(1), 1–18.

Mentzer, J. T., Stank, T. P., & Esper, T. L. (2008). Supply chain management and its relationship to logistics, marketing, production, and operations management. *Journal of Business Logistics, 29*(1), 31–46.

Min, S., Mentzer, J. T., & Ladd, R. T. (2007). A market orientation in supply chain management. *Journal of the Academy of Marketing Science, 35*(4), 507–522.

Norrman, A., & Jansson, U. (2004). Ericsson's proactive supply chain risk management approach after a serious sub-supplier accident. *International Journal of Physical Distribution and Logistics Management., 5*, 434–450.

Olson, E. M., Slater, S. F., & Hult, G. T. M. (2005). The performance implications of fit among business strategy, marketing organization structure, and strategic behavior. *Journal of Marketing, 69*(3), 49–65.

Patel, P. C., Azadegan, A., & Ellram, L. M. (2013). The effects of strategic and structural supply chain orientation on operational and customer-focused performance. *Decision Sciences, 44*(4), 713–753.

Peck, H. (2005). Drivers of supply chain vulnerability: An integrated framework. *International Journal of Physical Distribution and Logistics Management, 35*(4), 210–232.

Pettit, T. J., Croxton, K. L., & Fiksel, J. (2013). Ensuring supply chain resilience: Development and implementation of an assessment tool. *Journal of Business Logistics, 34*(1), 46–76.

Polyviou, M., Croxton, K. L., & Knemeyer, A. M. (2019). Resilience of medium-sized firms to supply chain disruptions: The role of internal social capital. *International Journal of Operations and Production Management, 40*(1), 68–91.

Ponis, S. T., & Koronis, E. (2012). Supply chain resilience: Definition of the concept and its formative elements. *Journal of Applied Business Research, 28*(5), 921.

Ponomarov, S. (2012). *Antecedents and consequences of supply chain resilience: a dynamic capabilities perspective.*

Resilinc. (2018). *Resilinc study: 32% of the S&P 500 impacted in 2017.* Retrieved August 15, 2019, from https://www.resilinc.com/news/resilinc-study-32-sp-500-impacted-2017/

Resilinc Corporation. (2020). Geopolitics, trade wars, and pandemic – analyzing the supply chain impact. https://www.resilinc.com/?webinar5virtual-panel-geopolitics-trade-warsand-the-pandemicanalyzing-the-supply-chain-impact. Accessed 10 Dec 2020.

Richey, R. G. (2009). The supply chain crisis and disaster pyramid: A Theoretical framework for understanding preparedness and recovery. *International Journal of Physical Distribution and Logistics Management, 39*(7), 619–628.

Sáenz, M. J., & Revilla, E. (2014). Creating more resilient supply chains. *MIT Sloan Management Review, 55*(4), 22–24.

Schminke, M., Ambrose, M. L., & Cropanzano, R. S. (2000). The effect of organizational structure on perceptions of procedural fairness. *Journal of Applied Psychology, 85*(2), 294.

Scholten, K., & Schilder, S. (2015). The role of collaboration in supply chain resilience. *Supply Chain Management: An International Journal, 20*(4), 471–484.

Sharp, J. M., Irani, Z., & Desai, S. (1999). Working towards agile manufacturing in the UK industry. *International Journal of Production Economics, 62*(1/2), 155–169.

Sheffi, Y. (2020). *The new (Ab) normal: Reshaping business and supply chain strategy beyond Covid-19*. MIT CTL Media.

Sheffi, Y. (2021). What everyone gets wrong about the never-ending COVID-19 supply chain crisis. *MIT Sloan Management Review, 63*(1), 1–5.

Sheffi, Y., & Rice, J. B., Jr. (2005). A supply chain view of the resilient enterprise. *MIT Sloan Management Review, 47*(1), 41.

Soni, U., Jain, V., & Kumar, S. (2014). Measuring supply chain resilience using a deterministic modeling approach. *Computers and Industrial Engineering, 74*, 11–25.

Stecke, K. E., & Kumar, S. (2009). Sources of supply chain disruptions, factors that breed vulnerability, and mitigating strategies. *Journal of Marketing Channels, 16*(3), 193–226.

Stock, G. N., Greis, N. P., & Kasarda, J. D. (2000). Enterprise logistics and supply chain structure: The role of fit. *Journal of Operations Management, 18*(5), 531–547.

Swift, C., Guide, V. D. R., Jr., & Muthulingam, S. (2019). Does supply chain visibility affect operating performance? Evidence from conflict minerals disclosures. *Journal of Operations Management, 65*(5), 406–429.

Treiblmaier, H. (2018). Optimal levels of decentralization for resilient supply chains. *The International Journal of Logistics Management, 29*(1), 435–455.

Trent, R. J. (2004). What everyone needs to know about SCM. *Supply Chain Management Review, 8*(2), 52–59.

Troy, L. C., Szymanski, D. M., & Varadarajan, P. R. (2001). Generating new product ideas: An initial investigation of the role of market information and organizational characteristics. *Journal of the Academy of Marketing Science, 29*(1), 89–101.

Uvet, H., Celik, H., Cevikparmak, S., & Adana, S. (2021). Supply chain collaboration in performance-based contracting: An Empirical study. *International Journal of Productivity and Performance Management, 70*(4), 769–788.

Vargo, J., & Seville, E. (2011). Crisis strategic planning for SMEs: Finding the silver lining. *International Journal of Production Research, 49*(18), 5619–5635.

Wagner, S. M., & Neshat, N. (2010). Assessing the vulnerability of supply chains using graph theory. *International Journal of Production Economics, 126*(1), 121–129.

Wieland, A., & Marcus Wallenburg, C. (2013). The influence of relational competencies on supply chain resilience: A relational view. *International Journal of Physical Distribution and Logistics Management, 43*(4), 300–320.

Chapter 9
Supplier Risk Tower: The Vigilant Eye on Supply Chains

Heiko Wöhner, Florian Schupp, Max Arnold, Barno Kholikova, and Andreas Schick

Abstract The disruptions in international supply chains caused by the COVID-19 pandemic highlight the importance of considering risk in supply chain management. Using an action research approach, we examine supply chain risk management at a tier-1 automotive supplier. We focus on the inbound supply risk of this supplier and introduce the new Supplier Risk Tower risk assessment. The Supplier Risk Tower combines vulnerability indices specific to the supply chain, supplier feedback on the current risk situation, and impact assessment from the tier-1's perspective. What is novel about this approach is that risk is calculated as an absolute number which provides guidance, especially for rare but severe disruptions. This approach also expands the understanding of lean management regarding the raison d'être of buffer stocks in supply chains. Because risks materialize.

1 Introduction

The COVID-19 pandemic has not only caused significant worldwide health issues for humans, but it has also severely impacted the global supply chains by demand fluctuations and supply interruptions (Flynn et al., 2021; Donaldson, 2020; Miroudot, 2020). In today's supply chains which are complex networks that rely

H. Wöhner (✉) · M. Arnold
Schaeffler Automotive Buehl GmbH & Co. KG, Bühl, Germany
e-mail: heiko.woehner@schaeffler.com; max.arnold@schaeffler.com

F. Schupp
Schaeffler Automotive Buehl GmbH & Co. KG, Bühl, Germany

Jacobs University Bremen, Bremen, Germany
e-mail: F.Schupp@jacobs-university.de

B. Kholikova
Jacobs University Bremen, Bremen, Germany

A. Schick
Schaeffler AG, Herzogenaurach, Germany
e-mail: andreas.schick@schaeffler.com

© The Author(s), under exclusive license to Springer Nature Switzerland AG 2023
O. Khan et al. (eds.), *Supply Chain Resilience*, Springer Series in Supply Chain Management 21, https://doi.org/10.1007/978-3-031-16489-7_9

on effective, on-time, and smooth flows of information and material (Khojasteh, 2018; Ivanov, 2020), managing risk has become a crucial challenge for supply chain managers (Daultani et al., 2015) and purchasing (Accenture, 2020). This is especially applicable to automotive manufacturing networks where buyer–seller relations are multifaceted and interconnected to a web of multitier suppliers (Fortune, 2020). Risks and uncertainties frequently interrupt the operational efficiency of the supply chain and hence adversely impact a firm's profits (Kumar et al., 2010). Even before the COVID-19 pandemic, organizations considered business interruptions and supply chain disruptions to be the most important risk factor that companies have to face in the year 2020 (AGCS, 2019). Research provided supply chain risk management approaches and tools to manage risks before and during their occurrence (Tang, 2006; Thun & Hoenig, 2011; Ritchie & Brindley, 2007). However, there still is a lack of investment into risk management and business continuity planning in the industry (Zsidisin & Ritchie, 2009)—despite the intensified exposure to risk (Snyder et al., 2016; Heckmann, 2016) and the consequently enhanced likelihood of disruption supply chains in today's global networks (Behnezhad et al., 2013). Focusing on purchasing and supplier selection particularly, risk management is either avoided or practiced to a limited extent and remains under-investigated until today (Zsidisin & Ritchie, 2009). The example of the COVID-19 pandemic highlights the importance of supply chain risk management as a mean to assess, mitigate, and handle supply chain risks, and provides the chance to learn from the insufficient application in the past for more robust and at the same time more agile supply chains in the future.

Investigating the weaknesses and improvements of supply chain risk management application in practice, this chapter focuses on automotive supply chains from a tier-1 supplier perspective. Further, we concentrate on the supply side of the tier-1 supplier, because the systems that the tier-1 supplier provides to the car producers (OEMs) on short notice call-offs typically require many components and parts from a broad and global supplier base. Therefore, this part of the automotive network is rather vulnerable to supply chain disruptions. One could argue that the emergence of such a destructive health crisis as the COVID-19 pandemic could not be subject to identification before its occurrence (FCG, 2020), but even after risk materialization, risk mitigation measures, if taken timely, could prevent or limit severe consequences (KPMG, 2020). Therefore, we focus on the bridge between risk assessment and risk mitigation for rare-but-severe events such as the COVID-19 pandemic.

Manufacturing companies have to monitor their inbound supply chains in order to ensure smooth supply inflow and to avoid production stoppage. However, when looking for supply chain risk assessment tools, literature review reveals a significant gap in practicable and easy-to-implement solutions: data mining relies on repetitive operations and therefore cannot contribute to mitigation of rare-but-severe risks (Zsidisin & Ritchie, 2009), Failure Mode and Effect Analysis (Wehbe & Hamzeh, 2013) and simulations (Zsidisin & Henke, 2019) address expected risk but do not provide guidance for unexpected risks that have materialized. Therefore, the target of this paper is to provide answers to the question: How to measure inbound supply chain risk during a rare-but-severe disruption in practice? More specifically, the problem to be examined will be how a manufacturing company in a complex supply chain environment can assess the risk of its suppliers during a risk situation in order to focus risk mitigation activities on the most critical cases.

In this chapter, we build on fundamentals of supply chain risk management including definitions of supply chain risks, risk assessment processes, and mitigation strategies. We follow an action research approach that offers insights into the measurement of inbound supply risks during the COVID-19 pandemic. A tier-1 automotive manufacturer established a new risk assessment framework, called the Supplier Risk Tower. We summarize the lessons learned from of the case study and present conclusions for supply chain risk management.

2   Supply Chain Risk Management

Risks materialize. In 2008, the Global Financial Crisis arose out of speculations with subprime mortgages in the United States and caused insolvencies of banks and companies around the globe. The fall in demand, reduced inventories, and lengthened payment to suppliers spread through supply chains, affecting countless numbers of suppliers throughout the world (Chauffour & Farole, 2009). Major consequences of the financial crisis in global supply chains were primarily in three areas: financing problems, logistical problems, and cost increase (Pisani-Ferry & Santos, 2009). In 2010, the eruption of the volcano Eyjafjallajökull Island led the governments on both sides of the Atlantic to suspend flight traffic in that area with impact on transport networks between Europe and North America. The major "express" logistics and distribution companies such as TNT, FedEx, and DHL were profoundly affected (Jones & Mendoza, 2011). Switching to land-based trucking services across Europe and sea-based deliveries for intercontinental shipments increased the waiting times and thus disrupted supply chains. In 2011, Earthquakes and Tsunamis halted the car production in Japan of Mazda, Nissan, and Mitsubishi (Mojonnier, 2011) with serious impacts on global automakers such as Ford, Chrysler, Volkswagen, BMW, Toyota, and GM that depend on Japanese paint color (Schmitt, 2011). The critical component part shortages shut down operations at GM, Ford, and Chrysler plants in the United States subsequently (Bunkley, 2011). In 2015, an explosion of hazardous chemicals at the port of Tianjin in China killed 173 people and led to a massive destruction of nearby warehouses, buildings, and stored goods. As a result, production facilities of companies like Toyota, John Deere, and GlaxoSmithKline had to suspend operations and shipments to the port were seriously disrupted. According to estimations, the economic damage that was caused by this event amounts to $1.2 billion (Fu & Yan, 2016; Avittathur & Ghosh, 2020). These and further local, regional and global disasters that have happened during the last years have in common that the occurrence of the event at that point of time was unexpected by most of us, but the impact was so severe that many were affected, including a contagion effect to other regions than the primary risk materialization (Miroudot, 2020). While one could accept the missing anticipation and preparation for individuals, managers should be expected to include rare-but-severe risks in their business strategies (Flynn et al., 2021). However, the presented examples reveal a missing preparedness in today's supply and distribution networks. Estimating the future as an extrapolation of history, managers might find themselves in the same situation as Edward Smith, the first and only captain of the Titanic who described his "experiences in nearly 40 years at sea, uneventful" and added "I never saw a wreck and have never been wrecked, nor was I ever threatened to disaster of any sort" (Heckmann, 2016). But sometimes rare-but-severe risks materialize.

The consequences of disruptions are often severe because supply chains comprise numerous companies on different levels of the value creation. Automotive supply chains represent complex, multitier structures of supplier relations from the car manufacturer (OEM) over tier-1 systems suppliers, tier-2 components suppliers to tier-n raw material suppliers (Slack et al., 2009). The number of tier-1 suppliers, delivering to a car manufacturer, can range from 1500 to 4500 (Unger, n.d.) with up to 465 trillion of possible configurations per model of a single passenger car (Scavarda et al., 2008). To manage this variance of configurations, automotive supply chains are typically nested and determined regarding the set-up of companies in the supply chain. The high flexibility on the product level can only be realized by a low flexibility in the supply chain set-up. This dependency between partners in the supply chain also results from high-quality standards in the automotive business that requires each supplier to prove its quality capability to the customer (Merkel, 2011).

Another characteristic of an automotive supply chain is the strive for efficiency and cost reduction (Cagliano et al., 2004). Lean manufacturing principles, which originate from the Toyota Production System, target at eliminating major sources of waste and are widely used by automotive companies (Abdulmalek & Rajgopal, 2007). Examples of lean principles include Just-in-Time or Just-in-Sequence, which both allow companies to synchronize supply with production demand in an efficient manner. On the downside, this philosophy of avoiding any redundancy in the supply chain, such as safety stocks, comes with a price. Studies have shown that companies are more vulnerable to supply chain disruptions, when lean practices are applied (Snyder et al., 2016; Heckmann, 2016; Ivanov & Dolgui, 2020). To increase supply chain resilience, suggested methods therefore include implementing a certain level of redundancies and to deploy supply chain risk management (Park et al., 2016; Tomlin, 2006; Zsidisin & Wagner, 2010; Miroudot, 2020).

The understanding of supply chain risk management (SCRM) builds on understanding the terms of *supply chain* and *risk*. First, mentioned by Oliver and Weber (1982), supply chain was used to describe "all activities associated with the flow and transformation of goods from raw materials to end users." According to Ganeshan and Harrison (1995), a supply chain is a network of facilities and distribution options that performs the function of procurement of materials, transformation of these materials into intermediate and finished products, and the distribution of these finished products to customers. In contrast to the term "chance" that can either refer to a statistical likelihood of favorable or unfavorable event, the term "risk" has got a negative connotation. The Oxford English Dictionary defines risk as "a chance of bad consequences, loss or exposure to mischance." In supply chain context, "risk is the chance, in quantitative terms, of a defined hazard occurring"

(Norrman & Lindroth, 2004). Thus, the term *supply chain risk* describes "the potential occurrence of an incident or failure to seize opportunities with inbound supply in which its outcomes result in a financial loss for the purchasing firm" (Zsidisin & Ritchie, 2009). The purpose of SCRM is to predict events causing disruptions and to foster flexibility against unwanted threats. SCRM focuses on coordination or collaboration among supply chain partners to ensure profitability and continuity (Tang, 2006), and to identify and reduce risk along the supply chain (Thun & Hoenig, 2011). Therefore, it is required to quantify the risk (Heckmann et al., 2015). While some determinations include several dimensions, e.g., the occurrence, the severity, and the likelihood of detection of a risk event (Ritchie & Brindley, 2007), a basic assessment for a quantitative definition of supply chain risk is the product of probability and impact (Mitchell, 1995).

$$Risk = Probability \times Impact$$

Supply chain risk management consists of different components from risk identification to risk assessment, risk monitoring, and mitigation activities to organizational learning (Zsidisin & Ritchie, 2009). For the question at hand, risk identification and risk assessment are the most relevant components.

First, risk identification entails the process of determining risks that could prevent a planned execution or program from achieving its objectives. Risks are typically clustered according to focus of the SCRM activities. Categorization into *internal* and *external* risks differentiates whether uncertainties arise from sources inside the supply chain such as machine breakdowns, forecast error, and malfunction of information technology and communication systems, or from external sources such as transportation delays due to cross border issues or natural disasters (Waters, 2007). The categorization can include the affected part of the supply chain: *supply risks, demand risks*, and *process risks* (Khojasteh, 2018) or the nature of the risk: *supply cost, commitment, continuity*, and *rare-but-severe risks* (Zsidisin & Henke, 2019). Because this paper focuses on activities during a risk materialization, i.e., when an unfavorable event has taken place or is taking place, we focus on external rare-but-severe supply risks. Such *macro risks* like natural disasters, terrorist attacks, financial crises or pandemics are rare but have tremendous influence on international supply chains in case of materialization. As an example, the "Great East Japan Earthquake" in 2011 led to a halt in production in northeastern Japan's semiconductor chips, random-access memory (RAM) and xirallic pigments production, causing significant disruptions in domestic and global supply chains (Park et al., 2013). The exposure of a supply chain to serious disturbance arising from supply chain risks and affecting the supply chain's ability to effectively serve the end customer market is described by *supply chain vulnerability* (Mason-Jones & Towill, 1998). Therefore, implementing appropriate actions in order to decrease supply chain vulnerability is an essential task in SCRM (Jüttner et al., 2003).

Second, *risk analysis, risk assessment, and impact measurement* are processes of identifying a risk, assessing its likelihood, and predicting the potential damage. Tools perform risk assessment in an efficient and timely manner to project risks accurately, to eliminate redundant expenses, and to avoid business interruptions. Risk assessment methods in the automotive industry vary with respect to the source of the risk (Zsidisin & Ritchie, 2009). The *Failure Mode Effect Analysis (FMEA)* involves a cyclical system of tasks to identify possible failures, their causes, their severity and their likelihood of occurrence. In addition, it assesses the likelihood of detecting these failures. Finally, failures are prioritized based on their severity, occurrence and detection probability, and risk minimization actions are derived. FMEA has been widely used in the manufacturing industry to study potential failures of products and processes along with their impacts and to suggest remedial measures at the look ahead planning level (Wehbe & Hamzeh, 2013). However, this method is an in-depth assessment of certain products or processes and a broad range of possible risks, but less suitable once a certain risk has materialized and multiple aspects need to be assessed. Likewise, the *PESTLE Risk Analysis* clusters external risk factors into Political, Economic, Societal, Technological, Legal, and Environmental forces (Bush, 2020). This can be supportive in qualitative risk prediction but of little contribution if one of the factors is in the focus. *Data mining* is a data processing method to uncover sources of risk that may otherwise remain unnoticed prior to risk occurrence. Data mining analyses historical data, recognizes patterns, and predicts what will happen next. However, because data mining builds on historical data and improves its prediction power with the number of data sets, it is suitable for highly frequent but less severe supply chain risks (Zsidisin & Ritchie, 2009). *Simulation* techniques allow for integration of sub-supplier's data into discrete event simulations for a better assessment of the supply chain risk of the tier-n suppliers, e.g., by Monte Carlo simulation to simulate the linear risk scenario models (Zsidisin & Henke, 2019). Simulation can provide insights into supply chain vulnerability. Vilko and Lättilä (2013) suggest that supply chain vulnerability depends on both the complexity of the supply chain as well as the disruption risks inherent in it, and different simulation software assess manufacturing and logistics systems in "what-if" scenarios. Simulation frameworks apply hybrid modelling approaches that combine discrete-event modelling with system dynamics modelling with objectives of: (1) simulating feedbacks of supply chain activities in social system mechanisms, (2) enabling management simulation in long time terms, and finally (3) clarifying requirement specifications toward supply chain management gaming (Umeda, 2007).

To summarize, each of the risk assessment tools outlined above has its own strengths and their suitability depends on the application case. However, during a crisis in which a risk has already materialized, these risk assessment tools face certain limitations. Considering the fast-evolving events during a rare-but-severe risk event, e.g. during the COVID-19 pandemic, these tools are not responsive enough for assessing inbound supply chain risk in a complex and changing supply chain environment. Moreover, they lack the integration of direct feedback from upstream supply chain partners, which is beneficial for obtaining a broader supply chain risk view (Zsidisin & Henke, 2019). Therefore, we present a methodology for assessing inbound supply chain risk during a rare-but-severe disruption that has been applied in the case of a tier-1 automotive supplier.

3 Our Research Methodology Is Action Research

Our research object, here the supply chain of a multinational automotive tier-1 supplier, obviously lives in a natural setting. Focussing on an inter-connected and inter-woven supply chain, our research team faced a real and active network of suppliers that deliver to multiple plants of an automotive tier-1 company. This network represents the setting and scope of our research. In other words, we were facing an ecosystem that is similar to an organism—and in this context the organism somehow fell sick. As we could not set-up this complex supply situation in vitro, we chose to go into the scene and tried to answer our questions in an in vivo case. Here our target was to develop an action research-based performance measurement system (Schmidberger et al., 2009). As already pointed out by Dunn et al. (1993) and Mentzer and Kahn (1995), especially the field of logistics requires more action research approaches as the present logistics and supply problems are of complex as well as distant nature and are influenced by real-world mediators and moderators. Such an action research approach is especially beneficial to cover and discover all relevant perspectives on the investigated research objects and their corresponding dynamic networks under real-world problems (Alvesson, 1996). By being in the real world of logistics and supply management and maybe only by moving around in this real world, we could gather first-hand information, feedback, and input to our model with the target to gain knowledge inside out (Näslund, 2002). Hameria and Paatela (2005) suggest that corresponding researchers should even be professionally involved in the concerned industries which in our case is given as four of us work in the supply chain that is being analyzed. Also, the request of Bourne et al. (2000) is fulfilled by adding a process consultant in action research approaches who acts as a coordinator. This aspect was and is fulfilled by managing the dynamic data collection on a regular and high frequency by a centrally installed process management function at the buying firm. In addition, some members of our research group from time to time got out of the scene and shifted roles from active participants to observers in order to be able to view the problems from a distance and to adjust direction and measurement system (Näslund, 2002; Smith & Smith, 2007; Ottosson, 2003). Action research is characterized by a collaborative and cyclical nature in a recurring cycle of planning, acting, observing, and reflecting (Altrichter et al., 2002; Zuber-Skerritt, 2001). We used this approach on the one hand as we are used to acting like this in a production and operations-related context when buying goods and services for the automotive production. On the other hand, we adjusted our approach and measuring system within the risk tower several times to increase both effectiveness of conclusion values and efficiency during data gathering and compilation. After going through our research presented in this paper, we therefore would even add "adopting" as a fifth step to the findings of Altrichter et al. (2002) and Zuber-Skerritt (2001) in the sense of readjusting our problem-solving model. Or how Frederike Otto would probably say, we wanted to and did create a real-time attribution study (Otto, 2019). More technical or definitory we found ourselves in a multi-stage adjustment process that has led to a successful development, testing, and finally also implementation of our model (Neely et al., 2000). We called our solution Supplier Risk *Tower* as we found the wish in many business leaders to be able to overlook the scene from a higher point and to be able to steer the dynamics of the supply chain. Of course, our research team is convinced that supply chains of complex nature cannot be controlled or decisively influenced from only one single spot (Wöhner, 2018; Schupp, 2020), but at the same time we wanted to add to the "influence model" of Nash and Handfield (2020) that suggests how purchasing as a function can increase its influence in the decision-making process of a firm while acknowledging executive intelligence as described by Menkes (2006). In other words, for those of you who watched the movie or who have played the game Jumanji, we as a research group found ourselves inside the game, forced to find a way out by learning and adjusting our approach. Looking back, we learned to understand and to play the game by action research. However, if we really master the game or the game masters us, we do not know yet. We might need further iterations and therefore decided to continue playing it.

While this chapter presents a single case study from the perspective of the buying focal firm with a focus on supply chain disruptions in the automotive industry during the COVID-19 pandemic, the involved suppliers are numerous and represent a wide supply chain. We therefore can probably say that the case can be seen in a wider perspective to learn about risk assessment approaches and tools in a scenario that has already materialized but neither predicted nor assessed beforehand while only a single case study would be employed to understand current events, conditions, and practices in detail. Following the case study research approach advocated by Yin (2017) we evaluated quantitative and qualitative information. In addition to information provided by the selected buying company, we conducted interviews with Gartner Consulting Inc. to also receive external feedback on the approach of the buying company and to embed the findings in our approach.

4 Conceptual Frame of Supply Risk

The present study builds on the automotive division of a globally operating company that functions as a tier-1 supplier. Complex supply chains connecting 3914 suppliers, sub-suppliers, and sub-contractors to produce and deliver high-precision components and modules to automotive manufacturers. Companies in the automotive industry typically follow a single sourcing strategy. They select only one supplier for a particular product (Treleven & Schweikhart, 1988). A survey in the automotive industry reveals that in 71.2% of the cases tier-1 companies do not have an alternative source of supply for a specific product available (Merkel, 2011). The company in the presented case has got the strategic option to change the source for 94% of the purchase volume. However, a second supplier has been released for only 15% of the purchasing volume and only for less than 1% of the purchasing volume dual sourcing is in place, in a sense that two suppliers are delivering the same product in the same period. Such predominance of single sourcing is also confirmed by Mueller et al. (2008) after conducting interviews with several German automotive manufacturers.

The purchasing department of the company is not only responsible for the commercial relationship with the supplier base, but also for supplier quality, supply management, including logistics alignment, and supplier technology. The tier-1 supplier applies a category management which groups suppliers by the kind of product they supply. A systematical risk management takes place twice per year including the assessment of multifactor supplier risks. The collaborative environment established between the company and its suppliers ensures a smooth flow of inbound goods. However, the well-controlled situation changed when in 2020 the COVID-19 pandemic resulted in worldwide disruptions of supply chains.

The COVID-19 pandemic has infected more than 108 million people and taken away 2,386,717 lives worldwide between December 2019, when it was first reported, and February 2021 (WHO, 2021). The outbreak spread from the Chinese city Wuhan to more than 180 countries and territories—affecting every continent except Antarctica (ECDC, 2021). Despite the global presence, a characteristic of the pandemic is that hot spots of infections are regional or local. To contain the pandemic, governments all around the world have imposed, to varying degrees, lockdowns and social distancing measures, further disrupting economic activity (UN, 2020). Similar to the changing hot spot locations, those measures have national, regional, or local validity. The decline in economic activity in the 2nd quarter of 2020 is likely to be the steepest since WWII (McKinsey & Company, 2020). Stimulus packages provided by governments to mitigate COVID-19 impact already exceeded $10 trillion in the first half of 2020—an amount three times higher compared to the global economic crisis in 2008 (McKinsey & Company, 2020).

The COVID-19 pandemic impacted the global automotive industry in an unprecedented manner. Registrations of new passenger cars in the EU dropped in the first half of 2020 by 38.1% compared to the same time frame in 2019 (ACEA, 2020). In terms of production figures, the losses of the European automotive industry amounted to 3.6 million vehicles—representing a monetary value of approximately 100 billion euros (ACEA, 2021). The tier-1 supplier saw a correlated decline in its automotive business. Lockdowns of OEM customers in Europe and America resulted in a suboptimal capacity utilization and volume-related negative effects on production costs.

The integrity of the company's inbound supply chains was not only influenced by the infection status of the individual suppliers but also by the effect of the COVID-19 pandemic on the region or country in which the suppliers were located. Whereas in January and February 2020 the virus was mainly impacting China, the subsequent spread of COVID-19 in Europe and America deteriorated the situation. To name a few specific occurrences, Italian authorities imposed a nationwide lockdown on March 9th shutting down all non-essential business for over 1 month. The government of Spain declared a state of emergency on March 14th. A further tightening of the measures followed on March 28th when all non-essential workers were ordered to remain at home for 2 weeks. First announced in mid-March, the production shutdowns in Mexico were extended until May 30th. Thus, the virus hot spots are local, but due to worldwide connections and contagion effect, the impact is global (see also Wulf, 2015; Miroudot, 2020).

Looking at concrete numbers for the company's supply chain, 14% of the company's suppliers had a complete shutdown of their production middle of April 2020. An additional 18% operated on less than half of their production capacity. Beginning of May 2020, still every fourth supplier responded that available capacities are below 50%, mainly due to lack of workforce. As a result, purchasing and supply management of the tier-1 supplier was facing the challenge to ensure supply for production despite the precarious circumstances. Measures to mitigate the impact included:

- Requesting suppliers to inform proactively about the infection status of their plants and potential delays in shipments.
- Delivery ahead of schedule for material from suppliers located in COVID-19 hot spot countries.
- Supporting financially unstable suppliers by temporarily offering liquidity.
- Focusing not only on suppliers but also on sub-suppliers.
- Supporting suppliers to get special production permissions from local authorities.
- Information events in the form of supplier conference calls, in which the company shared important news with its suppliers such as information about the demand situation and the status of its production plants.

For the coordination and implementation of the above-mentioned measures the establishment of an interdisciplinary task force team was of major importance. The inclusion of specialists from different departments—in particular, Purchasing, Supply Chain Management, and Health and Safety—and representatives from all regions ensured the implementation of timely and companywide responses to the fast-evolving situation.

From the perspective of risk management, one major problem for the tier-1 supplier was to aggregate the scattered information of its suppliers into a complete overview. This overview was required to dedicate available resources to places where they generate the largest positive impact. The existing risk management process, which is performed twice per year, was of no use during this situation. Therefore, the company set up a novel supplier risk management approach, the Supplier Risk Tower, that allowed it to get and maintain information about the risk level of its inbound supply chains and to develop the right risk mitigation activities.

5 The Supplier Risk Tower

The Supplier Risk Tower is a new risk assessment accommodating up-to-date, first-hand reliable analysis of inbound supply chain risk. The Supplier Risk Tower provides, on a weekly basis, both an aggregated view on the exposure to supply risks as well as drill down options for selected internal interest groups. The Excel-based tool calculates risk scores by combining static and dynamic factors. Input data

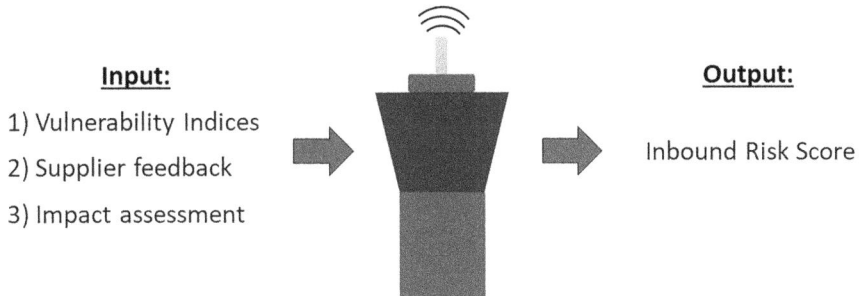

Input:

1) Vulnerability Indices

2) Supplier feedback

3) Impact assessment

Output:

Inbound Risk Score

Fig. 9.1 Schematic representation of the Supplier Risk Tower

include vulnerability indices for each category of supplied material (static), risk materialization status per supplier (dynamic, weekly updated), and classifications of suppliers into different risk groups based on the misfit of supply and demand (dynamic, weekly updated). Thereby, the Supplier Risk Tower draws on different sources of information: assessment of purchasing management for static values, weekly updated survey results from suppliers, and impact assessment by purchasers and supply chain managers. Based on these data, the Supplier Risk Tower calculates the risk score for the inbound supply chain (Fig. 9.1).

The following section explores the above-mentioned input factors of the Supplier Risk Tower. First, the risk assessment uses a Vulnerability Index V_i which represents the general supply chain risk inherent to the specific material category. The index has been determined for each category at the implementation of the Supplier Risk Tower. The Vulnerability Index considers the following factors:

1. Complexity of the category's supply chains and production steps:

    (a) Number of parts
    (b) Production complexity

2. Time required to find a substitute for the existing supplier.
3. Cost of switching to an alternative supply source.

For each material category, these factors are evaluated using a scale from 1 (low) to 5 (high). Factors are rated for each category relative to the other categories. The qualitative assessment is performed by purchasing managers. According to the relevance of the above-mentioned factors, a weight is assigned to each factor. As a result, the Vulnerability Index of each category is calculated with the following formula:

$$V_i = (c_i * 0.5) + (t_i * 0.25) + (o_i * 0.25) = ((n_i * 0.5 + p_i * 0.5) * 0.5) + (t_i * 0.25) + (o_i * 0.25)$$

V_i = vulnerability index of category i
c_i = complexity of the supply chains and production steps in category i

Table 9.1 Quantitative assessment of Vulnerability Index sub-criteria

		Vulnerability for sub-criteria from 1 (low) to 5 (high)				
		1	2	3	4	5
t_i	Time to second source in weeks	0 - 4	5 - 12	13 - 26	27 - 52	> 52
o_i	Money to second source in Mio. € per part #	< 0,05	0,05 - 0,1	0,11 - 0,2	0,21 - 0,5	> 0,5
n_i	Number of parts	0 - 50	51 - 200	201 - 500	501 - 2000	> 2001
p_i	Number of production steps per part *	1 - 2	3	4	5	> 5
p_i	Sub-suppliers managed by supplier *	1	2	3	4	> 4

* Use the greater value of criterion 4 and 5 for p_i: level of supplier production complexity of category i

$t_i = $ *level of time to second source for category i compared to all categories*

$o_i = $ *level of costs (money) to second source for category i compared to all categories*

$n_i = $ *level of number of parts in category i compared to all categories*

$p_i = $ *level of supplier production complexity of category i compared to all categories per part.*

The levels are defined through a quantitative approach for each category of purchased material as shown in the Table 9.1. Each factor receives an integer value between 1 and 5.

Second, in addition to this static factor, the approach includes dynamic input data about the status of suppliers. The tier-1 supplier chose to integrate direct feedback from suppliers into the risk assessment framework in order to cope with the fast-changing spread of the COVID-19 pandemic. This direct feedback provided valuable insights about the infection status of the supplier plants in the different regions to enable the anticipation of containment measures that are imposed by regional or national authorities. The target was to identify potential supply shortages in advance. To collect the data from its supplier base, the company started weekly supplier surveys in March 2020. Distribution of the questionnaire and collection of supplier feedback takes place via the survey function of a B2B supplier web platform which the company applies to communicate with its supplier base. The survey uses Likert scales and percentage measurements to assess the impact of COVID-19 on suppliers' production capacity. The suppliers answer the following four questions weekly:

1. Please indicate the infection status of your plants relevant for production of our parts.
2. Do you have a production shutdown or plan a shutdown?
3. Is your shipping department operational during this shutdown?
4. For the following 4 weeks, what percentage of your production capacity is available with respect to the capacity that is usually reserved for our parts?

As displayed in the following figure, the number of suppliers responding to the survey rose from 748 in calendar week 15 (beginning of April 2020) to a peak of 922 in calendar weeks 25 and 26 (middle of June 2020). Overall, the response rate of

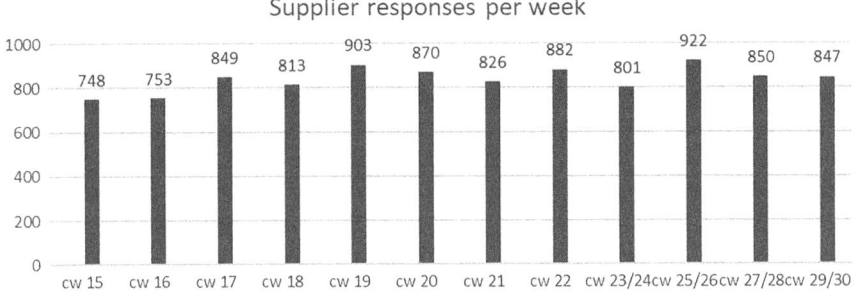

Fig. 9.2 Number of supplier responses to the company's survey in 2020 per week

Financial Risk		Number of suppliers			
		March 2020		July 2020	
high	10	3	62	5	82
	9	4		4	
	8	12		19	
	7	43		54	
medium	6	130	437	136	440
	5	171		187	
	4	136		117	
low	3	91	139	75	116
	2	41		31	
	1	7		10	

Fig. 9.3 Deterioration of the financial status of the company's major suppliers between March and July 2020

suppliers in the period from April to July 2020 was rather stable. From calendar week 23 onward, the tier-1 supplier changed the frequency of the surveys to biweekly due to a decreasing inbound supply risk (Fig. 9.2).

Third, the tier-1 supplier monitors the financial stability of its suppliers. There is a special focus on 638 "A suppliers," which account for 80% of the purchasing volume. Based on an internal multifactor financial risk assessment including external risk scoring data, these suppliers are assessed on a scale from 1 (no financial risk) to 10 (very high financial risk). As displayed in Fig. 9.3, the financial status of a significant number of suppliers deteriorated during the COVID-19 pandemic. Whereas in March 2020 the financial stability of 62 suppliers was evaluated with a grade of 7 or higher, which means high or very high financial risk, this number increased to 82 until July 2020. This rapid growth of financially unstable suppliers was treated by the company very seriously. The purchasing department paid special attention to the most critical suppliers and provided support by offering liquidity.

The tier-1 supplier collects all above-mentioned dynamic input data about the status of suppliers in a supplier database. The list displays for each supplier detailed information about risk-related factors like available production capacities, potential plant shutdowns, functionality of the shipping department, and financial stability. Purchasing uses this information in close cooperation with the supply chain management function to compare it with the production demand for parts of each individual supplier. As a result, the responsible purchasers classify each supplier in one of the following four risk groups on a weekly basis. The purchasers use the lowest classification, "baseline risk," for suppliers who do not face a risk materialization. If the purchaser is aware of a risk materialization at the supplier but does not have an indication about the impact on the own company, he/she will classify the supplier as "low risk." Likewise, the classification will increase to "medium risk" if the purchaser, based on all cross-functional information, expects a risk for the own company's production. He/She will use the highest classification "high risk" for suppliers that are expected to cause shipment interruptions to the company's customers.

Combining the Vulnerability Index with the risk classification, the inbound supply risk of each supplier, the Supplier Risk Score, is calculated:

$$\text{Supplier Risk Score}_{ijk} = V_i * a_{jk}$$

$V_i = $ *vulnerability index of category i*
$a_{jk} = $ *integer variable based on the risk classification of supplier k in week j:*

   3 in case of high risk (supply to customer at risk)
   2 in case of medium risk (production at risk)
   1 in case of low risk (Risk indicated but not proven)
   0 in case of baseline risk (only a general risk but no supply risk out of materialized risks)

Summarizing the formula, the Supplier Risk Score of a specific supplier is calculated by multiplying the Vulnerability Index of the supplier's category with a variable representing the current supplier's risk level for the assessed week. The Total Inbound Risk Score for the company in a given calendar week is determined by the sum over all Supplier Risk Scores:

$$\text{Total Inbound Risk Score}_j = \sum\nolimits_{k=1}^{n} \text{Supplier Risk Score}_{ijk}$$

The Total Inbound Risk Score expresses risk as a concrete and absolute number. It is used to inform all internal stakeholders about the current risk situation and serves as a reference value for deciding when additional measures are necessary. For example, the company changed the frequency of its supplier survey from weekly to biweekly when the Total Inbound Risk Score dropped below 1100 points in calendar

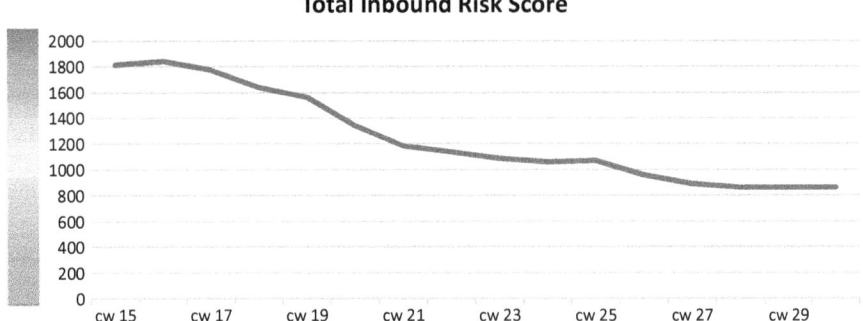

Fig. 9.4 Development of the Total Inbound Risk Score of the company in 2020

week 23. Figure 9.4 displays the development of the company's Total Inbound Risk Score between April and July 2020. After reaching a peak score of 1842 points middle of April, the diagram shows a decreasing trend and the risk value stabilizes at a level of approximately 900 points during July 2020.

The Total Inbound Risk Score provides aggregated information about the risk in the company's inbound supply chain. For managerial actions, sub-scores can be calculated that take only part of the whole supply chain into account. Application examples are the management of plants, the evaluation for specific material categories, or the assessment of risks in geographical areas.

To conclude, the process of risk assessment through the Supplier Risk Tower is established in the upstream supply chain. Results are regularly discussed within the mentioned task force and are also shared with internal stakeholders in form of weekly reports. The Supplier Risk Tower is key element in the company's supplier risk management going forward.

6   Reflection

This section aims to reflect on the measures presented in the case study to measure inbound supply chain risk during a rare-but-severe disruption. The presented Supplier Risk Tower builds on the basic assessment of risk according to Mitchell (1995). However, as the application targets at measuring risks *during* the disruption, the probability of occurrence is no longer questioned. Thus, the focus of the Supplier Risk Tower is the assessment of the impact. The Supplier Risk Tower takes a novel approach to integrate first-hand information from the upstream supply chain partners as proposed by Zsidisin and Henke (2019). The weekly survey collects and summarizes information from the supplier base for further processing. Additional external information is integrated into the assessment of supplier financial risk. Such a measure is proposed by a CAPS Research survey of 115 companies: In order to accurately anticipate supply chain disruptions and develop risk mitigation action plans, monitoring the suppliers' financial status is crucial (CAPS, 2020). In the case study, the suppliers' financial situation worsened from March to July 2020. Noteworthily, measures to mitigate the impact consequently included offering liquidity to financially unstable suppliers.

Because of the single sourcing approach in the presented case and the obstacles to change suppliers on short notice in automotive supply chains, the Supplier Risk Tower increases visibility of disruption impacts and vulnerable parts of the supply chain. Such increased surveillance on their multitier supply chain is reported during the COVID-19 pandemic (CAPS, 2020). In the case study, the combination of supplier's view, external financial views, and internal information from multiple departments and the task force as well as the combination of static and dynamic elements increases the impact of transparency for the company and allows for resource allocation for mitigation activities. Likewise, in other cases, status information on the upstream supply chain is used to increase visibility, such as suppliers' inventory, production, and purchase order fulfillment status (Deloitte, 2020). The clear definition of criteria, their measurement, and the logic to calculate the Total Supplier Risk Score is an advantage of the Supplier Risk Tower and can be seen as a new standard to calculate supply chain risk. The Total Supplier Risk Score provides a comprehensive view of reports where the inbound perspective is an important perspective within the corporate risk management. Thus, the Supplier Risk Tower is a well-working example of how to measure inbound risk during the COVID-19 pandemic.

Summarizing, advantages of the Supplier Risk Tower are standardized collection and aggregation of suppliers' information including production capacities through the automated survey, integration of different data sources, calculation of a Total Inbound Risk Score, use of Category Vulnerability Indexes to quantitatively differentiate between material categories, and resulting increased transparency for managing the risk in mitigating activities. Disadvantages are the lack of systematic information about tier-2 to tier-n suppliers and the manual activities during the data update in the database. The latter can and will be improved through further digitalization and software improvements.

7   Conclusion and Managerial Implications

The presented method to assess inbound supply risk provides novel insights into supply chain risk management. First, the presented new risk assessment framework for calculating inbound supply risk introduces measurement of the risk as an absolute number. The risk cannot be talked down by measuring it as a ratio of risk to other factors such as, for example, total purchasing volume. Because risks materialize and hit supply chains, the measurement and expression of risk shall reflect the risk: Inbound supply risk is absolute.

Second, the applied measurement of risk takes the structure of the supply chain in terms of single source, multiple sources, and the switching options into account. The factors "time to second source" and "cost/money to second source" provide a quantitative assessment of switching options. Thus, making second sources available has a value and provides a balance to the disadvantages of diversified sourcing (Miroudot, 2020). This allows for several improvements in managerial practice. Managers can actively decrease the inbound supply risk by providing switching options and lowering switching barriers. Looking at the purchase price of goods only, single source supply chains are mostly economical because building and maintaining a second source comes with duplicated tooling and set-up cost, more complex supply chain operations, and the loss of economies of scale. The value of second source options in the presented risk management balances this view. Second sources get a quantitative value.

Third, lean management requires risk management. The efficiency of no-inventory supply chains is waisted if disruptions cause severe impacts. During the COVID-19 pandemic, freight rates for air shipments out of China more than tripled (Baertlein & Kirton, 2020). The price that supply chains, which are dependent on short-term supply due to lack of buffers, pay to mitigate risks becomes visible. Lean management must not be misunderstood as a no-inventory approach. Planned inventory buffers that exist for a calculable and valuable reason (see also Simchi-Levi et al., 2018) as well as structural risk mitigation, e.g., by second sources, are no waste but fundamental parts of lean management.

Fourth and because of these insights, supply chains with high interdependencies in a worldwide network of companies and lean management applications to remain competitive, such as the automotive industry, must invest in risk management. This includes inbound supply risk management. Without novel risk management approaches, supply chains are not lean and will therefore not be competitive in the long run.

Summarizing, an absolute measurement of inbound supply risk that combines internal and external sources with first-hand supplier information enables supply chain risk management for different stakeholders, especially during rare-but-severe disruptions. Thus, this measurement allows for application of balanced second source applications as well as flexible and robust lean management—because risks materialize.

References

Abdulmalek, F., & Rajgopal, J. (2007). Analyzing the benefits of lean manufacturing and value stream mapping via simulation: A process sector case study. *International Journal of Production Economics, 107*(2007), 223–236.

Accenture. (2020). *COVID-19: Managing the impact on procurement for resilience and growth.* Retrieved March 13, 2021, from https://www.accenture.com/ae-en/insights/consulting/corona virus-procurement-recovery-growth

ACEA – European Automobile Manufacturers' Association. (2020). *Passenger car registrations.* Retrieved August 27, 2020, from https://www.acea.be/press-releases/article/passenger-car-registrations-38.1-first-half-of-2020-22.3-in-june

ACEA – European Automobile Manufacturers' Association. (2021). *Coronavirus/COVID-19*. Retrieved March 14, 2021, from https://www.acea.be/news/article/coronavirus-covid-19

Allianz Global Corporate and Specialty. (2019). *Allianz risk barometer: Top business risks for 2019* (pp. 10–16). Retrieved from https://www.allianz.com/de/presse/news/studien/190115_allianz-risk-barometer-2019.html

Altrichter, H., Kemmis, S., McTaggart, R., & Zuber-Skerritt, O. (2002). The concept of action research. *The Learning Organization, 9*(3), 125–131.

Alvesson, M. (1996). Leadership studies: From procedure and abstraction to reflexity and situation. *Leadership Quarterly, 7*(4), 455–485.

Avittathur, B., & Ghosh, D. (2020). Supply chain risk management. In *Excellence in supply chain management*. Routledge.

Behnezhad, A., Connett, B. I., & Nair, M. (2013). The evolution of supply chain risk management. *Journal of Supply Chain and Operations Management, 11*(1), 77–89.

Bourne, M., Mills, J., Wilcox, M., Neely, A., & Platts, K. (2000). Designing, implementing and updating performance measurement systems. *International Journal of Operations and Production Management, 20*(7), 754–771.

Bunkley, N. (2011). Piecing together a supply chain. *New York Times*. Retrieved October 2, 2011, from http://www.nytimes.com/2011/05/13/business/global/13auto.html

Bush, T. (2020). *PESTLE analysis in risk management*. Retrieved August 27, 2020, from https://pestleanalysis.com/pestle-analysis-in-risk-management/

Cagliano, R., Caniato, F., & Spina, G. (2004). Lean, Agile and traditional supply: How do they impact manufacturing performance? *Journal of Purchasing and Supply Management, 10*(2004), 151–164.

CAPS Research. (2020). *Supply management responds to the pandemic*. Webinar May 21, 2020. W. P. Carey School of Business at Arizona State University.

Chauffour, J.-P., & Farole, T. (2009). *Trade finance in crisis: Market adjustment or market failure?* Policy Research Working Paper #5003, The World Bank.

Daultani, Y., Kumar, S., Vaidya, O. S., & Tiwari, M. K. (2015). A supply chain network equilibrium model for operational and opportunism risk mitigation. *International Journal of Production Research, 53*(18), 5685–5715.

Deloitte Development LLC. (2020). *COVID-19: Managing supply chain risk and disruption*. Retrieved July 28, 2020, from https://www2.deloitte.com/content/dam/Deloitte/global/Documents/About-Deloitte/gx-COVID-19-managing-supply-chain-risk-and-disruption.pdf

Donaldson, T. (2020, February 4). China sourcing, shipments face 'severe disruptions' amid coronavirus epidemic. *Sourcing Journal.*

Dunn, S., Seaker, R., Stenger, A., & Young, R. (1993). *An assessment of logistics research paradigms*. Working paper. The Pennsylvania State University, State College, Pennsylvania.

European Center for Disease Prevention and Control (ECDC). (2021). *Communicable disease threats report* (pp. 1–3). Retrieved February 15, 2021, from https://www.ecdc.europa.eu/sites/default/files/documents/communicable-disease-threats-report-13-feb-2021.pdf

Flynn, B., Cantor, D., Pagell, M., Dooley, K., & Azadegan, A. (2021). Introduction to managing supply chains beyond COVID-19—Preparing for the next global mega-disruption. *Journal of Supply Chain Management, 57*, 3–6.

Fortune. (2020). *94% of the Fortune 1000 are seeing coronavirus supply chain disruptions: Report*. Retrieved March 30, 2020, from https://fortune.com/2020/02/21/fortune-1000-coronavirus-china -supply-chain-impact/

Fu, G., & Yan, M. (2016). Anatomy of Tianjin port fire and explosion: Process and causes. *Process Safety Progress, 35*(3), 216–220.

Ganeshan, R., & Harrison, T. P. (1995). *An introduction to supply chain management*. Technical Report; Department of Management Science and Information Systems, The Pennsylvania State University.

Hameria, A.-P., & Paatela, A. (2005). Supply network dynamics as a source of new business. *International Journal of Production Economics, 98*, 41–55.

Heckmann, I. (2016). *Towards supply chain risk analytics* (pp. 206–240). Springer Fachmedien Wiesbaden.

Heckmann, I., Comes, T., & Nickel, S. (2015). A critical review on supply chain risk—Definition, measure and modeling. *Omega, 52*, 119–132.

Ivanov, D. (2020). Viable supply chain model: Integrating agility, resilience and sustainability perspectives—Lessons from and thinking beyond the COVID-19 pandemic. *Annals of Operations Research*. https://doi.org/10.1007/s10479-020-03640-6

Ivanov, D., & Dolgui, A. (2020). Viability of intertwined supply networks: Extending the supply chain resilience angles towards survivability. A position paper motivated by COVID-19 outbreak. *International Journal of Production Research, 58*, 2904–2915. https://doi.org/10.1080/00207543.2020.1750727

Jones, S., & Mendoza, E. (2011). *Natural disasters and business: The impact of the Icelandic volcano of April 2010 on European logistics and distribution—A case study of Malta* [Ebook] (pp. 4–5). Retrieved August 5, 2020, from http://www.ftp://ftp.repec.org/opt/ReDIF/RePEc/msm/wpaper/MSM-WP2011-20.pdf

Jüttner, U., Peck, H., & Christopher, M. (2003). Supply chain risk management: Outlining an agenda for future research. *International Journal of Logistics: Research and Applications, 6*(4), 197–210.

Khojasteh, Y. (Ed.). (2018). *Supply chain risk management*. Springer Nature Singapore Pte Ltd. https://doi.org/10.1007/978-981-10-4106-8_1

KPMG. (2020). *Recalibrating your strategy*. Retrieved July 22, 2020.

Kumar, S. K., Tiwari, M. K., & Babiceanu, R. F. (2010). Minimisation of supply chain cost with embedded risk using computational intelligence approaches. *International Journal of Production Research, 48*(13), 3717–3739.

Mason-Jones, R., & Towill, D. R. (1998). Shrinking the supply chain uncertainty circle. *Control, 24*(7), 17–22.

McKinsey & Company. (2020). *Covid-19 global health and crisis response* (pp. 4–30). Retrieved August 3, 2020, from https://www.mckinsey.com/~/media/McKinsey/Business%20Functions/Risk/Our%20Insights/ COVID%2019%20Implications%20for%20business/COVID%2019%20July%2023/COVID-19-Facts-and-Insights-July-23.pdf

Menkes, J. (2006). *Executive intelligence: What all great leaders have*. Harper Collins.

Mentzer, J., & Kahn, K. (1995). A framework of logistics research. *Journal of Business Logistics, 6*(1), 231–250.

Merkel, J. (2011). *Dual Sourcing – Entwicklung eines Entscheidungsrahmens für ein 1st Tier-Unternehmen im Automobilzuliefergeschäft*. Betriebswissenschaftliches Institut der Universität Stuttgart.

Miroudot, S. (2020). Reshaping the policy debate on the implications of COVID-19 for global supply chains. *Journal of International Business Policy, 2020*(3), 430–442.

Mitchell, V. W. (1995). Organisational risk perception and reduction: A literature review. *British Journal of Management, 6*(2), 115–133.

Mojonnier, T. (2011). *Reducing risk in the automotive supply chain*. Business Theory. Retrieved December 15, 2016, from http://businesstheory.com/reducing-risk-automotive-supply-chain-2/

Mueller, F., Stahl, K., & Wachtler, F. (2008). *Upstream relationships in the automotive industry: A contractual perspective*. Study of University of Mannheim. Retrieved March 14, 2021, from https://www.vwl.uni-mannheim.de/media/Lehrstuehle/vwl/Stahl/MueStaWa_2016_03_19.pdf

Nash, T., & Handfield, R. (2020). Purchasing's role as an influencer of business outcomes. In F. Schupp & H. Wöhner (Eds.), *The nature of purchasing*. Springer Nature Switzerland AG.

Näslund, D. (2002). Logistics needs qualitative research: Especially action research. *International Journal of Physical Distribution and Logistics Management, 32*(5), 321–338.

Neely, A., Mills, J., Platts, K., Huw, R., Gregory, M., Bourne, M., & Kennerley, M. (2000). Performance measurement systems design: Developing and testing a process-based approach. *International Journal of Operations and Production Management, 20*(10), 1119–1145.

Norrman, A., & Lindroth, R. (2004). Categorization of supply chain risk and risk management. In C. Brindley (Ed.), *Supply chain risk* (pp. 14–27). Ashgate Publishing.

Oliver, R. K., & Weber, M. D. (1982). Supply-chain management: Logistics catches up with strategy. In M. L. Christopher (Ed.), *Logistics: The strategic issues* (pp. 63–75). Chapman and Hall.

Otto, F. (2019). *Wütendes Wetter* (3. Auflage). Ullstein Buchverlage.

Ottosson, S. (2003). Participation action research: A key to improved knowledge of management. *Technovation, 23*(2), 87–94.

Park, Y. W., Hong, P., & Roh, J. (2013). Supply chain lessons from the 2011 natural disasters in Japan. *Business Horizons, 56*(1), 75–85.

Park, K., Min, H., & Min, S. (2016). Inter-relationship among risk taking propensity, supply chain security practices, and supply chain disruption occurrence. *Journal of Purchasing and Supply Management, 22*(2016), 120–130.

Pisani-Ferry, J., & Santos, I. (2009). Reshaping the global economy. *Finance and Development*, (March), 8–12.

Baertlein, L., & Kirton, L. (2020). *Air freight rates skyrocket amid passenger flight cuts, Chinese factory restarts.* Retrieved March 2, 2021, from https://www.reuters.com/article/us-health-coronavirus-airlines-freight-idCAKBN20Y062

Ritchie, B., & Brindley, C. (2007). Supply chain risk management and performance: A guiding framework for future development. *International Journal of Operations and Production Management, 27*(3), 303–322.

Scavarda, L., Schaffer, J., Schleich, H., da Cunha Reis, A., & Carneiro Fernandes, T. (2008, May 9–May 12). *Handling product variety and its effects in automotive production.* In: POMS 19th Annual Conference, La Jolla, CA.

Schmidberger, S., Bals, L., Hartmann, E., & Jahns, C. (2009). Ground handling services at European hub airports: Development of a performance measurement system for benchmarking. *International Journal of Production Economics, 117*, 104–116.

Schmitt, B. (2011). *Japanese parts paralysis: The shiny paint is leaving the building.* Retrieved October 2, 2011, from http://www.thetruthaboutcars.com/2011/05/japanese-parts-paralysis-the-shiny-paint-is-leaving-the-building/

Schupp, F. (2020). Elements of purchasing in nature. In F. Schupp & H. Wöhner (Eds.), *The nature of purchasing.* Springer Nature Switzerland AG.

Simchi-Levi, D., Wang, H., & Wei, Y. (2018). Increasing supply chain robustness through process flexibility and inventory. *Production and Operations Management, 27*(8), 1476–1491.

Slack, N., Chambers, S., & Johnston, R. (2009). *Operations management* (6th ed.). Prentice Hall.

Smith, M., & Smith, D. (2007). Implementing strategically aligned performance measurement in small firms. *International Journal of Production Economics, 106*, 393–408.

Snyder, L. V., Atan, Z., Peng, P., Rong, Y., Schmitt, A. J., & Sinsoysal, B. (2016). OR/MS models for supply chain disruptions: A review. *IIE Transactions, 48*(2), 89–109.

Tang, C. S. (2006). Perspectives in supply chain risk management. *International Journal of Production Economics, 103*(2), 451–488.

The Ferrari Consulting and Research Group LLC. (2020). *Predictions for industry and global supply chains.* Retrieved August 4, 2020, from https://theferrarigroup.com/supply-chain-matters/research-center/

Thun, J.-H., & Hoenig, D. (2011). An empirical analysis of supply chain risk management in the German automotive industry. *International Journal of Production Economics, 131*(1), 242–249.

Tomlin, B. (2006). On the value of mitigation and contingency strategies for managing supply chain disruption risks. *Management Science, 52*(5), 639–657.

Treleven, M., & Schweikhart, S. B. (1988). A risk/benefit analysis of sourcing strategies: Single vs. multiple sourcing. *Journal of Operations Management, 7*(4), 93–114.

Umeda, S. (2007). IFIP international federation for information processing. In J. Olhager & F. Persson (Eds.), *Advances in production management systems* (Vol. 246, pp. 329–336). Springer.

UN. (2020). World economic prospects monthly. *Economic Outlook, 44*(S1), 1–33. https://doi.org/10.1111/1468-0319.12458

Unger, T. (n.d.). *Automotive industry and reach—Strategy and challenges for authorization.* Retrieved March 14, 2021, from https://echa.europa.eu/documents/10162/13587/candidate_list_industry_unger_hyundai_en.pdf

Vilko, J., & Lättilä, L. (2013). *Vulnerability in supply chain risk management.* In The 5th International Conference on Logistics and Transport, Kyoto.

Waters, D. (2007). *Supply chain risk management: Vulnerability and resilience in logistics.* Kogan Page.

Wehbe, F., & Hamzeh, F. (2013, January 2013). *Failure mode and effect analysis as a tool for risk management in construction planning.* Conference Paper. https://doi.org/10.13140/RG.2.1.3935.4409

Wöhner, H. (2018). Digitalisierung in der Lieferantenanbindung. In F. Schupp & H. Wöhner (Eds.), *Digitalisierung im Einkauf.* SpringerGabler.

World Health Organisation. (2021). *COVID-19 weekly epidemiological update* (p. 22). Retrieved February 10, 2021, from https://www.who.int/publications/m/item/weekly-epidemiological-update%2D%2D-16-february-2021

Wulf, A. (2015). *Alexander von Humboldt und die Erfindung der Natur.* C. Bertelsmann. isbn:978-3-570-10206-0.

Yin, R. (2017). *Case study research and applications: Design and methods* (6th ed.). Sage.

Zsidisin, G., & Henke, M. (Eds.). (2019). *Revisiting supply chain risk.* Springer Nature. isbn:978-3-030-03813-7.

Zsidisin, G., & Ritchie, B. (Eds.). (2009). *Supply chain risk: A handbook of assessment, management and performance.* Springer Science and Business Media, LLC. isbn:978-0-387-79934-6.

Zsidisin, G., & Wagner, S. (2010). Do perceptions become reality? The moderating role of supply chain resiliency on disruption occurrence. *Journal of Business Logistics, 31*(2), 1–20. https://doi.org/10.1002/j.2158-1592.2010.tb00140.x

Zuber-Skerritt, O. (2001). Action learning and action research: Paradigm, praxis and programs. In S. Sankaran, B. Dick, R. Passfield, & P. Swepson (Eds.), *Effective change management using action research and action learning: Concepts, framework, processes and applications.* Southern Cross University Press.

Part III
Lessons Learned

The lessons we have learned from the COVID-19 pandemic will help to shape the way future supply chains are structured. COVID-19 affected supply chains in many ways, such as labor shortages, government restrictions, and the significant shifts in volume demand for a myriad of products and services. The pandemic led to disruptions that exposed weaknesses in networks around the world—some known and some unknown—and on a scale we hopefully will not witness again. COVID-19 has also bred innovation, given us the benefit of hindsight and much needed clarity and insight.

The chapters in the final part of this book highlight some of the key learnings from the pandemic. There are recommendations for new models of resilience and suggested improvements for supply chain risk methodologies. There is also a much-needed call for bridging the gap between scientific research and industry approaches. Technology will of course play an important role and that role too is further scrutinized from the initial insights provided in Part II.

Chapter 10, *A rethink of supply chain risk management*, addresses how governments and other disaster management organizations could modify their stockpiling approach to create a more robust approach to disasters. The paper is set against the backdrop of COVID-19 which raised serious questions about preparedness for future pandemics, not least in the United States where the Strategic National Stockpile (SNS) for medically critical items proved inadequate in the first half of 2020. To that end, the authors argue that a strategic reserve of medically vital resources should be held to deal with rare public health emergencies, as well as standby capability.

To deal with the highly skewed demands of such scenarios, the authors present a three-tiered approach that is made up of stockpile inventory, backup capacity and standby capability to manufacture. They add that by taking this approach, public health or disaster agencies would use the stockpile inventory as the first line of defense in case of a viral epidemic and the backup capacity if the epidemic grew to a pandemic (or the disaster grew in size and scope). The final tier is used in cases where infections continue to grow, using manufacturing capability to create and increase backup capacity.

Chapter 11, *Supply chain configuration in a post-pandemic world*, looks into how supply chains can be remodelled post-COVID-19. During the pandemic, governments the world over enacted new border regulations for people and goods, some of which are still in effect as at the time of writing this book. The paper argues that modern global supply chains are highly vulnerable in the context of such changes, while trade wars often restrict import and export capacities leading to increased prices. This leads managers to temporarily localize production—which has created a public debate on the value of less globalized supply chains.

The chapter looks at how this configuration of supply chains can be understood in terms of their structure and key attributes, dividing the attributes into functional (such as those for procurement and distribution) and structural types (such as the topography of the supply chain, its integration and coordination). The authors examine how supply chains can be reconfigured post-COVID-19, using the functional and structural framework as a basis for analysis that directly contributes to the continued debate on developing future supply chains.

Chapter 12, *Building Resilient Post-Pandemic Supply Chains Through Digital Transformation*, describes that digital technologies can be used to create more resilient supply chains that are better able to cope with future, large-scale disruptions such as COVID-19. Throughout the chapter, the authors present current industry best practices, looking into blockchain, digital platforms, analytics, and digital twins, aiming to provide actionable insights for decision makers. They suggest that emerging digital technologies hold the potential to address weaknesses in the supply chain, creating resilience against future large-scale disruptions. This approach to digital resilience can be applied to improve supply chain visibility, flexibility, and redundancy.

The authors cite several interesting avenues of enquiry, including blockchain which has been used to enable authenticity and traceability in the supply of vaccines, and digital platforms that are used to efficiently allocate and coordinate a variety of resources and services, facilitating operational flexibility. The paper also highlights the increased level of investment in advanced analytics tools such as AI and machine learning, both of which contribute to better forecasting, automation, and increased visibility. The use of digital twins—digital mirrors of physical objects or processes—is also discussed, with the authors highlighting its capacity to improve the speed and quality of decision-making.

Chapter 13, *Can you fix the supply chain? Pitfalls and stepping stones in pandemic risk management and research for a better supply chain*, reflects on what is and what is not new about the risk impact of the COVID-19 pandemic. It considers stepping-stones for structurally improving supply chain management after the pandemic and the pitfalls in the change process involved.

The pandemic, the author says poses significant questions about supply chains. Will it prove to be a once-in-a-lifetime risk event resulting in a return to pre-pandemic comfort zones? Or will it become a turning point in supply chain management, a critical stepping-stone to break through bottlenecks and strategic inertia?

The author suggests that the pandemic gave companies both familiar risks and less familiar risk circumstances, the result of which were new risk management techniques developed at a speed not normally considered feasible. This, he says, provides input into the ongoing efforts to develop more structurally robust risk management capabilities.

This situation, the author argues, makes it incumbent on researchers to grow the body of research and social value by studying the innovations so that supply chain managers can meet future demands. With that in mind, he considers what is new, what is not so new, and what this implies for managers navigating supply chain risks as well as for supply chain researchers.

It is likely the pandemic will be the defining risk event of a generation. Against a backdrop of rapid social change, digital disruption, and the emergence of sustainability as a key business driver, COVID-19 has delivered a sizeable shake-up that has accelerated the re-calibration of supply chains. There is a strong argument that the pandemic has served as a wake-up call for more seismic shifts to come in the way we do business. To that end, the lessons we have learned are positive.

It is important to remember that the process of building greater resilience from here is iterative—in truth it always has been. The lessons contained within this chapter—and this book as a whole—are starting points, markers from which to begin phases of improvement. That can only come from trial and error. Failure, as we saw with COVID-19, is part of the process, as well as part of the success story. Always fail forward, fail better and keep improving. Learn the lessons and move on.

Chapter 10
Supply Chain Configuration in a Post-pandemic World

Sascha Düerkop and Michael Huth

Abstract Shortly after the outbreak of the global COVID-19 pandemic in early 2020, governments around the world enacted new border regulations for people and goods, some of which are still in effect 2 years later. Modern supply chains, which often span the entire world, have shown to be vulnerable to such changes. Additionally, trade wars often restrict import and export capacities or lead to increased costs. This in turn might trigger managers to increase, where possible, local production. Such new capacities were designed to be temporary, but a public debate to configure less globalized supply chains has already started. This configuration of supply chains can be understood as the supply chain structure (the supply chain units and the links between them) and the key attributes of the supply chain. These key attributes can be divided into functional attributes, such as the procurement and the distribution type, and into structural attributes, such as the topography of a supply chain and the integration and coordination. The chapter analyses how supply chains might be reconfigured in the aftermath of the COVID-19 pandemic. It uses the framework of functional and structural attributes as a basis for the analysis. This analysis will directly contribute to the ongoing debate about the configuration of tomorrow's supply chains.

1 Introduction

The COVID-19 pandemic, which has been ongoing since early 2020, has had a significant impact on supply chains in addition to its human health implications. At the beginning of the pandemic, the perceived threat often led to hoarding purchases. Surgical masks and toilet paper, as well as dry food such as pasta, flour, and yeast, were in extreme demand, leading to shortages in supermarkets. However, these demand shocks were only temporary in nature. In principle, the products in demand were available in sufficient quantities, so that supply chains functioned normally

S. Düerkop (✉) · M. Huth
Fulda University of Applied Sciences, Fulda, Germany
e-mail: sascha.dueerkop@w.hs-fulda.de; michael.huth@w.hs-fulda.de

again after a short time and the supply of all products to the population was restored (Lerch et al., 2020).

But global supply chains, regardless of its product group, were also affected by the pandemic. The effects were not immediately noticeable for the population, but were clearly felt within the various sectors and were of much longer duration. Difficulties arose due to production restrictions up to and including (temporary) plant closures, but also due to trade barriers erected at the political level to contain the COVID-19 pandemic, which significantly limited the effectiveness of supply chains. Carrera and Duthoit (2021) show that in the automotive industry, well over 40 % of companies had or have to cut production due to supply bottlenecks; manufacturers of household appliances, the mechanical engineering sector, and the electronics industry also report that more than 30 % of companies had or have to cut production due to supply problems. Supply problems mainly occurred due to delays in cross-border land transport, delays in air transport, and delays in critical deliveries (Elliott, 2021). This highlighted the vulnerability of global and thus often complex supply chains.

Due to this vulnerability of supply chains the option of "de-globalization" of supply chains is periodically discussed in politics and in the public. The idea behind de-globalization is to replace key actors within supply chains, whose failure might affect the effectiveness of the supply chain and who are not based in the target country, with national actors (Heckmann et al., 2015). In this way, supply chains can be made independent of trade restrictions and other events that threaten supply security. In other words, adjusting the supply chain configuration should lead to lower vulnerability and thus higher resilience to adverse events.

The objective of this chapter is to examine the effectiveness and feasibility of such supply chain configuration adaptation approaches. The results show, which options for supply chain configuration are realistic for increasing resilience.

In order to achieve this goal, the following section develops the necessary fundamentals. The section explains the question of what is meant by supply chain configuration and which forms of adaptation of the supply chain configuration are conceivable. Building on the theoretical foundations, individual adaptation options are then examined and evaluated in terms of their effectiveness and feasibility. The chapter ends with an outlook on the extent to which supply chain configuration adjustments will be made in the future in order to become more resilient to undesirable events.

2   Relevant Basics of Supply Chain Configuration

The basis for the following analysis and evaluation are supply chains. A supply chain is understood to be "[...] a network of organizations and processes wherein a number of various enterprises [...] collaborate [...] along the entire value chain to acquire raw materials, to convert these raw materials into specified final products, and to deliver these final products to customers" (Ivanov et al., 2019).

The configuration is then usually understood as the strategic choice of all actors, links, and processes along the supply chain. According to a seminar paper by Fisher (1997), such choices are regularly made as a function of the final product. For functional goods, which have a low margin but a well-predictable and stable demand, the primary goal of supply chain configuration is efficiency, i.e., to produce the final product as cheaply as possible. For so-called innovative products, which are characterized by fluctuating demand and high margins, the supply chain is designed to respond to the market to meet demand as best as possible, even if this is not always cost-effective.

The ability of a supply chain to adapt to disruptions can be measured in two different ways, as detailed by Bundschuh et al. (2003). They define reliability "as the probability that a system or a component performs its specified function as intended within a given time horizon and environment." Applied to supply chain configurations, this means that the supply chain is considered reliably configured if it is highly unlikely to malfunction, i.e., fail to deliver goods to consumers. In contrast, they define robustness as "as the extent to which a system is able to perform its intended function relatively well in the presence of failures of components or subsystems." Applied to supply chain configuration, this means that a supply chain is robust if it manages to deliver a good percentage of its intended performance even in the face of failures along the supply chain.

This configuration of supply chains can be understood as "a set of supply chain units and links among these units defining the underlying supply chain structure and the key attributes of the supply chain network" (Chandra & Grabis, 2016). These key attributes can be divided into categories of functional attributes, such as the procurement and the distribution type, and structural attributes, such as the topography of a supply chain and the integration and coordination (Meyr & Stadtler, 2015), as shown in Table 10.1.

Identifying and classifying supply chain attributes, as shown in Table 10.1, help identify options for supply chain configuration. The following section uses selected attributes to discuss whether and how adjustments in supply chain configuration can lead to higher levels of resilience.

3 Analysis and Evaluation of Supply Chain Configuration Approaches

The COVID-19 pandemic, as well as other global or continental supply chain disruptions such as the blockade of the Suez Canal in 2021, have led to volatile demand for products generally considered functional goods. Demand for face masks tends to be stable in "normal times," and profit margins for these goods are low. As a result, supply chains for face mask have been configured in the most efficient manner, but have not been able to respond to a dramatically and globally changing market. While supply chains may be reliable, as it is highly unlikely that a global

Table 10.1 Functional and structural attributes of supply chains (Meyr & Stadtler, 2015)

Functional attributes		Structural attributes	
Categories	Attributes	Categories	Attributes
Procurement type	Number and type of products procured Sourcing type Flexibility of suppliers Supplier lead time and reliability Materials' life cycle	Topography of a supply chain	Network structure Degree of globalization Location of decoupling point(s) Major constraints
Production type	Organization of the production process Repetition of operations Changeover characteristics Bottlenecks in production Working time flexibility etc.	Integration and coordination	Legal position Balance of power Direction of coordination Type of information exchanged
Distribution type	Distribution structure Pattern of delivery Deployment of transportation means Loading restrictions		
Sales type	Relation to customers Availability of future demands Demand curve Products' life cycle Number of product types Degree of customization Bill of materials (BOM) Portion of service operations		

crisis could cause a failure, they did not prove to be robust, as a significant bottleneck was the result of a supply chain failure.

Due to the severe consequences of supply shortages, particularly for health commodities needed to address the global health crisis of the COVID-19 pandemic, various options to make supply chains for functional commodities more resilient are currently being discussed by policymakers, academics, and the public. To structure the range of possible adaptations, both through potentially new policies and through strategic choices made by supply chain owners, the following analysis is structured along the supply chain typology of Meyr and Stadtler (2015). In this context, individual structural and functional attributes of the typology are singled out and examined for feasibility and impact with regard to resilience in supply chains. These relate to the drivers of potential vulnerability described as "typical" in Alicke et al. (2020a), namely the question of planning and the supplier network.

3.1 Structural Attributes: Network Structure

According to Meyr and Stadtler (2015), the network structure describes "the material flows from upstream to downstream entities." This definition, which is still not very clear, is concretized by Feldmann and Olhager (2019). With a focus on production activities in a supply chain, it is about "the relationship between component plants and assembly plants, focussing on the material flows within the internal manufacturing network for a product group." Based on real production networks, Feldmann and Olhager (2019) derive four types of networks: linear, divergent, convergent, and mixed.

Determining a suitable network structure for a supply chain of a specific product is part of the supply chain design and thus a strategic decision. In particular, the network structure is usually rigid and is only adjusted when the production process or external circumstances change. Aylor et al. (2020) argue that such an adjustment of the network structure (including the near- and reshoring discussed below) is primarily determined by two factors: the "impetus to change," such as primarily economic but also political pressure, and "the ease of adjustment," i.e., how easy or difficult it is to replace selected suppliers or how high the capital costs are for the geographic relocation of sites in the network.

If adjustments are made that change the network structure, this does not necessarily affect all partners along a supply chain. Often, partners along a supply chain do not have an overview of the entire supply chain, but only know their immediate upstream and downstream neighbors. As a result, many companies do not know where they stand in the supply chain.

From a manager's perspective, however, it is of great importance to know at which level in a supply chain one's own company is located. A study by the Fraunhofer Institute for Systems and Innovation Research ISI shows that companies at the (customer) end of the supply chain experienced greater delivery difficulties than companies at a lower level of the supply chain (Lerch et al., 2020).

A McKinsey study on the vulnerability of supply chains analyzes five different areas: While most of these areas the vulnerability of the individual company—also due to increased financial resilience—is below the industry benchmark, an individual company is significantly more vulnerable, especially in the area of network structure (Alicke et al., 2020b). A first step to mitigate this vulnerability by building higher resilience is to know the network structure and its points of vulnerability (Alicke et al., 2020b). However, the prerequisites for this are currently low because there is little transparency of the supply chain. A study by the German Association of Supply Chain Management, Procurement and Logistics (Bundesverband Materialwirtschaft, Einkauf und Logistik e.V.) shows, for example, that while the first supplier level is still transparent to 70 % of companies, the second supplier level is transparent to less than 41 % of companies; earlier supplier levels are only taken into account by a company's SCRM in 30 % of cases (Huth et al., 2020). The most urgent task for companies is therefore to increase the transparency of their supply chain (and thus the network structure), to know their suppliers not only at the first level, and thus to create a basis for sound and detailed risk identification, analysis, and assessment. Only then can risks arising, for example, from single sourcing relationships (see below) be reduced through appropriate measures.

3.2 Structural Attributes: Degree of Globalization

Closely related to the network structure is the degree of globalization of a supply chain. A de-globalization of supplies, in particular of critical goods such as medical supplies and pharma goods, was widely discussed among policy makers (Kuroczik, 2020), industry leaders (Hüttemann, 2020), and scholars. Two possible concepts were considered possible options for the future: (1) Nearshoring and (2) reshoring, sometimes also referred to as nationalization.

Nearshoring essentially means outsourcing production steps along the supply chain to supply chain partners in the vicinity. Proximity in this context can refer to geographical distance, but also to cultural, administrative, or economic proximity (van Hassel et al., 2021). While the concept originates from the 1980s and 1990s, when production steps were increasingly outsourced and proximity was conceived as a potential factor in this step, it is now revisited as one option to bring back already outsourced production steps into the proximity of the market to avoid disruptions like those experienced during the COVID-19 pandemic. van Hassel et al. (2021) discuss nearshoring as a potential relief to global crisis such as the pandemic, while Jovanović et al. (2021) go a step further and propose such a nearshoring production hub for the European market, the Western Balkans. Finally, Putri and Hudaya (2021) take a look at one specific sector, the automotive and electronic industry, and explore the potential for nearshoring or reshoring production steps that are currently done offshore in Mainland China.

Reshoring or nationalization goes one step further and (re-) organizes the supply chain so that all steps of the chain are carried out in the same country. Complete relocation of production would minimize the risk of supply chain disruption due to a global crisis, but it is usually associated with high costs. Due to the common European market, it also has little advantage compared to relocation within the common market area. Nevertheless, Zhu et al. (2020) consider a full nationalization of at least certain "crucial industries" as a likely outcome of the lessons from the COVID-19 pandemic.

In general, both, nearshoring and reshoring are being (re-) considered for the design of post-COVID-19 supply chains, as they simply remove the biggest barrier that caused the shortages that happened during the pandemic: The collapse of intercontinental trade due to closed or partly closed borders for goods and people. Thus, they directly address the lessons learned and are indeed one option to tackle possible risks caused by future pandemics. According to a survey by McKinsey, 40 % of supply chain managers are planning nearshoring and increasing supplier base (Alicke et al., 2020c). Another survey of more than 1,100 decision makers shows that just under 15% of companies are planning reshoring (Allianz Research and Euler Hermes Economic Research, 2020). However, both come at a cost, in this case literally. Nearshoring, e.g., to the Western Balkans for goods consumed within the European Union, results in higher production costs than producing in the Far East, but they reduce the numbers and the complexity of border crossings required. Reshoring naturally entirely removes the need to cross any border, but subsequently comes at even higher costs. In addition to these immense capital costs of building modern facilities associated with reshoring, the need for highly trained employees (at least in high-tech industries) can also make reshoring difficult (Aylor et al., 2020). This trade-off between production costs and robustness to global crisis will eventually decide if the production of a good is reshored, nearshored, or left unchanged. This is clearly illustrated by new data from a survey conducted by the Association of German Chambers of Industry and Commerce, according to which 15% of the companies surveyed are planning to relocate their production or parts of their production to a new site (Deutscher Industrie- und Handelskammertag e. V., 2021). The outcome will likely be determined by the good itself, e.g., by its value, its criticality, especially in the case of a global crisis, and the political will of actors to subsidize either near- or reshoring. Because this chapter focuses on pandemics, cost is one of the most important factors for near- or reshoring. Apart from cost, other factors should also be considered; see, for example, the extensive list of relevant decision factors provided by Ellram et al. (2013).

The above-mentioned study by the Fraunhofer Institute for Systems and Innovation Research ISI, however, also provides a strong argument against nearshoring or reshoring, as it directly addresses the question of whether global supply chains are more susceptible to a shock such as the COVID-19 pandemic than more local supply chains. For this purpose, the supply chains of the participating companies were examined. A disadvantage of global supply chains in contrast to regional supply chains was not observed: "The robustness of a network does not seem to be determined by the degree of internationalization in the case of the COVID-19 pandemic" (Lerch et al., 2020, pp. 5–6).

Another approach in the context of supply chain configuration with the potential to increase the resilience of supply chains is the sourcing type. Meyr and Stadtler (2015) define this as the number of suppliers from which a specific material (raw material, component, etc.) is procured. A distinction can be made between single sourcing and multiple sourcing: While in single sourcing the material is procured from a single supplier, in multiple sourcing it is procured from a large number of suppliers. Due to risk aspects, but also capacity issues, a third sourcing type, dual sourcing, has become established. In this case, the material is procured from two suppliers.

Realized risks such as the COVID-19 pandemic, but also the Fukushima disaster, for example, have shown that supply chains in which procurement is largely based on single sourcing can be disrupted in such a way that they no longer function. In the winter of 2020, for example, the Volkswagen Group had to cut production at its main plant in Wolfsburg because a supplier had failed (tagesschau.de, 2020). This was a supplier of foam parts or components for seats that has its production site in

Germany (IDG Business Media GmbH, 2020). The example shows the fundamental problem that exists with single sourcing: as soon as the only supplier—for whatever reason—can no longer deliver, the supply is interrupted. Although the remaining stocks of required materials can be used for the company's own production, when these are exhausted, nothing can be produced due to the lack of materials—the supply chain breaks down. A short-term change to another supplier is often not possible and depends on the answer to a multitude of questions: Is another supplier available—do they have the technologies and know-how to produce the materials as required, do they have the necessary capacity? How long does it take to qualify a supplier (both technically and formally)? For example, in pharmaceutical supply chains, the costs are particularly high: the establishment of a "second source" can take up to 5 years here due to the regulatory ancillary conditions (Lücker & Seifert, 2017). Is it permissible to choose a different supplier with regard to one's own customers? An example of this is Toyota, which also had to cut production in Europe after the earthquake in Fukushima, as parts deliveries were produced in Fukushima Prefecture (Süddeutsche Zeitung, 2011). In such cases, the inherent risk is accepted.

Multiple sourcing, on the other hand, leads to a reduction in risk and to greater resilience in the supply chain. If a supplier—for whatever reason—is unable to deliver, the share of material to be procured is allocated to one or more of the other suppliers. A shortage up to an out-of-stock situation is not excluded, but unlikely. At the same time, there are certain disadvantages associated with such an approach: In principle, transaction costs are higher with multiple sourcing than with single sourcing. Supplier management is significantly more complex—starting with the search and selection of suppliers and extending to monitoring and quality control of suppliers. These costs must already be taken into account in the supply chain configuration.

This also applies to dual sourcing, which on the one hand is intended to reduce the likelihood of an out-of-stock situation occurring, but on the other hand is also intended to result in excessively high transaction costs and the realization of economies of scale. In a survey by McKinsey on measures planned by companies to strengthen the resilience of supply chains, 53 % of supply chain managers mentioned the implementation of dual sourcing (Alicke et al., 2020c) (Despite the risk reduction, it is possible that both suppliers fail—a rare occurrence, it should be noted: In an expert discussion as part of the "BME Logistics Survey 2020" conducted by Huth et al. (2020), one interviewee explained that the supply chain configuration called for two suppliers—one in the Wuhan region of China, one in Lombardy, Italy; both areas were initial hot spots in the COVID-19 pandemic in the spring of 2020, so both production facilities were closed and unable to deliver).

3.3 Functional Attributes: Sourcing Type (Stockpiling Versus Just in Time)

One aspect that is not explicitly addressed in Meyr's and Stadler's typification is the question of whether the procurement process is based on stockpiling or just-in-time supply. This point is significant because the issue of stockpiling has been increasingly discussed, especially since the beginning of the COVID-19 pandemic.

In principle, the question of the extent to which inventories can help to generate resilience and the extent to which just-in-time supply leads to low resilience is easy to answer: The inherent strengths and weaknesses of the two procurement principles are described in almost every basic book on logistics or SCM: Thus—among others—one of the main reasons for holding inventories is the "buffering of uncertainty" (Bowersox et al., 2010). Stock procurement is thus a control measure in the sense of risk management that generates resilience. Accordingly, 47 % of the supply chain managers surveyed by McKinsey plan higher inventories for critical products (Alicke et al., 2020c). However, there are costs associated with stockpiling. These include capital commitment costs for the stored products, costs for warehousing as a service (inventory management, insurance), storage costs (costs for the physical warehouse, handling of the products), and risk costs, for example, for damaged or expired products (Rushton et al., 2017). Such costs often represent a high proportion of total logistics costs (Rushton et al., 2017) As such, they conflict with one of the major trends in logistics and SCM that has existed for a long time and is essential to supply chain decisions—cost pressure. The last two empirical surveys of the German Logistics Association (Bundesvereinigung Logistik e.V.) showed cost pressure among the three most important trends: Thus, Kersten et al. (2017) found that cost pressure had the highest relevance of all considered trends for the companies surveyed. In the subsequent survey, cost pressure was also the third most relevant trend for the companies surveyed, with a value of 4.1 (on a scale of 1–5) (Kersten et al., 2020). Cost pressure is therefore one of the decisive trends that many companies in supply chains have to face and bow to. Higher inventories with the corresponding costs are usually diametrically opposed to this trend. The question, therefore, arises as to whether this trend, which has after all dominated supply chain management for years—despite all other developments—is abating, so that stockholding in the sense of inventory procurement appears to make more sense.

The fact that stockpiling runs counter to the basic entrepreneurial idea of profit maximization due to the costs mentioned is already made clear by the terminology: goods held in stock within a supply chain are usually referred to as "safety stock"—i.e., stock that ensures that the entire supply chain is "safeguarded" against unforeseen events (for example Collier, 2017). Conversely, however, the term can also be interpreted in such a way that a change in the feeling of security (among companies, politicians, or even society) almost inevitably leads to an adjustment and thus an increase in the safety stock. The crucial question, which has not yet been answered conclusively, is whether the feeling of security will continue to change after the COVID-19 crisis has subsided. Statements made in expert interviews conducted by Huth et al. (2020) give no reason to assume that risk aversion will increase.

On the other hand, regardless of all just-in-time approaches, there often seem to be (quasi-hidden) inventories in a supply chain that reduce an out-of-stock situation: Tempelmeier (2005) tributes this primarily to the fact that many software systems for inventory management assume by default and incorrectly that demand is normally distributed and the vast majority of supply chain actors are or become aware of this miscalculation and accordingly, based on empirical knowledge, create additional inventories in order to increase their own service level. Studies by McKinsey & Company show that in the automotive industry the inventory range, added up over the entire supply chain, is 40–70 days and that in the pharmaceutical industry the inventory range, also as the addition of the ranges at the individual stages in a supply chain, is 230–320 days (Alicke et al., 2020a). Companies should therefore identify these (often invisible) inventories and use them as a buffer (Alicke et al., 2020a).

4 Discussion and Outlook

The drastic consequences of realized risks such as the COVID-19 pandemic are increasing public, political, and also corporate risk awareness.

Increasing risk awareness, especially in the case of security-relevant or "critical" goods, is suitable for creating a regulatory framework in the future that will require at least system-wide risk management, but also might require regional production or stockpiling under certain circumstances. Such a framework seems to be particularly relevant for products that have a high social value (which the monetary value might not necessarily be high as well): For goods, such as medical consumables like face masks, the costs to society in the event of a crisis are significantly higher than for producers and other actors along the respective supply chain, as the COVID-19 pandemic has shown. Accordingly, producers are not expected to build up regional production worldwide or build up safety stocks on their own initiative—the costs would probably significantly exceed the benefits, given the rarity of such crises. Conversely, politicians in many places have initiated debates on how exactly these steps can be taken, since they have a great interest in preventing the social costs of a shortage in the event of a crisis in the future. Nevertheless, these considerations harbor imponderables: If the value chains are anchored more strongly within a region for precautionary reasons, this could lead to a reallocation of production factors, which would require a redefinition of the optimum of the international division of labor. The model of global division of labor could disintegrate into competing economic blocs. This would entail a real welfare loss, but one to be paid in the case of reduced dependence (Kolev & Obst, 2020). Such a welfare loss, based on foreclosure of the European Union, can be up to 3.6 % permanently for the countries in the European Union, and even up to 4.9 % in the case of a trade war due to a reaction to the foreclosure by the countries outside the EU (Felbermayr et al., 2020).

The opposite is the case for high-priced, high-margin, and socially less relevant goods. For example, the closure of an automobile plant harms the economy in which it is located, but not directly to society as such. The economic damage to the operator of the plant, on the other hand, is enormous. It can therefore be assumed that the newly identified risks will change the risk awareness of the players in the supply chain itself and that corporate strategy adjustments will follow. As a first step, it is to be expected that companies will address the issue of risk management much more thoroughly than before and also demand greater transparency along their supply chains. It is also conceivable that companies currently pursuing a single sourcing strategy will at least identify and qualify other possible suppliers.

In summary, it seems unlikely that supply chain managers will completely abandon the previous maxim of territory and optimize processes in the future so that the supply chain is as robust as possible. It is more likely that a certain degree of robustness will be incorporated as an additional restriction in future supply chain management considerations to a greater extent than has been the case to date.

Many consequences of the COVID-19 pandemic will only be measurable in the coming years and after the end of the crisis. For example, as soon as industry-specific analyses of the corporate and societal costs of the pandemic appear to be backed up by corresponding studies, there will be a great need for further research into which best practices have led to companies and supply chains coping well with the crisis. Finally, there is a need for regionally focused research to assess how the pandemic affected different parts of the world differently and which regions might even benefit in the long run.

References

Alicke, K., Azcue, X., & Barriball, E. (2020a). *Supply-chain recovery in coronavirus times—Plan for now and the future*. McKinsey & Company. Retrieved from https://www.mckinsey.com/~/media/McKinsey/Business%20Functions/Operations/Our%20Insights/Supply%20chain%20recovery%20in%20coronavirus%20times%20plan%20for%20now%20and%20the%20future/Supply-chain-recovery-in-coronavirus-times-plan-for-now-and-the-future.pdf?shouldIndex=false. Updated on March 18, 2020, checked on January 15, 2021.

Alicke, K., Barriball, E., Lund, S., & Swan, D. (2020b). *Is your supply chain risk blind—Or risk resilient?* McKinsey & Company. Retrieved from https://www.mckinsey.com/~/media/McKinsey/Business%20Functions/Operations/Our%20Insights/Is%20your%20supply%20chain%20risk%20blind%20or%20risk%20resilient/Is-your-supply-chain-risk-blind-or-risk-resilient.pdf?shouldIndex=false. Updated on May 14, 2020, checked on January 15, 2021.

Alicke, K., Gupta, R., & Trautwein, V. (2020c). *Resetting supply chains for the next normal*. McKinsey & Company. Retrieved from https://www.mckinsey.com/~/media/McKinsey/Business%20Functions/Operations/Our%20Insights/Resetting%20supply%20chains%20for%20the%20next%20normal/Resetting-supply-chains-for-the-next-normal.pdf?shouldIndex=false. Updated on July 21, 2020, checked on January 15, 2021.

Allianz Research, & Euler Hermes Economic Research (Eds.). (2020). *Search of post-Covid-19 resilience*. Global Supply Chain Survey. Munich, Paris. Retrieved from https://www.eulerhermes.com/content/dam/onemarketing/ehndbx/eulerhermes_com/en_gl/erd/publications/pdf/2020_10_12_SupplyChainSurvey.pdf. Checked on December 18, 2020.

Aylor, B., Datta, B., DeFauw, M., Gilbert, M., Knizek, C., & McAdoo, M. (2020). *Designing resilience into global supply chains*. Boston Consulting Group. Retrieved from https://web-assets.bcg.com/8d/6f/993b0da4424dac2931263f02df1c/bcg-designing-resilience-into-global-supply-chains-july-2020.pdf. Checked on January 15, 2021.

Bowersox, D. J., Closs, D. J., & Cooper, M. B. (2010). *Supply chain logistics management* (3rd ed., International ed.). McGraw-Hill/Irwin (The McGraw-Hill/Irwin series operations and decision sciences).

Bundschuh, M., Klabjan, D., & Thurston, D. L. (2003). *Modeling robust and reliable supply chains.* Retrieved from https://citeseerx.ist.psu.edu/viewdoc/download?doi=10.1.1.399.3 672&rep=rep1&type=pdf

Carrera, J. B., & Duthoit, A. (2021). *The big squeeze. Supply chain disruptions pressure manufacturing margins in the US and Europe.* Allianz Research & Euler Hermes Economic Research (Eds.). Retrieved from https://www.eulerhermes.com/content/dam/onemarketing/ehndbx/eulerhermes_com/en_gl/erd/publications/the-watch/2021_10_28_Sector-profitability.pdf. Checked on November 23, 2021.

Chandra, C., & Grabis, J. (2016). *Supply chain configuration. Concepts, solutions, and applications* (2nd ed.). Springer. Retrieved from http://gbv.eblib.com/patron/FullRecord.aspx?p=4454243

Collier, D. A. (2017). *OM. A student-tested, faculty-approved approach to teaching and learning operations management* (6th. ed, student ed.). South-Western Cengage Learning.

Deutscher Industrie- und Handelskammertag e. V. (Ed.). (2021). *Neusortierung von Lie-ferketten. Sonderauswertung des AHK World Business Outlook Herbst 2021.* Berlin. Retrieved from https://www.dihk.de/resource/blob/62046/ebd89f041be671ecd292c6dffff7c5da/wbo-sonderauswertung-lieferketten-data.pdf. Checked on November 26, 2021.

Elliott, R. (2021). *Supply chain resilience report 2021.* Business Continuity Institute BCI. Everstream Analytics. Retrieved from https://www.thebci.org/static/e02a3e5f-82e5-4ff1-b8bc61de9657e9c8/BCI-0007h-Supply-Chain-Resilience-ReportLow-Singles.pdf. Checked on November 11, 23, 2021.

Ellram, L. M., Tate, W. L., & Petersen, K. J. (2013). Offshoring and Reshoring: An update on the manufacturing location decision. *Journal of Supply Chain Management, 49*(2), 14–22. https://doi.org/10.1111/jscm.12019

Felbermayr, G., Sandkamp, A., Mahlkow, H., & Gans, S. (2020). Lieferketten in der Zeit nach Corona. In IMPULS-Stiftung für den Maschinenbau, den Anlagenbau und die Informationstechnik (Eds.), *Kurzgutachten im Auftrag der IMPULS Stiftung.* Institut für Weltwirtschaft (IfW Kiel). Retrieved from https://www.ifw-kiel.de/fileadmin/Dateiverwaltung/IfW-Publications/-ifw/Policy_Papers/2021/Lieferketten_in_der_Zeit_nach_Corona_Endbericht.pdf. Checked on September 6, 2021.

Feldmann, A., & Olhager, J. (2019). A taxonomy of international manufacturing networks. *Production Planning and Control, 30*(2–3), 163–178. https://doi.org/10.1080/09537287.2018.1534269

Fisher, M. L. (1997, March–April 1997). What is the right supply chain for your product? *Harvard Business Review.*

Heckmann, I., Comes, T., & Nickel, S. (2015). A critical review on supply chain risk—Definition, measure and modeling. *Omega, 52*, 119–132. https://doi.org/10.1016/j.omega.2014.10.004

Huth, M., Knauer, C., & Prang, J. (2020). BME-Logistikumfrage 2020. *Supply chain risk management.* Bundesverband Materialwirtschaft, Einkauf und Logistik e.V. (BME) (Ed.).

Hüttemann, D. (2020, March 16). Arzneimittel: Produktion zurück nach Europa holen. *Pharmazeutische Zeitung* (Online). Retrieved from https://www.pharmazeutische-zeitung.de/produktion-zurueck-nach-europa-holen/. Checked on November 17, 2021.

IDG Business Media GmbH (Ed.). (2020). *Volkswagen drosselt wegen Corona die Produktion. Lieferant für Schaumstoffteile ausgefallen.* Retrieved from https://www.cio.de/a/volkswagen-drosselt-wegen-corona-die-produktion,3649750. Updated on December 14, 2020, checked on November 16, 2021.

Ivanov, D., Tsipoulanidis, A., & Schönberger, J. (2019). *Global supply chain and operations management. A decision-oriented introduction to the creation of Value* (2nd ed.). Springer International Publishing (Springer texts in business and economics).

Jovanović, B., Ghodsi, M., van Zijverden, O., Kluge, S., Gaber, M., Mima, R., et al. (2021). *Getting stronger after COVID-19: Nearshoring potential in the Western Balkans.* The Vienna Institute for International Economic Studies (Ed.) (Research report, 453). Retrieved from https://wiiw.ac.at/getting-stronger-after-covid-19-nearshoring-potential-in-the-western-balkans-dlp-5814.pdf. Checked on November 18, 2021.

Kersten, W., Seiter, M., von See, B., Hackius, N., & Maurer, T. (2017). *Trends and strategies in logistics and supply chain management. Digital trans-formation opportunities.* Bundesvereinigung Logistik e.V. (BVL) (Ed.). Retrieved from https://www.bvl.de/misc/filePush.php?id=39660&name=BVL2017-TAS-Digital-Transformation-Study.pdf. Checked on November 18, 2021.

Kersten, W., von See, B., Lodemann, S., & Grotemeier, C. (2020). *Trends und Strategien in Logistik und Supply Chain Management.* Entwicklungen und Perspektiveneiner nachhaltigen und digitalen Transformation. Bundesvereini-gung Logistik e.V. (BVL) (Ed.). Retrieved from https://www.bvl-trends.de/wp-content/uploads/2020/07/BVLD20-TUS-Auswertung-1.pdf. Checked on November 18, 2021.

Kolev, G., & Obst, T. (2020). *Die Abhängigkeit der deutschen Wirtschaft von internationalen Lieferketten.* Edited by Institut der Deutschen Wirtschaft. Köln (IW-Report, 16/2020). Retrieved from https://www.iwkoeln.de/fileadmin/user_upload/Studien/Report/PDF/2020/IW-Report_2020_Lieferketten.pdf. Checked on 9/6/2021.

Kuroczik, J. (2020, April 20). Verschärfte Lieferengpässe bei Medikamenten. *Frankfur-ter Allgemeine Zeitung.* Retrieved from https://www.faz.net/aktuell/wissen/medizin-ernaehrung/verschaerfte-lieferengpaesse-bei-medikamenten-in-deutschland-16730952.html. Checked on November 17, 2021.

Lerch, C., Jäger, A., & Heimberger, H. (2020). *Produktion in Zeiten der Corona-Krise. Welche Auswirkungen hat die Pandemie heute und zukünftig auf die In-dustrie?* Fraunhofer-Institut für System- und Innovationsforschung ISI (Ed.). Karls-ruhe (Mitteilungen aus der ISI-Erhebung, 78). Retrieved from https://www.isi.fraunhofer.de/content/dam/isi/dokumente/modernisierung-produktion/erhebung2018/PI_78_Produktion_in_Corona_Web.pdf. Checked on November 16, 2021.

Lücker, F., & Seifert, R. W. (2017). Building up resilience in a pharmaceutical supply chain through inventory, dual sourcing and agility capacity. *Omega, 73,* 114–124. https://doi.org/10.1016/j.omega.2017.01.001

Meyr, H., & Stadtler, H. (2015). Types of supply chains. In H. Stadtler, C. Kilger, & H. Meyr (Eds.), *Supply chain management and advanced planning. Concepts, models, software, and case studies* (5th ed., pp. 55–70). Springer (Springer texts in business and economics).

Putri, R. A., & Hudaya, M. (2021). Reimaging post COVID-19 global value chain: Case study of automotive and electronic companies in China. *Global Strategies, 15*(2), 255–286. https://doi.org/10.20473/jgs.15.2.2021.255-286

Rushton, A., Croucher, P., & Baker, P. (2017). *The handbook of logistics and distribution management* (6th ed.). Kogan Page.

Süddeutsche Zeitung. (2011). *Toyota stellt Fertigung in Europa vorübergehend ein.* Retrieved from https://www.sueddeutsche.de/wirtschaft/japan-folgen-der-naturkatastrophen-toyota-stellt-fertigung-in-europa-tageweise-ein-1.1084536. Updated on April 13, 2011, checked on November 17, 2021.

tagesschau.de. (2020). *VW muss Produktion drosseln.* Retrieved from https://www.tagesschau.de/wirtschaft/unternehmen/hr-boerse-story-25193.html. Updated on December 14, 2020, checked on November 16, 2021.

Tempelmeier, H. (2005). *Bestands management in Supply Chains.* BoD—Books on Demand.

van Hassel, E., Vanelslander, T., Neyens, K., Vandeborre, H., Kindt, D., & Kellens, S. (2021). Reconsidering nearshoring to avoid global crisis impacts: Application and calculation of the total cost of ownership for specific scenarios. *Research in Transportation Economics,* 101089. https://doi.org/10.1016/j.retrec.2021.101089

Zhu, G., Chou, M. C., & Tsai, C. W. (2020). Lessons learned from the COVID-19 pandemic exposing the shortcomings of current supply chain operations: A long-term prescriptive offering. *Sustainability, 12*(14), 5858. https://doi.org/10.3390/su12145858

Chapter 11
Rethinking the US Strategic National Stockpile for Future Pandemics with Inventory, Capacity, and Capability

ManMohan S. Sodhi and Christopher S. Tang

Abstract The response to COVID-19 as a public health emergency raised questions about preparedness against future pandemics. The US Strategic National Stockpile (SNS) with medically critical items such as ventilators and personal protection equipment for major public health emergencies proved to be inadequate in the first half of 2020. We seek to address how governments or other disaster management organizations should modify their stockpile approach for a more robust response to disasters than was the case in 2020. To this end, we argue that a "strategic reserve" against rare public health emergencies must not only have inventory but also backup capacity and standby capability. With a highly skewed "demand" distribution reflecting a rarely occurring pandemic or other disasters, we present a three-tiered approach comprising stockpile inventory as the first tier, backup capacity as the second, and standby capability to manufacture as the third.

1 Introduction

Stockpiling is a common strategy against disasters. However, COVID-19 exposed the shortcomings of the inventory-based US Strategic National Stockpile of ventilators, personal protection equipment (PPE), and other critical items to fight major public health emergencies. Not only were the stockpile quantities inadequate but also many items in stock had expired or become otherwise unusable. Makeshift reactive efforts to bolster ventilator stocks by tapping into the in-country manufacturing capabilities in the auto industry also foundered. This chapter addresses *how to redesign stockpiling for major public health emergencies or*

M. S. Sodhi
Bayes Business School (Formerly Cass), City, University of London, London, UK
e-mail: m.sodhi@city.ac.uk

C. S. Tang (✉)
UCLA Anderson School of Management, UCLA, Los Angeles, CA, USA
e-mail: chris.tang@anderson.ucla.edu

© The Author(s), under exclusive license to Springer Nature Switzerland AG 2023
O. Khan et al. (eds.), *Supply Chain Resilience*, Springer Series in Supply Chain Management 21, https://doi.org/10.1007/978-3-031-16489-7_11

other disasters, building on the current inventory-only approach for a more robust response by adding domestic capacity and capability as "additional tiers."

We argue that financially viable stockpiles for pandemics or other disasters should be designed and built around a three-tiered "reserve" with inventory, backup capacity, and standby capability to manufacture. With such a multitiered stockpile, public health or disaster management authorities would use inventory as the first line of defense in case of a viral epidemic (or other disasters) as is the current practice. If the epidemic turned into a pandemic (or the disaster expands in scope), the authorities could allow the use of backup capacity to produce more inventory. Furthermore, if the number of affected people kept growing, the government would call upon manufacturing capability within the country to create more backup capacity. Such a three-tiered response could be more cost-effective than the one based on inventory alone, especially when the annual "demand"—the need for medically critical items based on the total number of people hospitalized—is such that highly impactful events are very rare but low impact events are quite common across the years.

The managerial implication for a stockpile-based approach such as the US Strategic National Stockpile is that there is potential to reduce the currently targeted inventory in the inventory-only approach in practice today and use the savings to reserve domestic capacity and invest in domestic capability. For disaster management, the practical implication of our work is that the use of capacity and capability can not only lower the average annual cost of having pre-positioned inventory in anticipation of disasters. Building "domestic" capacity and capability can also help develop the target countries to escape the "vicious cycle" of disasters and vulnerability (Sodhi, 2015).

The rest of the chapter is as follows: Sect. 2 provides the pertinent literature and our contribution, while Sect. 3 gives some background on the US National Stockpile and the challenges for the stockpile during the first half of 2020 with COVID-19. Section 4 presents our three-tiered approach—we refer the reader to Sodhi and Tang (2021c) for a mathematical analysis of a three-tier system with proofs and numerical illustrations. Section 5 then provides some practical aspects on how to build and use capability, say, for the United States reserve before the conclusion in Sect. 6.

2   Literature

This chapter is related to different streams of the research including supply chain risk management, strategic stockpile design, humanitarian logistics, as well as inventory and capacity management.

2.1 Supply Chain Risk and COVID-19

COVID-19 created a research opportunity for disaster management and a wake-up call for supply chain management. Researchers are trying to infer opportunities and shape future research. Sodhi and Tang (2021a) argue that COVID created "extreme" conditions going beyond disruptions as considered in supply chain risk, while Chopra et al. (2021) present the use of "commons" to mitigate such extreme conditions. Use different theories—resource dependence theory, institutional theory, game theory, and others—to draw out research questions, offering ways for simultaneous transformation and resilience, i.e., *transilience*. Besides resilience and robustness discussed in the literature, additionally bring up the notion of viability (i.e., survivability) of a supply chain network in the face of disruptions. Use a structured review of papers in the OM and OR literature by examining the impact of epidemics or pandemics on supply chains to outline a research agenda for supply chain management. Their agenda is based on an adaptation to reallocate supply; preparedness; ripple effects in supply chains; recovery; sustainability (including humanitarian relief); and adopting digital means. See "a window of opportunity" for sustainability as a result of COVID. Our contribution to this literature is a way for a better (lower cost and more effective) stockpile with a three-tier "reserve" to bolster the response against a highly skewed demand distribution.

2.2 The US Strategic National Stockpile

We also contribute to the literature on the US stockpiles. In this literature, develop a decision support system to mitigate the effects of the disruption to healthcare supply chains during a pandemic by categorizing individuals in communities by vulnerability. Handfield et al. (2020) list the shortcomings of the Strategic National Stockpile. They propose a national contingency supply chain cell to manage the medical materials supply chain for the Strategic National Stockpile for governance and response all the way to county level. They also propose a national material control tower for real-time material status and location. Mehrotra et al. (2020) use stochastic "demand" for ventilators from different states in the United States at different stages of COVID-19 spread and a two-stage stochastic linear programming model for centralized allocation. Allocation can be done at a regional level with Huang et al. (2017) providing a detailed demand model for ventilators for the state of Texas with state-level centralized and distributed stockpiles under different scenarios of severity of influenza. Similarly, though not tied to the stockpile, consider the twin problems of unexpectedly high demand and the constrained supply of essential goods and offer a nonlinear programming model to guide the manufacturer develop an optimal recovery plan. Our contribution to this literature is stylized expected cost models with the three-tier "reserve" for the stockpile, changing the SNS to what Sodhi and Tang (2021b) term as the Strategic National Emergency Reserve.

2.3 Disaster Management with Humanitarian Supply Chains

Pre-placing inventory with near- and long-term projections is an important area in humanitarian logistics (e.g., Whybark, 2007; Tavana et al., 2018); see Dhamija et al. (2021) for a review of the wider humanitarian supply chain management literature. For disasters that are predictable in timing though not in intensity like floods, pre-positioned inventory can be used. For instance, Sodhi and Tang (2014) propose using micro-retailers for last-mile delivery. A network of pre-placed inventory in a network of warehouses acts as a two-tier system—meet the need from inventory from warehouses when the disaster strikes, and then trans-ship the goods laterally treating the other warehouses as a "reserve capacity" (Davis et al., 2013). Toyasaki et al. (2017) focus on the lateral stock trans-shipments between depots comprising the World Food Program-run United Nations Humanitarian Response Depot. The "Depot" in this case a network of depots in strategic locations around the world to transport emergency relief items on behalf of member humanitarian organizations.

Overall, the literature takes an inventory-only based approach for supply chains that respond to disasters. Our contribution is to bring attention to manufacturing capacity (not just "reserve" capacity from lateral trans-shipment) and production capability to bolster these supply chains. Doing so can reduce average annual costs and possibly circumvent misaligned incentives by reducing trans-shipments between depots (Toyasaki et al., 2017). Moreover, our chapter could contribute to a multi-echelon network of inventory in the humanitarian context (Tavana et al., 2018) with one echelon being manufacturing capacity or even capability, close to vulnerable areas. For pre-positioned inventory for floods, a second echelon of production capacity in an unaffected area can be used for replenishment of inventory in affected areas. Building capacity and capability also adds to the regional economy in a way that pre-positioned inventory cannot, and a better economy can counter the vicious cycle of disasters (Sodhi, 2015).

However, more research is needed to apply production capacity and capability as proposed in this chapter to humanitarian operations at large, and we defer such investigation to further research.

2.4 Inventory and Capacity

In the classical OM literature, determining the right level of inventory to meet uncertain demand has been studied extensively—see the comprehensive review by Zipkin (2000). Cohen et al. (1990) determined spare parts inventory at different locations to meet uncertain demand that is related to our chapter. However, our chapter examines a three-tiered system that integrates all three mechanisms: *inventory planning* (Zipkin, 2000), *capacity reservation* (Brown & Lee, 2003), and *capability conversion* (Sodhi & Tang, 2021b, 2021c).

In terms of reservation of backup capacity, Brown and Lee (2003) examined capacity reservation contracts in the semiconductor industry. Under the reservation contract, the buyer can pay an upfront and nonrefundable unit cost to "reserve" the capacity from the supplier. Then the buyer can exercise this contract by paying an additional unit cost to the supplier for producing up to the reserved capacity. Brown and Lee (2003) showed this capacity reservation contract was beneficial when implemented at a US-based electronics company, Xylinx. In the fashion industry, buyers often need to commit to the order quantity before the start of the selling season because of long production lead time. Because of this inflexibility, buyers cannot leverage the realized demand information obtained during the season to adjust its order quantity. To overcome this shortcoming, Eppen and Iyer (1997) examined a backup agreement that can be described as follows: The buyer commits to a certain capacity in advance and places its first order before the start of the season. Then the buyer can place its second order (up to the remaining capacity) after observing some sales information. The buyer pays the price for unused capacity.

Specifically, in addition to deciding on the amount of stock x for the National Stockpile, we need to decide not only on the backup capacity level y, but also the standby capability level z. Further, our objective function is also different. In the multi-echelon inventory literature, the objective is to determine optimal inventory planning policy at each echelon so that the system can satisfy stationary (but uncertain) demand according to a particular service level at a minimal cost. In the case of a pandemic, our objective is to design our system by choosing x, y, and z by considering the trade-off between the system's performance (stockout probability and the expected shortfall), and the total relevant cost (inventory purchasing and hold cost, the cost of establishing and exercising the backup capacity, and the cost of developing the standby capability as well as the cost of converting the capability to capacity).

The objective for a stockpile or, more generally, any response, is not only to reduce the expected total annual cost of any inventory—plus any capacity and capability—in the long run, but also the cost of any lives lost. Loss of life entails a penalty for not meeting demand. In health economics, there are two notions used to justify the amount of investment in saving a life *value of a statistical life* (VSL). For the United States, a typical number used is $10 million (Kniesner & Viscusi, 2019). A related notion encompassing the quality of life is *quality of life years* (QALY) saved. The point is that a trade-off needs to be made between the cost of intervention and the value of a life (or quality life years) saved, and using a penalty is a way of handling that.

We contribute by showing how *standby capability* integrates with inventory and capacity. The notion of developing capability at the "knowledge level" that can be converted into actual production level has not been examined in the OM literature. Moreover, to our knowledge, there is no known study—other than Sodhi and Tang (2021b, 2021c)—that examines a three-tiered integrated system that involves stockpile inventory, backup capacity, and standby capability. Our chapter is an explanation of integrating three different mechanisms—pre-positioned inventory, backup capacity, standby capability—into a tiered approach for response to public health emergencies.

From a practical viewpoint, unlike the reactive and makeshift responses of the government discussed in Sect. 3 regarding PPE and ventilators, our approach is "proactive." The proposed tiers of domestic capacity and capability need to be put in place well before a pandemic. We discuss stockpile-based preparedness next and the reactive—and ultimately ineffective—measures taken to turn capability into capacity.

3 The US National Stockpile and Pandemic Preparedness

For a tangible example of a stockpile, we provide some background information about the US Strategic National Stockpile as well as the shortage of ventilators and PPE during COVID-19. Handfield et al. (2020) provide more details on the shortcomings of the stockpile during the pandemic in early 2020.

3.1 Preparation: The US Strategic National Stockpile

The Strategic National Stockpile (SNS) is a massive inventory-based approach as a response to public health emergencies in the United States to meet demand surges of medically critical items. The stockpile is maintained by the US Department of Health and Human Services (HHS) and had an annual budget of $603 million for FY 2019 as part of the $2.3 billion budget for the Assistant Secretary for Preparedness and Response. In case of a large-scale public health incident including with an unknown cause, a broad range of pharmaceuticals and medical supplies can be sent from strategically located warehouses throughout the United States to any state in 50-ton containers within 12 h according to the federal deployment decision. All states in turn have plans to receive and distribute these quickly to local jurisdictions. In general, HHS is responsible for planning and maintaining inventory and responding to public health crises are well defined by way of (a) planning and preparation, (b) maintenance of the inventory, and (c) response to a public health emergency (see Box 11.1 for details).

Box 11.1 Responsibilities of the US Strategic National Stockpile

1. *Planning and preparation*

   (a) Conducting strategic planning, with a 5-year budget forecast.
   (b) Getting needed medicines and supplies into the stockpile.
   (c) Making sure the right amounts and types of medications and supplies are available to respond to an emergency.
   (d) Ensuring the stockpile can resupply state and local public health agencies in a catastrophic health event.

2. *Maintenance*

   (a) Managing quality control of the stockpile's inventory and IT support of inventory management systems.
   (b) Maintaining day-to-day situational awareness, ensuring the stockpile is ready to respond.
   (c) Serving as a point of contact for federal agencies, non-governmental organizations, and commercial partners for stockpile initiatives.

3. *Response in an emergency*

   (a) Managing the stockpile's response activities during a public health emergency.
   (b) Coordinating information sharing with states and locals during public health emergencies to determine the most efficient way to respond.
   (c) Working with partners inside and outside of the government to support the optimal distribution of medical countermeasures during public health emergencies.

3.2   Awareness: Potential Shortage of Ventilators

Following SARS-1 in 2003, the General Accounting Office (GAO, 2003) noted that: "few hospitals have adequate medical equipment, such as the ventilators. . . [in numbers needed in a pandemic]." Even when HHS developed the Pandemic Influenza Plan in 2005, a Congressional report noted a shortage of ventilators following the Avian flu, and NIH and CDC estimated a "deficit" of about 70,000 ventilators. After the swine flu in 2009 took more than 12,000 American lives, the US federal government contracted with a small California-based company, Newport, to develop and manufacture inexpensive ventilators. However, the government eventually cancelled the contract at the supplier's request after Newport was taken over by other firms a couple of times.

Thus, when the pandemic struck in early 2020, HHS was informed that there were only 12,700 ventilators stored in the SNS. As the number of cases of COVID-19 rose rapidly, in March 2020, the US government estimated the COVID-related likely need was 90,000 ventilators for the stockpile (additional to what was already in use in hospitals). Consequently, there was a rush to order more ventilators, but worldwide demand was going up and the total annual manufacturing capacity was nowhere near the estimated need in March. As such, the US government sought to create ad hoc domestic capacity with similar efforts in the United Kingdom.

3.3 Response: Capability Development as a Reactive Attempt

When the pandemic struck, the US government realized that the inventory in the stockpile is grossly insufficient. As a reactive measure, the US government sought to tap the manufacturing capability on the fly among domestic manufacturers from various sectors to create or reallocate capacity to produce large numbers of ventilators quickly. Similarly, the UK government attempted to tap into domestic manufacturing capability as a reactive measure. Industry in the United States attempted to rise to meet the national need of producing ventilators quickly by creating consortia, with the President Trump's use of the Defense Production Act[3] facilitating the supply of ventilator components. One consortium was GM and Ventec, a medical equipment maker, who planned to build ventilators at a GM plant in Kokomo, Indiana. At the same time, Michigan-based Creative Foam Corp. and Minneapolis-based Twin City Die Castings, both auto industry suppliers, repurposed their capacity to provide parts at high volume for the GM-Ventec endeavor. At first, the consortium planned to produce 30,000 of Ventec's premiere product with 700+ components for which it had identified most of the suppliers. The government balked at the $1 billion price tag. Hence, GM and Ventec switched to a more straightforward design with half the cost, but only the single ventilator function without oxygen-related features. The consortium shipped 600 ventilators by mid-April and was on schedule to produce 30,000 ventilators by August end.

Although existing ventilator manufacturers and auto companies such as Ford and GM attempted to meet the government's need as a reactive measure, the products produced were not the ones most needed. For example, the ventilators made by Ford and GM were basic mechanical ventilators, not those advanced electrical invasive ventilators that can help support a patient's breathing while their body fights off the effects of the virus. Similarly, the US government asked Hanes to retrofit its factories in the United States to produce masks. However, Hanes lacked any capacity to make non-woven filters to block minute particles. As such, the company could only manufacture basic masks, not the N95 masks that effectively protect healthcare workers.

Without any plans established in advance, the reactive use of capacity and capability of the auto and other sectors, in general, failed to the national need in terms of product specifications. As another example, without proactive planning for capacity and capability, it was impossible for these firms to produce surgical or N95 marks as there was no capacity to produce melt-blown fabric, a key component. As such, the ad hoc efforts foundered despite early claims of success.

The inability to turn capability into capacity for the government's supply chain of needed products was not limited to the US government. Across the Atlantic, facing a rising death toll, the UK government estimated another 20,000 ventilators would be needed and issued the Ventilator Challenge in March 2020 to industry to provide 20,000 ventilators "designed from scratch" to be delivered "as soon as possible." A two-page indicative specification list included the requirement that the ventilator "be made from materials and parts readily available in the UK supply chain." Additionally, the Medicines and Healthcare Products Regulatory Agency (MHRA) said it could allow medical devices quickly "without formal regulatory approval." Within 2 weeks, three consortia responded: the aerospace sector, led by Meggitt, and two from the automotive industry, led by Nissan and McLaren, respectively.UK manufacturers Vauxhall and Airbus (AIR.PA) announced they would re-purpose their factories and use 3D-printing technology to create parts for ventilators to treat coronavirus patients. Aircraft engine maker, Rolls Royce, and vacuum cleaner manufacturer, Dyson, also jumped into the fray to produce a basic ventilator.

None of the UK government-initiated basic Ventilator Challenge designs were eventually needed as the NHS was able to meet demand during and past the mid-April peak of the pandemic. The estimated total need for more ventilators was excessive despite having been revised downwards in early April. In a rush to get production started, the government ignored or downplayed warnings from a panel of experts about basic designs. The experts felt that such designs would only result in "the need for more ventilators,..., more staff and almost certainly worse patient outcomes." Also, the MHRA upgraded specifications a month after the challenge began. With much of the money already given to the various consortia, the government eventually cancelled outstanding orders. UK manufacturer Dyson had already spent £20m in design and equipment when the government cancelled their order. With the pandemic peaking in April, the promised August deliveries of ventilators would have been too late, at least for the first wave of the pandemic.

3.4 Lessons Learned

We draw lessons from the US government's reactive response to the pandemic as follows:

1. *Need good inventory management of the stockpile.* The government supply chain for pandemics requires managing a stockpile of medical equipment for two to three decades. In turn, the government needs to ensure that all items are in good working order. All inventory must be checked and replaced periodically to ensure usability during a future emergency. Over 2000 ventilators in the US stockpile were either expired or faulty so they were unable to be deployed in early April.

Some states received unusable—expired, rotting, or not working—masks, gloves, ventilators, and other essential equipment for COVID-19 from the national stockpile. Consequently, there are questions about how well the Strategic National Stockpile has managed its inventory over the years.

2. *Need a consistent public policy across the years.* Because the stockpile is rarely used, a consistent policy across successive administrations is needed. For example, California built a considerable stockpile, including ventilators, in 2005 under Governor Schwarzenegger. But the stockpile had to be dismantled in 2011 to cut costs owing to a massive budget deficit in 2011. In 2020, the state announced it would going build up the stockpile again because of the pandemic. Even reserve capacity for producing ventilators for a massive surge can be quite expensive if kept unused for decades in anticipation of a pandemic.

3. *Need to identify and reserve manufacturing capacity proactively.* Panic led to the reduced use of whatever inventory there was due to over-ordering by states and hoarding. Medtronic's CEO Geoff Martha commented in April that "The numbers that they were asking [Medtronic to produce] were orders of magnitude bigger than the entire [ventilator] market." In both the United States and the United Kingdom, the fear of having too few ventilators resulted in the manufacture of under-specified new units. Also, expert opinion was ignored in a rush to get ventilators initially, despite reports in the United States that the bottleneck was the skills for using ventilators rather than the number of ventilators.

4. *Need to identify sources and develop suitable capabilities proactively.* The government and the various manufacturing consortia would have been more effective in turning capability into capacity for its supply chain had there been a shared resource of knowledge and capabilities within the country. The shared resource would be R&D, know-how, advanced process development and engineering skills, and manufacturing competencies. This kind of standby capability is essential during a global pandemic because foreign suppliers may not even be allowed by their respective governments to export certain items. For example, due to worldwide shortages of surgical masks and N95 masks, China suspended its exports of not only masks but also a key component, melt-blown fabric, between late February and late March (Sodhi et al., 2021). US manufacturers could not produce such masks as there were no domestic factories of melt-blown fabric.

4   Preparation with Inventory, Capacity, and Capability

A risk-based approach can help us decide how to respond to a public health emergency of any scale. As in any risk map, risk mitigation decisions depend on the potential impact (need) of a future emergency and the likelihood or frequency of such public health emergencies. A higher likelihood would require an inventory-based approach. Rare occurrences would warrant a capability-based approach on the grounds of cost as we saw earlier.

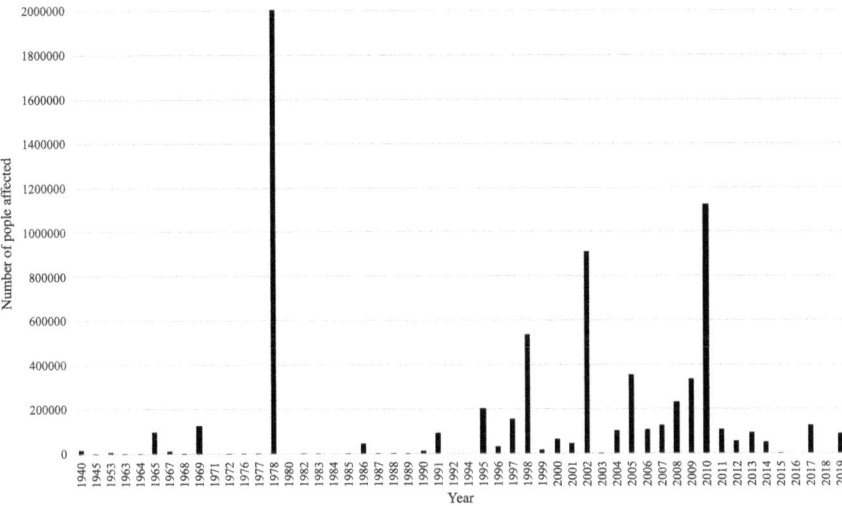

Fig. 11.1 Number of people affected per year by a virus-related disaster. Data source: EMDAT

4.1   Demand Distribution

Let us examine the number of people affected each year by virus-related infections worldwide. As a proxy for the annual impact of epidemics and pandemics, we obtained annual data from 1940 till 2019—thus excluding COVID—on the number of people affected by a virus-related disaster from the Emergency Events Database (EMDAT) (Fig. 11.1).

Taking the cumulative distribution of the annual demand over different years, we find that the number of affected people requiring assistance per year fits a 2-parameter *Pareto* distribution (k = 220,000, α = 2.955)) or even the single-parameter *exponential* distribution that has (λ = 1/125,000) (Fig. 11.2). Note that tail probabilities are identical for either distribution but the smaller values on the left that are not interesting (Fig. 11.2).

There are two points worth mentioning. First, autocorrelation across the years in the number of affected people is quite low over this period at −0.05, so we could assume annual impact of viruses to be *i.i.d* as a first approximation. Second, pandemics can go well beyond a year as COVID has done. Still, our argument is qualitative, and this analysis suffices to show that small-impact occurrences have a higher frequency while big impact occurrences like COVID are extremely rare. Flus of different sizes occur every year, but a pandemic may occur only once in, say, 10–30 years. The last pandemic before COVID in 2020 was the swine flu of 2009–2010, which took some 12,000 American lives.

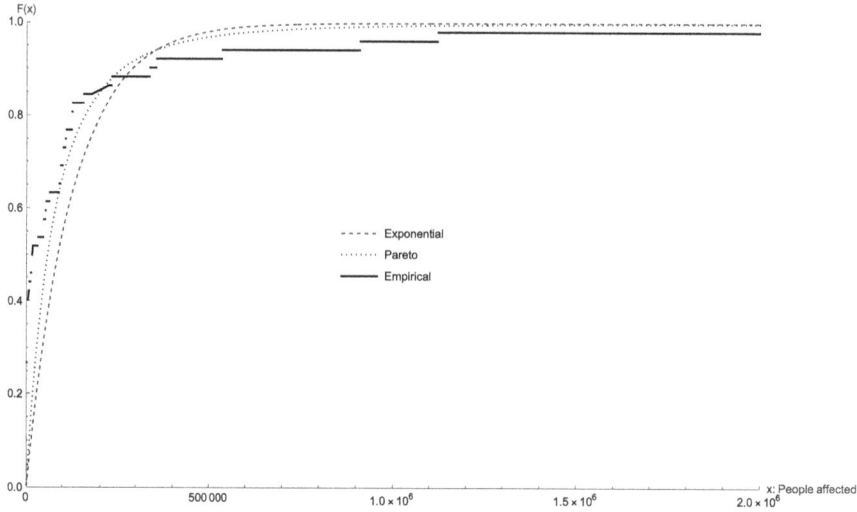

Fig. 11.2 Cumulative empirical distribution of the number of people affected in any year (1940–2019) in a virus-related disaster worldwide indicating a Pareto (dotted line) or an exponential probability distribution (dashed line). Data source: EMDAT

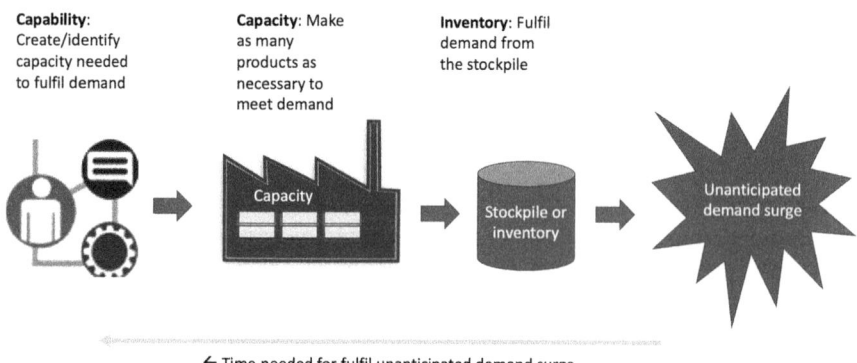

Fig. 11.3 Inventory-, capacity-, and capability-based approaches to meeting a demand surge from a public health emergency

4.2 Response and a Risk Map

We propose that inventory be supplemented by capacity and capability (Fig. 11.3). An inventory-based approach uses inventory alone like the Strategic National Stockpile, the other two are "mixed" approaches:

1. An *inventory*-based approach works best for meeting the demand "fits" with high-frequency, (relatively) low-impact occurrences of public health emergencies in line with the total cost argument.

Table 11.1 Public health emergency risk map with frequency and size of possible occurrences, showing the fit with primarily inventory-, capacity-, and capability-based approaches

Uncertainty regarding quantity and type of need →	*High*: Low quantifiability of risk, so quantity is unknown; additionally, type of goods that will be needed is uncertain	*Moderate*: Moderate quantifiability of risk, with a range of the quantity known; also, type of goods known	*Low*: High quantifiability of risk, so a narrow range for quantity is known and type of goods is also known
Frequency of occurrence →	*Rarely occurring*, say, once in 10–30 years	*Moderately occurring*, say, once in 2–3 years	*Frequently occurring*, say, once a year or seasonal
Impact of each occurrence ↓			
Massive: pandemic	Capability-based approach		
Moderate: regional epidemic		Capacity-based approach	
Low: local health risk			Inventory-based approach

2. A *capacity*-based approach requires some inventory to meet the demand surge up to a certain level to give time for the capacity to be kick-started. This approach works best for occurrences of moderate frequency and impact.
3. A *capability*-based approach entails capacity and inventory to meet the surge initially while capability is being deployed to create additional capacity immediately when it is estimated that both capacity and inventory are insufficient to meet demand. This approach works best for rare but high-impact occurrences.

Given the high frequency of low-impact events and rarity of high-impact events, we can use the idea of a risk map quite naturally to match the approach to the severity and frequency of the public health emergency based on lower total (expected) costs (Table 11.1).

An obvious question is how much inventory, ready capacity, and capability the United States should have to meet needs related to public health emergencies of various scales. Sodhi and Tang (2021c) provide numerical illustrations with reasonable numbers shows a three-tier optimal solution covers 52nd percentile of the demand distribution with inventory, 96.7th percentile with inventory and capacity, and 99.5th percentile with inventory, capacity, and capability. The optimal cost is 30% lower than that of an inventory-only stockpile that would require inventory to cover up to 88th percentile of the demand distribution. These numerical illustrations suggest we need inventory for frequently occurring "outbreaks" (one in 1- or 2-year events), while capacity would be called for more infrequently occurring events (say, once in 5–10 years), and capability in rare cases, say, once in 20–30 years. Of course, in all cases we would have all three tiers, so even in a rare pandemic, the inventory would be exhausted first, then the capacity, and only then would the capability be drawn upon, in line with the risk map in Table 11.1.

Technology further shifts the balance from inventory to capacity to capability, lowering the unit cost and the time to respond. Technology may also mean a change in the production method. Consider that 3D printing with fast response to make a unit but with a high cost per unit—while capacity is being readied to produce parts in high volume at low unit cost. And technology, and therefore capability, can lower unit marginal costs in the long run.

5   Building and Using Standby Capability

Building standby capability at the national level requires creating an ecosystem of various actors. These include designers, engineering and manufacturing capacity owners, design approvers, R&D units, and those who estimate what will be needed by way of the items produced. Knowledge creation and knowledge sharing are critical elements of this. Standby capability requires individual firms' capabilities for design and manufacturing within the country. We also need other companies, "including suppliers of advanced materials, tools, production equipment, and components" that together comprise the *industrial commons* that support and shape an entire industry (Pisano & Shih, 2009). Just as the commons in an English village can sustain the people in the village and their animals, industrial commons can sustain an entire industry. Such commons include "R & D knowhow, advanced process development and engineering skills, and manufacturing competencies related to a specific technology."

5.1   Developing Standby Capability in Advance

One example of a node of an ecosystem of "capability," rather than the ecosystem itself, is the Fraunhofer Institute for Material Flow and Logistics located adjacent to the Technical University of Dortmund, Germany. Funding comes from the German government's financial support and such companies as automaker BMW. Technical University researchers and students can engage in smart manufacturing of spare parts using 3D printing. They can also carry out smart logistics projects using drones, advanced robotics, and blockchain in manufacturing and logistics.[1]

Another example of developing a "capability" node, in this case for the textile sector, the Hong Kong government investing heavily in the Institute of Textiles and Clothing at Hong Kong Polytechnic University to offer education and research

---

[1] Fraunhofer Institute. https://www.iml.fraunhofer.de/en/istitue_profile.html

programs in fashion, textiles, and design.[2] Another node in these industrial commons is The Hong Kong Research Institute of Textiles and Apparel Limited (HKRITA). This node has enabled the sector to move up to high-value-added manufacturing and servicing activities using technology.[3] The knowledge and capability helped HKRITA develop the 6-layer washable face mask, the CuMask+, that offers high protection against droplets and, therefore, infectious diseases such as COVID-19.[4]

A third example, closer to an entire ecosystem of capability, is America Makes, an Ohio-based non-profit,[5] that "supports the transformation of manufacturing in the United States through innovative, coordinated additive manufacturing (AM) and 3D Printing Technology Development and Transition, and Workforce and Educational Development." As of this writing, the organization seeks to coordinate 3D printing capability with the US healthcare providers' PPE needs in collaboration with the FDA, NIH, and the Veterans Health Administration (VHA). The VHA got the first design of a 3D printed mask approved by the FDA (Sodhi et al., 2021).[6] The NIH also has a 3D Print Exchange to curate PPE designs for individuals to be printed at home. The organization enables the creation of approved PPE designs that can be manufactured with additive manufacturing capability within the country. Members include US government departments, private companies, and universities. America Makes floats projects with open calls for furthering capability. Furthermore, a knowledge-sharing platform, Digital Storefront, gives access to the latest information to members. The Storefront is "an online platform where members can access member-exclusive information, project data, and intellectual capital assets, including project deliverables and artifacts along with their association to the Technology Roadmap." By developing this kind of capability in advance, we can convert to production capacity when needed.

5.2 Deploying Standby Capability to Respond

Any government—and indeed, any company—should follow a blended approach with inventory, capacity, and capability. What might a mixed approach look like? Let us revisit the National Stockpile (Box 11.1) and adjust these responsibilities as we shift the balance from inventory-based to a hybrid of inventory-, capacity-, and capability-based approaches for different scales of emergencies. As shown in Box

---

[2] Keh, E. and Tang, C.S. 2020. Smart thinking, smart technology required to reindustrialize HKSAR, China Daily, Aug. 16. Accessed at [https://www.chinadailyhk.com/article/140231].

[3] Hong Kong Research Institute of Textiles and Apparel. https://www.hkrita.com/about.php

[4] CuMask+. https://www.qmask.gov.hk/about

[5] www.americamakes.us

[6] e.g., 3D printed mask developed by the Veteran Hospital Administration. Accessed at [https://governmentciomedia.com/fda-approves-first-3d-printed-mask-covid-19-support].

11.2, with standby capability, we are trading off maintaining physical goods against keeping information and knowledge (i.e., the blueprint and the know-how).

Box 11.2 Responsibilities of a Proposed US Strategic National Emergency Reserve Compared to that of the US Strategic National Stockpile (Differences from the Existing Inventory-Only Based Approach of the SNS in Box 11.1 Are Highlighted by Underlining)

1. *Planning and preparation*

   (a) Conducting strategic planning for inventory, capacity, and capability, with a 5-year budget forecast.
   (b) Getting needed medicines and supplies into the stockpile for the short term, and contracting or otherwise ensuring availability of capacity as well as industry-commons capability within country.
   (c) Making sure the right amounts and types of medicines and supplies, the right amount of capacity, as well as standby capability, is available to respond to an emergency within an adequate time.
   (d) Ensuring the stockpile of inventory, capacity, and capability can resupply state and local public health agencies in a catastrophic health event in a reasonable time.
   (e) Conduct stress tests and/or simulation runs to ensure a proper mix of inventory, capacity, and capability is available to respond to an emergency within the required time.

2. *Maintenance*

   (a) Managing quality control of the stockpile's inventory and IT support of inventory management systems, ensuring operability of capacity as well as capability.
   (b) Maintaining day-to-day situational awareness, ensuring the stockpile is ready to respond across the board (inventory, capacity, and capability).
   (c) Serving as a point of contact for federal agencies, nongovernmental organizations, and commercial partners for stockpile (broadly speaking) initiatives.

3. *Response in an emergency*

   (a) Managing the stockpile's response activities during a public health emergency.
   (b) Coordinate the creation of inventory from capacity and capability.
   (c) Coordinating information sharing with states and locals during public health emergencies to determine the most efficient way to respond.

Working with partners inside and outside of government to support optimal distribution of medical countermeasures during public health emergencies.

6 Conclusion

We described the challenges of the response to the pandemic from the US Strategic National Stockpile as well as from the ad hoc efforts to create capacity for ventilators and PPE. To improve a stockpile-based approach, we proposed a three-tiered "reserve" with inventory, (domestic) backup capacity, and (domestic) manufacturing capability. Assuming an exponentially distributed demand motivated by data on viral infections, we characterized the optimal solution in terms of the quantities of inventory, capacity, and capability.

As likelihood and impact are inversely correlated, we couched our argument in terms of high-frequency low-impact events needing an inventory-based response and a low-frequency high-impact event like COVID-19 necessarily drawing upon capability (including capacity). A capability-based approach entails capacity and inventory to meet the surge initially while capability is being deployed to create additional capacity immediately when it is estimated that both capacity and inventory are insufficient to meet demand. This approach works best for rare but high-impact occurrences.

Some ideas for further research are:

1. *Other uses of capability*: Our chapter looks at capability only from the narrow viewpoint of being able to manufacture items needed for the pandemic. In reality, capability is about the ability to manufacture a wide variety of products, entailing many people to be trained in or training others. As such, further research could consider how capability could be used for responding to a wide set of times of sharply increased unanticipated need—whether due to pandemics or other disasters—and for subsequent recovery.
2. *Product and volume flexibility afforded by capability*: Many have bemoaned the loss of manufacturing capability, which we brought up in this chapter. Offshore manufacturing capacity lowers the ability to respond to changes in demand. True, agility is afforded by inventory, but also by nearshore manufacturing capacity. Further research could extend the idea of flexibility and responsiveness to include capability. We used a rather simple model of capability, so further research could develop the notion analytically as well as empirically. See Chopra et al. (2021) for an argument about the flexibility afforded by "industrial commons," if these refer to capabilities shared by companies across different sectors.
3. *Humanitarian logistics and preparedness*: Humanitarian operations should involve pre-positioned inventory for meeting the needs of the occurence of a large disaster of any size were to occur anywhere in the region under consideration. The effort is then on the logistics to ensure this inventory is made available. Our chapter argues for inventory to be traded off for capacity and capability for pandemics. The natural question that arises then is whether the ideas here, particularly on capacity and capability to bolster inventory can be used for *strategic* humanitarian operations for responsiveness as well as long-term recovery.

The matter of designing the right stockpile to prepare for future pandemics is a matter of urgency for all countries and even for pan-national global collaborations like Covax. This chapter, supported by Sodhi and Tang (2021b, 2021c), argues that rather than focusing on inventory, we must consider capacity and capability, especially in the context of rare high-impact risk events. Supplementing inventory with capacity and capability can be an exciting area of research for not only pandemic response but for strategic humanitarian operations in general.

References

Brown, A. O., & Lee, H. L. (2003). The impact of demand signal quality on optimal decisions in supply contracts. In J. G. Shanthikumar, D. D. Yao, & W. H. M. Zijm (Eds.), *Stochastic modeling and optimization of manufacturing systems and supply chains* (International Series in Operations Research & Management Science) (Vol. 63). Springer. https://doi.org/10.1007/978-1-4615-0373-6_12

Chopra, S., Sodhi, M., & Lücker, F. (2021). Achieving supply chain efficiency and resilience by using multi-level commons. *Decision Sciences, 52*(4), 817–832.

Cohen, M. A., Kamesam, P., Kleindorfer, P., Lee, H., & Tekerian, A. (1990). Optimizer: IBM's multi-echelon inventory system for managing service logistics. *Interfaces, 20*(1), 65–82.

Davis, L. B., Samanlioglu, F., Qu, X., & Root, S. (2013). Inventory planning and coordination in disaster relief efforts. *International Journal of Production Economics, 141*(2), 561–573.

Dhamija, P., Gupta, S., Bag, S., & Gupta, M. L. (2021). Humanitarian supply chain management: A systematic review and bibliometric analysis. *International Journal of Automation and Logistics, 3*(2), 104–136.

Eppen, G., & Iyer, A. (1997). Backup agreements in fashion buying—The Value of Upstream Flexibility. *Management Science., 43*(11), 1469–1477.

GAO. (2003, May 7). *Improvements to public health capacity are needed for responding to bioterrorism and emerging infectious diseases: Statement by J. Heinrich.* Retrieved from https://www.gao.gov/assets/110/109932.pdf on 20 Dec. 2020

Handfield, R. Finkenstadt, D. J., Schneller, E. S., Godfrey, A. B., & Guinto, P. (2020). A commons for a supply chain in the post-COVID-19 era: The case for a reformed strategic national stockpile. *The Milbank Quarterly.* Retrieved from December 20, 2020 https://onlinelibrary.wiley.com/doi/10.1111/1468-0009.12485

Huang, H. C., Araz, O. M., Morton, D. P., Johnson, G. P., Damien, P., Clements, B., & Meyers, L. A. (2017). Stockpiling ventilators for influenza pandemics. *Emerging Infectious Diseases, 23*(6), 914–921.

Kniesner, T. J., & Viscusi, W. K. (2019). *The value of a statistical life.* Oxford Research Encyclopedia of Economics and Finance. Retrieved from https://doi.org/10.1093/acrefore/9780190625979.013.138 or on SSRN at https://ssrn.com/abstract=3379967

Mehrotra, S., Rahimian, H., Barah, M., Luo, F., & Schantz, K. (2020). A model of supply-chain decisions for resource sharing with an application to ventilator allocation to combat COVID-19. *Naval Research Logistics, 67*(5), 303–320.

Pisano, G. P., & Shih, W. (2009, July–August). Restoring America's competitiveness. *HBR.*

Sodhi, M. S. (2015). Natural disasters, the economy and population vulnerability as a vicious cycle with exogenous hazards. *Journal of Operations Management, 45*(1), 101–113.

Sodhi, M. S., & Tang, C. S. (2014). Buttressing supply chains against floods in Asia for humanitarian relief and economic recovery. *Production and Operations Management, 23*(6), 938–950. https://doi.org/10.1111/poms.12111

Sodhi, M. S., & Tang, C. S. (2021a). Supply chain management for extreme conditions: Research opportunities. *Journal of Supply Chain Management, 57*(1), 7–16.

Sodhi, M. S., & Tang, C. S. (2021b). Rethinking industry's role in a national emergency. *MIT Sloan Management Review, 62*(4), 74–78. Retrieved from https://sloanreview.mit.edu/article/rethinking-industrys-role-in-a-national-emergency/

Sodhi, M. S., & Tang, C. S. (2021c, February 16). *Preparing for future pandemics with a reserve of inventory, capacity, and capability*. Retrieved from SSRN: https://ssrn.com/abstract=3816606.

Sodhi, M., Tang, C. S., & Willenson, E. T. (2021). Research opportunities in preparing supply chains of essential goods for future pandemics. *International Journal of Production Research*. https://doi.org/10.1080/00207543.2021.1884310

Tavana, M., Abtahi, A. R., Di Caprio, D., Hashemi, R., & Yousefi-Zenouz, R. (2018). An integrated location-inventory-routing humanitarian supply chain network with pre-and post-disaster management considerations. *Socio-Economic Planning Sciences, 64*, 21–37.

Toyasaki, F., Arikan, E., Silbermayr, L., & Falagara Sigala, I. (2017). Disaster relief inventory management: Horizontal cooperation between humanitarian organizations. *Production and Operations Management, 26*(6), 1221–1237.

Whybark, D. C. (2007). Issues in managing disaster relief inventories. *International Journal of Production Economics, 108*(1–2), 228–235.

Zipkin, P. (2000). *Foundations of inventory management*. McGraw-Hill/Irwin.

Chapter 12
Building Resilient Post-pandemic Supply Chains Through Digital Transformation

Maximilian Klöckner, Christoph G. Schmidt, and Stephan M. Wagner

Abstract The COVID-19 pandemic has created a challenging environment for firms on a global scale. Due to policies aiming to contain the spread of the virus, firms across all industries are forced to quickly adapt to highly dynamic changes in supply and demand, while simultaneously managing internal production disruptions. Most companies experience severe financial consequences during the supply chain disruptions. Digital technologies can be used to create more resilient supply chains that are able to better cope with future large-scale disruptions. In this chapter, we present current industry best practices, related to blockchain, digital platforms, analytics, and digital twins, to provide actionable insights for decision makers.

1 Introduction

The COVID-19 pandemic disrupts firm operations across multiple industries and functions at an unprecedented scale. Response policies are important to limit the spread of the virus, but substantially shake firms worldwide. There are many and diverse examples of COVID-19-induced disruptions, such as strained goods movements between borders, production delays and halts due to physical working restrictions, or unexpected demand shifts in both directions due to rapidly changing customer and business partner behavior. Clearly, the crisis initiated a new paradigm shift for firms, from profit optimization to survival (Ketchen & Craighead, 2020).

Being a widely unexpected event with low probability but high consequences, the COVID-19 pandemic can be depicted as a "black swan" event for global supply chains (Yang et al., 2021; Knemeyer et al., 2009). Further, the pandemic is arguably different from previous supply chain disruptions, as the pandemic is not a geographically restricted phenomenon, it clearly affects both supply *and* demand, and it is an exogenous shock, implying that it is not caused by the behavior of the affected firms themselves (Craighead et al., 2020; Yang et al., 2021). This different—and

M. Klöckner · C. G. Schmidt · S. M. Wagner (✉)
Department of Management, Technology, and Economics, Swiss Federal Institute of Technology (ETH Zurich), Zürich, Switzerland

unprecedented—disruption requires new mitigation strategies, and challenges previous best practices of crisis management and supply chain resilience. Unlike any other disruption, the COVID-19 pandemic has ruthlessly identified and exacerbated the weaknesses in firms' supply chains (Choi et al., 2020). An evident weakness is insufficient supply chain visibility, which can be a driver of resilience. Visibility is crucial to identify and assess risks, and helps firms to address disruptions before they occur or before their impact worsens (Williams et al., 2013; Skorna et al., 2009; Kleindorfer & Saad, 2005). However, at the moment, numerous firms are lacking the necessary supply chain visibility to effectively and quickly respond to the COVID-19 pandemic. In contrast, only a minority of firms with such knowledge were able to react appropriately, partially mitigating the negative impact of the crisis (Choi et al., 2020). Another substantial trend of global supply chains is the orientation toward efficiency-focused network designs. While minimizing operating costs, such networks are also associated with lower levels of flexibility and redundancy. Beyond visibility, both flexibility and redundancy are important drivers of supply chain resilience (Zsidisin & Wagner, 2010; Sheffi & Rice, 2005).

Emerging digital technologies hold the potential to address these weaknesses, contributing to the resilience of firms, especially with a view to future large-scale disruptions. Under the emerging concept of *digital resilience*, we subsume novel digital tools that help to mitigate the negative impact of disruptions (Boh et al., 2020). We argue that emerging digital technologies can be applied to improve (1) supply chain visibility, (2) flexibility, and (3) redundancy, thereby making supply chains more resilient to disruptions.

For instance, firms are exploring blockchain to substantially increase supply chain visibility. During the COVID-19 pandemic, blockchain is also being discussed as an enabler for authenticity and traceability in the vaccine supply chain. Another promising avenue are digital platforms, which help firms to efficiently allocate and coordinate a variety of resources and services, facilitating operational flexibility. Furthermore, firms are increasingly investing in advanced data analytics tools, such as artificial intelligence and machine learning. Presenting opportunities for increased visibility, robust, and efficient automation, or smarter forecasting, these tools may further contribute to the resilience of firms, especially in a data-intensive business environment. Finally, digital twins—digital mirrors of physical objects or processes—provide the opportunity to drastically increase visibility and flexibility in industrial settings. Digital twins that capture high volumes of product- or process-related data and properties allow firms to remotely monitor and manage their assets, and to simulate the course and impact of supply chain disruptions, enabling managers to make quick and informed response decisions.

In the following, we present the background on the COVID-19 pandemic, and offer insights on how firms may use different digital technologies to boost supply chain resilience.

2 The COVID-19 Pandemic and Digital Resilience

2.1 The COVID-19 Pandemic

A public health crisis at global scale, the COVID-19 pandemic impacts individuals and organizations substantially. As of February 2022, more than 400 million COVID-19 cases have been counted and more than 5.5 million COVID-19-related deaths registered.[1] Arguably, such numbers inevitably evoke strict political responses, targeting a containment of the virus spread. Consequential policies occur worldwide, characterized by human mobility restrictions (e.g., border closings and night-time curfews), limitations of physical gatherings (e.g., cancellation of events and remote working obligations), and rules on the usage of personal protective equipment (e.g., hygiene masks and hand sanitizer).

Clearly, these political responses impact firm operations across multiple industries and functions (Foss, 2020; Klöckner et al., 2021). Beyond the severity of restrictions, which surely affect operations, firms are facing an immensely high and temporally prolonged level of uncertainty. Political responses that need to be dynamic to effectively adapt to the course of the COVID-19 pandemic increase the difficulty for firms to conduct effective planning. First studies show an excessive increase in "panic buying" behavior, significantly driving demand uncertainty and challenging forecasting, which is crucial for supply chain planning (Islam et al., 2021). Examples of demand-based disrupted manufacturing supply chains include typical consumer staples with exploding demands, such as toilet paper or hand sanitizer, but also products with massive demand drops, such as cars or luxury goods (e.g., Craighead et al., 2020; Govindan et al., 2020).

Furthermore, mobility restrictions strain the flow of goods and services, constraining the supply of raw materials and production capacities. Consequential domino effects may lead to disruptions at downstream supply chain tiers, for instance, collapses of production processes (Paul & Chowdhury, 2021; Bode & Wagner, 2015). Multiple global manufacturers had to shut down production plants during 2020, driven by either upstream (i.e., supply) or downstream (i.e., demand) disruptions. Prominent examples are production stops at Volkswagen plants across Europe (Taylor & Schwartz, 2020), Apple's delayed 2020 iPhone production ramp-up (Kubota, 2020), and Dow Chemical closing plants in the United States and Europe in late 2020 (Duckett, 2020).

Finally, the COVID-19 pandemic and the political responses have changed the way people and firms work (Narayanamurthy & Tortorella, 2021). In many cases, the working environment of individuals has changed to digitally enabled remote working. In instances, where this is not possible, firms need to ensure safe working conditions, including the application of distancing rules and personal protective

---

[1] *John Hopkins University Coronavirus Resource Center.* https://coronavirus.jhu.edu/map.html. Accessed on February 11, 2022.

equipment. The severe consequences of the COVID-19 pandemic, oftentimes of operational nature, inevitably raise the question of supply chain resilience.

2.2 Digital Resilience

Supply chain resilience is key to mitigate the adverse impact of disruptions, and to help firms quickly recover from disruptions (Ambulkar et al., 2015; Zsidisin & Wagner, 2010). Hence, unsurprisingly, supply chain resilience, relating to the containment of and recovery from disruptions (e.g., El Baz & Ruel, 2021; Sheffi, 2005), has always been a key pillar of supply chain management research and practitioner interest. Numerous empirical studies demonstrate that supply chain resilience can be effectively managed, and identify several mitigation factors. These factors include firm size (Hendricks & Singhal, 2003), financial slack, diversification (Hendricks et al., 2009), supply chain complexity (Bode & Wagner, 2015), and among many others.

In the context of the COVID-19 pandemic, the first studies address the question on supply chain resilience. For instance, Ivanov (2022) proposes a conceptual resilience framework, highlighting the role of a proactive management of firm assets and capabilities, especially digital technologies. In another piece, the same author emphasizes the importance of supply chain viability, understood as the "ability of a supply chain to maintain itself and survive in a changing environment" (Ivanov, 2021, p. 1), to navigate a disruption like the COVID-19 pandemic. To achieve supply chain viability, the study suggests different adaptation strategies, such as intertwining supply chains or substituting crucial sources (Ivanov, 2021). Leveraging an empirical survey approach, El Baz and Ruel (2021) show that supply chain risk management practices are a viable source of supply chain resilience and mitigate the negative impact of the COVID-19 pandemic. The authors specifically highlight the importance of supply chain risk identification, providing the groundwork for supply chain visibility (El Baz & Ruel, 2021).

Likewise, media reports and practitioner articles have emphasized the role of supply chain visibility during the COVID-19 pandemic (Choi et al., 2020; Loten, 2020a). Especially in crisis situations like the COVID-19 pandemic, early transparency is key to effectively mitigate and respond to disruptions. However, in quite contrast, many companies were unprepared during the beginning of the pandemic in 2020, wasting valuable time and resources due to tough data collection and assessment processes. A minority of firms, which had already invested in visibility and mapping tools, appeared to be better prepared (Choi et al., 2020). Digital technologies provide clear opportunities to address these visibility shortcomings, and hence boost resilience. Unsurprisingly, many firms adjusted their tech budgets and increased digitalization investments, despite or more likely, because of, the disruptions of the pandemic (Loten, 2020b; McKinsey & Company, 2020). Emerging technologies like blockchain or artificial intelligence (AI)-based analytics promise increasing supply chain visibility, which in turn helps to improve resilience. General

Motors, for instance, has a long history of investing in technologies to enhance supply chain mapping, enabling the firm to quickly and accurately react to disruptions (Linton & Vakil, 2020).

Beyond supply chain visibility, digital tools may further increase flexibility. Cloud-based solutions and communication tools, like Microsoft Teams, Slack, or Zoom are on the rise during the pandemic, clearly facilitating flexible remote working in uncertain environments. Communication, video conferencing, real-time file sharing, and editing maintain productivity and mitigate the negative impact of dynamic mobility and gathering restrictions (Leonardi, 2021). Emerging platform solutions further boost flexibility by enabling real-time sharing and allocation of crucial resources, such as manufacturing capacities or delivery services.

Finally, strategic redundancies are another important driver of supply chain resilience (Zsidisin & Wagner, 2010; Sheffi & Rice, 2005). Emerging digital technologies might enable such redundancies in supply chains, without drastically increasing costs. For example, blockchain functions as a distributed data repository, where copies of critical digital assets are locally stored on every network member's server. This natural redundancy reduces the risk of costly outages substantially. Digital twins of physical objects and processes themselves are also a valuable second source of important object- and process-related data, further increasing redundancy.

In sum, the COVID-19 pandemic clearly highlights the role of the *digital* dimension as a key enabler of supply chain resilience, which has yet received little attention from academia. However, it seems crucial to understand how digital technologies may help to mitigate and respond to major disruptions like the COVID-19 pandemic, and hence contribute to a firm's *digital resilience* (Boh et al., 2020).

3 Industry Best Practices

Advancing the understanding of the digital resilience dimension, we present exemplary industry best practices and forward-looking use cases for the implementation of digital technologies that foster supply chain resilience during and after the COVID-19 pandemic. Specifically, we present four prominently discussed technological concepts and corresponding use cases, (1) blockchain, (2) platforms, (3) analytics, and (4) digital twins. Table 12.1 provides an overview of how these technologies may facilitate supply chain resilience.

3.1 *Blockchain*

Blockchain is gaining increasing attention in supply chain management, with recent empirical studies finding positive financial implications of blockchain initiatives (Klöckner et al., 2022). Frequently debated and promising use cases include supply

Table 12.1 Overview of selected technologies and exemplary use cases

Resilience driver	Blockchain	Platforms	Analytics	Digital twins
Visibility	• Authentication of COVID-19 vaccines or other drugs • Traceability of products, eliminating blind spots	• Improved (market) overview of business partners, suppliers, and (potential) customers	• Advanced demand forecasting, enhancing upstream visibility • Enabling predictive maintenance and/or remote machine monitoring	• Remote visibility, simulation and condition monitoring of physical and procedural assets • Simulations of disruption spillovers and consequences
Flexibility	• Ensuring safe and efficient peer-to-peer payments between multiple supply network members • Smart contract-based automation of order processes	• Efficient trading and booking of services like manufacturing capacity or delivery • Sharing of critical products, such as medical equipment or cooling infrastructure	• Automation of manual processes, such as document processing • Remote warehouse management	• Remote management of (digital) assets and manufacturing systems • Immersive training to onboard supply chain employees
Redundancy	• Distributed data structure of crucial digital assets (copy on every supply chain network node)	• Availability of multiple sourcing partners (e.g., suppliers) • Easier access to larger (potential) customer base	• Identification of reasonable strategic redundancies (e.g., second sources) • Automated supplier relationship management, enabling more cost-efficient second sources	• Additional security layer, as digital assets themselves are an additional (redundant) representation

chain traceability (e.g., Hastig & Sodhi, 2020), inventory management (e.g., Babich & Hilary, 2020), or additive manufacturing (e.g., Kurpjuweit et al., 2021). As a distributed database for transactional records (i.e., "ledger"), blockchain provides the opportunity to immutably and transparently store information about products or processes in a distributed architecture (Schmidt & Wagner, 2019; Klöckner et al., 2022).

In the context of the COVID-19 pandemic, blockchain has been proposed for a variety of use cases. One prominent example is the COVID-19 vaccine supply chain. Since some of the vaccines require special cooling conditions (e.g., Moderna's vaccine −20 °C and BioNTech/Pfizer's vaccine −70 °C), a blockchain infrastructure might help to securely log the actual condition data, most importantly the temperature (Korin, 2020). Startups like the Swiss-based firm modum.io are working on such solutions for supply chains.[2] With a transparent record of immutable product data, different actors in the vaccine supply chain would be able to easily check and monitor historic condition data. This blockchain use case is not limited to vaccine temperature data. For instance, manufacturers may track vaccine delivery, distributors provide various other product condition data, hospitals could effectively manage stocks, and individual vaccine recipients or physicians would be able to check vaccine authenticity (Korin, 2020).

---

[2] https://www.modum.io/

Beyond facilitating supply chain visibility, blockchain may also help firms to increase efficiency and flexibility, both contributing to resilience. As blockchain allows secure and quick transactions in a peer-to-peer network, firms could bundle several types of supply chain data in a single and transparent data source. Examples are purchase and sales orders, payment processing, or insurance data, eliminating manual intervention (Hewett & Mølbjerg, 2020; Nandi et al., 2021).

Finally, as a distributed database, the blockchain architecture itself creates digital redundancy. Specifically, in a blockchain network, the whole database including all transactional information is copied to every network member. This inherent redundancy contributes to blockchain's high-security levels (Babich & Hilary, 2020; Kumar et al., 2020). As part of the digital supply chain infrastructure, blockchain can facilitate supply chain resilience, making crucial information available even in the case of multiple outages (Kumar et al., 2020).

3.2 Platforms

In the wake of platform economy trends, digital platforms are becoming increasingly relevant in the business world. Arguably, platforms can improve resilience, as their fundamental idea is the bundling of different types of stakeholders and their respective physical and digital assets, enhancing operational flexibility.

For example, during the COVID-19 pandemic, the availability of personal protective equipment or cold storage infrastructure for vaccines or treatment drugs has become critical. Firms can leverage platforms to flexibly share and trade such assets (Nandi et al., 2021). Another conceivable sharing asset is production capacity. Due to restrictions and hygiene regulations, firms could be forced to shut down production plants, to guarantee employee safety and to control operating costs. Especially during such extreme situations, shared factory platforms, where production capacities can be traded, provide a viable and cost-efficient opportunity for manufacturing up- (e.g., buying of additional capacity to produce high-demand items, such as hygienic masks or ventilators) or down-sizing (e.g., selling of excess capacity to control operating costs due to shrinking demand), while maintaining high production capacity utilization (Kurpjuweit et al., 2021).

In the business-to-customer segment, digital platforms are also an attractive concept to maintain or even increase sales during disruptions like the COVID-19 pandemic. A prominent example is e-commerce platforms, which are surging during the pandemic. For instance, Walmart's e-commerce sales doubled during the pandemic in 2020 (Wahba, 2020). In times of increased uncertainty, restrictions on mobility and closures of physical stores, digital platforms are an important channel to maintain cash flows, which are essential for firm survival and recovery in crisis situations. Likewise, many small and medium-sized businesses, which do not have the financial power to run their own e-commerce platforms, rely on third parties to digitally access their customer bases during the COVID-19 pandemic. One illustrative and well-known example is Uber Technologies, whose platform Uber Eats can be leveraged by (smaller) restaurants. A recent study empirically demonstrates that small restaurants could significantly increase order volume and activity during the COVID-19 pandemic by joining the platform (Raj et al., 2020).

3.3 Analytics

While data is becoming omnipresent, businesses are increasingly leveraging advanced data analytics tools, such as machine learning or artificial intelligence (AI)-based algorithms, to ultimately sustain or create competitive advantages (Choi et al., 2018).

The COVID-19 pandemic has clearly demonstrated that uncertainty comes at a high cost. Emerging analytics tools are developed and designed to cope with uncertainty, allowing managers to make optimal decisions in unstable environments. One prominent example is the rapidly changing customer behavior during the COVID-19 pandemic. While some products experienced extreme drops in demand (e.g., passenger cars or luxury goods), the demand for others quickly multiplied (e.g., medical equipment or consumer staples). Arguably, such volatility challenges traditional forecasting methods in supply chain planning. The case of deploying data analytics (e.g., machine learning) for demand forecasting has already been discussed and developed before the COVID-19 pandemic hit the economy. However, experts estimate that while machine learning approaches in demand forecasting were able to lead to a 15% accuracy improvement, when compared to traditional forecasting methods, the pandemic has only expanded that lead to 40%. Of course, such improvement indications could be trailblazing for inventory management and working capital optimization (Herzog et al., 2021).

Another promising case for advanced analytics solutions might be document processing. In today's supply chains, many transactions involve paper-based standard documents and manual processing, providing immense opportunities for automation. This would not only reduce errors, but also streamline and shorten processing times, enhancing the resilience of supply chains. During the COVID-19 pandemic, the fintech BlueVine, for instance, applied machine learning tools to automate loan application processes for small businesses. In this way, the company was able to equip over 150,000 small businesses with loans within a shorter time period and with higher accuracy than before (Kass-Hout, 2020). Likewise, the service HelloWorks offers analytics-based document processing solutions, streamlining interactions with customers. During the pandemic, it further helps to limit in-person interactions with customers that were necessary before, reducing the physical exposure of customers, while simultaneously saving process costs (Kass-Hout, 2020).

The COVID-19 pandemic further intensified investments in data and analytics tools in the manufacturing sector. For example, the Norwegian aluminum manufacturer Norsk Hydro implemented analytics tools to remotely monitor shop floor machinery, increasing the automation degree and maintaining worker safety compliant with mobility restrictions (Loten, 2020a). Beyond remote monitoring, advanced analytics tools are said to allow quicker production ramp-ups, reduction of waste, and avoidance of downtime through smart maintenance algorithms (Loten, 2020a).

3.4 Digital Twins

Digital twins are digital representations of physical objects or processes, including key properties and historic object or process data (Liu et al., 2021; Ivanov & Dolgui, 2021; Schleich et al., 2017). In industrial ecosystems, the concept of "digital twinning" is gaining increasing traction. Mirroring their physical counterparts, digital product twins provide immense opportunities for supply chain visibility. Ideally, a digital product twin contains all relevant properties of the physical object and all interaction data with the object, throughout the entire object lifecycle. A commonly debated use case for digital twins is 3D printing. A digital twin of a 3D printed part, for example, a sensitive aircraft component, could transparently store all relevant object data, such as raw material information, printing properties, safety certificates, or ownership transfers (Kurpjuweit et al., 2021; Klöckner et al., 2020). This would enable flexible and cost-efficient monitoring, part traceability, and provide the groundwork for product analytics. In case of a supply chain disruption, such levels of visibility can be crucial time and cost savers, drastically increasing the responsiveness of tailored response actions.

The value of digital twins can be of descriptive or predictive nature. While the descriptive value relates to the real-time visualization of the current state of any mirrored object or process, facilitating remote management and flexibility, the prescriptive value relates to the possibility of predicting the future state of the corresponding object or process (Dohrmann et al., 2019). General Electric, for example, deploys digital twins for wind power plants to simulate and predict the expected levels of electricity output (Dohrmann et al., 2019).

Beyond physical objects, such as products or machines, digital twinning may also be applied to more abstract entities like processes or networks. For instance, digital supply chain twins can be defined as "computerized models that represent the network state for any given moment in time and allow for complete end-to-end SC visibility to improve resilience and test contingency plans" (Cavalcante et al., 2019, p. 87; Ivanov & Dolgui, 2021). Fed with key supplier and customer network data, such as locations of supply chain actors, order quantities and frequencies, transportation modes, warehouse capacities, among others, a digital supply chain twin can be leveraged to realistically simulate the course and the consequences of disruptions. Clearly, this level of visibility can be crucial to not only minimize response times, but also to assess different what-if scenarios, enhancing the effectiveness of a specific disruption response (Ivanov & Dolgui, 2021). Another promising avenue are digital process twins in manufacturing. Organizations like Tetra Pak or Schneider Electric are actively pursuing digital process twin strategies to virtually represent manufacturing systems, enabling more flexible remote management, monitoring, and driving process improvement opportunities (Andaluz, 2017).

4   Implications and Conclusion

Digital technologies are justifiably claiming to be viable sources of supply chain resilience. Based on four different technologies, we highlight the role of the digital resilience dimension in today's business environment. As such, blockchain may particularly help to enhance supply chain visibility. Digital platforms hold the potential to efficiently share and trade assets, and are already used to facilitate flexibility for firms. Data analytics are on the rise to eradicate blind spots, improve forecasting, and automate numerous manual processes. Firms may further use digital twins to flexibly monitor assets remotely, or to simulate the course and consequences of supply chain disruptions. The latter particularly facilitates response time and accuracy, increasing the supply chain resilience of firms. Self-evidently, the digital transformation, which is ongoing in industries worldwide, is not limited to these technologies, but rather includes a diverse set of tools and process adjustments.

Most importantly, however, the key requisite for a successful digital transformation that may ultimately help to facilitate resilience and sustain competitive advantages is the human dimension. A plethora of studies has demonstrated that it will be crucial to adequately sensitize and train workforce to successfully transform businesses digitally, and to establish an open and forward-thinking corresponding firm culture (e.g., Kurpjuweit et al., 2021; Kache & Seuring, 2017). Furthermore, as emerging technologies and associated business process adaptation are complex endeavors, oftentimes spanning organizational boundaries, it may help to create and leverage networks. These networks could include business partners, such as suppliers or business customers, industry peers, or sources of technological expertise, like tech startups or universities.

It seems quite clear that the digital transformation of businesses will reshape supply chains, redesign networks, and redistribute work processes. Information flows and data are becoming increasingly valuable assets that need to be carefully safeguarded, especially when moving across organizational boundaries (Holmström et al., 2019). While technologies like blockchain claim to provide promising solutions in this regard, the role of data security and privacy will most likely become even more prominent in the future. Hence, it appears essential for firms to simultaneously develop and design corresponding security solutions for each use case, and to engage with regulators, legal, and cyber security experts early on in the development process, minimizing the risk of unintentional information leakage or non-compliance with data privacy regulations.

Finally, for businesses, it seems reasonable to start simple, and begin with smaller pilot projects, but in greater numbers to explore technological diversity. This not only mitigates investment and budget risks. On the long and iterative journey of designing appropriate technology use cases that add actual business value, clearly, some projects will fail, but promising initiatives can be easier identified from a pool of pilot projects, and then gradually developed further.

References

Ambulkar, S., Blackhurst, J., & Grawe, S. (2015). Firm's resilience to supply chain disruptions: Scale development and empirical examination. *Journal of Operations Management, 33*, 111–122.

Andaluz, E. (2017, October 23). The process digital twin: A step toward operational excellence. *Microsoft Industry Blogs*.

Babich, V., & Hilary, G. (2020). OM Forum—Distributed ledgers and operations: What operations management researchers should know about blockchain technology. *Manufacturing and Service Operations Management, 22*(2), 223–240.

Bode, C., & Wagner, S. M. (2015). Structural drivers of upstream supply chain complexity and the frequency of supply chain disruptions. *Journal of Operations Management, 36*, 215–228.

Boh, W. F., Constantinides, P., Padmanabhan, B., & Viswanathan, S. (2020). Call for papers—MISQ special issue on digital resilience. *MIS Quarterly*, pp. 1–3.

Cavalcante, I. M., Frazzon, E. M., Forcellini, F. A., & Ivanov, D. (2019). A supervised machine learning approach to data-driven simulation of resilient supplier selection in digital manufacturing. *International Journal of Information Management, 49*, 86–97.

Choi, T. M., Wallace, S. W., & Wang, Y. (2018). Big data analytics in operations management. *Production and Operations Management, 27*(10), 1868–1883.

Choi, T. Y., Rogers, D., & Vakil, B. (2020, March 27). Coronavirus is a wake-up call for supply chain management. *Harvard Business Review Digital Articles*.

Craighead, C. W., Ketchen, D. J., Jr., & Darby, J. L. (2020). Pandemics and supply chain management research: Toward a theoretical toolbox. *Decision Sciences, 51*(4), 838–866.

Dohrmann, K., Gesing, B., & Ward, J. (2019, June 27). Digital twins in logistics: A DHL perspective on the impact of digital twins on the logistics industry. *DHL Trend Research*.

Duckett, A. (2020, October 5). Dow will close chemicals plants on top of job cuts. *The Chemical Engineer Digital Articles*.

El Baz, J., & Ruel, S. (2021). Can supply chain risk management practices mitigate the disruption impacts on supply chains' resilience and robustness? Evidence from an empirical survey in a COVID-19 outbreak era. *International Journal of Production Economics, 233*, 107972.

Foss, N. J. (2020). Behavioral strategy and the COVID-19 disruption. *Journal of Management, 46*(8), 1322–1329.

Govindan, K., Mina, H., & Alavi, B. (2020). A decision support system for demand management in healthcare supply chains considering the epidemic outbreaks: A case study of coronavirus disease 2019 (COVID-19). *Transportation Research Part E: Logistics and Transportation Review, 138*, 101967.

Hastig, G. M., & Sodhi, M. S. (2020). Blockchain for supply chain traceability: Business requirements and critical success factors. *Production and Operations Management, 29*(4), 935–954.

Hendricks, K. B., & Singhal, V. R. (2003). The effect of supply chain glitches on shareholder wealth. *Journal of Operations Management, 21*(5), 501–522.

Hendricks, K. B., Singhal, V. R., & Zhang, R. (2009). The effect of operational slack, diversification, and vertical relatedness on the stock market reaction to supply chain disruptions. *Journal of Operations Management, 27*(3), 233–246.

Herzog, C., Jost, F., & Greiner, N. (2021, May 10). Machine learning has revolutionized forecasting during COVID-19. *Oliver Wyman Insights*.

Hewett, N., & Mølbjerg, R. W. (2020, June 19). This is how blockchain can be used in supply chains to shape a post-COVID-19 economic recovery. *World Economic Forum*.

Holmström, J., Holweg, M., Lawson, B., Pil, F. K., & Wagner, S. M. (2019). The digitalization of operations and supply chain management: Theoretical and methodological implications. *Journal of Operations Management, 65*(8), 728–734.

Islam, T., Pitafi, A. H., Arya, V., Wang, Y., Akhtar, N., Mubarik, S., & Xiaobei, L. (2021). Panic buying in the COVID-19 pandemic: A multi-country examination. *Journal of Retailing and Consumer Services, 59*, 102357.

Ivanov, D. (2021). Supply chain viability and the COVID-19 pandemic: A conceptual and formal generalisation of four major adaptation strategies. *International Journal of Production Research, 59*(12), 3535–3552.

Ivanov, D. (2022). Lean resilience: AURA (Active Usage of Resilience Assets) framework for post-COVID-19 supply chain management. *The International Journal of Logistics Management.* https://doi.org/10.1108/IJLM-11-2020-0448

Ivanov, D., & Dolgui, A. (2021). A digital supply chain twin for managing the disruption risks and resilience in the era of Industry 4.0. *Production Planning and Control, 32*(9), 775–788.

Kache, F., & Seuring, S. (2017). Challenges and opportunities of digital information at the intersection of big data analytics and supply chain management. *International Journal of Operations and Production Management, 37*(1), 10–36.

Kass-Hout, T. A. (2020, November 19). Automating business processes with machine learning in the COVID-19 pandemic. *AWS Machine Learning Blog.*

Ketchen, D. J., Jr., & Craighead, C. W. (2020). Research at the intersection of entrepreneurship, supply chain management, and strategic management: Opportunities highlighted by COVID-19. *Journal of Management, 46*(8), 1330–1341.

Kleindorfer, P. R., & Saad, G. H. (2005). Managing disruption risks in supply chains. *Production and Operations Management, 14*(1), 53–68.

Klöckner, M., Kurpjuweit, S., Velu, C., & Wagner, S. M. (2020). Does blockchain for 3D printing offer opportunities for business model innovation? *Research-Technology Management, 63*(4), 18–27.

Klöckner, M., Schmidt, C., & Wagner, S. M. (2021). The impact of the COVID-19 pandemic on shareholder value. *Academy of Management Proceedings, 2021*(1). https://doi.org/10.5465/AMBPP.2021.45

Klöckner, M., Schmidt, C. G., & Wagner, S. M. (2022). When blockchain creates shareholder value: Empirical evidence from international firm announcements. *Production and Operations Management, 31*(1), 46–64.

Knemeyer, A. M., Zinn, W., & Eroglu, C. (2009). Proactive planning for catastrophic events in supply chains. *Journal of Operations Management, 27*(2), 141–153.

Korin, N. (2020, November 20). Using blockchain to monitor the COVID-19 vaccine supply chain. *World Economic Forum.*

Kubota, Y. (2020, April 27). Apple delays mass production of 2020 flagship iPhones. *The Wall Street Journal Digital Articles.*

Kumar, A., Liu, R., & Shan, Z. (2020). Is blockchain a silver bullet for supply chain management? Technical challenges and research opportunities. *Decision Sciences, 51*(1), 8–37.

Kurpjuweit, S., Schmidt, C. G., Klöckner, M., & Wagner, S. M. (2021). Blockchain in additive manufacturing and its impact on supply chains. *Journal of Business Logistics, 42*(1), 46–70.

Leonardi, P. M. (2021). COVID-19 and the new technologies of organizing: Digital exhaust, digital footprints, and artificial intelligence in the wake of remote work. *Journal of Management Studies, 58*(1), 249–253.

Linton, T., & Vakil, B. (2020, March 5). Coronavirus is proving we need more resilient supply chains. *Harvard Business Review Digital Articles.*

Liu, M., Fang, S., Dong, H., & Xu, C. (2021). Review of digital twin about concepts, technologies, and industrial applications. *Journal of Manufacturing Systems, 58*, 346–361.

Loten, A. (2020a, June 2). Pandemic to jumpstart spending on data tools at manufacturers. *The Wall Street Journal Digital Articles.*

Loten, A. (2020b, April 16). Companies devote shrinking tech budgets to cloud, AI. *The Wall Street Journal Digital Articles*.

McKinsey & Company. (2020, October 5). *How COVID-19 has pushed companies over the technology tipping point—and transformed business forever*. McKinsey & Company.

Nandi, S., Sarkis, J., Hervani, A. A., & Helms, M. M. (2021). Redesigning supply chains using blockchain-enabled circular economy and COVID-19 experiences. *Sustainable Production and Consumption, 27*, 10–22.

Narayanamurthy, G., & Tortorella, G. (2021). Impact of COVID-19 outbreak on employee performance–moderating role of industry 4.0 base technologies. *International Journal of Production Economics, 234*, 108075.

Paul, S. K., & Chowdhury, P. (2021). A production recovery plan in manufacturing supply chains for a high-demand item during COVID-19. *International Journal of Physical Distribution and Logistics Management, 51*(2), 104–125.

Raj, M., Sundararajan, A., & You, C. (2020). COVID-19 and digital resilience: Evidence from Uber Eats. *arXiv preprint, arXiv*, 2006.07204.

Schleich, B., Anwer, N., Mathieu, L., & Wartzack, S. (2017). Shaping the digital twin for design and production engineering. *CIRP Annals, 66*(1), 141–144.

Schmidt, C. G., & Wagner, S. M. (2019). Blockchain and supply chain relations: A transaction cost theory perspective. *Journal of Purchasing and Supply Management, 25*(4), 100552.

Sheffi, Y. (2005). *The resilient enterprise: Overcoming vulnerability for competitive advantage*. MIT Press.

Sheffi, Y., & Rice, J. B., Jr. (2005). A supply chain view of the resilient enterprise. *MIT Sloan Management Review, 47*(1), 41–48.

Skorna, A. C. H., Bode, C., & Wagner, S. M. (2009). *Technology-enabled risk management along the transport logistics chain*. In S. M. Wagner & C. Bode (Eds.), *Managing risk and security: The safeguard of long-term success for logistics service providers* (pp. 197–220). Haupt.

Taylor, E., & Schwartz, J. (2020, March 17). Volkswagen suspends production as coronavirus hits sales. *Reuters*.

Wahba, P. (2020, August 18). Walmart's e-commerce sales nearly double as shoppers go beyond groceries in online orders. *Fortune Digital Articles*.

Williams, B. D., Roh, J., Tokar, T., & Swink, M. (2013). Leveraging supply chain visibility for responsiveness: The moderating role of internal integration. *Journal of Operations Management, 31*(7–8), 543–554.

Yang, J., Xie, H., Yu, G., & Liu, M. (2021). Antecedents and consequences of supply chain risk management capabilities: An investigation in the post-coronavirus crisis. *International Journal of Production Research, 59*(5), 1573–1585.

Zsidisin, G. A., & Wagner, S. M. (2010). Do perceptions become reality? The moderating role of supply chain resiliency on disruption occurrence. *Journal of Business Logistics, 31*(2), 1–20.

Chapter 13
Can You Fix the Supply Chain? Pitfalls and Stepping Stones in Pandemic Risk Management and Research for a Better Supply Chain

Remko van Hoek

Abstract This chapter reflects upon what is and what is not so new about the risk impact of the COVID-19 pandemic. We consider stepping stones for structurally better supply chain management coming out of the pandemic and pitfalls in the change process involved. Additionally, we call for researchers to more actively impact this change with relevant, timely, and actionable findings.

1 Introduction

A question that we need to consider is if the pandemic will proof a once in a lifetime risk nightmare that we will simply get beyond and move on from. Or will it prove to have been a turning point in supply chain management? Will we revert back to our pre-pandemic comfort zones and strategies, something that we have done to a large degree in prior risk crises? Or was the pandemic a critical stepping stone to break through bottlenecks and strategic inertia?

The pandemic provided companies with familiar risks and less familiar risk circumstances and new risk management techniques and approaches were developed with a pace of change greater than normally considered feasible. These innovations provide input to the ongoing efforts to structurally develop and implement more robust risk management capabilities. As researchers, we owe it to the heroic supply chain managers that navigated the pandemic risk environment to grow our research impact and societal value by studying and publishing these innovations so they can impact the supply chain management work ahead. It is for these reasons that this chapter aims to consider what is new, what is not so new and what this implies for managers navigating supply chain risks as well as for supply chain researchers.

This chapter is structured as follows: the next two sections will consider what is and what is not new about the risks experienced during the COVID-19 pandemic.

R. van Hoek (✉)
Sam M Walton College of Business, University of Arkansas, Fayetteville, AR, USA
e-mail: rvanhoek@walton.uark.edu

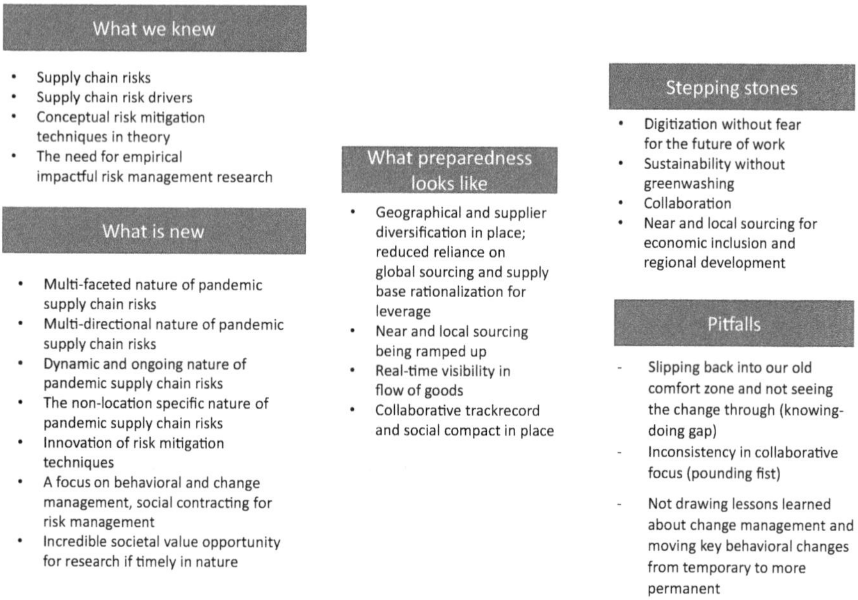

What we knew

- Supply chain risks
- Supply chain risk drivers
- Conceptual risk mitigation techniques in theory
- The need for empirical impactful risk management research

What is new

- Multi-faceted nature of pandemic supply chain risks
- Multi-directional nature of pandemic supply chain risks
- Dynamic and ongoing nature of pandemic supply chain risks
- The non-location specific nature of pandemic supply chain risks
- Innovation of risk mitigation techniques
- A focus on behavioral and change management, social contracting for risk management
- Incredible societal value opportunity for research if timely in nature

What preparedness looks like

- Geographical and supplier diversification in place; reduced reliance on global sourcing and supply base rationalization for leverage
- Near and local sourcing being ramped up
- Real-time visibility in flow of goods
- Collaborative trackrecord and social compact in place

Stepping stones

- Digitization without fear for the future of work
- Sustainability without greenwashing
- Collaboration
- Near and local sourcing for economic inclusion and regional development

Pitfalls

- Slipping back into our old comfort zone and not seeing the change through (knowing-doing gap)
- Inconsistency in collaborative focus (pounding fist)
- Not drawing lessons learned about change management and moving key behavioral changes from temporary to more permanent

Fig. 13.1 Overview of the chapter

We consider what markers of more prepared companies are and use this as a basis for suggesting stepping stones for structurally, not temporarily, improving supply chain capability to navigate risks and improve performance. We finally offer pitfalls in the change process involved in driving this structural improvement. Figure 13.1 offers an overview of the storyboard for this chapter.

2   What Is Not Unique About the COVID-19 Pandemic?

What is *not* unique about the pandemic is the types of risks experienced. Risk types such as supply, demand, financial, and transportation risks from earlier works of Christopher and Peck (2004), Ho et al. (2015) and Mena et al. (2018) are among those experienced (van Hoek, 2020a). Drivers of these risks such as the globalization of supply chains, the reliance on a highly rationalized supply base and a few factories and the proliferation of products and services are well known (Pettit et al., 2019). And the pandemic revealed that companies may have overfocused on creating negotiating leverage with suppliers by rationalizing the supply base and seeking low-factor cost global sourcing options (van Hoek, 2021a). In fact, it could be argued that the pandemic did not cause any of these risks but that it clarified their existence, as a consequence of how supply chains have been built and structured across the past few decades.

What is also not new is the risk mitigation techniques considered. Techniques suggested by Pettit et al. (2010) such as inventory buffering, introducing alternative sources of supply, and digitization are widely considered as part of pandemic risk mitigation (Van Hoek, 2020b). And these techniques from literature are broadly relevant across different supply chains, geographies, and industries in the context of the pandemic, as is typically the case. But it should be noted that these recommendations from literature come largely conceptual and somewhat high-level prescriptive (see, for example, Manu & Mentzer, 2008; Rao & Goldsby, 2009) and in fact there have been consistent calls for more empirical research on risk management (Ho et al., 2015).

It may be due to the time lag between empirical data collection, analysis, and paper writing and publishing but many initial publications about risk management in the pandemic have been conceptual and non-empirical (Craighead et al., 2020; Flynn et al., 2021; Wieland, 2021) just like earlier risk management literature. This reduces the ability of research to impact pandemic risk management; either findings are delayed or not theoretical and not informed by lessons learned in the real world. Herein reside opportunities to benefit from the unique opportunities that the pandemic provides to grow societal value of research.

3   What Is Unique About the COVID-19 Pandemic?

What is different about risk management in a pandemic, when compared to risk management scenarios more commonly experienced, is firstly the multifaceted nature of the risks experienced. This is not a port strike that causes a temporal transportation bottleneck or a plant quality issue that impacts manufacturing risks only. There are risks in supply, demand, transportation, finance, and manufacturing all at the same time. And these risks and their drivers are experienced in multiple directions with dynamics over time. Rolls Royce has seen a massive and continued drop in demand (van Hoek & Loseby, 2021) while e-commerce companies have seen rapid growth in demand and transportation risks have increased substantially during the first year of the pandemic. Rolls Royce also designed, implemented, ran, and dismantled a temporal ventilator supply chain in a matter of weeks (van Hoek & Loseby, 2021). Whereas there were shortages of PPE and sanitization supplies at the start of the pandemic, these were largely resolved just a few months into the pandemic. The third unique aspect of risks during the pandemic is that unlike a natural disaster or a transportation delay, pandemic risks are not location and time specific. Pandemic risks are experienced around the globe, in all supply chains and over a longer period of time (van Hoek, 2021a).

Perhaps most interesting is the fact that new approaches and risk management scenarios are being developed to expand upon existing risk mitigation techniques. As part of reshoring considerations, for example, a new reshoring scenario that has been introduced is that of having global sourcing suppliers set up new in-market operations to provide an alternative local source for their manufacturing customers (van Hoek & Dobrzykowski, 2021). This is alternative to more typical approaches of engaging new local suppliers or growing volumes with existing local or nearshore suppliers. Additionally, managing through the incredible dynamics and supply chain disruptions does not only require risk techniques and approaches. It also requires behavioral and change management efforts (van Hoek, 2021b) which are not to be underestimated. These apply to the management or internal supply chain teams but also to the relationships with key suppliers. During the early stages of the pandemic, many supply chain managers found themselves spending a lot more time with their suppliers working through order books, inventory positions, and shipment updates, they collaborated to navigate an uncertain and new environment, deprived of traditional travel and meeting options. And while change in supply chain management can be complex and slow, in particular in a cross-border, cross-company setting (van Hoek et al., 2010), they did it fast and collaboratively. The social contract with suppliers, the unwritten collaborative compact with suppliers, was key in this process; do we trust each other, do we know each other well, and are we going to put the written contract to the side if the risks faced requiring different approaches? In particular, in down markets, such as that of Rolls Royce, the formal contract for volumes that were not going to be needed anytime soon will not suffice as a basis for ensuring supply chain continuity. Blockchain technology has also seen a rise in attention (van Hoek & Lacity, 2020) and this represents a newer use-case for blockchain (Van Hoek, 2020c) to digitization as a well-known risk mitigation technique.

It is for these reasons that supply chain researchers do face a massively larger than normal opportunity to not only conduct relevant but also impactful research that has tremendous societal value potential. If the time lag for conducting and publishing empirical research about lessons learned by pioneers in the face of the pandemic can be reduced, then research can help supply chain managers risk mitigate and innovate to keep their supply chains running. The good news is that there are new publication options coming available to researchers to publish in a timelier manner. There are online journals such as logistics and sustainability of MDPI aimed at fast tracking the publication process and their open-access publishing standard makes findings easily accessible also for non-academics. And there are new sections in existing journals aimed at fast-tracking impactful innovations such as the innovators and transformers section of the *International Journal of Physical Distribution and Logistics Management* and impact pathway papers in the *International Journal of Operations and Production Management. The Journal of Purchasing and Supply Management* also has a "notes and debates" paper category that does not require fully completed empirical research papers but rather seeks relevance and impactful insights. Table 13.1 summarizes what is and what is not new about risk management and research during the COVID19 pandemic.

Table 13.1   What is and what not new about risk management and research during a pandemic

	What is not new	What is different
Risk types	Supply, demand, transportation, financial risks	Multifaceted nature of the risks experienced
Mitigation techniques	Inventory buffering, supply base diversification, digitization	New scenarios, digitization use cases and greater reliance on behavioral, change management and social contracting
Risk drivers	Globalization, supply base rationalization, and proliferation of products and services	Multidirectional and dynamic nature of the risks experienced
Supply chain relevance	Broad relevance across supply chains, geographies, and industries	Non point in time and space specific longer lasting and more sweeping impact
Research approach	Conceptual and theoretical recommendations	Opportunity to not only conduct relevant research but also grow societal value of research by supporting managers managing through the pandemic
Research contributions	There is a substantial time lag between events occurring and empirical research being published	New paper and journal types that can accelerate the publishing process for it to be timelier

4   Markers of More Prepared Companies

When studying pandemic risk management across companies and supply chains several markers of companies that were in a better position going into the pandemic can be identified. These companies were more capable of responding to the risks faced and as a result provide a part template for companies seeking to develop a structurally more robust risk management capability.

Based upon our research into pandemic risk management we can offer Nike as an example of a company that had started a strategic focus and programmatic transformation effort to diversify its supply base geographically and to move away from concentrating on global sourcing highly concentrated volumes with maximum unit cost benefits only. The company had started implementing near market and even in-market sources. Turkey and Eastern European suppliers supply Nike's EMEA business and Latin American suppliers supply its North American business. The demand responsiveness benefits the supply base diversification aimed to achieve became only more valuable during the start of the pandemic. And the reduced reliance on global shipping became equally greater when transportation risks and costs started increasing further into the pandemic. Other companies had already started diversifying to India and other Asian sources in response to the US tariffs on Chinese imports. And while did not necessarily drive a move away from global sourcing and shipping, this reduced the reliance of these companies on a limited number of suppliers and source locations did enable them to navigate supply risks better by being able to shift orders between geographies and suppliers (van Hoek, 2020a).

During the early stages of the pandemic supply chain managers found themselves spending a lot more time with suppliers considered (potential) bottlenecks. Going back and forth about product in transit and planned order releases. They buffered inventory where possible and supported better payment terms to enable suppliers to secure materials with tier 2 and 3 suppliers. For some companies, this was a largely manual, and as a result, time-intensive war room-type effort. For those companies that had (partial) automation In place this was a more doable endeavor and those that were implementing technology already could accelerate these efforts to get closer to real-time visibility into the flow of goods (van Hoek, 2021a).

On top of that, companies that had established a collaborative track record with their key suppliers were in a better position. Suppliers can see risks coming ahead of their customers and together with customers these risks can be reduced or avoided. So those supply chain managers that were already engaged in joint risk mapping and contingency planning with suppliers were more prepared and had part of the social compact and contract already in place before the pandemic impact began to be felt (van Hoek, 2021b).

5 Stepping Stones

Whether companies were prepared or not, whether supply chain researchers have started research aimed at supporting pandemic risk management or not, the pandemic environment provides incredible stepping stones for progress in practice and science. The disruption of the supply chain has both enabled much accelerated change as well as forced through many potential levels of resistance and inertia in structural supply chain improvements. A VP of supply chain from Nordstrom, the US retailer, described the pandemic change appetite as: *"Your five year plan became this year's plan."*

In the spirit of "never waste a good crisis" Rolls Royce is investing in an event management system that helps digitize part of risk management. Using more real-time risk data from a number of sources will hopefully enable the company and its suppliers to become more proactive, reducing the need for reactive firefighting. These capabilities are good examples of how automation can augment work and capability, not necessarily automate the work away and can help reduce employee fear of the future of work and possible job consequences from automation. Supply chain managers at Rolls Royce would love to have this new capability enable them to spend less time chasing orders and shipments, being able to focus on relationships instead (van Hoek & Loseby, 2021).

Sustainability ambitions in supply chains have benefited from the pandemic risk environment. Commuting and travel, for example, are major drivers of carbon emissions so clearly the carbon reduction ambitions of many companies were aided by the no travel/work from home pandemic environment. And several companies, including Google, have announced an ongoing work from home/anywhere option for parts of their workforce. The implication of this is that the short-term pivot to the pandemic environment may have triggered a structural step forward to a new operating environment that brings companies closer to carbon reduction ambitions, possibly ahead of plan. In addition to that, geographical rebalancing of the sourcing network to include less global sourcing and reliance on global shipping by introducing more local and near sources will aid scope 3 carbon emissions. All of these elements of progress move beyond greenwashing approaches (more PR-centric sustainability efforts that do not necessarily tie closely to change in day-to-day operations) to drive meaningful change.

Supplier relationship management and supplier-enabled innovation has for some time been more of an aspiration than a common practice and capability in procurement (Mena et al., 2018; van Hoek et al., 2020a). The intensity, dynamics, and complexity of pandemic risks made it mandatory overnight for companies to engage with many more suppliers that had become bottleneck suppliers. Equally so, critical dependencies on tier 2 or 3 materials suppliers, for example, steel and CPUs became visible and taking the approach of win-lose hard bargaining negotiations to navigate these shortages proved ineffective. Not only are tier 2 and 3 suppliers not receptive to bargaining, suppliers also needed to decide which shipment to prioritize in the face of limited capacity and they will likely prioritize their customers of choice, not necessarily the ones that pound their fist on the table the hardest.

Accelerating digital, sustainable, and SRM capability development does not only make procurement an even more exciting part of the supply chain. It also raises the bar on future-proof skills and capabilities. Leaders have had to rely on the creativity, entrepreneurialism, and communication effectiveness of their teams to navigate risk dynamics in collaboration with suppliers (van Hoek et al., 2020b). Developing temporal supply chains and responding to unforeseen circumstances cannot be done with business-as-usual processes, governance, and policies. Talented supply chain managers have had to step up to problem solve, design, and implement new operations and even supply chains (van Hoek & Loseby, 2021). As a result, change has come faster than it normally might and the learnings about how to change and how to operate effectively outside of normal process and procedure may be both beneficial to professionals and their organizations.

6   Pitfalls

If companies were familiar with the type of supply chain risks experienced and with risk mitigation approaches, why were they not more prepared for pandemic risks? Partially because there are unique aspects to the risks experienced and part because of the knowing-doing gap. While we understand risks and risk mitigation techniques and while we have faced these risks before, that does not mean that we have acted upon them. And part of that is understandable; after a risk crisis it is tempting to want to hit pause and return to our pre-risk comfort zone. And there are already some early indicators that this might happen with the COVID-19 pandemic also (van Hoek, 2021b).

There is much work ahead to address structural improvement opportunities. Developing new digital capability and rolling this out across the supply chain and finding, adopting and ramping new suppliers and sources takes time. Hopefully, companies will not stop short of seeing these improvements through and resist the temptation to return to simply global sourcing strategies and leveraged price negotiations to drive savings and efficiencies only.

A social contract and collaborative compact with suppliers is not developed overnight, but it can be broken in an instant. If, when bottlenecks are removed, buyers move away from collaborative approaches and start pounding their first seeking discounts, that violates social contracts and might put much of the progress at risk. And, perhaps most importantly, reduce, not improve, risk readiness to levels lower than those going into the pandemic. It will also be important for managers to take stock of lessons learned on change management and draw conclusions about which governance and policy adjustments made during the pandemic need to be moved from temporary to more permanent. The Google work from home example is but one small aspect of the many learnings about governance and behavioral operations that can be learned and carried forward. We obviously hope that research can inform the hard work ahead and the drawing of lessons learned as part of a concerted effort to grow societal value of research with impactful and actionable insights.

7 Conclusion

While supply chain risks have been widely understood for some time and while conceptual risk mitigation techniques have been available many companies faced unique risk scenarios during the COVID-19 pandemic. The accomplishments of supply chain managers in facing these risks are highly commendable but also far from over. To "fix the supply chain" managers need to avoid reverting to pre-pandemic comfort zones, strategies, processes, and governance. Instead, there are critical lessons being learned that can inform a much-enhanced supply chain capability, if managers make temporal changes more permanent and fully execute new strategies around near and local sourcing, supplier collaboration, and digitization. We obviously hope that research can inform the hard work ahead and the drawing of lessons learned as part of a concerted effort to grow societal value of research with impactful and actionable insights.

References

Christopher, M., & Peck, H. (2004). Building the resilient supply chain. *International Journal of Logistics Management, 15*(2), 1–13.
Craighead, C. W., Ketchen, D. J., Jr., & Darby, J. L. (2020). Pandemics and supply chain management research: Toward a theoretical toolbox. *Decision Sciences, 51*(4), 838–866.

Flynn, B., Cantor, D., Pagell, M., Dooley, K. J., & Azadegan, A. (2021). From the editors: Introduction to managing supply chains beyond Covid-19—Preparing for the next global mega-disruption. *Journal of Supply Chain Management, 57*(1), 3–6.

Ho, W., Zhengb, T., Yildizc, H., & Talluri, S. (2015). Supply chain risk management: A literature review. *International Journal of Production Research, 53*(16), 5031–5069.

Manu, I., & Mentzer, J. T. (2008). Global supply chain risk management. *Journal of Business Logistics, 29*(1), 133–155.

Mena, C., van Hoek, R., & Christopher, M. (2018). *Leading procurement strategy*. Kogan Page.

Pettit, T. J., Fiksel, J., & Croxton, K. L. (2010). Ensuring supply chain resilience: Development of a conceptual framework. *Journal of Business Logistics, 31*(1), 1–21.

Pettit, T. J., Croxton, K. L., & Fiksel, J. (2019). The evolution of resilience in supply chain management: A retrospective on ensuring supply chain resilience. *Journal of Business Logistics, 40*(1), 56–65.

Rao, S., & Goldsby, T. J. (2009). Supply chain risks: A review and typology. *International Journal of Logistics Management, 20*(1), 97–123.

Van Hoek, R. (2020a). Responding to COVID-19 supply chain risks—Insights from supply chain change management, total cost of ownership and supplier segmentation theory. *Logistics, 4*, 23.

Van Hoek, R. (2020b). Research opportunities for a more resilient post-COVID-19 supply chain-closing the gap between research findings and industry practice. *International Journal of Operations and Production Management, 40*(4), 341–355.

Van Hoek, R. (2020c). Developing a framework for considering blockchain pilots in the supply chain—Lessons from early industry adopters. *Supply Chain Management an International Journal, 25*(1), 115–112.

van Hoek, R. (2021a). Larger, counter-intuitive and lasting—The PSM role in responding to the COVID-19 pandemic, exploring opportunities for theoretical and actionable advances. *Journal of Purchasing and Supply Management, 27*. https://doi.org/10.1016/j.pursup.2021.100688

van Hoek, R. (2021b). Exploring progress with supply chain risk management during the first year of the COVID-19 pandemic. *Logistics, 5*(4), 70. https://doi.org/10.3390/logistics5040070

van Hoek, R., & Dobrzykowski, D. (2021). Towards more balanced sourcing strategies—Are supply chain risks caused by the COVID-19 pandemic driving reshoring considerations? *Supply Chain Management, 26*(6), 689–701.

van Hoek, R., & Lacity, M. L. (2020). How the pandemic is pushing blockchain forward. *Harvard Business Review*. https://hbr.org/2020/04/how-the-pandemic-is-pushing-blockchain-forward

van Hoek, R., & Loseby, D. (2021). Beyond COVID-19 supply chain heroism, no dust settling yet—Lessons learned at Rolls Royce about advancing risk management thinking. *International Journal of Operations and Production Management*. https://doi.org/10.1108/IJOPM-03-2021-0141

van Hoek, R., Johnson, M., Godsell, J., & Birtwistle, A. (2010). Changing chains. *The International Journal of Logistics Management, 21*(2), 230–250.

van Hoek, R., Sankararaman, V., Udesen, T., Geurts, T., & Palumbo-Miele, D. (2020a). Where we are heading and the research that can help us get there—Executive perspectives on the anniversary of the Journal of Purchasing and Supply Management. *Journal of Purchasing and Supply Management, 26*(3). https://doi.org/10.1016/j.pursup.2020.100621

van Hoek, R. I., Gibson, B., & Johnson, M. (2020b). Talent management for a post-COVID-19 supply chain—The critical role for managers. *Journal of Business Logistics, 41*(4), 334–336.

Wieland, A. (2021). Dancing the supply chain: Toward transformative supply chain management. *Journal of Supply Chain Management, 57*(1), 58–73.

Milton Keynes UK
Ingram Content Group UK Ltd.
UKHW020607201123
432904UK00002B/17

9 783031 164910